Women's Letters from Ancient Egypt,
300 BC–AD 800

Women's Letters from Ancient Egypt, 300 BC–AD 800

ROGER S. BAGNALL *and* RAFFAELLA CRIBIORE

with contributions by
EVIE AHTARIDIS

THE UNIVERSITY OF MICHIGAN PRESS
Ann Arbor

2009   2008   2007   4   3   2

A CIP catalog record for this book is available from the British Library.

Library of Congress Cataloging-in-Publication Data
Bagnall, Roger S.
  Women's letters from ancient Egypt / Roger S. Bagnall and Raffaella Cribiore ; with
contributions by Evie Ahtaridis.
     p.   cm.
  Includes bibliographies and index.
  ISBN-13: 978-0-472-11506-8 (cloth : alk. paper)
  ISBN-10: 0-472-11506-5 (cloth : alk. paper)
  1. Women—Egypt—History—To 1500—Sources. 2. Women—Egypt—Correspondence.
3. Letter-writing, Egyptian—History—To 1500. I. Cribiore, Raffaella. II. Ahtaridis, Evie.
III. Title.

HQ1137.E3B34   2006
932'.02—dc22

                                                                    2005055947

Acknowledgments

T he creation of this collection has been a collaborative venture of the authors, but it has also involved help from many others. We are deeply indebted to all those who have supplied photographs, slides, and digital images of the papyri included here and who have given permission for them to be included in this work. These include particularly Revel Coles and Gideon Nisbet for the Oxyrhynchus Papyri and other papyri of the Egypt Exploration Society in the Sackler Library; Rosario Pintaudi and Franca Arduini for the Biblioteca Medicea Laurenziana; and Günter Poethke for the Staatliche Museen zu Berlin (Ägyptisches Museum und Papyrussammlung). Some of the digital photography (at Berkeley, Columbia, and Michigan) was made possible as part of the Advanced Papyrological Information System (APIS), which has been funded in large part by the National Endowment for the Humanities.

Much of the work of converting our files into a form usable over the Web was carried out by Stamenka Antonova, Ceylan Tözeren, and Evie Ahtaridis, graduate students at Columbia University, to whom we are grateful. This work was financed by the Faculty Cluster for Information Technology and by the Stanwood Cockey Lodge Foundation of Columbia University. Once the project was accepted for inclusion in the American Council of Learned Societies' History E-Book Project, Nancy Lin of the New York University Press helped define the final database format for us. Our graduate assistants Jinyu Liu and Giovanni Ruffini helped with many tasks, including rounding up the images not yet obtained, checking images systematically against the database, and reading the database and introduction. Phyllis Lee, an undergraduate assistant, also helped in final checking of the database and images. Without the help of these sharp eyes, many more of our errors would have survived.

The Stanwood Cockey Lodge Foundation bore the cost of most of the imaging work necessary for the project; additional help came from the Dunning Fund of the Department of History, Columbia University.

Part of the texts were ready in time to be used in a Summer Seminar for College Teachers directed by Roger Bagnall in the summer of 1999. This seminar, "Culture and Society in Roman Egypt," was funded by the National Endowment for the Humanities. We are grateful to the endowment and the participants in the seminar for serving as a testing panel, whose comments, both during and after the seminar, helped us to shape the commentaries and introduction.

We also owe a debt of gratitude to those who afforded us audiences for discussing this project as it developed. The intellectual biography of the book is described in chapter 1. Those who figure in it without being named are among our creditors, including Diana Kleiner and Susan Matheson for the invitation to speak at Yale in the I, Claudia symposium and Janet Martin and her colleagues for the ability to do so at Princeton.

Part or all of the book has been read by various colleagues, to whom we are very grateful for their time, critical engagement, and numerous improvements: Adam Bülow-Jacobsen, Julie Crawford, Hélène Cuvigny, Nikolaos Gonis, Kim Haines-Eitzen, AnneMarie Luijendijk, George Parássoglou, and Terry Wilfong. Mark Depauw, Ursula Kaplony-Heckel, and Brian Muhs also offered valuable advice on Demotic texts. As always in a work of this scale and complexity, we know that even with the help of all of these colleagues we have undoubtedly been responsible for many sins of omission and commission. We will appreciate readers' comments that may improve subsequent versions of the electronic publication and the book.

August, 2003

Contents

෴ ෴ ෴

෴ ෴ ෴

List of Letters

༄ ༄ ༄

Illustrations

CHAPTER I

Introduction: This Book and How It Came to Be Written

This book collects all of the letters known to us, as of the middle of 2003, preserved on papyrus or ostracon (potsherd or flake of limestone), that can be identified as having been written by women in Egypt, during the period from the arrival of Alexander the Great (332 BC) to the end of the relevant Coptic documentary evidence somewhere in the later eighth century of our era.

This printed book is the offspring of an electronic book, published as part of the American Council of Learned Societies' History E-Book Project (http://www.historyebook.org). The e-book has the advantage of allowing much richer illustration of the letters, fuller commentaries, and extended versions of the introductory chapters, as well as links to digitized Greek texts. The images are particularly important because we recognized that a part of what we had to say about women's letters depended on looking at the papyri themselves, not just at texts or translations of them. We will be asking who actually wrote the letters and what level of competence as writers they had. Those who get interested in the letters by reading this book will find that every aspect can be pursued in greater depth in the e-book, which is not as subject to the constraints of space as a printed volume. We hope that in this way the digital and printed versions will complement one another.

HOW THIS BOOK CAME TO EXIST ⁓

Chapter 2 describes why we think this project makes sense and can yield useful results. First, however, we plan to tell the reader how we came to produce this book. Its earliest ancestor was Bagnall's involvement in the creation of *Women and Society in Greek and Roman Egypt: A Sourcebook*, edited by Jane Rowlandson (Cambridge 1998). That sourcebook was the product of eleven scholars who decided to create a collection of a wide variety of types of primary evidence concerning women's lives in Hellenistic and Roman Egypt. Although the papyrus documents are neither innocent of bias nor self-interpreting, they are, by and large, far less problematic in these respects than our literary sources in Greek and Latin, and they broaden the social range of ancient individuals and families about whom we may know something very considerably.

During the same period, Cribiore was finishing *Writing, Teachers, and Students in Graeco-Roman Egypt* (American Studies in Papyrology 36, 1996). Much of the work involved in that book concerned the close observation, analysis, and classification of handwritings—the attempt to get inside the head of the writer and see just what writing entailed for him or her. "Him or her" is not just polite contemporary language, for one of the results of the book was an argument in favor of the view that there was more education of upper-class women than has sometimes been thought; another was the closer identification of a group of women who were themselves teachers.

During 1995–96, a sabbatical in Oxford gave Bagnall the chance to try out some approaches to these issues on a sample of letters from the Oxyrhynchus Papyri, with the advantage that the Ashmolean Museum possessed either the originals or photographs of virtually all of them, so that the visual side of the work was relatively easy. This sondage resulted in a paper given to the Oxford Philological Society. In 1996, while Cribiore's book was in press, we began to discuss the applicability of the palaeographic discoveries of this book to women's letters—the possibility that one could really discern the difference between autograph and dictated letters, for example, and what one might learn by doing so for the entire body of women's letters.

Versions of the Oxyrhynchos sondage were presented in the fall of 1996 to the I, Claudia symposium at Yale University and the colloquium Feminism and Classics: Framing the Research Agenda at Princeton University. The conversations at all of these gatherings helped to shape further work and raise questions, perhaps most importantly about the typicality of the Oxyrhynchos letters and their social matrix. A conference on women in Graeco-Roman Egypt held in Brussels and Leuven (November 1997) and a collective volume on women's voices in literature provided opportunities for Cribiore to look closely at the archive of Apollonios the strategos, the single largest group of women's letters to be published to date (Cribiore 2001b, 2002). Work on *Gymnastics of the Mind* (Cribiore 2001a) also brought the education of women back into focus and contributed to the work on what is now chapter 7.

A large part of the material was presented to a Summer Seminar for College Teachers, sponsored by the National Endowment for the Humanities, in June and July 1999. Conversations in the seminar were decisive in shaping the organization of the introduction and to some degree of the documents themselves. The rest of the Greek texts were (apart from a few strays) finished during the fall. The Coptic letters took some months more. In the four years since, we have written the introduction and gathered images from scores of institutions.

THE ORGANIZATION OF THE BOOK ～

The book as it now stands, then, is the product of a long period of preparation, in the course of which we have repeatedly had new influences and stimuli both about the substance of the work and about the form it might most usefully take. We first (chap. 2) ask what we can actually hope to learn from reading these letters, a much more complex matter than was thought when the first— and, until now, only—study of these letters was published more than seventy years ago or even quite recently. From this we proceed to more descriptive chapters, setting out in chapter 3 what letters have survived and why the record is so uneven from period to period and century to century. Chapter 4 discusses late medieval English letters, which (we argue) help us to think about key questions such as palaeography and social location of the writers. In chapter 5 we look at the mechanics of letters, how they were written, delivered, and read. Handwriting is looked at in more detail in chapter 6, where we explain what we think we can learn from it and why we have given descriptions of the hands of each letter. The same attention is given to language in chapter 7. In chapters 8 and 9 (the latter by Evie Ahtaridis) we turn to look at some of the information that analysis can elicit from the letters about the economic and social location of the women who wrote these letters and about how they led their lives. These chapters are inevitably highly selective. Our purpose is not to give an exhaustive account of these subjects but to help the reader interpret the texts. The final chapter (10) is given to other forms of reader assistance, describing a number of practical and technical aspects of ancient life such as forms of address, names, dating methods, and money. In translating, we have kept many technical terms, rather than replacing them with modern "equivalents" that might mislead more than enlighten.

The texts themselves are arranged in two broad groups. The first consists of papyri organized by archives and dossiers, which include individuals, families, and find groups. The second is thematically driven. A detailed discussion of these groups is given in the last part of chapter 3. For each text we provide whatever information is available about the place of writing, the place of finding, and the date of the papyrus or ostracon. In many cases none of these is known with any exactness. Relatively few letters are dated to year, month, and day (see chap. 10 on this topic), and for the most part we must rely on handwriting, which is very approximate (chap. 6). We know the place where the papyrus was found more often than where it was written. Most of the time the find place was probably the same as the original destination, but that will not always have been true, and only occasionally are real addresses given (chap. 5). Papyri acquired on the antiquities market cannot in many cases be given even a place of finding (chap. 3).

The introductions to individual texts deal to varying degrees with handwriting, language, and contents. The electronic version has more extensive discussions of handwriting and language, as well as more information about the current location of the physical objects and bibliography about them. The notes after the translation aim only to explain allusions that may be unclear to the reader and to call attention to difficulties in the interpretation of the text.

CITATIONS AND IMAGES ∾

Each letter is identified in this book by a single reference to a volume of texts and item number. These are given with standard papyrological abbreviations, which can be found in the *Checklist of Editions* either online or in print form (Oates et al. 2001). The texts we translate are not always the same as the standard edition. The e-book gives full documentation of the bibliography standing behind these divergences. We have been able to print images of thirty-two of the letters, aiming to give as wide a variety of objects and handwritings as possible.

CHAPTER 2

Why Women's Letters?

L etters make up one of the largest categories in the body of surviving texts on papyrus (and related materials, cf. chap. 5). They have from the earliest days of papyrology caught the attention of scholars from a range of disciplines, as well as of a broader public. Their immediacy and sense of direct access to the personal lives of people who lived two millennia ago account for part of their appeal, particularly because such texts are almost entirely lacking for most other times and places in antiquity. Their everyday language has drawn much interest from scholars intent on mining them for parallels to the vocabulary, syntax, idiom, and life of the early Christian world. Along with this appreciation, however, has come a degree of ambivalence. Part of this reserve stems from the difficulties that the letters pose to the editor, some of which will be apparent to readers of these letters. Much more, however, comes from the frustrations that their contents offer to anyone moved to approach the daily life of antiquity through them. Out of frustration has been born a considerable degree of neglect.

There is no doubt that the papyrus letters very rarely display that willingness to put the author's inner life down on paper that we find in modern letters and which we value so highly—indeed, that is a central part of our definition of modernity. Ancient letters are, rather, filled with greetings, including those to everyone in the household; inquiries after and information about the health of the writer, recipient, and their families; information and instructions about goods acquired, received, to be dispatched, or to be sought; and exhortations to write back or complaints about previous failures to do so.

It is probably because our other evidence for women of the ancient world so rarely allows us direct contact with their thoughts, unfiltered by men, that some of the most optimistic statements about the potential of letters have come from feminist thinking about women's letters. The earliest is the enthusiastic response of Maria Mondini (1916: 29): "Moreover, these represent perhaps one of the very few most sincere testimonies of ancient women, at least of ordinary women, not certainly of those who sat on the throne of Arsinoe or of Cleopatra . . . In the papyrus letters, by contrast, we find women directly represented, and women of the people, who speak sincerely of what interests and stirs them, so that we can follow on the paper the traces of the feminine hand, sometimes uncertain and unpracticed, which sketched those signs, which represented, one might say, an emancipation."

In this book we will find reason to challenge some of Mondini's assumptions about the character of the letters. But what is most striking about this foresighted passage is that it could equally well have been written sixty years later and been at home in the discourse of academic feminism of the 1970s. Its optimism about the texts can be reformulated in a fashion more congenial to modern theoretical expression, as it has been by Amy Richlin (1993: 293): "All these 'texts' serve the postcolonial theorist's program of locating the subaltern's speech." She might better have said "could serve," as no one has yet made an attempt to get women's letters on papyrus to disclose such subaltern speech. For that matter, women's letters of other periods have not had the kind of attention that they might and everyday letters are almost entirely absent from modern theoretical discussions of women's writing, ancient or modern (with the significant exception of Watt 1993).

WHOSE VOICES ARE WE HEARING?

Before we consider how to read the letters, the assumption that the private letters reveal the unmediated voices of ancient women must be interrogated. Quite apart from deeper questions about differences among women and the meaningfulness of gender as a category, topics which will be discussed below, there are two critical and difficult technical issues. First, did women write these letters themselves? And, second, if they did not, how likely are they to represent the actual words of the nominal authors?

It is by now, in the wake of William Harris's influential book on literacy (1989), widely accepted that the vast majority of the ancient population was unable to write; women were still less likely to be literate than were men. In looking at women's letters, therefore, we may feel compelled to start from the assumption that in most cases they did not write the letters themselves. If, as we argue, the letters come almost entirely from the top quintile of society, the chances of literacy are much higher than if they were the product of a cross section of society.

In many cases, it turns out to be remarkably difficult to be sure who wrote the letters. Some women, it turns out, were able to write with ease, but they are also those most likely to have been able to afford to own or hire an amanuensis. It is, ironically, those most capable of writing who are least likely to do so; like wealthy people of other periods, they tend to limit their own writing to greetings and signatures on letters prepared by others from dictation.

The occasional longer addition to the end of a letter is for this reason exceptionally valuable in understanding how particular letters were written.

The hands of those secretaries are often recognizable by their regularity. Highly educated writers who were not professional secretaries did not use these regular, scribal hands very much. The person dictating the letter might be a fast writer, but not a neat or regular one. When we find the kind of handwriting characteristic of papyrus contracts, we are certainly dealing with a professional—but one using his skills inappropriately, because letters were supposed to be written in a slower, clearer hand. These letter hands are widely represented in our corpus and in most cases must be the work of paid staff.

Much more difficult to categorize turn out to be the letters written in less polished hands. It is a facile assumption that many women who had to write letters themselves, for want of an amanuensis, were not very skilled at writing and thus did it awkwardly. But much the same is true when women had recourse to family members to do the writing for them; many men also did not reach very high levels of education, and sometimes internal evidence allows us to identify the struggling writer as definitely male.

Modern readers often assume that it should be possible to identify particular handwritings as female, an assumption stemming from the fact that twentieth-century schoolchildren have to a considerable degree been trained in penmanship in a highly gendered fashion. But to the extent that this observation is true, it is entirely the product of cultural conditioning. Detailed study of the history of handwriting in America (Thornton 1996) has shown that the governing assumptions of the teaching of handwriting changed repeatedly from the eighteenth to the twentieth century. Distinctive styles of female penmanship have been the product of shifting ideologies of gender difference. We have not found any solid basis for identifying such a link between gender ideology and handwriting styles in the papyri.

In the absence of such a link, therefore, we must fall back on the detailed analysis briefly described earlier. Sometimes we can be confident that a letter was dictated; much of the rest of the time, we cannot tell. Only occasionally can we be confident that a letter is written in a woman's own hand. It is, however, possible, in reading the letters, to distinguish fairly readily between those written in a polished style and those of an essentially oral character (see chap. 7 for discussion). This distinction is also found in early modern English letters, where an oral style predominates, just as it does in the Greek and Coptic letters. In the absence of a widespread habit of producing drafts of letters, it is not likely that secretaries normally took down rough copy and then rewrote it as a polished composition. Rather, the more polished compositions are probably the result either of a highly educated writer, deliberately dictating with great care, or (more commonly) of a professional secretary told to write a letter to a particular person with specified content, then left to compose the letter himself. It should follow that those letters that display a more oral style are the product of direct reproduction by the amanuensis of the author's dictation, with only a relatively modest degree of neatening and correcting. This is what our detailed analyses (see chap. 7) of the language of the letters mostly suggest.

On the whole, then, the results of the palaeographic study of the letters tend to be negative or agnostic for the question of actual female handwriting, with occasional but highly significant exceptions; but the examination of the language, by contrast, leads us to believe that in most cases the interposition of an amanuensis had relatively little effect on our ability to discern the actual words of the author or something very close to them. As the latter is more important for the larger project of recovering what women had to say about their lives, our conclusion is thus broadly optimistic.

WHICH WOMEN? ～

That optimism, however, concerns only part of society, a portion of the women of Hellenistic and Roman Egypt. It has become customary, even obligatory, in recent scholarship to point out that "women" do not form a self-explanatory category. Gender is one of the most important characteristics through which we may understand individuals and groups (see the classic article of Scott 1986), but statements assuming that all women—or all men—shared any particular set of experiences are almost certain to be wide of the mark. The habit of analyzing society in terms of affinity groups is characteristic of modern Western thought; class, ethnicity, and gender have been the most salient of such group identifications. It is doubtful that people in antiquity thought of themselves in such terms very much; at least, this cannot be taken for granted. By and large, ancient society was organized around families, and beyond the family there were complex networks of patronage and dependence, means of linking together those occupying higher and lower stations in a highly stratified world.

The degree to which it is meaningful to speak of class in this setting, therefore, has been much debated. Even though the concept of class in the ancient world has thus perennially been a controversial one, there is no doubt that ancient societies were very hierarchical, with differentiation by economic standing and social order playing a large part in determining everyone's life experience. "Class" has therefore been recognized as one of the main ways in which women's experience was differentiated. Nonetheless, no matter what measure one uses, the indications of the women's letters clearly are that their authors predominantly belonged to elite families. Both direct and indirect marks of wealth are found in a large number of the letters (see chap. 8 for examples), and mentions of family tenure of magistracies and other public offices (chap. 9) confirm the sense that we are often dealing with the top part of society.

"Ethnicity" has also played an important part in the modern analytic disaggregation of the population. The applicability of the idea of ethnicity to Graeco-Roman Egypt, and the nature of ethnicity in this society, have received extensive comment in recent decades. There was certainly in the Ptolemaic period a significant correlation between Greekness and membership in the higher strata of society, but there were Egyptian elites throughout the reigns of the Ptolemies, particularly connected to the temples. Moreoover, even Greekness is a problematic notion, even though the Ptolemies enshrined it in law. As Egyptians learned Greek and found means of getting access to money and power through the royal system, the tidiness of legally established ethnic designations broke down; intermarriage also certainly contributed to the emergence of a considerable body of elite population that was to some degree both Greek and Egyptian at the same time. It is probably fair to say, however, that the very highest rungs in society continued to be occupied by those most Greek in culture.

The terms *Greek* and *Egyptian* are even less easy to define in the Roman period. Some of the possible complexities, and their relationship to gender, are explored in chapter 3. With the reemergence of written Egyptian, in the form of Coptic, late antiquity makes it possible once again to think about written language as an indicator of culture. Even then, however, interpretive problems remain acute, for we shall see that the writers of the shorter Coptic letters of late antiquity give every impression of belonging to the same groups as those who produced the Greek letters of the Roman period.

Although most of the authors of the letters collected here are of the upper strata, then, it would be unwise to take anything for granted about their ethnic background. And even economic standing is not to be assumed uncritically; there are in fact some letters in which little or nothing tells us about the writers' wealth or status, and some in which the indicators are ambiguous (see chap. 8).

THE DISTINCTIVE VALUE OF LETTERS ◔

Letters are by no means the only documentary texts from Egypt that inform us about women's experience. A wide range of these texts has been collected in Rowlandson 1998. Two characteristics set the letters apart from this mass of other documentation. First, they are constrained only to a very limited degree by formalism, even though to some extent they use formulaic language (see chap. 7). In this respect they differ greatly from legal documents, which impose a predetermined structure of roles on the parties instead of explaining their actions. For example, it would be difficult to tell from leases alone whether a woman who owned agricultural land took an active part in managing it or delegated that entirely to a male member of the family.

Second, the letters are the one genre in which women are definitely expressing themselves on their own behalf and not through a male who controls the representation of their thought. From the analysis in chapters 6 and 7, it can be seen that this is true even where a woman has used dictation in order to have her words recorded on papyrus. The exceptions are likely to have been cases in which the content was relatively formal and impersonal, particularly where a secretary was given only a sketch of the contents of a business note and left to compose the actual text on his own.

To a limited degree petitions to administrative or judicial authorities also form an exception to the norms of impersonality and intermediation, and they are worth much more study than they have had so far. But anyone reading petitions can see that they do not, unlike letters, represent a fairly straightforward recording of oral language from dictation. Rather, they are highly rhetorical, with a large amount of stereotyped expression, undoubtedly the product of rhetorically educated males, writing for other men and women of similar background and status.

GENERALIZATIONS AND PARTICULARS ◡

Despite everything we have said, the letters allow us to get closer than any other category of document to a significant part of the ancient female population: not, as Mondini said, those who sat on the throne, and not peasants either, but a considerable segment of the propertied and literate population, a much broader group than the literary texts provide access to. The authors of these letters were not middle class; in modern terms, they were upper class and upper middle class.

Collecting these letters is in some degree an attempt at an ethnography of the past. But a sourcebook is a particular type of work, and we have chosen it deliberately rather than writing a synthetic account of what we have found. We hope in this way to give back to these women of another era the chance to speak to the present without the burden of faulty generalizations. This is in its pure form an impossible aspiration, and the existence of this introduction may be taken as our own form of generalization, inevitably faulty to some degree. Moreover, our own views of ancient society and our own interests have shaped the organization of the material, the presentation of the letters, and the choice of subjects to comment on. No doubt they have also affected the views we have taken of some of the texts and the ways in which we have translated them. There is no such thing as an entirely innocent way of presenting these materials.

Nonetheless, this is a sourcebook, and the reader can readily check whether the translations seem to support our generalizations. In preparing the editions, we have sought to stay as close to the language of the originals as possible and to avoid paraphrases that might import more of our own thought than necessary into the letters themselves. We have preferred to think that the authors of the letters had ideas they wanted to communicate and that they were not the incompetents that frustrated editors have sometimes made them out to be. We know that we have not succeeded in recovering what they were trying to say in all instances, but we hope that this book represents some progress toward that goal. All the same, we are well aware that translation cannot avoid the replacement of Greek and Egyptian idioms with English or the importation of our own assumptions about Egyptian society of Greek and Roman antiquity.

Most importantly, however, we hope that this collection will allow us to retain the variety of voices of the authors of the letters in all their granularity. Providing the texts themselves can be seen as a form of resistance to the tendency, shared by the historian and the anthropologist, to take our description of a culture or a society as being more widely applicable than it realistically can be. The letters we have collected here are far less rich in some ways than we might wish, but they can offer opportunities to see the women of Hellenistic and Roman Egypt as agents, faced with disparate circumstances and prepared to make choices. Letters are peculiarly susceptible to this kind of microhistorical approach and particularly rich in this ability to complicate our generalizations about ancient cultures. We have tried to avoid obliterating the singularity of the individual letters, commenting extensively on their physical embodiments.

CHAPTER 3

About the Corpus of Letters

W hat is a letter? The ancient writers reflected on this question in rhetorical handbooks on letter writing (Malherbe 1988) and occasionally in their personal letters. They all agreed on one point: a letter is a dialogue with someone who is absent, a written conversation that should have an aim and take into account the character of the person to whom it is addressed, using the same expressions that one would use if that person were present. A letter should strive for clarity, avoiding obscurities and covert allusions, and should be relatively brief. Letters could be composed in one of a number of styles, according to the specific circumstance and the aim of the writer. Sometimes a mixed style was better suited for covering several subjects.

But insofar as a letter was a written and not a spoken conversation, the ancients conceded that it had a less ephemeral character and should be composed with some care. It was a sort of gift that the writer sent the recipient, and it could be saved and reread. Writers such as Cicero and Seneca occasionally expressed their conviction that in writing to their friends and reading their letters they felt as though they were in their company (e.g., Cic. *Att.* 12.53; Sen. *Ep.* 40.1). Undoubtedly, however, in spite of claims of sincerity and spontaneity, ancient literary letters are far more formal and studied than most letters of common people that have been preserved from the ancient world.

The women's letters in this collection are full of standard topics and introductory and concluding expressions. Scholarly reactions to the relative uniformity of the structure and language of letters have varied from W. Schubart's conviction (1918: 211, 397) that these expressions were the result of the teaching of letter writing in the schools and the use of professional letter writers to whom people dictated their correspondence to P. Parsons' assumption (1980–81: 8) that people thought in clichés. It is true that some stereotyped topics such as the complaint that no correspondence had been received, the request to write often, or the joy at receiving a letter are part of human experience and are sometimes present even in Cicero's correspondence (Cugusi 1983: 73–104). On the other hand, it is not unreasonable to suppose that students practiced letter writing in school contexts.

The actual evidence for copying epistolary expressions in elementary Greek schools, however, is extremely scanty (cf. Cribiore 1996: no. 147). In Coptic school contexts, by contrast, beginners regularly copied and practiced on introductory parts of letters. At higher levels, when students were able to express themselves more easily in writing, it is conceivable that they practiced corresponding with their families: some evidence in this direction might be found in letters that students who were away from home to study sent their parents (Cribiore 2001a: 215–19). Practicing epistolary formulas, moreover, was part of the routine in schools for apprentice scribes. Not much information exists about the timing and character of such education, but it should be noted that the preserved scribal exercises show relatively experienced hands.

Obviously, the women who personally wrote letters in Egypt did not attend professional or business schools. The texts of their letters are mostly simple and straightforward, without rhetorical niceties. Nonetheless, these women knew very well that a letter was intended as an effective instrument of communication, however they may have learned that. They indeed conceived of the messages that they penned or dictated as private dialogues with distant persons, but in general, and especially in the Roman period, they do not show much concern for careful editing or expressing their thoughts with unusual turns of phrase. Allusions and ambiguous expressions were perfectly comprehensible to the actual addressees and were the result of the fundamental lack of privacy of ancient letters and the desire to conceal some situations and the identity of certain persons. The women's letters, moreover—and letters from Graeco-Roman Egypt in general—are perfect examples of what the epistolary theorists called the mixed style. They are practical letters that address specific family, business, or work concerns, convey news, ask the recipient to send certain items, or accompany the dispatching of gifts and supplies. Only in very few cases is the tone of a letter more uniform and focused on a single main subject.

The section of this book called "Archives and Dossiers" includes women's letters that are part of archives of documents that were formed in antiquity and dossiers, which are groups of letters revolving around certain individuals or environments that have been identified and classified in modern times. Even though the letters in section B are classified according to the main theme around which they revolve, they often cover and illuminate other topics as well. The largest group of letters in this section is formed by what Ps.-Libanius calls "the request letters." In these, women ask their recipients to send them, or to bring with them when they visit, a number of items, such as clothes, foodstuffs, or furnishings, that are presumably difficult to find in the writer's place of residence. These letters sometimes end up being mere shopping lists, at times quite detailed in their requests. Writers often reciprocate by dispatching something in turn: these are often products of home activities such as cooking, preserving, weaving, and manufacturing clothes.

Other identifiable types of letters are messages conveying urgent or important news, the opposite end of the spectrum from polite letters analogous to modern Christmas cards containing only greetings. Once again it is difficult to fit these letters into neat categories. In general, in urgent messages not much time is spent in lengthy introductory and concluding stereotyped expressions, and salutations to and from other relatives and friends are dispensed with. Quite the opposite is true in polite cards. These were often inspired by the presence of an opportune letter carrier, allowing people to get in touch with distant relatives, or they might be the result of a genuine desire to communicate with someone in spite of no real news to disclose. In the ancient world people who lived far from each other needed periodic reassurance about reciprocal well-being. In this case, therefore, salutations were fundamental ingredients of a message. People who noted a lapse rightly protested, as did Aline, who was concerned about her daughter (*P.Giss.* 78) or a daughter annoyed at her father's forgetfulness (*P.Grenf.* 1.53). It should be noted that sometimes people sent their greeting cards with a few supplies, but the main reason for their letters was to get in touch.

Another large category of texts that can be distinguished, even though we chose to do so only to a limited extent, is that of letters that are from Christian milieus or which allude to the religious beliefs of the writers. The subsection called "Religion" includes only a handful of letters, those that touch on religious themes and were not included in other groups. But many other letters also illuminate the topic of religion. The letters to clergy and holy men and those to Bishop Pisentius testify to the Christian faith of the writers, their desire to obtain help, and the contacts existing between clergymen and monastics and common people. Some of the Coptic letters from Kellis contain striking expressions originating from Manichaean milieus. Other letters testify to the habit of paying homage to the gods of the country in the name of the recipient, gods such as Serapis, Souchos, or Zeus Kasios or those indicated with the expression "our ancestral gods" or "the local gods". Sometimes it is even possible to appreciate the flavor and nuances of religious faith. The letters of Eudaimonis, the mother of the strategos Apollonios, are arresting testimonies of her desire to stir the gods in the direction she wants.

Far from conforming to stereotyped models, the women's letters communicate genuine concerns for a number of issues. Even though in the Byzantine period letters achieved more formality, they were still conversations of a different kind from that envisaged by the epistolary theorists. Roman letters in particular contain a number of topics that are often only mentioned in passing, names thrown around casually, others hidden on purpose, plenty of allusions to obscure events and issues, and occasionally some strong feelings: all this is unedited life.

CHANGES IN LETTER WRITING FROM PTOLEMAIC TO BYZANTINE TIMES ❧

Greek and Egyptian in the Ptolemaic Period

The women's letters of this period are a smaller part of the preserved Greek papyri than in the Roman period. There are several possible explanations for this situation. It is possible that letter writing was not particularly widespread among women in Hellenistic times. Since letters more often revolved around official, administrative, and business matters and were less concerned with personal and family affairs, letter writing may seem to have been a man's prerogative. The extreme scarcity of letters by women in Demotic Egyptian might be taken to reinforce this impression. We have included only 4, 2 each from the Ptolemaic and the early Roman period, and know of 1 other not yet published. From a body of roughly 675 Demotic letters, this is a remarkably small number, less than 1 percent. The paucity is even more striking given the presence of letters by women in Egyptian letters of earlier periods, particularly of the Ramesside period (Dynasty 19). Of the 470 letters preserved or cited from Deir el-Medina, for example, about 5.7 percent are written by women. It would be surprising to find no echo of this tradition in the Egyptian population of the Ptolemaic period. The total number of preserved Demotic letters, however, is sufficiently large that it is unlikely that the shortage of letters by women is entirely the product of the circumstances of survival.

By contrast, a shortage of Greek women's letters might well be, in the main, a product of the archaeological circumstances of the preservation of Ptolemaic papyri, which have favored government records, tax receipts, and private contracts over personal correspondence. Some caution is therefore required in drawing broad conclusions from our limited sample of letters. However, in light of the relative formality of letters in this period and of the perceptible change later on in favor of more spontaneity, one might view letter style as one factor in the lower frequency of letters written by women. Before the Roman period, letter writing may have seemed less easily approachable because it had to obey rather precise rules; women might as a result have sent fewer letters.

Formality in Ptolemaic Greek Letters

The letters sent by women in this period can be divided into two groups, the letters that are part of the archive of Zenon (an agent of Apollonios, the finance minister under Ptolemy II) and a few personal letters sent by women to relatives. These two groups stand apart with regard to the identity of the writers and linguistic and structural characteristics. All the letters included in the first group can be considered petitions of some sort, addressed to Zenon by women of relatively low station: female dependents in the complex organization revolving around Apollonios, the mother who claimed that her son, a member of the retinue of Apollonios, had been mistreated, and two old women who asked Zenon to redress some alleged wrongs. Most of the letters in this group are centered around a specific request. They are composed with a simple style but carefully and correctly, and they abound in minute details of a specific affair. Absent any personal relationship, the letters skip greetings and conclude abruptly.

In personal letters sent to family members, one might expect less care in diction and structure, but the contrary is true. These letters open with elaborate, formulaic expressions of greeting and wishes for good health, sometimes also adding lengthy closings. The body of the message is expressed in a periodic style, in which each sentence flows with rhythm from the preceding one and leads to the next. Conjunctions and connective particles are abundantly employed, and so are complex sentences of various kinds and a proper and rich vocabulary that display to the full the writer's good command of the language. Salutations to and from relatives naturally complement these private messages. The women themselves might have penned some of these letters (*P.Bad.* 4.48 and 51, *P.Münch.* 3.57), but in other cases they dictated them to relatives or professional scribes. At any rate, the writers of the entire group show a definite awareness that a specific style was appropriate for a letter and that this style would be modified according to the identity and status of the recipient.

A Colloquial Style in Roman Times

The vast majority of the women's letters written in Greek belong to the Roman period. Most Roman letters are centered around minor business and work matters, family relationships, and solicitation of favors, gifts, and supplies. Women seem to have become more at ease with the epistolary medium and to have been more willing to use it, both to break their isolation by establishing contacts with loved ones and to improve the quality of their own lives.

The frame of a Roman letter is itself revealing. The relatively long introductory expressions of the Ptolemaic letters give way to brief, stereotyped openings, more varied than those of the Ptolemaic period. Those expressions, though generic, hinted at personal relationships by disclosing the longing that distance created and alluding to the remembrance that the writer kept of the addressee. A larger space is often reserved for salutations to family members and friends who might have shared the content of a letter. These salutations provide a long coda to many letters, but they are sometimes introduced at the very beginning, revealing the writer's focus. Once a message is communicated, the letter closes abruptly with a "farewell" formula; its impersonal nature is also revealed by the frequency with which it is abbreviated.

The letters of Isidora, written in 28 BC, which form part of the archive of Asklepiades, already show these characteristics (BGU 4.1204–1207). Even though she seems to spend a bit more than average time in greetings, her letters are practical messages packed with information and injunctions. Other women's letters reveal the same tendency toward brevity and efficiency. Writing a letter had become equivalent to talking. A few stereotyped formulas were sufficient concessions to an epistolary style. The use of more care and formality is exceptional. Aline, the wife of the strategos Apollonios, for example, usually sent informal letters packed with information and directions, but she opted for a more sophisticated and pensive style in the letter she sent her husband, who had just left for the war (P.Giss. 19).

Reversion to a Formal Style in the Early Byzantine Period

Relatively few Greek letters written by women are preserved from after the fourth century. The reasons are not entirely clear (see the next section), but it is possible that the more formal style in which letters of this period are usually written was a factor. For both men and women, Greek letters were no longer considered a vehicle for simple, spontaneous messages. Greek letter writing became more ambitious, demanding knowledge of artificial formulaic expressions and the ability to put together complex sentences in a periodic style beyond everyday speech, sometimes embedding biblical allusions. The writing of letters was entrusted therefore to specialists both in formulating a letter and in penning characters as ornate and flamboyant as the texts themselves. Probably women without easy access to professional scribes refrained from sending such letters altogether, but even women with access to them considered letters something exceptional, reserved for real need. The fact that no archive or dossier of letters sent by one woman or by women in the same family survives reinforces this perception.

Delegation of writing to a scribe makes recovering signs of a woman's personal expressions and vocabulary much harder than before. When a woman acted as spokesperson for a larger group, such as her whole family or a monastic group, a scribe may have found it easier to preserve the occasional switching between singular and plural pronouns. Literate women of high station may have had more control over the text of their letters. SB 18.13762, for example, seems to preserve a bit of the real speech of Phoibasia in the sporadic repetitions when she intended to emphasize something.

The distance between a woman and the text of her letter, moreover, may have increased as time progressed. *CPR* 14.53, from the eighth century, is the product of a very capable scribe who used high-flown expressions and rephrased the whole dictated text into a web of elaborate sentences with reminiscences from the Scriptures. But at the end the woman who sent this letter seems to resurface in a domestic detail left as dictated: "We did not receive the pepper."

WOMEN'S LETTERS IN COPTIC ～

The same elaborate and formal style that characterizes Byzantine letters written in Greek is a feature of some of the letters written in Coptic. Most Coptic letters, however, maintain a relative simplicity and abruptness. Their authors felt free to express themselves in a rapid and colloquial style, aiming at the efficient and pragmatic quality now largely lost in Greek letters.

Most of the Coptic letters that are formally written address clergymen, even bishops. Although these letters usually contain a mixture of elaborate formulaic expressions and prayers combined with practical matters, everything is rephrased and becomes stiff and bloated. *P.Pisentius* 28, sent by a group of seamstresses in charge of preparing various garments for the bishop, opens and closes with high-flown expressions of greetings and reverence. Then the main reason for sending the letter is explained at length and in detail but with courteous and conventional expressions. As the letter proceeds, it assumes the tone of a petition. The author's prayer becomes personal and heartfelt, leaving plural pronouns behind. The deferential, conventional tone seems to be justified by the distance between writer and addressee.

But in other cases a formal style imposes itself in spite of the close relationship of sender and recipient, showing that letter writing was often considered an activity that had to obey precise stylistic canons and conventions. Like their Greek counterparts, women who wrote extensive Coptic letters with lavish greetings and complex constructions most often had to use the services of a scribe or a male relative or acquaintance with a strong command of language and fluent handwriting. It is uncertain, for example, who wrote *P.Kell.Copt.* 42, a letter on a wooden board that a woman and her daughter sent to their respective son and brother. The writing is not completely regular but is the work of a proficient hand, beginning with a long-winded mixture of greetings and fervent prayer.

Shorter Coptic letters skip ample greetings and extensive prayers in favor of going straight to the point, plunging directly into the midst of business. The ending is equally abrupt. These letters are invariably written on ostraca. These concise Coptic letters are often difficult to interpret because they are meant exclusively for the parties in question, and their content is often obscure and full of allusions. That is not to say that everything is clear in more elaborate Greek and Coptic letters, but short messages were jotted down to respond to the need of the moment and leave much unsaid. They continue the tradition of Roman informal letters.

THE CHRONOLOGICAL DISTRIBUTION OF
THE LETTERS ∿

As the preceding discussion has stressed, a very striking characteristic of the Greek letters is their uneven distribution over the centuries of the Hellenistic, Roman, and Byzantine periods (see Bagnall 2001 for a fuller discussion of this phenomenon and its causes). There is a great rise from the modest numbers of letters in the Hellenistic period to much larger numbers in the first four centuries of Roman rule, then a collapse from the fifth century on. But this is too simple a description, because women's letters are not alone in following a course of rising and falling.

If we leave aside the extremes of our millennium, where archives distort the picture, we find that down to the fourth century AD, private letters as a percentage of the total papyri remain relatively constant, with only the second century BC falling outside a range of 8.8 to 12.8 percent. Private letters form a relatively stable part of the total documentation from the late Hellenistic period until late antiquity. Women's letters as a percentage of the letters vary somewhat more, but as a percentage of total documentary papyri there is a remarkable stability from the first century BC to the fourth century AD, with the percentage right at 1 percent of the total, plus or minus a tenth of a percent. Because the numbers are relatively small, of course, there is a real possibility of distortion—that is, that the percentages are not statistically reliable—and for this reason we would not make too much of the second century BC (where official texts are proportionately more numerous than later) or of the poorly documented fifth century AD.

The stability of the five central centuries makes it all the more striking when we come to the late antique drop, which begins perhaps in the fifth century but is very clear and striking in the sixth and seventh centuries. Women's letters as a share of total Greek documents drop to a tenth of their previous level, amounting to just one-tenth of one percent of all documents for the sixth through eighth centuries. Letters as a whole, however, drop in percentage terms by a much more modest amount. Women simply disappear as writers of letters in Greek after the fourth century.

It does not seem possible to explain the pattern only by what we know about the archaeology of papyrus discoveries or the physical characteristics of Byzantine letters (see the e-book for more discussion of these points). We are thus led to ask if there are deeper sociological explanations available. Were women's letters particularly the product of a society strong in social mobility, and did such mobility decline in late antiquity? Does the flourishing of women's correspondence in the Roman period represent a period of greater social freedom for women, which closed in under Christianity? These explanations too have problems, for late antique society seems to have maintained a high degree of social mobility and continuity with preceding centuries, despite the spread of Christianity (see Keenan 1975; Beaucamp 1990–92).

From what has been said already, it is obvious that we cannot leave the role of Coptic letters out of consideration. Their number is considerable, with at least sixty-five identified so far. There is no data bank for Coptic documentary papyri, so it is difficult to calculate percentages of all letters or all documents as we have done for Greek. In general, it looks very much as if women's letters amount to a little over 1 percent of the surviving Coptic documentary texts. But Coptic documents have a much higher proportion of letters than the Greek documents by a factor of about four. If looked at against the aggregate of documents, the women's letters in Coptic are roughly in line with, or barely higher than, the level of Greek women's letters in the period of their greatest numbers, the first century BC to the fourth century AD. This is at first glance somewhat surprising, because these letters survive largely on ostraca found at monastic sites in the nearer desert—Deir el Bahri, Epiphanius, Bawit, and so on. All of the sites in question were very heavily male, and indeed the women's letters in Coptic are largely written to men. This fact may help explain why women's letters in Coptic are a lower percentage of total letters than is the case with Greek letters. But it makes it difficult to get any good sense of what place women's letters in Coptic had in the context of ordinary urban and village settlements, the societies from which the Greek letters of the Ptolemaic and Roman periods come. This is particularly true because it is likely that some of the letters to male monastics come from female monastic communities, which were certainly atypical environments, both in the social and economic status of many of the women ascetics (see Wipszycka 2002b) and in the potential opportunities for education that monasteries offered.

The recently published volume of Coptic letters from Kellis, which are written on papyrus and date to the middle of the fourth century—very early for Coptic letters—forms an interesting comparison and a rare opportunity to look at Coptic in a settlement context. Four and perhaps five of the thirty-five letters are by women, and a very high percentage of letters is addressed to women. The contrast with the volume of Greek papyri from Kellis, where no letters from women figure among the twenty-four letters, and only one is addressed to a woman, is striking. Most of these letters were written in the Nile Valley by male members of the family who were away on business of one sort or another, to the women at home. The fact that there are so many by women in this Coptic assemblage is thus really noteworthy.

At this point the change in letter style described earlier should be remembered: the tradition of short, informal letters, not requiring a professional scribe's intervention, which we find in the Greek letters of the Roman period, is carried on in the Byzantine period by the shorter Coptic letters, almost entirely on ostraca. We may therefore offer a hypothesis: when Coptic became available as a letter-writing language, women largely switched from Greek to Coptic for their everyday letters. On this hypothesis, the switch began by the middle of the fourth century and was essentially complete by the fifth, after which very few women's letters in Greek appear. That does not mean that men did not also write letters in Coptic in considerable numbers—there are far more published Coptic than Greek letters by men for the period from the sixth to eighth centuries—in both familial and external contexts, but men also still produced substantial numbers of Greek letters in the later centuries.

It should be remembered, too, that the period of the peak production of women's letters in Greek was also the period from the decline of Demotic Egyptian as a documentary language, which began in late Hellenistic times and was pretty much complete by the middle of the first century AD, until the appearance of Coptic. During those centuries, there was for most people no means of having a letter written in Egyptian, for literacy in Demotic was uncommon and largely restricted to the more learned members of the Egyptian clergy. An Egyptophone had to write in Greek, dictate in Greek, or find someone to turn Egyptian dictation into written Greek. When Coptic arrived and came to be accepted as a language for letters—our earliest published examples (all from male monastic milieus) are apparently from the 330s—this lack of means to have letters written in Egyptian came to an end.

Women's preference for Coptic may be rooted in the fact that men operated extensively in the public world, where Greek was in late antiquity still the language of administration, power, commerce, and the world at large. Women's lives were, though by no means confined to the home, much more defined by the domestic world, where Egyptian was at least on a par with Greek and perhaps dominant. This male/female, outside/inside, public/private binary opposition should not be pushed too far. One does not need to see it in absolute terms. Indeed, we are inclined to think that women of the social strata responsible for most of the letter writing had far more freedom of movement and action than modern scholars have generally been willing to ascribe to ancient women (see chap. 9). In these families there were women with a Greek education. But that there was a difference between men and women in the proportion of time spent in such spheres is at least plausible. Monasticism, it is true, provided an environment with both public and private characteristics, and to the extent that women's letters originated in monastic communities it is hard to classify them simply in the public/private typology. The evidence of the letters leads to the suggestion that the gendering of name giving reflects not only different social roles but a real division in patterns of language use, in which women in families in which the men were active in public and were unmistakably Greek in culture were in many instances more comfortable with Egyptian than with Greek.

ARCHIVES, EXCAVATIONS, AND PLUNDERING ᷡ

Something must be said here about how we come to have our texts. Papyri and ostraca have come to us through a complex process of deposition, discovery, and editing. Although it is commonplace to invoke chance and randomness in describing the survival of ancient texts, the process was not mainly one of chance. Rather, it represents the complex interplay of choices and environments. The physical environment creates the broad framework of physical survival. Artifacts with ink writing rarely survive in legible form in the Egyptian Delta—least of all from Alexandria—or in the regularly inundated parts of the Nile Valley. Those texts that we have come from places in the desert, or on its edge, or from high mounds not reached by the flood or groundwater. In judging the representativeness of the women's letters gathered here, the loss of Alexandria and the Delta is the most important gap; although we have a fair number of letters written in Alexandria, we have hardly any written to the capital. Almost every other part of the Nile Valley is represented to some degree in the surviving texts, though no doubt not in any proportion to ancient populations. The deficiencies of our documentation are more subtle in such areas. For example, we have many letters found at Oxyrhynchos, but none found in the Oxyrhynchite countryside. As a result, there are many instances of letters written on country estates to the city but few identifiable cases of the reverse.

Even where letters do survive the ravages of water, slow or fast, choices of various sorts come into play. People may save letters in boxes or jars or they may toss them away; accumulated letters may be left in a house or taken out to the dump with other trash. Where excavations have concentrated on dumps (as at Oxyrhynchos), letters deliberately sent out in the trash have fared better than those kept in the house or taken to the country estate. As we have noted, an entire period is underrepresented as a result of such choices: a high proportion of the surviving documents from the Ptolemaic period comes from papyrus reused to wrap mummies. Because the easiest way to acquire large quantities of such papyrus was to get it from the paper-generating government (whether directly or indirectly), not from individuals with only a few sheets, private letters are proportionately poorly represented in the Ptolemaic finds.

Modern choices have also played a part. Just to give one example, there are far more papyrologists capable of editing Greek texts than there are scholars specializing in Demotic or Coptic. As a result, Demotic and Coptic are underrepresented in publications. Although letters form only a modest part of the published Demotic texts, this fact is probably a result in part of the fact that Demotic went out of use for most day-to-day purposes in the early part of the Roman period. That is, the period in which women seem to have used letters most freely is one in which Demotic was no longer in widespread use. The period when Demotic letters were probably written in the greatest quantity is precisely the Ptolemaic period, when circumstances were unfavorable for the survival of letters on papyrus.

The archaeological history of papyri and ostraca has also had a profound impact on our material. We have commented elsewhere on the fact that we are hardly ever in the position of having a large enough body of material from one family or milieu to get a clear sense of individuals in the way that early modern letters allow us to do. But we do have a number of clusters of texts that come from a particular individual or family or that belong to a particular setting (like a military camp or a monastery). In some cases these groups of texts were found together in scientific excavations. The Coptic letters from the Monastery of Epiphanius near Jeme are an example. In other cases the texts were found in unauthorized digging and dispersed on the antiquities market, requiring scholars to reconstitute the assemblages by means of painstaking detective work. The Zenon archive is a famous example of such a group.

Many other papyri come from excavations, scientific or not, on ancient habitation sites, dumps, or tombs, without this digging's having yielded obvious archives. Sometimes, however, such nonarchival material yields small clusters of texts connected with the same person or milieu. These dossiers are more difficult to identify, but they are often interesting because even a limited ability to see an individual or setting from more than one angle is worthwhile. But the majority of published papyri fall, as far as we can tell, into neither the large archives nor these small dossiers. No doubt some of these actually were part of clusters, but the illegal plundering of ancient sites of their artifacts has disrupted these clusters and lost all of the contextual information that could have helped us reconstitute less obvious groups.

HOW THIS BOOK IS ORGANIZED ❧

The organization of this collection takes the complex survival history of the letters into account. The first part is composed of letters from archives or other related groups. These vary considerably in coherence, ranging from the family letters of the women connected with the strategos Apollonios to loose groupings of Greek letters of the Ptolemaic and Byzantine periods, which are collected together because of their comparative rarity. These dossiers (in the broadest sense) are arranged in rough chronological order. Many of them are very small and fall into the category of reconstituted clusters (Didyme and the Sisters is an example).

The second part is organized thematically around the contents of the letters and subjects referred to, particularly women's activities. This section ends with groupings of fragmentary Coptic and Greek letters not distributed to other groups. It is obvious that one letter might fall into two or even several categories, not only among the thematic sections but between the archival and thematic sections.

CHAPTER 4

Late Medieval Letters as Comparative Evidence

T he letters written by women in Hellenistic and Roman Egypt that still survive offer a number of challenges to the interpreter, challenges that can be seen from the analysis of chapter 3. We think that the single most difficult problem is not so much the uneven distribution of the letters by century or period but the fact that relatively few of them constitute dossiers of letters written by a single person or within a single family. Most of the archives and dossiers here are very small, and the larger groups are the most loosely constituted or defined. This lack of density in the documentation is compounded by the fact that we also do not generally have much other evidence for the women or families who appear in the papyri. Our context for them is usually supplied from contemporary documents unconnected with the individuals and families in question and is thus very unspecific. We know nothing directly about the education or wealth of most of the women whose letters figure in this collection.

As one means of alleviating this lack of context, we have turned to comparative evidence, in particular letters written in late medieval England. There are earlier medieval letters preserved, but these come largely from "women who live in a male world of secular or religious government (even if they are in convents), of scholarly investigation or documentation" (Ferrante 1997: 10). They are fundamentally different in character from the letters we have collected. It is not until the fifteenth century that we begin to get something more comparable. But how, one may wonder, can letters of a thousand years later help us understand ancient Egypt? The answer is precisely that the late medieval letters in question come from larger ensembles of family papers, and we have a far better chance of knowing the circumstances of these families than of those of Hellenistic and Roman Egypt. That is not, of course, to say that we know everything about them or even as much as we might about more recent individuals; even with the Pastons, the best known of the lot, we are still in the position of "reinventing the characters" rather than seeing them directly (see Richmond 1996: 7–52 on the difficulties presented by the Pastons). But what looks like a dossier full of holes to a late medieval historian would be a delight to any ancient historian. We can trace the Pastons' activities from year to year, from month to month, sometimes even from day to day. We can therefore see much better how patterns that we find in the letters fit into the structures of their lives. Obviously, we cannot turn and treat second-century Egypt as if it were fifteenth-century England. But we can ask ourselves if some of the structural patterns we find in another premodern and hierarchical society may reappear in some fashion. The study of the comparative evidence is thus an exercise in devising questions and hypotheses that we may take back to the ancient evidence. We are not guaranteed the ability to test such hypotheses, but at least we may have some sense of what the range of possibilities is.

As well as possessing its own gaps, comparative evidence is always a tricky business because its representativeness is not assured. In the case of letters, one problem is that the means by which fifteenth-century letters came to survive to the present were not neutral, not even as neutral as the ways in which papyri were deposited and found. The four earliest bodies of surviving English letters are those of the Cely, Paston, Plumpton, and Stonor families. (See the bibliography for a listing of the editions used here. The first volume of *Paston Letters* is also available online; see http://etext.lib.virginia.edu/collections/languages/english/mideng.browse.html.) Of these, probably all except the Paston papers survived because they had some role as evidence in lawsuits. Only the Paston papers survived because of family continuity into a document-oriented age. Whether the atypicality of the Pastons' durability makes their papers any less representative is difficult to say, but we cannot take it for granted that they are typical of their period. The problem of representativeness, however, is less acute if we are looking for a range of possible behavior and some hypotheses for testing than if we were seeking a single description of letter-writing habits in this period.

For our purposes, limiting the comparative material to this earliest group of vernacular letters has a significant advantage, for in later centuries the ethos of letter writing starts to change, particularly in the direction of the expression of the writer's personal feelings. By contrast, the tone and subjects of the fifteenth-century letters are strikingly reminiscent of the letters of antiquity, most of all of those of Roman Egypt. The letters of Margaret Paston in particular are full of requests to her husband and sons for goods she needed from London, where they spent long periods on legal business. Such "shopping lists" are found in the papyrus letters already in the Hellenistic period. It should be kept in mind, however, that on the whole the Roman Empire may have been a more cosmopolitan and integrated world than Europe in the time of the

Pastons and Stonors, and we cannot take it for granted that the outlook of the individuals involved would be similar.

Our discussion will focus on three areas that figure importantly in the introduction to our collection: social and economic standing (chap. 8), handwriting and literacy (chap. 6), and the degree to which the language of the letters is a direct representation of the author's thoughts (chap. 7).

FOUR WEALTHY FAMILIES ∾

The Paston papers are much the largest and most famous of these groups and certainly that in which the women figure most prominently. They were a wealthy landowning family of coastal Norfolk, who rose over a considerable period to reach a point at which they had access to court and some of their men were knighted. Like many such gentry families, they were often short of cash as they worked to extend their landholdings. (On the Pastons see the classic work by Bennett [1932], the article by Carpenter [1986], and the two recent volumes by Richmond [1990, 1996].)

The Stonors were wealthy landowners and knights of Oxfordshire, established since at least the thirteenth century, with estates in other counties as well, closer to royal power struggles than the Pastons but skilled at avoiding disasters and generally more conservative in behavior than at least some of the Pastons. Their house in the Chilterns still stands in a great park. After the Reformation, they ran afoul of the Crown because of their Catholicism, but they survived many vicissitudes and are a rare case of family continuity in their class down to the present day.

The Plumptons were landowners in Yorkshire, knights as early as the thirteenth century, and often connected to court politics. Like the Pastons, they found themselves sometimes overmatched in litigation about their property, which extended over several counties, and a combination of bad luck, sharp practice, and bad judgment often left them in difficulties. The Celys were of a lower stratum than the other three, mainly wool merchants in London and Calais rather than landed gentry, but it is only compared to the Pastons or Stonors that they would appear to be anything except wealthy and well connected.

Taking these families at face value, we would certainly be encouraged to suppose that women who wrote letters were of the elite. A look at women who wrote letters to the Pastons will only reinforce this view: apart from four of their own relatives, who were roughly of their own standing, we find nine members of the titled nobility, two widows of knights, and an abbess. About the remaining four we have little information. Women in the Stonor correspondence, other than family members, are uniformly members of titled or knighted families. The situation is similar in the Plumpton correspondence, although some women are unidentified. The Cely letters contain only two by women, both exceptionally interesting, but this archive preserves little that is not related to the wool-staplers' business, thus differing importantly from the Pastons, in whose correspondence family property and estate operations are the central points.

The reasons for the different quantities and characters of the surviving letters in these archives are complicated, but they are not important to us here. Letters were in any event mostly written not for the pleasure of writing but because business required them to be written. Possibly women in the cities did not need to write such letters as often as those in the country, being in places where goods of a broad range (particularly elaborate clothing and other textiles, as well as other craft products) were more readily available and being separated from their menfolk less frequently. The role of the woman as custodian of the household's stores, which figures so largely in the Paston letters, as in the papyri, is thus much more likely to be central on the country estate than in the city. At all events, all of these groups fall into the stratum of society below the very top but still provided with property and income far above the average.

HANDWRITING ∼

In the domain of handwriting, the two smaller groups may be left aside. The original Plumpton letters do not survive, and only two of the Cely letters are by women. The two larger collections produce rather divergent impressions. It is perhaps best to start by looking at the writing behavior of the Paston men, who were mostly university educated. In public business, drafting petitions and business letters, they all used a mixture of composition in their own hand, of writing by staff or junior family members, and of drafts in the hand of a member of his staff corrected in the sender's own hand. Seven of John I's letters to his wife are written by a clerk, but completions, additions, and signatures are autograph. Of the equally modest number of family letters we have from William II, 8 are autograph, 2 subscribed, and just 1 apparently in a clerk's hand throughout. John II and John III, homonymous brothers, have left us 130 family letters, of which 126 are autograph; 4 of John II's letters are subscribed. All of the letters of William III are autograph. It seems fair to say summarily that family letters are either autograph or (less commonly) dictated but subscribed and sometimes addressed (where "Dear Mother" would stand today) in the author's own hand. What we do not find, except rarely, is letters from literate men that contain greetings but are written in their entirety by their secretaries.

Women's Letters from Ancient Egypt

With the Paston women the situation is much different (see *Paston Letters*: I:xxxvii). Despite the more optimistic conclusions of earlier students of the letters, not a single letter by a woman is certainly autograph. In Margaret's large correspondence, the hands of ten individuals have been identified, seven of them family retainers and agents (often of fairly high social standing) and three of them family members. An even larger number of unidentified hands also occur, some nineteen of them, but none demonstrably or even probably hers. Perhaps more strikingly, not a single item has even a subscription in Margaret's hand; all subscriptions are in the same hands as the bodies of the letters. In any event, Margaret participated fully in the operations of the literate society around her, even if through others, just like many men and women in antiquity.

The situation with her mother-in-law, Agnes, is similar, except that the hands are largely unidentified. With Margery, however, although all of the letters are written by clerks, half of the six have autograph subscriptions, written in what Davis called a "distinctively halting and uncontrolled hand, as of someone beginning to learn to write" (ibid.). The pattern is followed even where we would regard the contents as personal. When Margery Paston wrote to her husband (417), "Ser, I prey you if ye tary longe at London þat it wil plese to sende for me, for I thynke longe sen I lay in your armes," it was dictated to their steward Richard Calle, but Margery signed it in her own beginner's hand.

There are two possible conclusions. One is that argued for by Davis, "that the [Paston] women could not write, or wrote only with difficulty, and so called on whatever literate person happened to be most readily at hand," leading him to conclude "that the women of this family whose letters survive were not, or not completely, literate" (*Paston Letters*, I:xxxviii); he is of course referring to writing literacy, not reading. (Keith Thomas [1986] has made the point that in early modern England the ability to read printed text was more widespread than either the ability to write or the ability to read script. The archives discussed here belong essentially to a world before printing became a widespread and dominant technology.) Margery's three subscriptions are in this view to be seen as the first attempts of a woman trying to cross the boundary into writing literacy. The other possibility is that a different code operated: literate women might dictate letters but not bother to subscribe them. This notion was suggested, but not strongly argued for, by Watt (1993: 124–25), who supposes that even those women unable to write were able to read. Against this can be offered not only Margery's clear wish to subscribe her letters but the intrinsic likelihood that (as Margery's attempts show) women would, if they could, follow the same pattern that their menfolk did. It may well be that Margaret belonged to a generation in which women did not learn to write and that Margery marks the beginning of a transition to a society in which women felt the need to have at least some command of the medium. But our sample is not large enough to bear the freight of such a generalization.

The editor of the Stonor letters summarized his views on their writing as follows: "Sir William Stonor, his father, and brothers . . . wrote their own letters and spelt passably well. Jane Stonor wrote tolerably but spelt atrociously. Her daughter-in-law Elizabeth generally employed an amanuensis, but could write well enough if she pleased; any difficulty there is in her letters seems to be due to the fact that they were dictated" (*Stonor Letters*, xlvii = 75). But matters are—even apart from the fact that English spelling was hardly standardized in this period—more complicated. There are three letters definitely from Jane. Each is written in a single hand throughout, including the signature, but no two of the three hands are the same. Any one of them might be Jane's, but equally (and more likely) none of them may be hers. It is thus misleading to attribute the tolerable writing but atrocious spelling to Jane. It is perhaps most probable that, like Margaret Paston, she did not write any of her preserved letters in her own hand.

Elizabeth Stonor, the wife of Sir William, presents a different picture. Her letters are indeed for the most part dictated, with signature and (often) concluding subscription written in a different hand from that of the body of the letter. In one case, the entirety of the letter is certainly in a single hand, somewhat irregular, with a number of blots and the lines not straight, but written with vigor and speed. It may be that another letter is also holograph. Because the subscription constitutes a small sample of writing, there is sometimes room for doubt in the case of a particular letter. Overall, it is clear that Elizabeth routinely dictated her letters and then signed them, probably writing the entirety only under exceptional circumstances. Her own hand is not neat or professional, but it is very practiced and fluent.

We may summarize these findings as follows. Women of the propertied classes tended to adopt one of three practices: (1) Dictate a letter in its entirety to a literate person, usually an employee; (2) dictate the body of a letter but add the concluding signature and usually a greeting (as well as any postscripts); and (3) write the letter in its entirety. It looks from our limited sample as if women of the generation of Margaret Paston and Jane Stonor, who may have been unable to write themselves, used the first of these. Women who reached adulthood a little later, in the 1470s and later, were more likely to use the second of these possibilities, reserving the third for unusual situations in which they did not have access to a secretary or did not wish to use one. From a practical, editorial point of view, distinguishing (1) and (3) is in principle impossible if one has only one letter from an individual. The more letters from a given individual one has that are written entirely in a single hand the more likely it is that we are dealing with a nonwriter who dictated all letters. Moreover, the evident preference of literate women for (2) over (3) suggests that we should be cautious in seeking to identify women's letters as holographs. At the same time, it is noteworthy that women's hands cannot be stereotyped simply as slow and halting. They may be slow or fast; what they are not is professional and standardized. The same was true of most men. Similar points will emerge from the detailed analysis of the papyri in chapter 6.

LANGUAGE ∾

Identifying the language of the letters with direct expression by women poses one set of problems; trying to find a distinctive language of women is still thornier, famously so. A first point of great importance is the issue of dictation. We do not know a priori if those who wrote from dictation cleaned up what they heard as they turned it into written form. Most people, even educated ones, do not normally speak in complete paragraphs or even in complete grammatical sentences. The editor of the *Paston Letters* expressed a generally agnostic position about the relationship between author and words: "It is seldom possible to know whether a letter written by a clerk was taken down verbatim at dictation or composed more or less freely on the basis of instructions given by the author" (*Paston Letters*, I:xxxviii). But he points to a number of errors that must reflect mishearing on dictation. Early writers on the Paston letters thought they could define an entire set of linguistic phenomena, particularly of phonology and morphology, on the basis of the forms in the women's letters. A closer look, alas, showed that most of these phenomena were editorial errors (Davis 1949). More recently, Diane Watt (1993) has described the use of plain style and colloquialisms for narrative vividness in the letters of Margaret Paston but with the pointed reminder that the same features occur at times in men's letters also. These features of style point to the oral character of epistolary language, whether dictated or written autograph. But they do not obviously yield something distinctively characteristic of women.

That does not mean that it is not worth looking. Certainly Tobias Smollett thought there was a difference; he therefore distinguished the various letter writers who make up the characters of *Humphrey Clinker* (1771) by their syntax, orthography, and vocabulary, as well as by the substance of their letters. Tabitha Bramble is a kind of burlesque Margaret Paston, always concerned with getting goods, taking care of the home from which she is absent, keeping the domestics in line, and acquiring money. Smollett's characters' language is distinctive both by gender and by status. But of course Smollett wrote in a different era. The gendering of epistolary language may therefore itself be a product of a particular period, not a universal that we ought to look for at all times.

Overall, it seems most likely that in the early English letters we have predominantly the reflection of the spoken language of the propertied class, with gender playing at best a modest role. Individual self-identification is mainly with the household and its interests, not with maleness or femaleness. But if we can proceed with some degree of confidence that we are in identifiable cases hearing the actual voice of the author, even if not witnessing her handwriting very often (other than in signatures), there may be more nuances to be picked up.

CHAPTER 5

Writing and Sending Letters

WRITING MATERIALS ∽

I
n Ptolemaic and Roman Egypt letters were mostly written on papyrus, and
the women's letters in Greek are no exception. Only very occasionally
and in some specific circumstances did women write Greek letters on
ostraca. The reverse is true for Coptic letters of the early Byzantine period;
these, judging from the surviving evidence, were rarely written on papyrus
and commonly on ostraca. Moreover, single instances occur of parchment and
a wooden board displaying letters.

Papyrus as a letter material offered considerable advantages over sherds,
notably its smooth surface and light weight. Since the cost of papyrus was not
an issue, as will be shown subsequently, it is not surprising that women preferred it. Papyrus letters could be rolled and folded and offered some degree
of secrecy: writers tied a string around them and might even seal them with
a clay seal or draw a saltire pattern or similar design on and around the string
that could prevent undetected opening (cf. Vandorpe 1995). If the recipient
intended to preserve papyrus letters, moreover, it was possible to glue them
side by side into a roll.

Letters on papyrus usually occupied one side, with the back containing the
address. Most women's letters of the Roman period were written on a tall and
narrow piece of papyrus, with a width of 8 to 12 cm and an average length of
about 30 cm, the height of the standard papyrus roll. Apparently there was
no standard size for pieces used for correspondence. A very limited number of
letters were extremely narrow, with a width below 7 cm. Such narrow pieces
presented the inconvenience that writers were forced to break words very
often. Equally rare were squarish letters of varying size that could contain
either short notes or long letters or even more than one letter together. Only
twenty of sixty-five Coptic letters were written on papyrus. As a rule, these
letters appear to be more formal and more extensive than letters on ostraca.
They include letters to important clergymen and family letters that communicated detailed, lengthy messages.

Ostraca—pieces of pottery or slices of limestone—were the second common material to which women entrusted their written messages. Greek and Coptic usages, however, differ considerably; when a letter addressed a relatively important recipient and was particularly long, ostraca were not considered suitable material in any language and environment. A man's Coptic letter on an ostracon from the monastery of Epiphanius (O.Mon.Epiph. 281) is instructive. Paul apologized to the anchorite Apa Pson for not writing sooner, repeatedly blaming lack of papyrus for the delay. Although the letter on the ostracon is hardly short, he said that he had told his message to a priest who was going to repeat it in detail to the monk, "mouth to mouth." Apologies for using ostraca rather than papyrus are a cliché of Coptic letter writing.

Very few women's letters in Greek are written on ostraca, only eight in all. These letters come mainly from locations in the Eastern Desert, and the reason for the choice of material is no doubt a shortage of papyrus at a remote location; the military environment of the desert generated thousands of such letters on ostraca, but few of their authors were women.

As noted earlier, in late antiquity the situation changes. Two-thirds of women's letters from this period were written on ostraca. In large part this proportion reflects the dominance of Coptic in women's letters of this period (see chap. 3) and the dominance of ostraca in Coptic letter writing. Limestone pieces were used occasionally for the more formal among them, such as the letter of a wretched widow to the bishop Pisentius. In general, even though some letters on ostraca were short and ephemeral, it was not the length of a message to communicate that dictated the use of an ostracon.

Parchment was very rarely used for letters in Egypt. Only one woman's letter (P.Iand. 2.12) is written on a piece of parchment, and we know of only three letters by men on this material (PSI 3.208, PSI 9.1041, and SB 3.7269). Likewise, only one woman's letter is written on a wooden board, P.Kell.Copt. 5.42. Its size was so small as to be able to fit into a hand. It is difficult to know whether this letter actually was sent or whether it was only a draft, as the absence of an address might indicate. In Rome small, easily portable tablets were sometimes used for drafts of letters and notes. Cicero, for instance, jotted down the draft of a letter at a dinner party while lying on the couch (Fam. 9.26), and Pliny did the same during boar hunting, while he was waiting by the nets (1.6).

The women's letters on papyrus confirm N. Lewis's view (1974: 129–34) that papyrus was not regarded as expensive in social circles above that of peasants and unskilled laborers. The vast majority of these letters, in fact, are written on sheets used for the first time: the main text appears on the front and is inscribed along the fibers, and the address is on the back, which is left mostly unwritten. Very occasionally, as in SB 14.12085 and P.Oslo 2.52, remnants of a documentary text are visible on the back together with the address. Since there is every reason to believe that the women who wrote and sent letters belonged for the most part to a propertied elite, it is only to be expected that they could easily afford fresh, blank sheets.

Papyri that already had another text on the front were reused on the back by women in just 7 percent of cases. The front carried a private document or an account that a woman might easily have found among her papers and was cut to the desired size. Writers in general used completely blank sides of sheets. Only once (*P.Oxf.* 19) did the person who wrote a short note share the same side occupied by an obsolete documentary text. This writer, perhaps the woman herself, took a small piece that already contained a receipt, tried to wash out the text, gave up, turned the sheet, and used the small available space for the letter.

Letters from Graeco-Roman Egypt occasionally contain requests for papyrus. Such solicitations are too rare to be of much significance for the question of the cost and availability of this writing material (Skeat 1995). Two women's letters include such requests or complaints about unfulfilled requests. One was found at Wadi Fawakhir, a mining camp in the Eastern Desert, and no doubt was written in a similar milieu. In the second letter, *P.Wash.Univ.* 2.106, Dionysia complains to her "brother" Panechotes that he did not write to her and did not even send her "a sheet of unwritten papyrus (*kollema agraphon*)". We do not know where she lived, but no doubt Panechotes, who was in Oxyrhynchos, could easily purchase papyrus.

Besides the fact that most women who wrote letters belonged to the more comfortable strata, a further reason why the cost of papyrus for correspondence did not represent a problem for them was that letters were relatively short and required a moderate quantity of papyrus. It is likely that letter writers sometimes obtained writing material by cutting an unwritten piece from an old papyrus. Rolls with literary works, for instance, often had an unwritten part (*agraphon*) at the end. The habit of cutting from a used papyrus is documented for school exercises. This form of reuse is hard to detect in letters, because adult writers may have done a better job at cutting a piece than students. But it is not clear how else one obtained just enough papyrus for a single letter. A person might go to a scribe, who would cut a piece from a roll or would even write the letter on the roll and cut it afterward. But how would a literate woman proceed in order to write the letter herself? Did she always have a full roll at her disposal? And how about the woman who asked a friend or a relative to pen her letter? Were some people purchasing single sheets besides whole rolls? Responding to these questions is not easy. The papyri sometimes mention sums of money paid for papyrus sheets, even half a sheet. Three letters, one from a woman (*P.Wash.Univ.* 2.106) and two from men (*SB* 6.9017–15; and *P.Flor.* 3.367), mention individual sheets used for correspondence. It appears that people could find on the market papyrus stationery and could purchase individual pieces, whether whole sheets or not, and not only rolls. Even if manufacturers sold only by the roll, retailers must have cut rolls up in order to have sheets available for sale.

LETTER WRITING: DUAL LETTERS ∾

There are eight, possibly nine, dual letters on a papyrus sheet, a group to which *P.Brem.* 61, which includes three letters, should be added. Dual letters can originate from various situations. A woman might decide to write to two people who lived in the same household or not far from each other (*SB* 20.14032; *P.Oxy.* 31.2599; *P.Grenf.* 1.53; and *P.Oxy.* 36.2789). Conversely, two or more people might join their efforts in writing to the same person (*BGU* 2.615; *P.Oxy.* 62.4340; *P.Giss.* 81; and *P.Brem.* 61). But someone might also decide to reply to a letter by using the same sheet (*P.Leid.Inst.* 42; and possibly *SB* 16.12981 and *P.Benaki* 4–5).

Since most of these letters were dictated, even when there was more than one sender, a single writer penned both letters. An interesting case is represented by the three letters of *P.Brem.* 61, a papyrus by several hands. Apollonios's sister took the initiative of dictating a letter for him, adding salutation in her hand. The scribe also penned another letter of one of Apollonios's friends, who subscribed in his own hand. Apollonios's uncle then penned his message entirely in his hand, showing his customary independence. This papyrus shows to the full the disparate mechanisms that regulated the writing of more than one letter on the same sheet.

When a letter prompted a reply, one would naturally expect the latter to be in a different hand than that of the first. This is probably what happened in *SB* 16.12981: the addressee of the first letter, Serapion, used the back of the papyrus for a very fragmentary letter. But the case of *P.Leid.Inst.* 42 is more intriguing. Two letters are written on the front of this papyrus in a hand that is not entirely fluent: the hand of the courier himself. A woman, Heras, dictated a letter to her sister, in which she reproached her for never replying and urged the courier to bring an answer back. A different circumstance and pen, and perhaps some haste, are responsible for some variations in the handwriting of the reply, but the writer is unmistakably the same. In another case, *BGU* 2.615, the person who took down the dictation of two letters from a woman and a man may have been responsible for taking the letters to their destination.

Multiple letters issuing from the same sender or from different senders to the same recipient need to be considered together, almost as single texts. They refer to people who had close relationships among themselves and often belonged to the same family and therefore form small archives. We can surmise that they were read one after the other so that the single or multiple addressees were aware of both texts. But even when two letters addressed people who did not have a close relationship, and one of the addressees was actually an antagonist, as in *P.Grenf.* 1.53, the letters belong together as a unit. The format of this papyrus makes this particularly evident. Artemis wrote a letter to her husband, then enclosed a letter for the soldier Sarapion, the father of two "naughty" girls. In the same way the two letters (*P.Oxy.* 36.2789) that Kleopatra wrote to her father and Moros, a man with whom she had a business relationship, were probably not meant to be detached but have to be considered one and the same text.

GETTING LETTERS DELIVERED ❧

Letter writers in the ancient world usually had them delivered informally, through friends or acquaintances who traveled to a certain location. Only rarely was there the possibility of using an official letter carrier. This fact, coupled with the vague information contained in addresses, made a letter's delivery less than certain. The complaint about lack of a prompt reply to one's written messages often occurs in ancient letters, both in those from renowned writers such as Cicero and in those from common people from Graeco-Roman Egypt. It is so frequently expressed that it can almost be considered a cliché. It is part of human experience that receiving personal correspondence brings a degree of pleasure and expectation. And yet, in the erratic state of mail delivery in antiquity, one suspects that such complaints were often based on real problems.

While Cicero and his addressees often traveled in the provinces and encountered difficulties in sending and receiving a steady flow of correspondence, people in Graeco-Roman Egypt wanting to communicate with others who lived in different parts of the country often encountered the same difficulties. In *P.Mert.* 2.82, Nike, who is ill, writes to her sister primarily to defend herself from the accusation that she had neglected to send a letter. "Was I so boorish as not to write to you?" Nike says. The word she uses, *amathes*, denotes an uneducated person unable to handle the written word even indirectly. Nike concludes that her letters probably were not delivered. It is also significant that the women in the archive of Apollonios do not level this accusation at each other. Not only is it likely that they corresponded with some regularity, but they probably did not encounter particular difficulties in sending their letters to their destination.

Addresses were usually added on the back of a letter, and, if that side already contained some other text, they coexisted with it. Their utter simplicity and lack of detail presupposed personal knowledge on the part of the courier. As a rule, in fact, they consisted of a slight variation of the first line of a letter, the prescript: "to so-and-so" (the addressee) "from so-and-so" (the sender). In very few cases would an address supply more detailed information. In *W.Chr.* 100 Serenilla described her father by name and patronymic and mentioned the man who was going to deliver the letter; in *P.Bad.* 2.35 the sender supplied a geographical location, Ptolemais Hermeiou. The same happened in *P.Oxy.* 14.1773, which Eutychis addressed to the Camp, a quarter of Oxyrhynchos. Sometimes the sender herself may have been aware that an address was incomplete and unclear, as in *BGU* 1.332, which carries two addresses. But usually a letter was at the mercy of the person who delivered it, who had received oral instructions about its destination.

More complicated is the scenario evoked by another letter, *P.Mich.* 8.514. Isidora, the writer, furnishes the address of an Apollos, since she is in Alexandria, away from home. The letter is addressed to Onnophris the priest and not to the actual addressee Sarapias. The address of a third letter, *P.Tebt.* 2.414, written by a woman to her sister, introduces the latter as the "wife of the potter." Men seem to have been more readily identifiable and locatable parties.

Men sometimes also displaced women as senders in addresses. A response then would be sent to the more visible male sender. Like Isidora, in *P.Mich.* 8.507 Artemis may have stayed in Alexandria in the house of Harpakysis, who appears in the address. The same might be true in the case of Zoe in *BGU* 3.827. The address identifies the sender as Petronius the *dromadarius*, who may have been Zoe's host or may have written the whole of the letter that was subscribed by her.

It is not rare to find women's—and men's—letters without an address. One might suppose that some letters were never sent, but it is likely that the absence of an address was mostly due to other reasons. In some cases addresses are missing because letters are not entirely preserved. But when a letter without an address is complete, other scenarios are possible. A letter might have been included in a parcel containing various goods with an outer address. A letter without an address might also have been a copy that a sender kept for her personal file. This, for instance, is likely the case in *P.Oxy.* 59.3993, written by a man and a woman to their children.

Since couriers were mostly friends and acquaintances who were conveniently traveling to a certain place, a sender might have thought that an address was not strictly necessary, especially because she had already furnished the courier with oral indications. Because most of the time addresses consisted of a repetition of the first line of a letter, with the name of the sender and of the addressee, if a letter was not strictly confidential and was entrusted to someone well known, the sender might not have felt the need to seal it. Addresses on ancient letters were thus part of epistolary convention but were often non-essential elements that on some occasions could be dispensed with.

A person delivering a letter was usually simply described as "the man who is bringing you this message." The knowledge that someone was ready to travel to a certain location encouraged people to send messages to distant relatives and friends. When the message carried a certain urgency and there was something to communicate besides salutations we may surmise that people actively looked for a courier. Very occasionally a woman writer might use an official courier, variously called *epistolaphoros*, *grammatephoros*, or *symmachos*. *Epistolaphoroi* were carriers of official correspondence and were organized by nome. Most private people would not have had access to one of them. Beginning in the fourth century AD, official couriers were also called *grammatephoroi*. This term could also indicate a more informal service. In a letter written by a man, *P.Heid.* 7.411, the *grammatephoros* was a woman, certainly not an official. Since women traveled commonly for various reasons (see chap. 9), it is only natural that sometimes they carried with them letters to be delivered. A woman, for instance, is the carrier of the letter and clothes that Apia sends to her mother Serapias (*P.Oxy.* 14.1679).

Very often a letter accompanied the sending of goods. These could consist of foodstuffs of various kinds, clothes, material, money, or even a donkey (*P.Oxy.* 14.1773). The items dispatched were listed in a letter so that the recipient could be aware if something was missing. Some apprehension in this regard can be perceived in the words of Ammonous, who was sending a basket to her father (*BGU* 2.615): "If the man bringing you the letter brings you a basket, I am sending it." The lack of a dependable carrier sometimes prevented people from dispatching goods. Thus, Euthalios and Mike could not find a reliable friend or relative to take things to their mother before Lent started and opted not to send anything (*SB* 12.10840).

Letter carriers are sometimes presented as people coming and going in a great hurry, as, for instance, in *BGU* 2.615. When in *O.Florida* 14 a woman tells her recipient that the person delivering the ostracon was going to return to her, it is difficult to know how soon that was going to happen and whether delivering the letter had been this man's main task. In *P.Oxy.* 14.1773, Eutychis tells her mother expressly "not to detain even one hour" the men who were bringing her letter and goods. There is no information concerning carriers' speed in delivering letters, but it must have varied considerably according to circumstance and means of transportation. It is instructive in fact that two letters probably written from the Herakleopolite to Memphis by Isidora to Asklepiades (*BGU* 4.1206 and 1207) were sent three days apart but were received in reverse order of sending.

In spite of all the difficulties a writer encountered in getting her letters delivered, some women seem to have been successful in establishing regular epistolary contacts. Isidora, a lady of means, was one of them. But regular contacts also existed between the slave Aphrodite and her mistress (*P.Tebt.* 2.413). "We are behind-hand in sending you letters," Aphrodite writes to Arsinoe, "because of having no one . . . . " A suitable letter carrier must be hidden in the lacuna of the papyrus.

CHAPTER 6

Handwriting

In a felicitous expression, Herbert Youtie described the hand of *SB* 16.12589 as a hand "which breathes," that is, a hand with characters well spaced and unconstrained by their proximity to others. One might extend this definition of "breathing hands" to epistolary hands more generally. A letter hand is typically less uniform and more personal than most documentary hands. Letter hands—including the most proficient—often exhibit a pace of execution that varies from section to section as well as a palpable struggle for legibility. Clarity and legibility are almost universal characteristics, in contrast to the handwriting taught to women in the eighteenth century, which was slow but ornamental and difficult to read (Thornton 1996: 55–63).

Naturally, these traits are more evident in the less smooth and homogeneous hands, those of secretaries or of individuals who did not write on a daily basis. The private hands in particular, and the less experienced among them, show all the immediacy—the struggle, the successes, and the failures—of the hands that penned school exercises. These "breathing" hands are unpredictable: they may triumphantly assert some limited expertise and then collapse into quivering and throbbing characters.

In what follows, we have divided letter hands into broad categories. About a third of these hands stand out because they are particularly proficient. These should be distinguished from those hands (approximately another third) that are experienced but not as smooth and flowing as the first group; some might have belonged to secretaries. The remaining third are personal hands; they show some discontinuities and probably belonged to individuals for whom writing was not a daily concern. More than half of these hands exhibit serious difficulties in handling the pen.

In terms of the identities of all these writers, however, these categories may overlap considerably, as our employment of the scholar's usual adverbs of reservation shows. While the extremely proficient hands of professional scribes are conspicuous, there is some uncertainty concerning the people who penned the letters in the second category and the most experienced hands in the last. There must have been different levels of expertise among scribes. Not every individual who earned a living writing documents displays superior ability. Location of the writer and the recipient of a letter may have played a role. In the Zenon archive, for instance, or among Roman chancery hands, papyri destined for higher spheres were written more formally than others. But a study of scribal hands according to provenance, destination, and type of document is still a desideratum (cf., on early Christian scribes, Haines-Eitzen 2000). It is therefore difficult to define the boundary between mediocre scribes and accomplished secretaries.

Another possibility that unfortunately we were not able to verify is that some of the letters were penned by women who functioned as scribes and secretaries. Haines-Eitzen (2000: 41–52) pointed to evidence of women scribes in the Roman world and Christian monastic settings, but our women's letters do not disclose anything in this respect. It remains possible that some women were employed as secretaries in wealthy households and that women teachers (Cribiore 2001a: 78–83) lent their hands on need.

TYPOLOGY ∾

Professional Hands: Epistolary, Documentary, and Literary

Probably at least two-thirds of the women's letters in Greek were written by someone other than the named author, mainly from dictation. The difficulty of identifying proficient women writers accounts for the imprecision of this estimate. The reasons for dictation have been discussed already and are fairly evident; it is more difficult to discover the motivations of people who opted for personally handwritten letters. We know something of the writing habits of ancient literary figures. In the Roman world an etiquette of correspondence existed among the elite (cf. Horsfall 1995; McDonnell 1996). Quintilian urged Romans to practice penmanship to develop a clear and legible hand. Cicero, Atticus, Cornelius Nepos, and Fronto apologized to addressees who were close friends or social superiors when illness or some other circumstance prevented them from writing in their own hands. This was not merely a rhetorical device; it shows that they were normally expected to pen their own letters to these people, at least until old age and poor eyesight intervened. Dictation of letters to other categories of addressee was, however, always the rule, and salutations in one's own hand guaranteed the participation of the sender. About earlier Greek correspondence, we know little, but in the fourth century AD Libanius dictated his letters to a secretary and added salutations at the bottom (e.g., Ep. 1223). It is curious that Libanius, who gives so many details about his letter writing, never mentions that he wrote a letter in his own hand and never apologizes for not doing so.

While letters generally aimed at being easily legible to eyes that might not be accustomed to reading fast handwriting, such comfortable legibility was not always achieved. Among the "professional" hands, the unabashedly documentary ones stand out. These are hands such as those of *P.Oxy.* 9.1217 or *P.Haun.* 2.18, which are not particularly concerned with legibility. In these letters generally the high quality of the language matches that of the handwriting. In the Roman period only a small percentage of letters are written in such rapid, ligatured cursives. In the Byzantine period, however, highly polished scribal hands dominate in the longer letters on papyrus, for reasons we have already described. Byzantine documentary hands, though at first sight as difficult as Roman ones, are in fact usually larger and slower, developing all the constitutive strokes of a character with flowing and graceful movements.

The presence of fast documentary hands among letters, however, does not justify evaluating typical epistolary hands by their standards. Most writers obviously strove for clarity and legibility. The occasional division of words into syllables and the separation of words, both sometimes occurring in men's and women's letters, are signs not only of slow writing but also of a writer's desire to accommodate the reader's needs.

Whether the most elegant and fluent letter writers were professional scribes or very accomplished secretaries cannot be said with any certainty. "Professional" in this context does not mean fast; some of these hands seem to have been able to perform with no difficulty at a faster level of scribal expertise but chose not to. Instead, they produce a leisurely, perfectly clear and attractive epistolary style. Some even had to struggle to maintain a slow pace. Hands such as those of *P.Bour.* 23, *P.Col.* 8.212, or *P.Lond.* 3.988 appear to have checked their speed repeatedly in order not to lose clarity. In these hands the choice of a clear epistolary style was deliberate; occasion—not only ability— shaped handwriting.

A still lower percentage of letters is written in professional chancery hands, which might have appealed to a letter writer for their easy legibility. These writers incorporated only some features of the chancery style; the highly stylized hands of the most prestigious chancery offices are entirely absent. Fewer still are the examples of literary hands.

Secretarial Hands

In this category, legible, well-spaced handwriting is dominant. Whether the addressee read a letter personally or asked someone in the immediate circle of relatives and friends to do so, it still had to be highly accessible. The approachable handwriting of letters corresponds to their relatively simple content. With a document, it was usually enough to be able to recognize initial formulas, names, sections, or witnesses; the message in the body of a letter had to come across.

Legibility depends on a set of interrelated characteristics: speed, size, and relative autonomy of the characters. Letter hands are generally much slower than documentary ones, or at least they start slowly, though sometimes losing some control as they proceed. A letter is usually not written at a uniform pace. The opening with the names of sender and addressee is very deliberate. Speed increases a bit in the first part of the message and continues at a relatively slow pace; line openings are written very slowly, but the writer gains velocity as lines progress. The salutations are often in faster, semicursive characters, probably because names could be recognized without much trouble. Speed further increases in the farewell, but the address is the slowest part of a letter.

Letter size is also variable. Letter hands are generally larger than documentary ones, but size is not maintained throughout. The largest size tends to appear in a letter opening, in the address, and at the beginning of lines, when the writer periodically renews his or her vows to legibility. When the pace increases, size usually decreases, so that the final farewell is often in minute characters.

With their slow pace of execution and large size, characters in a letter tend to maintain their individual identity, remaining separate from adjacent ones. Ligatures are kept to a minimum, generally consisting of simple strokes that link some vowels to a following letter. They rarely transform a letter's basic appearance. A reader with limited literacy could thus hop from syllable to syllable with relative ease. The typical letter hand was probably more easily legible even than a book hand. As in school exercises, the linking strokes and proximity of characters in a letter hand eased the reader's eye in gliding through a text.

About one-third of all the women's letters are in what we have called a secretarial hand, experienced but without the degree of elegance and professionalism of a scribal hand. The women's letters in the archive of Apollonios offer examples of such hands. The evidence from this archive shows how difficult it is to separate professional and secretarial hands into mutually exclusive categories. The family matriarch Eudaimonis dictated eight of her letters, sent over a period of eight years. Among these it is possible to identify at least five different hands. Three are very accomplished and fine examples of "professional" hands; the writers of the first two letters may have been trained in writing literary texts, while the scribe of the third produced an unusually ligatured hand. The other four letters are in typically secretarial hands with clear and mostly separated characters showing occasional unevenness. The secretaries available in this wealthy household possessed an impressive range of skills.

Personal Hands

This category comprises approximately sixty hands of individuals for whom writing was not a daily activity. It is mostly here that one looks for women's hands. At the highest end of the spectrum there are hands only slightly less practiced than some of the secretarial ones, while at the lowest end there are those hands that can be defined, in the terms used for school exercises, as "evolving," and occasionally even "alphabetic." With few exceptions, personal hands—and particularly the most accomplished among them—do not have any trouble with individual letter shapes. The individual strokes can be fluent and even elegant and show that the writer continued to do some writing after leaving school. Producing an altogether attractive text, however, seems to have been beyond the capabilities of these hands. Several factors reveal lack of expertise: particularly unruly right margins, wildly varying line spaces, wavering lines of writing, clumsy corrections, and retracing of letters. A glance is sufficient to recognize texts that, though not too badly produced and even very extensive, have a definitely unprofessional air.

Who are the people behind these personal hands? Some, as we will discuss, were the women themselves, those who had not only the ability but also the desire to leave an entirely personal mark. Otherwise we can speculate about the existence of relatives, friends, or acquaintances who lent their hands. Only rarely is it possible to go beyond speculation and identify specific individuals. When Isias sent an earnest letter asking her husband Hephaistion to return home (*UPZ* 1.59), her brother-in-law penned the body of the message; his hand appears in another letter he wrote. In *P.Oxy.* 56.3860 it is Alexandros, Taesis's guest, who discharges some of his obligations by penning her letter. Toward the end, he reveals his role and his fatigue at writing: "I Alexandros wore myself out writing you the letter." In spite of many corrections, some clumsiness, and lines that are too crowded and not too symmetrical, Alexandros was able to maintain the identity of his hand till the end of this very long letter without visibly collapsing. It happens very often, however, that personal hands produce acceptable results at first but are then betrayed by the length of a text. In contrast to scribal hands, which seem to become more impatient and faster toward the end, personal hands are often overcome by the effort, just as are school hands.

Approximately half of the private hands exhibit severe and consistent problems with writing. Most of these hands are "evolving," only a few "alphabetic." Letters are not usually limited to just a few lines, as slow writers' subscriptions to contracts are and school exercises might be. Someone with limited experience was likely to embark upon the enterprise of penning a whole letter only after fully mastering the letter shapes. Thus, there are only a handful of letters such as *P.Köln* 1.56 or *P.IFAO* 2.7, in which the acute effort is visibly conveyed by characters that are isolated in their idiosyncrasy.

Different sections of a letter stand out at a glance: the opening, the body, the closing with the final farewell, and the address. Professional writers aimed at some elegance and symmetry in the opening, and less capable people sometimes tried to follow them. In the Byzantine period openings are longer (e.g., SB 20.14226); in Roman times a letter's initial section usually consists of two lines with the names of sender and addressee plus the greeting. Both lines might be in larger characters, aiming at some formality and style, as in P.Mert. 2.82, with its chancery letters, or only the initial characters of each line might be enlarged (e.g., P.IFAO 2.40). The first, or more commonly the second, line might also be conspicuous because words are separated (e.g., PSI 9.1080; and P.Lond. 3.988); indentation also adds to elegance (e.g., P.Oxy. 9.1217). Less experienced writers seem to have considered a formal opening very attractive and tried to imitate scribal conventions.

The body of a letter stands out only because it is framed by the opening and closing sections. Some of the same formality that appears at the beginning is sometimes repeated in the closing section. The address of a letter is like the title of a book. While it aims at being easily legible, it also intends to be a striking presentation of the message. In professional products, addresses were often written with a different style than the rest of a letter. Generally in the Roman period the letters in an address are straight even when the hand of the body leans to the right because the writer concentrates on forming slow, painstaking shapes. In a household well provided with proficient scribes, the last link in the chain may have been someone in charge of addressing and sending letters.

FINAL GREETINGS: SECOND HAND VERSUS SECOND STYLE ⟡

The greetings at the end of a letter were often penned more quickly than the rest. Addressees must have simply verified that greetings were there, recognizing them at a glance by their location and often the hand more than actually reading the individual characters. But the more cursive look of the farewell formula leads us to ask if the greetings were penned by a second hand or were simply in a different style, as most addresses were. Editors hurry to proclaim the existence of a second hand, but this may not be right. In letters written in professional or otherwise experienced hands, the scribes did not have legibility in mind when they penned the final greetings in fast characters. But a close look at these farewell expressions also indicates that the writer was the same throughout. What one concludes from countless examples is that professional scribes and secretaries wrote greetings at a faster pace but without altering their handwriting in the same way as they did in addresses.

In the category of the personal hands, several situations are possible. Greetings might be in the same stiff characters as the rest of a letter, as in P.Oxy. 14.1761, where the same writer wrote the whole thing. Neither style nor size distinguishes this from the main hand of the text. If the writer was different from the sender, he did not want or was unable to write faster greetings. If a woman herself wrote the whole message, she had not developed a faster style for greetings because she sent letters only occasionally.

Finally, there is a large group of letters in which the greetings are in a smaller and slightly different hand from that of the body. In some cases there is no way of knowing for sure how many persons were involved. P.Petaus 29 well exemplifies the dilemma faced by a papyrologist. The main hand, large and mainly detached, is not completely proficient; the greetings are faster and more cursive. Either Didymarion wrote the whole letter or another inexperienced writer wrote the body and she penned the greetings. At other times, however, one can reach relative certainty by two possible avenues: comparing other writings by the same woman and examining the dates that sometimes accompany the final greetings. The best way to identify greetings penned by a woman's hand is by comparing them to other writing samples of the same woman. The letters in the archive of Apollonios, which are a good testing ground for women's writing habits, allow one to identify the greetings of Eudaimonis (P.Flor. 3.332; P.Giss. 21; and P.Brem. 63) and Aline (P.Giss. 78). The complete letters show that both women added salutations in their own hands when they dictated a letter. When they wrote the whole message themselves, final salutations do not stand out but are incorporated in the letter. Eudaimonis and Aline knew how to write but followed the custom for letter writing that was prevalent in antiquity when a person belonged to a wealthy and cultivated household, where it was easy to find a secretary who could take down a letter on dictation (cf. Horsfall 1995).

When different writing samples by the same woman are not preserved, another way of determining whether the final greetings are in the hand of the sender or in that of a scribe or secretary is by comparing greetings and dates. Examples where these are written with the same characters and in the same size are numerous, spanning the Ptolemaic and Roman periods. Scribes who added a date to the final greetings did so at the same time without switching to a larger and slower hand (e.g., P.Oxy. 1.116 and 9.1215; and P.Haun. 2.18). The fact that they did not try to make dates slightly more legible than greetings might be surprising. But at the end of a letter, a scribe's hand was in high gear and not likely to slow down. Dates were written slightly faster than the text even when they appeared without final greetings (e.g., P.Col. 8.212). That dates and greetings possessed an identical rhythm and speed is also visible in writing samples of less proficient writers (e.g., *P.Bad.* 4.48; *P.Col.* 8.215; and *P.Köln* 1.56).

In a few letters, however, some discontinuity is apparent, with dates in the same hand as the text and greetings in a faster, smaller hand. This might help us identify a woman's hand. Isias enlisted her brother-in-law's help in writing *UPZ* 1.59. Text and date are written in the same characters, but the greetings are faster. The discrepancy would support Wilcken's supposition that Isias herself added the final salutations. *BGU* 16.2617 and 2618 preserve two letters of Tryphas that were written by proficient scribes. In both, the greetings are in smaller characters than the dates, which appear to have been written continuously after the text. The difference is particularly noteworthy in the second letter, which is written in a rounder and larger hand than the first. It is likely that Tryphas was an experienced enough writer and often appended greetings to a letter.

A WOMAN'S HAND ∾

Not enough is known about women's education in Greek and Roman Egypt— or in antiquity generally (Cribiore 2001a: chap. 3). The instances of exceptional women—of royal status or from extraordinarily educated families—who functioned at highly literate levels (Pomeroy 1977, 1984) do not shed much light on the rest of the female population. It is an easy assumption that in this respect women were in a disadvantaged position. Only a minority of men, after all, functioned at a completely literate level; others used literate modes through intermediaries, and even more were passive spectators. Women did not have the same access to schooling as men did and were excluded from education beyond the grammarian. In learning to read and write, wealth and high social status were more important prerequisites for women than for men. But even though it is clear that the women's letters emanate mainly from wealthy and propertied milieus (chap. 8), and many of the women who appear in them seem to be highly functioning members of society (chap. 9), one instinctively attributes a letter written in a well developed private hand to an educated man and only in passing entertains the idea that the writer might have been a woman. The women who were certainly able to write may be the tip of the iceberg but, ironically, come to light partly because of the limits of their skills. The superior writing skills of other women, who may have operated at high levels of education, are hard to detect (cf. the pessimistic view in Harris 1989).

In evaluating the instances of literate women, it is tempting to search for a Woman's Hand endowed with immutable characteristics different from a man's. This attempt is doomed to failure. In the same way, it is dubious that it is possible to define common features in the personal handwriting of men below the level of professional writers and secretaries. The numerous private hands that appear in the papyri are so dissimilar and betray so many levels of ability that distinguishing them according to periods and styles is not always feasible (Schubart 1925: 146–55). And yet the women's letters form a limited corpus, and the examples of women's handwriting are even fewer, so that one can at least entertain the hope of distinguishing a set of characteristics not common to all, but to enough, of them.

WOMEN WRITE: THE ARCHIVES ∿

The Archive of Apollonios

When several letters of the same woman are preserved, the chance of being able to recognize her own hand in a whole text or in the greetings is greater. While several archives yield good results, the archive of Apollonios presents unique evidence. We have noted that both Eudaimonis and Aline sometimes added fast greetings to their letters. Three letters of Eudaimonis allow us to go farther, detecting her own handwriting in a whole text (Kortus 1999: 52; Cribiore 2001b: 230). *P.Giss.* 22, 23, and 24 are written in the same large and mostly detached hand, which shows some skill in forming individual characters but betrays an overall inability to keep any rhythm. The addresses are written with a style and elegance that betray the work of one or more professionals. Eudaimonis may have been inspired by a desire to be even closer to her family during the Jewish War.

The minute, fast greetings that Aline appended to a letter she sent to a servant (*P.Giss.* 78) prove that she was relatively comfortable with writing. But distinguishing her handwriting in a whole letter with confidence is not possible. An interesting sample of a woman's handwriting appears in *P.Brem.* 61; a relative of the strategos added greetings and a date to the letter she sent. Even though she wrote slowly in separated characters, her hand possesses a certain flair and some of the grace of a book hand. The educated woman's hand resulted from school practice, from letters that she read and wrote, and from literary texts.

The Archive of Asklepiades

In 28 BC Isidora wrote four letters to her "brother" Asklepiades, who pasted them into a roll together with others (*BGU* 4.1204–1207). *BGU* 1204 and 1207 are the product of a scribe with a smooth and fast hand and a good knowledge of the language. This professional writer nevertheless respected Isidora's dictation and some of her idiosyncratic expressions; these recur in the other two letters, likely in her own hand (*BGU* 1205 and 1206), which is slower, larger, and much less polished than that of the scribe. Although it has a certain grace and the bilinearity of a book hand, it does not possess the rhythm and flow that come from frequent use, and it shows marked fatigue as the writing progresses. The same observations apply to her Greek, which is not as polished as in the other letters. The tone itself, which is imperious, condescending, and reproachful, suggests that Isidora had a further reason for writing herself: she may have preferred not to have a witness as she handled Asklepiades so roughly. Finally, the spelling and form of names distinguish these two letters. Isidora spells her name with a superfluous vowel and addresses Asklepiades with a familiar nickname, Asklas, which she did not use in dictating her other letters. All these factors together strongly suggest that Isidora wrote these two letters in her hand.

The Archive of Pompeius

This archive includes five letters in five different hands. Herennia, Pompeius's daughter, sent two of them, while three other women of the family sent the others. Herennia was literate, but it is uncertain whether the other women knew how to write; they used a variety of scribes, whose hands show a notable range of skills. *P.Fouad* 75 is the product of an elegant, professional hand; *SB* 6.9121 is at a lower level but is still written very competently; and the hand of *SB* 6.9120 is very experienced but struggles to maintain a slow speed. The level of Herennia's letters is entirely different. The hands of both *P.Mert.* 2.63 and *SB* 6.9122 belong to experienced writers. While the former is more tenaciously attached to letter shapes learned in school, the latter is able to maintain some speed and rhythm in spite of the mostly separated characters and wavering lines. This hand writes the text and the date, but Herennia herself adds the greetings. She must often have practiced her large, flowing salutation formula, and a serifed letter shows that she had some ambitions. Since Herennia knew how to write but did not subscribe *P.Mert.* 2.63, there is a good chance that she penned it in its entirety. This letter is a labor of love in many respects. It shows that Herennia was able to keep intact her identity as a writer till the end but was unable to increase her speed. As often in letters professionally written, her characters become much smaller in the date for lack of space but are written at the same painfully slow pace.

The Archive of Kronion: The Dossier of Diogenis

Among the women's hands appearing in the corpus, that of Diogenis is possibly the most fluent. Even though a whole letter written by this woman is not extant, the long salutations and further commands that she added to the two letters she dictated show a remarkable fluency. While the fast salutations and the date she pens in *P.Mil.Vogl.* 77 already reveal what a competent writer she was, the additions that she introduces in *P.Mil.Vogl.* 76 show that she would have been fully capable of writing the whole letter. Her impatience is palpable, and as she dictates new thoughts keep intruding. Before dictating further instructions, Diogenis adds her salutations, which go beyond the usual formulaic expressions. She mentions "little" Isidora—her daughter perhaps— and further business. Her hand is faster than her scribe's. It is smaller and more ligatured, and the inclination to the right is a further sign of speed. We can conjure up the picture of this woman quickly reading the final product and adding something else farther down. Diogenis's hand is a sad reminder of our inability to detect with certainty women as competent in writing as she was when we have only letters written entirely in one hand.

Klematia

Klematia, like Diogenis, was an active landowner, who gave peremptory in-structions to a subordinate. Like Tasoucharion, she had access to first-rate scribes with perfect mastery of Greek, as *P.Oxy.* 48.3407 shows. One rightly suspects, therefore, that she herself wrote her other letter, *P.Oxy.* 48.3406, which is of a very different quality. We are again measuring a woman's lack of full command of language and writing skills against our ability to detect her writing. This letter, in any case, is only moderately deficient. Klematia— if she is really the writer—produced an extempore message, which is strongly oral, and did so in an uneven, personal hand that is not entirely lacking in experience. Of course, one can envision circumstances that might have forced her to have recourse to an inept writer. But this is the limit of our investi-gation.

WOMEN WRITE: THE ISOLATED LETTERS ॐ

The difficulties mentioned above are magnified when only one letter of a particular woman is extant. Very few of these can be identified as surely able to write. But it is essential to recognize that this does not mean that women did not write and always asked others to do it for them. It is, rather, simply that we are unable to detect women writers. Most of the time we can only hope to ground more firmly our suspicions that certain hands might have been women's own. The surest way to appraise a woman's hand, as we have seen, is through final greetings and corrections that she added herself, particularly when the additions consist of more than formulaic expressions. Another pos-sibility is the divergence between a low quality of writing and evidently high culture, sometimes an indication that a woman did the writing. The content of a letter can also be a good indication of a woman's participation when the writing has an immediacy that reveals a particular woman's personal touch. Finally, there is the group of letters written throughout in unskilled hands that might—but need not—be women's.

Besides the letters that contain simple closing greetings in a woman's hand, a few others include longer and more significant additions. The extensive greetings appended by Claudia Dionysia to her letter (SB 5.7743) display a striking combination of cursive characters and serifs. Dionysia's hand is almost totally bilinear and reveals some experience with writing. She may have been influenced by the literary hand that penned the whole letter.

Longer and more interesting is the addition of Ammonous to PSI 12.1247. The letter she dictated consists mostly of unusual expressions of greetings, which are indicative of her cultured background. At the end of her letter, Ammonous does more than add personal greetings; she quickly alerts her brother to a thorny matter the letter carrier will explain in detail. Her desire to mention this affair without leaving it to the scribe is already significant of her confidence in writing, which extends beyond the linguistic aspects of the message. Lack of constant practice prevented Ammonous, like other women, from developing a fast, cursive hand, but her handwriting possesses unmistakable elegance and regularity. Doubtless, Ammonous could have penned the whole letter without excessive discomfort.

Toward the end of a long and elaborate letter dictated to a professional scribe in the Byzantine period (SB 18.13762), a poignant comment inserted above the line alerts us that the woman in question, Phoibasia, probably added it in her hand. Phoibasia must have gone through the letter herself and made sure to add that "what she had suffered" entitled her to visit Agapetos—probably her husband—in Alexandria. While the contrast between the professional hand of the letter and her own is striking, this woman's hand is by no means unpracticed, only of a very different quality. The characters are separated and inclined to the right and have some of the same grace of the literary hands of the period. Altogether this hand is similar to that of the relative of Apollonios in P.Brem. 61 and to that of Ammonous, even though these are separated by several centuries.

Finally, we are on even more unsure ground with the last group of hands, those written clumsily in their entirety, and in which poor writing skills match deficient linguistic knowledge. In such letters it is possible to delineate a clear picture of writers, although their identities remain uncertain. Everything that we can conjure up to evoke the image of a woman for whom writing was a painful affair can plausibly be applied to someone else, equally inexperienced, who lent his hand. But a modestly propertied household that did not own or regularly employ a competent secretary might not at any particular moment have access to someone skilled. The argument is thus open to objection. It may seem stronger in extreme cases: would Diodora (*P.Köln* 1.56) not see what a poor specimen her letter to Valerius Maximus was? This letter was occasionally illegible, and the writing degenerated and became even worse in the greetings. The force of this argument is undermined, however, by our lack of knowledge of criteria for acceptable handwriting among common people in antiquity.

COPTIC LETTERS ∾

A notable feature of the women's letters written in Coptic is the relative expertise of their hands and the rare occurrence of unskilled handwriting among them. The difficulty of distinguishing letters penned by women from those that were dictated to another party is thus greater than is the case with letters written in Greek. Even though the vast majority of these letters are penned by accomplished hands, there is considerable difference in the degree of expertise that they exhibit. It is possible to distinguish roughly three groups: the professional, cursive hands and the few literary ones on papyrus; the proficient but not completely even hands of some of the ostraca; and the few irregular hands, which are nevertheless fast and capable and appear on various materials. The letters written on ostraca, which represent two-thirds of all, pose a general problem. In most of the ribbed ostraca, the roughness of the material seems to have been partly or wholly responsible for the unevenness of the hands. The same writer who produced an irregular specimen on a rough surface (e.g., *O.Vind.Copt.* 225) might have looked much more fluent on a smoother material. Besides the obvious advantages offered by papyrus, the uniform surface of a flat clay sherd allowed more room for graceful strokes (as *O.Vind.Copt.* 181 shows); limestone pieces also let a writer perform better (see, e.g., *SBKopt.* 1.295).

The accomplished hands of the first group (e.g., *P.Mon.Epiph.* 433 and 489; *BKU* 416; and *P.Lond.Copt.* 530) are very similar to the fluent and expert hands that penned women's letters in Greek in the Byzantine period. They are large and clear but show some ligatured strokes, though to a lesser degree than the Greek hands. Some letters are greatly enlarged in them, and the vertical strokes of others trail below the baseline. They convey an impression of great skill, which was the result of constant, professional practice. Only a few hands show some literary traits such as serifs, marked bilinearity, and thickening of some strokes. These features are most pronounced in *P.Ryl.Copt.* 310, which was written by a first-class scribe, who was at home with writing literary texts.

The second group comprises the hands that appear most frequently on

Coptic ribbed ostraca, whatever their content. These hands are small, relatively fast (as might be expected, given the writing material), and mostly unligatured (e.g., O.Mon.Epiph. 199, 336; and O.Brit.Mus.Copt. add. 23). They sustain the effort of writing until the end and often maintain a regular alignment. At times, they achieve a printlike quality but are sometimes betrayed by the uneven surface or the thickness of the pen. In the latter case, the lines appear crowded and may wobble, letter size is inconsistent, and the overall result is not entirely accomplished. In spite of this slightly coarse look, however, these hands are trained and experienced and might have belonged to scribes.

We could call the hands that belong to the third group "private" or "personal" hands, but we have to keep in mind that these terms are purely descriptive and do not refer to specific groups of people who used this kind of handwriting. Again, it is possible that these hands belonged to individuals who wrote daily and helped others discharge their writing obligations. We do not know, for example, the identity of writers such as those who penned P.Kell.Copt. 43 and 50. Hands that clearly show difficulty writing are rare. There are no examples of "alphabetic" hands, and only two or three hands can be defined as "evolving." Effort is evident, for example, in O.Mon.Epiph. 293, which exhibits stains, extensive cancellations, and multistroke characters. Similarly, the quality of the handwriting is rather low in O.Brit.Mus.Copt. 68,4, which was written slowly by someone who strove to produce a better text but was unable to. Were these letters penned by the women who sent them? Of course, it is impossible to go beyond the realm of speculation.

There is, all the same, evidence that some women did pen their own Coptic letters. O.Mon.Epiph. 170 presupposes the existence of at least one, and possibly two, women writers, since the two letters on this ostracon are written in two different hands. It would be nonsensical to imagine that both Maria and Susanna asked two different people to help them. Interestingly, both hands display good familiarity with writing. On another ostracon of the same collection, moreover, O.Mon.Epiph. 386, Tatre announces that she wrote her letter in her hand. This remark, which appears rather infrequently, is an indication of pride in her accomplishment, and rightly so. This ostracon visibly demonstrates the value of practice, as Tatre produced a few clumsy lines but improved dramatically in the course of the letter.

DATING HANDWRITING ∾

In the absence of objective evidence (see chap. 10), dates for letters depend on the style of handwriting. Professional letter hands that are heavily ligatured can be dated by comparison with contemporary documents. While studies of documentary and literary hands exist, based on palaeographical characteristics that evolved over the course of time, there is no such study of hands that takes into account all letters, men's as well as women's. For all of these reasons, palaeographical dates are often very approximate.

Dating Ptolemaic and Byzantine women's letters is to some degree less problematic than dating Roman ones. In neither period was there a marked difference between the handwriting of letters and documents, if only because few unpracticed hands occur in the letters. But dating Greek hands in the Roman period, with a wider range of writers and a greater use of personal hands, can present problems. A letter hand written at a slow pace with unconnected characters can be as difficult to date as a school hand, because its writer has not yet acquired a style of penmanship that follows the fashion of the times and often clings to letter shapes learned in school. School hands, moreover, of both teachers and students, are conservative and tend to adopt new features of a certain script only when it is well established, and then they maintain them for centuries. Focusing on certain palaeographical details that might seem datable, therefore, is hazardous.

CHAPTER 7

Language

The letters collected in this book were written in Egyptian and Greek. These were by no means the only languages in use in Egypt during the millennium spanned by these letters. Egypt was located in a Levantine world where many other languages were spoken, including above all Aramaic and related Semitic languages and dialects. There can be no doubt that many of them were in use in Egypt, particularly in commercial centers like Memphis, Pelusium, and Alexandria, but we have relatively few texts from these places. Latin, the dominant language of the western Roman Empire, is moderately well represented in the papyri, but its use was mostly legal, official, and military; there are few private letters, all, so far, by men. There are, however, a number of letters by women from Britain preserved in the Vindolanda tablets found at Hadrian's Wall (see *T.Vindol.* II 257, 291–294, 324). After the Arab conquest, of course, there begin to be texts on papyrus and then paper in Arabic, but these fall almost entirely outside our time period.

The vast disparity in numbers of letters in Greek and Egyptian in our collection reflects to some degree the abilities and preferences of the modern scholars who have edited these texts. But to an even greater extent it displays the complicated history of the use of Egyptian in written form during this millennium (Bagnall 1993: chap. 7). At the start of the Ptolemaic period, three Egyptian scripts were in widespread use but for different purposes. Only the cursive Demotic script was used for such purposes as contracts and private letters. This had not always been the case. There are many letters surviving from earlier periods written in Hieratic, when that cursive script was the workhorse of daily life. An ample collection of these has been published in translation by Edward Wente, with dates ranging from the Old Kingdom to Dynasty 21 at the very end of the New Kingdom (Wente 1990). They display many of the characteristics found in letters on papyrus and ostraka from the Hellenistic and Roman periods and raise many of the same issues.

As chapter 3 indicates, the use of Demotic declined during the latter part of the Ptolemaic period, and after the first half century of Roman rule it largely

vanished from any role in the documentation of everyday life and legal transactions, despite its lively role in literature in the temples. Although Egyptian
was unquestionably the majority language of everyday speech in the countryside and probably even in the cities, for most people it had no regular means
of being recorded in writing. This period of silence in written Egyptian letters
corresponds with the peak period of Greek letter writing.

That situation ended only with the arrival of Coptic as a vehicle for recording letters composed in the oral Egyptian language, a process that on
present evidence should be dated to the second quarter of the fourth century,
although it is not impossible that earlier letters will come to light. The earliest
surviving correspondence in Coptic comes from monastic communities, but
the discovery of the Coptic letters from Kellis has narrowed the once considerable gap between monastic and nonmonastic letter writing in Coptic to a
matter of perhaps a couple of decades. Even this gap could disappear with
another discovery. There are few other substantial finds of letters from villages
from the beginning of the fourth century; the village archives for which this
period is known, like those of Aurelius Isidoros and Aurelius Sakaon, mostly
consist of official and business papers, not letters. The bulk of our Coptic
letters, however, comes from a considerably later period, the seventh and
eighth centuries, principally because the major sources are ostraca written in
and to the monastic communities of that era (see chap. 3). There is no reason
to believe that Coptic was not in widespread use in village and monastic
settings in the fifth and sixth centuries. But whether the same is true of cities
is harder to say.

GREEK AND EGYPTIAN IN LITERATE SOCIETY ❧

As we have indicated already, the authors of the women's letters on the whole
seem to belong to the upper social and economic strata of this society (see
also chap. 8). Connecting that social place to the sociolinguistic situation in
Egypt across these centuries is not easy, particularly because we are effectively
limited to the written use of language, having very little access to information
about the oral use of Greek and Egyptian. At the beginning of Macedonian
rule in Egypt, there was already a small cadre of Egyptians capable of using
Greek and probably also some Greeks competent in Egyptian. Most of these
had probably been in the service of the Persian government or active in trade,
and they were only the latest representatives of groups present in Egypt since
the seventh century BC. There is no reason to think the numbers of either
group were large, however. The arrival of thousands of Greek-speaking soldiers
in the employ of Ptolemy I after the death of Alexander the Great in 323 no
doubt expanded the Hellenic population considerably, for Alexander himself

had not left a large garrison or a sizable Greek-speaking administration. They were followed over the next century or more by large numbers of settlers from all over the eastern Mediterranean, not all of them Greeks by strict standards but using Greek as the common language of communication. What exactly "large numbers" means in this context is impossible to say, perhaps a few hundred thousand at most, a hundred thousand at a minimum.

It is difficult to distinguish the history of language from the history of society during the ensuing centuries. Histories of the Hellenistic period have within the last half century moved from positing a high level of cultural fusion to describing two cultural solitudes to lacking any simple, dominant theme. No doubt this less confident stance is more realistic than the earlier, simpler extremes, but it is hard to characterize. The last two decades have gradually made it clear that Greek and Egyptian documentation does not correspond in any simple fashion to underlying realities. The same individuals in some cases operated in both spheres for different purposes: Greek in royal service, often Egyptian in religion, but much more mixed in law and private relations. Long before the end of the Ptolemaic period, Greek was overtaking Egyptian as a means of communication in practically every sphere except the religious, and yet, at least until the late second century BC, private legal instruments in Demotic remained common.

What seems clear is that society contained a considerable spectrum of individual positions in the use of language, ranging from Greek settlers whose Egyptian was limited to a few words for talking to servants or tradesmen, to numerous Egyptian peasants who encountered Greek almost exclusively in the person of bureaucrats and even there used intermediaries as far as possible. Between these extremes were many more or less bilingual persons. In some general sense there was a positive correlation between knowledge of Greek and position in the social and economic hierarchy. But that correlation was far from perfect, and many people who had little Greek themselves no doubt had tax receipts in Greek in their files and Greek legal contracts, drafted and even signed by someone else, safely stored away. Generation of Greek documentation, in other words, extended by proxy much farther in society than did actual competence in Greek.

This pattern appears to have extended itself much farther under Roman rule, especially during the three hundred years when Greek was the only available means of written communication for most people, whether they did the writing themselves or not. The Romans' attitude toward languages other than Greek and Latin was less friendly than the Ptolemies' had been, and whatever difficulties Egyptians had found with legal instruments in languages other than their own in late Ptolemaic times certainly grew. But it is not necessary to imagine coercion as the engine of change. The dominance of Greek no doubt reinforced itself gradually.

The arrival of Coptic changed things only very slowly. Legal instruments and the entire operation of government continued to use Greek (except where Latin intruded at high levels). Although Coptic contracts are by no means uncommon in the sixth century, they did not become dominant until after the Arab conquest. It should be kept in mind that learning Coptic as a script implied learning at least some Greek, because most of the alphabet was Greek and a sizable fraction of the vocabulary was also borrowed. To learn Coptic thus certainly required at least command of the Greek alphabet, and it is doubtful that there was a truly separate Coptic educational system during the period of Roman rule.

The social location of Coptic users is also difficult to discern. There are good reasons for thinking that the early development of Coptic took place in privileged, bilingual milieus. Certainly some of the experimentation with writing Egyptian in Greek characters took place in the Egyptian temples, which were largely bilingual settings by the second century if not earlier, and the final development of a standardized writing system may well have been the work of bilingual Christian circles. Coptic in the fourth century is found exclusively in Christian milieus—including the Manichaean groups that clearly considered themselves Christian—and displays a dazzlingly rich Greek vocabulary. The Kellis letters have a number of greetings in Greek alongside the Coptic bodies of the texts, suggesting ready code switching between the languages and a deliberate use of Coptic for personal reasons rather than because of an inability to write in Greek.

These indicators are enough to show that it would be unsafe to suppose that Coptic was used by a lower stratum in society than Greek was. As its use broadened in later centuries, it is possible (but even then not certain) that this was the case, but early Coptic texts give the impression of coming from the same kind of circles that Greek letters do. Even when short, less elaborate Coptic letters become common, their writers resemble the authors of the shorter, more informal, Greek letters.

In reading the women's letters, then, we start with few certainties about the authors. We must try to deduce their status from internal evidence in the letters and information that they give about themselves or their addressees rather than imagining that a letter in Greek, Demotic, or Coptic tells us something of itself. Rather, access to writing (even if that means writing by others in most cases) was diffused fairly widely and was not limited to a small Greek-speaking elite.

DICTATED VERSUS COMPOSED VERSUS AUTOGRAPH: ORALITY OF LETTER PROSE ᵔ

An ancient letter needs to be carefully placed in the context of the person who composed the text and the person who wrote it, because they were not necessarily identical. A third party consists of the audience, that is, the recipient or recipients, who often remain behind the stage. Only when several letters survive by a single woman or more is known about her family and circumstances does the audience really come into play. No clear gender distinctions are discernible in the way males and females sent letters. In general terms, the relationship between a woman and her letter may fall at various points along a spectrum: rather distant, when she gives only some directions, leaving the composition of the text itself entirely to a second party; closer when she dictates her letter word for word; and very tight when she is able to articulate and pen the letter herself. It is useful to examine in detail these different scenarios, but one needs to be wary of generalizations because the distinctions between these different modes of expression are often blurred.

A woman who relies on a second party to have her letter written down is like a storyteller who spins her tale using the language of conversation, narrative, and sometimes reminiscence. Depending on her level of literacy and personal confidence and on the ability and authority of the text's writer, her story may be entirely retold, preserving only the bare outlines, or may bear the strong imprints of her language and personality. A literate woman was able to read and check the text of the letter written down by someone else: this can be verified for Eudaimonis (*P.Giss.* 21) and Phoibasia (*SB* 18.13762), who added remarks in their hands. Secretaries are likely to have respected the actual words of such women, but the opposite might happen not only when an illiterate woman left the written form of her letter entirely to the amanuensis but also when a woman employed a proficient scribe who was able to rewrite the text as he was hearing it. More commonly, the writer was not able or did not wish to do so and limited himself to taking dictation, and in this case a woman's "voice" is still detectable.

The term "voice" is sometimes abused in modern scholarship. In what follows, we will not use it to indicate a typical and distinctive female voice that reflects the style, concerns, and modes of expression of an essentialized Woman. We will, rather, use "voice" to refer to these women's individual ways of expressing themselves. Women's letters, however, also let emerge male voices, those of the various writers who articulated and sometimes transformed the texts they received.

A Woman Spins Her Tale

Some of the women's letters evoke a scenario like that of a classical Athenian speechwriter for a litigant: a skilled writer hears a woman's story and puts it down in his own words. Consider, for instance, a highly polished letter, *CPR* 14.53, which was composed and penned by a professional scribe for a group or community of women. The beginning of the text is particularly artful, stilted, and impersonal. As the scribe proceeds to expound the matter at hand, the narrative becomes less impersonal but still by no means the woman's own words. We know that she is there—for instance, when she reminds her recipient that she did not receive some pepper that he was supposed to send or when she abandons the first plural pronouns of the group in favor of a singular pronoun in the address. The writer, however, takes over almost entirely.

Another letter that shows to the full the expertise of the man who wrote and composed it is *P.Rain.Cent.* 70. The scribe, who has clear and elegant handwriting influenced by the chancery style, uses a sophisticated vocabulary and a polished style. This letter, which concerned a personal loss, allowed a capable writer to draw from his rhetorical resources and even to draw inspiration from model letters of condolence. Our knowledge of women's education indicates that they were not exposed to rhetorical instruction; it is thus very unlikely that a woman could compose in such an elegant and elaborate personal style.

The average letter was not so extensive as these two, covered more ordinary subjects, and presented fewer challenges, both for the woman who determined its content and the actual writer. Sarapias, who sent *PSI* 4.308, relied on a capable writer with a rather fast but clear and large hand. She may not have been literate, as she did not subscribe in her hand. Her message is very simple; she must have told the scribe or secretary only the names of the recipient and of those whom she wanted to salute. *P.Oxy.* 9.1217 presents a similar situation, with a scribe competently fleshing out a few greetings.

A letter with a more complicated content is *P.Oxy.* 48.3407, which deals with practical business matters that did not require elegant rhetoric. It was written in a rather fast cursive hand in the name of a lady, the same Klematia who probably penned *P.Oxy.* 48.3406 herself. Both letters contain instructions to dependents and use a brusque and practical style with almost no attention to polite introductory and concluding expressions. But the differences between the two texts are remarkable. Klematia had some difficulty with spelling and wrote in an oral, paratactic style without connectives. The man who wrote the other letter expressed himself in almost impeccable Greek, avoiding colloquialisms. Klematia must have given him quick directions about the text, but he displayed their relationships to the text by referring to her as "the landlady" rather than by name.

Dictated Letters

Most letters, however, show to different degrees the imprint of a woman dictating to a second party. They are written in fluent hands and belonged to experienced writers. Even so, these secretaries were not able or did not care to alter significantly the words that they heard. These letters are tinged with the colors of everyday speech. They often include direct discourse, reporting people's actual words. Not surprisingly, rather than smooth pieces of writing, with clauses tightly interconnected, they are fragmented in smaller, disconnected units connected by "and." The pace of the narrative is thus fast and jerky. Clauses pile up in succession: they look like crude lists of errands or statements and appear longer than they really are. A letter such as *P.Abinn.* 34, for example, shows a scribe with an experienced hand taking down the dictation of a woman speaking in short, nervous sentences. The writer introduced a good number of connective particles in order to produce a mellower prose but to no avail; the result is still very close to spoken Greek. In another letter, *P.Oxy.* 6.932, although the handwriting is clear, smooth, and even elegant, the scribe seems to have given up on the attempt to improve on the abrupt commands of Thais. Omissions that would be acceptable in oral language give her written text a sense of incompleteness.

It is important, in stressing the oral characteristics of dictated letters, not to lose sight of the fact that the orality of written texts, even letters of this type, is always incomplete. This point has been made very cogently by Deborah Sweeney (2001: 19–22) in her comparison of letters to conversations. In the letters we hear, by definition, only one side of the conversation, even if responding letters are preserved. The opening formulas are indeed reminiscent of one side of the call and response openings of many conversations, a feature perhaps less marked in English than in some other languages (Arabic comes to mind). But it remains true that the amanuensis serves as a kind of filter.

Repetitions—a feature of storytelling style—also characterize letters in which a woman's voice is still perceptible. Many of the letters consist of serial requests to send various items, directives, advice, and the nagging "don't neglect to . . ." In *P.Mert.* 2.82, for instance, Nike is worried that the letters she sent to her sister were not delivered. She refutes the accusation that she neglected to respond, lingers for half of her letter on this theme, and ends up giving little fresh news. Sarapammon, the man who wrote for her, faithfully took down the series of complaints and even a reproachful rhetorical question. In another letter, *P.Yale* 1.77, Eirene's voice is noticeable in the repeated expression "as I informed you." The annoying repetition, tolerable in oral language, contributes to compromising the letter's style.

Dictated letters frequently allow us to follow a woman's thoughts. Although a letter may contain matter of various kinds, its main concern is usually clear because a woman keeps on revisiting it in several ways. A reader wanders here and there but keeps on coming back to one nagging preoccupation. As the woman dictates, variations on the same thought come to her mind, and her narrative leads the scribe forward and backward. A good example of this feature of oral style is *P.Mich.* 8.473, for which Tabetheus used a very competent scribe with a proficient hand and an overall good command of Greek. The first part of the letter concerns this woman's son, Saturnilus, and the dispatching of provisions. But as the letter proceeds and other matters are introduced Saturnilus repeatedly takes center stage. The bits of reminiscences that occur out of chronological order let emerge a complete picture of his personality and let us glimpse his and particularly his mother's despondency about a murder he committed.

Afterthoughts are sometimes expressed in postscripts added by a scribe after a letter was complete with final salutations and farewell. Postscripts are frequent in the women's letters belonging to the archive of Apollonios (see, e.g., the eloquent addition in *P.Brem.* 61). Since postscripts are practically absent from the men's letters in this archive, one is tempted to conclude that they were a typical feature of letters dictated by women. But only an accurate survey of men's letters could confirm its validity.

A woman's personality sometimes surfaces in spite of the scribe's effort to order her narrative and present it in a more fluid manner. The scribe who wrote *SB* 3.6264 in a relatively fast, cursive hand may have believed that connectives had the capacity of conferring some style to a narrative; he sprinkled a bunch of them here and there, sometimes incorrectly. But the narration, with its unusual display of exasperated feelings, uncommon vocabulary, and direct speech is so vivid that it is difficult to credit him with it.

Another way to capture the personal contribution of a woman to her written text is through the precise details that abound not only in dictated but also in autograph letters. A woman's story suddenly zeroes in on the color of a dress, the exact shape of anklets, the layers of pickles in a jar, or an expensive bed for a child. These details often remain with the modern reader and give the flavor of what a woman's life was like. In the letter of Taesis to Tiron, *P.Oxy.* 56.3860, the careful attention to details concerning items of clothing or furnishings, such as leopard-pattern garments, shapes the outlines of a life of privilege.

A Woman Writes

Our remarks concerning the typical features of dictated letters apply even more to letters penned by a woman in her hand. Direct speech, paratactic style, lack of order in the structure, and repetitions abound in autograph letters and are accompanied by unusual numbers of mistakes and corrections. We remarked in chapter 6 on the difficulty of identifying these letters. One fortunate exception is *PSI* 12.1247, written by a scribe but containing a long subscription by the author, Ammonous. The civilized tone of the sentences that she adds permits us to identify the polite and idiosyncratic expressions of the first part as entirely hers. Ammonous handles the written word with competence, using correctly a formulaic expression and a connective particle. Her only errors—banal iotacisms—are easily forgiven.

Badly written texts, by contrast, seem to allow us more chances of recovering the direct writing efforts of women. What stands out immediately in them is the quantity of orthographic mistakes of various kinds, revealing writers who conflate pronunciation and the written form of a word. While phonetic mistakes are not uncommon even in texts written with competence, their concentration in these letters is accompanied by other orthographic and grammatical errors. The typical letter that is suspected as having been written by a woman embodies all the oral qualities of dictated letters described earlier, sometimes in a more extreme form.

Autograph letters, lacking the mediation of a second party, abound in omissions, allusions, and obscurities. *PSI* 9.1082, which may have been penned by Palladis herself, is a crudely written letter in which Palladis repeatedly alludes to someone designated as "him." Doubtless the letter's recipient did not have any trouble understanding, but for the outside reader it is a different story. It is also possible that a woman felt less intimidated in expressing some feelings when her words did not need to go through the ears and fingers of someone else. In *SB* 5.7572, Thermouthas, who is happily pregnant, writes to her mother. She mentions her husband Valerius and reveals that she is longing for him in her mind. The lack of intimate details in most women's letters may indeed come from the fact that most of them were not written by the women themselves. The letter of Thermouthas, which leaves much to be desired in every respect, ends with a date but does not contain a final farewell. Thermouthas, who probably wrote the text herself, did not have any need for this final convention because her letter was personal and eloquent enough. Lack of a final farewell in a badly written letter may thus be another pointer in identifying autograph letters.

This feature can be verified in one of the letters most likely penned by Eudaimonis. The letters this woman dictated usually contained a final farewell written by her. But, like Thermouthas, Eudaimonis ends *P.Giss.* 24 only with a date. Since she appears to have been better educated than Thermouthas and is better able to express herself correctly and competently, she incorporates the final salutation into the body of the letter. It is very likely that Eudaimonis penned two more letters herself, *P.Giss.* 22 and 23, which are written in a hand far from fluent, while the rest of her extant correspondence was dictated to several competent scribes. No considerable difference is perceptible between the two groups in terms of composition of the texts and vocabulary. These letters are all rather well written but show a somewhat simple structure, density of content, and a personal lexicon—Eudaimonis is powerfully present in all of them. Although she did not write most of her own letters, her correct observance of morphology, syntax, and orthography is an unmistakable sign of her good education. Unusually, for the most part, Eudaimonis was even able to avoid phonetic spellings.

Another rare occasion to compare texts dictated by a woman with others that she penned herself is offered by the letters of Isidora (*BGU* 4.1204, 1205, 1206, and 1207). Like Eudaimonis, Isidora could write fairly complex texts with less than perfect handwriting. Even though she used a variety of complex sentences, she made some phonetic and other orthographic errors and occasionally seems unsure about case endings. She appears to write rather fast and is not intimidated in the least by the written medium. She probably did not read and correct her letters, which even show missing syllables. The letters that she dictated are more polished, smooth, and stylish, with every sentence deftly connected.

ASSESSING LEVELS OF EDUCATION: THE USE OF RARE WORDS

Determining the level of education of women on the basis of the language used in letters is not a simple endeavor, even if one thinks that a letter represents a woman's own words. Where professional composition of the text is visible, the vocabulary is of course to be attributed largely to the secretary. In dictation or autograph letters, however, unusual words rarely found in the *koine* of the papyri may provide a window on her way of thinking and level of education. Determining the sources of a certain word, however, is often difficult. The classical poets? Literary or "lower" prose? The Old and the New Testament? We will examine here only the most significant examples. Such unusual, sometimes refined words in women's—and men's—letters are the exception, not the rule. Letters were relatively short texts, usually of a practical nature, by which people communicated with relatives, friends, and business acquaintances. Inevitably, therefore, letters employ a relatively simple and informal vocabulary suited to mundane affairs, even if some of the words connected with clothing and household objects are technical and even rare.

Once again, it is from archives that we have the best chance of guessing the outlines of a woman's background. The letters from the archive of Apollonios are as usual unique in this respect. From several instances it appears that both the matriarch Eudaimonis and Apollonios's wife Aline had received an education going beyond the rudiments, which allowed them to be ironic in writing, to use words with loaded meanings, and sometimes to take terms from literature. When, for example, Eudaimonis in *P.Flor.* 3.332 wants to express her irritation and anxiety about her brother, who was threatening Apollonios and herself with a lawsuit, what better way than to play the teacher, presenting him as a naughty, misbehaving, "disorderly" (*ataktos*) student who was acting with the help of the friends he met in his athletic activities. The term *ataktos* was connected to discipline (for example in the military) and education and was often used in the grammatical examples of the second-century grammarian Apollonius Dyskolos (*Syntax* I.111). It is suggestive to think that Eudaimonis, who made sure that her granddaughter persevered in her studies (*P.Brem.* 63), might have used this word ironically.

Naturally, isolated letters present a more fragmented picture. We have said (chap. 3) that letters of the Ptolemaic period betray more confidence and care and show a more complicated language structure than those of later periods. Thus, the letter of Dionysia (*P.Bad.* 4.48) shows a high level of ease with complex syntax and a more extensive vocabulary than usual. One is not too surprised when this woman employs words such as *pandeinos* (awful), a term that rarely occurs in papyri, or *anagoniatos* (free from worry), which is used only one other time, in a man's private letter, *P.Tebt.* 1.58, and does not occur in any other source.

It often happens that it is difficult to conjecture how a rare word found its way into a woman's vocabulary. Such is the case, for instance, of a term that is not part of the language of the papyri, *peripsema*. This word is postclassical and occurrs in biblical and patristic literature, in the lexicographers, and interestingly in the *Vita Aesopi*. In the papyri it appears only twice and both times in letters written by women: *P.Petaus* 29 and *P.Mich.* 8.473. Its meaning is not entirely clear. Since the verb *peripsan* means "to wipe clean," one supposes that it indicated something that was wiped off, canceled (such as a debt), or perhaps forgotten or lost. In both women's letters this term fits well the personality of the writer, who seems to be quite emotional and uses descriptive language.

There are cases in which it is harder to say whether the woman dictating or her secretary is responsible for the expressions used. *P.Hamb.* 2.192 and *P.Oxy.* 12.1581 are good cases in point. Both the handwriting and the quality of the prose in the first letter betray the professional. One imagines Demetria telling the text of her message to a scribe, who was able to put it into a good form. But when this woman describes her impatience at the skipper who left too soon, the word used, "accursed, damned" (*kataratos*) attracts our attention. It appears only one other time in papyri, in the lively and unusual letter of a man, *P.Oxy.* 36.2783, who was venting his frustration, like Demetria. But this word has a good pedigree and often occurred in comedy. While it seems certain that a scribe would not write such a strong word on his own initiative, one wonders whether he might have embellished a more colloquial term used by this woman or whether we are hearing her own voice.

In *P.Oxy.* 12.1581, the man who took down Apia's letter attempted to present her prose in the best possible way but was not always successful—she is still visible behind him. Apia's concern about a certain Sarapion, who was to be kept out of trouble, comes through powerfully. When she writes that he should not "roam aimlessly," she uses an unusual word, *rembesthai*, which rarely occurs in classical literature but appears in the Septuagint. This verb is present two other times in papyri, in the private letters *P.Cair.Zen.* 5.59852 and *P.Brem.* 48, which are both from educated individuals and use recherché language. One is tempted to suppose that this word emanated directly from Apia and that her scribe only used cosmetic measures in taking down her dictation.

CHAPTER 8

Economic and Social Situation

As the studies of palaeography and language in chapters 6 and 7 suggested, the authors of the women's letters are by no means a homogeneous group. Some have well-trained secretaries at their disposition, others do not. Some display educated vocabularies, but most do not. We may easily suppose that the economic and social circumstances of the women in question varied considerably. In the present chapter we look at some of the more direct evidence for questions of wealth and standing.

THE PTOLEMAIC LETTERS ᵔᵔ

We observed in chapter 3 what a small part of the total corpus the Greek letters of the Ptolemaic period constitute (the Demotic letters being too rare to lend themselves to generalization). They are also distinctive in character. The handful of women's letters from the Zenon archive are almost all petitions in the form of letters, complaining about some matter supposed to be in Zenon's power to put right. We see Greek petitioners who are complaining about their entitlements. These are evidently people who in the larger scheme of things are dependent on Zenon and his network of patronage, which extended ultimately up the scale to the finance minister Apollonios.

Two of the Egyptian correspondents, however, are of quite a different category, both being entrepreneurial women. The author of *P.Mich.* 1.29 is a beekeeper, concerned about transportation for the hives, while the writer of *P.Lond.* 7.1976 holds the retail beer concession for her village. It is clear that her gross revenues are considerable, and her concern in the letter is about the impact that the departure of her daughter may have on the level of revenues, because the daughter had been doing most of the work as the mother grew older. These women are clearly not of a very high stratum in society, but like Zenon's female Greek correspondents they have some resources and position. Both have capital and generate cash incomes, and both are much more significant sources of revenue to the crown than the average Egyptian woman.

The other Ptolemaic letters all seem to come from privileged milieus, mainly in or on the edge of the crown-employed cadres that ran the country. *BGU* 6.1300 is perhaps the most obvious, with its long list of luxury goods and mention of a slave girl, suggesting considerable wealth, but Kleon (*P.Petr.* 3.42H[8]) was a high-ranking royal engineer for the Fayyum irrigation and drainage system and a member of the Greek elite. The people of *UPZ* 1.59 belong to the military class. It appears that the addressee of *P.Bad.* 4.48 had claimed official or military status but did not actually possess it; he probably was in some kind of business closely tied to the government. These Greek letters all seem to come from members of the upper strata in society, a point that their generally high-quality writing confirms.

ROMAN ARCHIVES ↶

We have nearly a dozen archival groups of texts from the Roman period that give us a chance to see more than one view of an individual or a family. In other chapters we have stressed how critical these groups are for our ability to understand the context of the women who appear in them. That is not to say that valuable information does not also come from the more isolated documents, but sometimes these are not very informative about economic matters, just as they can be hard to assess for matters like the identity of the writer. In the case of the archives, we can in every case form at least some picture of the circumstances of the individual(s) at stake. The earliest two groups, the Isidora to Asklepiades file (A3) and the Athenodoros archive (A4) clearly come from well-off circles. Isidora talks of expensive furnishings, of a sum of 2,800 drachmas of silver (several years' income for an ordinary person), of a couple of boats that her correspondent—whom we suppose to be her husband—disposes of, and of substantial landholdings, including at least 1 kleros of 30 arouras. In the Athenodoros archive we get a whiff of grain speculation, hear about a pair of family slaves in jail because of a debt, and find mention of a stash of forty-three tree trunks, a matter of some value in wood-short Egypt. There can be no doubt that this cartonnage-derived material comes from well-to-do people who apparently belong to an entrepreneurial and landed urban family.

Probably the wealthiest family we encounter is that of Apollonios the strategos (A7), who is discussed in some detail at various points in this book. The fact that Apollonios held the office of strategos, the highest magistracy available in the second century AD to the metropolitan elites, is in itself probably enough to indicate large landholdings and considerable influence, and everything we find in the archive—which extends far beyond the women's letters included here—confirms this view. Diogenis (A11) is probably not far from being in the same category, a metropolitan landholder with a steward in charge of her country estates. Similarly, the Klematia who is the landowner in the fourth-century Papnouthis and Dorotheos archive (A15) is a metropolitan of considerable wealth.

Some of the other groups are not extensive enough to give us quite such a good view, but the Eirene (A9) who speaks of "our workman" and deals in sums like 340 drachmas is certainly well above middling means. Property is also important in the Pompeius family (A5) and with Tasoucharion (A10) and Thermouthas (A12). In the Tiberianus archive (A6) and the ostraca from the Eastern Desert (A8) we are in the milieu of the imperial household or the military. The individuals involved are not necessarily of high rank or particularly wealthy, but they are well connected to the privileged status groups involved in the imperial enterprise.

Overall, then, the archives appear to document a range of status and wealth from moderately privileged to very wealthy. We turn now to the nonarchival documents to see how far they confirm this picture. Some of the relevant aspects are dealt with in chapter 9, where the frequent references to travel (an expensive activity) are considered and where women's involvement in managing estates is analyzed. Similarly, women's dealings with public officials are discussed there. Two particular topics that turn up in many letters deserve to be singled out, however. One is the considerable amount of litigation mentioned, often before high officials (this material is mostly collected in section B3). This is certainly for the most part the domain of those with significant property and the means to pursue lawsuits, which, as they do today, cost a lot of money. Such litigation was not worthwhile except when substantial sums of money were at stake, whether in the ownership of land or the performance of public liturgies. The second critical point is the large number of letters apparently written in Alexandria. The bulk of these appear to result from the temporary displacement of individuals living in the upriver nomes to Alexandria for purposes of family business or litigation. It can be taken for granted that extended stays in the capital were not cheap. Others of these letters are no doubt the product of families in which some members lived in Alexandria and others nearer their landed property in the Arsinoite, Hermopolite, or Oxyrhynchite nomes—to name only those from which the bulk of our texts come. Such families were certainly of far above average wealth.

PROPERTY ∾

Many papyri refer directly or indirectly to landed property belonging to the writer or her family, including valuable investments like olive groves (*P.Mich.* 8.464), vineyards (*P.Fay.* 127), land with irrigation machinery (*P.Mich.* 3.221;

P.Col. 8.212), and cattle (*P.Mich.* 3.221; *P.Hamb.* 1.86). A number of letters appear to be addressed to persons helping to manage property, whether friends or hired stewards (e.g., *P.Ryl.* 2.243); there are references to tenant farmers and their rents (e.g., *BGU* 7.1675; *P.Oxy.* 14.1758; and *P.Oxy.* 33.2680). Section B5 collects some of the texts dealing with agriculture. In general, the management of estates appears to be part of the background taken for granted throughout much of the correspondence.

MONEY ◯

Sums of money are mentioned in many letters. For reasons discussed in chapter 10, it is not always easy to be sure how to interpret these sums given the only approximate dates we can assign to the letters. But we find mentions of money-lending frequently. A bank account figures in *P.Charite* 38, and substantial sums appear particularly in *P.Oxy.* 10.1295 (1,300 drachmas are spent on a son's expenses, the nature of which is not, alas, stated) and *P.Oxy.* 14.1773 (more than two talents, a really large sum if the date is indeed the third century).

MOVABLE GOODS ◯

Many of the papyri mention the acquisition, sending, or receipt of goods. Some of these are everyday staples like wheat or bread. But there are also many references to luxury goods, with clothing, other textiles, and the raw materials for making luxury textiles, including purple, all playing a prominent role. Among the texts where these things are particularly noteworthy are *PSI* 9.1082; *P.Oxy.* 14.1679; *P.Oxy.* 31.2593; *PSI* 14.1418; *P.Oxy.* 31.2599; *PSI* 9.1080; and *P.Mey.* 22. Items of jewelry or metal plate, typical stores of wealth in ancient society, appear in, for example, *SB* 16.12326; *P.Yale* 1.77; *SB* 14.12024; *P.Mich.* 3.221; and *P.Oxy.* 1.114, with its extraordinary list of valuables that have been pawned and are now to be redeemed. Expensive foodstuffs ranging from olive oil (*P.Hamb.* 2.192) to cheese (*P.Oslo* 2.52; *P.Stras.* 4.173) and other fancy foods (*SB* 5.7743 contains the most impressive list) appear from time to time.

OFFICES ◯

Some letters offer useful clues to the status of the writers' families or circles of acquaintances by virtue of mentioning public functions of one sort or another. Quite a few military men appear among the women's families, and enlistment is discussed on occasion (see, e.g., *P.Mich.* 8.464 and 514; *P.Bingen* 74; and *P.Grenf.* 1.53). The status and wealth of military men and veterans could vary considerably, depending on their branch of service and rank, but they are in all cases to be seen as of middling wealth or higher (see generally Alston 1995). Nemesion of Philadelphia (*SB* 14.11585) was a tax collector and friend of the local centurion, a large mass of whose papers has survived (see, e.g., Hanson 1989). Liturgical offices, which could be held only by men of sufficient financial means to give the government guarantees for performance, in the form of property to proceed against in case of failure in office, are mentioned in *P.Oxy.* 7.1067; *P.Ryl.* 2.232; and *SB* 5.7737. The husband of the author of *P.Oxy.* 56.3860 was an *officialis* on the staff of the *dux*, the military governor. Even apart from the archive of Apollonios mentioned earlier, another strategos's family is the source of *PSI* 12.1247.

But there are some less exalted people, too. The addressee of *P.Mich.* 3.202 is urged to take a wet-nursing job. Someone in *SB* 8.9930 is connected to a charioteer. *P.Oxy.* 2.300 is addressed to an oil supplier for the gymnasium. And it should be remembered that soldiers were by no means all people of wealth; most of them, indeed, were people of middling means, small landowners rather than large ones, although some veterans did well and became relatively prosperous. There is good reason to think that many of the writers came from families with modest resources or made their livings through entrepreneurial activities rather than living on rents.

It is important to single out the groups that we cannot identify in these letters. These are the tenant farmers, very small peasant landowners, and wage laborers, groups that cumulatively certainly amounted to a large part of the population, indeed, a substantial majority. Even when the less wealthy and non-wealthy are taken into consideration, therefore, the world of these letters is one located well above the median of this society.

AFTER THE FOURTH CENTURY ❧

Despite the social and economic range displayed by the letters of the Roman period, the reader perceives a kind of unity to the corpus. After the middle of the fourth century, this shared character begins to dissolve as the result of a number of late antique developments. The arrival of Coptic complicates matters, as we have described in chapter 3, and it is natural to look for differences between the Greek and Coptic material. Christianity, moreover, brings with it a particular rhetoric, and a high proportion of our letters of the fourth to seventh centuries comes from ecclesiastical and monastic settings. In these we find a language of supplication, full of requests for intervention either in this world or with God, and in this rhetoric the writer's dependency, wretchedness, and poverty are strongly emphasized. Among numerous examples are *P.Herm.* 17; *O.CrumST* 360; *P.Pisentius* 39; *SBKopt.* 1.295; and *O.Brit.Mus.* add. 23. The terms of equality on which the bulk of the letters from the Roman period are written are thus replaced by a language of inequality, and we cannot expect quite the frank discussion of family affairs that we get earlier. Moreover, a large chunk of letters, particularly from the Monastery of Epiphanius and the correspondence of Bishop Pisentius, comes from the period of the Persian occupation of Egypt. These letters reveal the widespread disruption and loss, both human and property, caused by this invasion, but in the process they make the writers appear more destitute than they normally were.

The small body of Greek letters from the fifth to eighth centuries certainly gives every sign of being the product of the high elite. Money in the form of gold coinage is at stake in some of them (*SB* 5.8092; *SB* 14.11492; *SB* 14.12085), and a banker is mentioned in the remarkable *SB* 18.13762, where all manner of expensive goods are mentioned. Stewards and nurses appear several times as dependents of the writers, the level of education and scribal craftsmanship displayed in texts like *CPR* 14.53 is very high, and expensive capital equipment for irrigation is mentioned in one papyrus.

But this should not lead us to suppose that the Coptic letters are proletarian productions. On the contrary. Many of the same marks of belonging to the propertied or entrepreneurial class that we found in the Roman period turn up. This should not be a surprise, for we have seen that these letters are the late antique equivalents of the ordinary shorter Greek letters of the Roman period. The Kellis letters, which are longer than the letters on ostraca, are not particularly devoted to business matters, but they make it clear that we are in a world of property, travel, money, and ownership of animals. The Nepheros archive, of which we have one representative (*P.Neph.* 18), reveals intensive connections between well-off people in Alexandria and the Monastery of Hathor, with a constant flow of goods from the capital to the monastery. The writer of *P.Nag Hamm.* 72 talks about her donkeys and orders up fodder for them in a tone suggesting that she was not short of money. Litigation is mentioned in a number even of the ostraca, where, if anywhere, one might imagine the less wealthy would appear (e.g., *O.Vind.Copt.* 258; cf. also *P.Ryl.Copt.* 310). Significant sums of money appear in *O.CrumVC* 115 and *P.Lond.Copt.* 530. The little cluster of letters from Christophoria to Count Menas (*P.Lond.Copt.* 1104–1106) appears to be the product of the mother of a convent to its patron. Perhaps the most remarkable item of all is the threat— ostensibly by someone in prison!—in *O.Mon.Epiph.* 177 to take six soldiers to go and enforce an obligation if necessary. Moneylending, indeed, is in other Coptic letters a pervasive theme, and it is at the center of a well-known archive belonging to a woman of Jeme who was a pawnbroker, following perhaps in the footsteps of her grandmother (Wilfong 1990; Bacot 1999).

In sum, if one adjusts one's expectations to take account of the sources of the Coptic texts, the circumstances in which they were written, their addressees, and the ends for which they were written, what is striking is just how much even the ostraca contain much the same kind of evidence that the papyri of the Roman period do. The authors are mostly not of very high status—rich people do not have to apologize for not being able to obtain papyrus for a letter—but they are very much of the same standing as the less wealthy authors of the letters of the Roman period, preoccupied with their modest landholdings, their loans, their valuables, their business travel, and their legal affairs, in short the entire range of everyday life of the moderately well off. These clues confirm the view, taken in chapter 3, that with the coming of Coptic only a relatively small number of the wealthier women continued to use Greek for correspondence and that the Coptic letters come from most of the rest of the spectrum of those women who were prone to producing letters in the Roman period, what we might be inclined to call an upper middle class.

CHAPTER 9

Household Management and Travel

The letters in this book bring to light an abundance of information about the daily activities and concerns of the women who were their authors. Although some of these activities belong to a stereotypical domain (such as those that deal with the family and work inside the home), other activities mentioned in the letters offer a window into less expected aspects of women's lives, namely, those that took women outside the home.

This chapter explores an assortment of subjects that surface in the letters. The topics include childbearing and rearing, weaving, and spinning, activities long considered the particular domain of women. We will also, however, look at women's active participation in managing household businesses and their occasional involvement in matters connected with public authorities. Last, we turn to the abundance of evidence for women leaving the confines of their homes and traveling to a range of places.

CHILDBIRTH

Women's lives have often been described in terms of a life cycle of personal and family events, beginning with birth and education, moving on to marriage and married life, and ending with sickness and death. The private letters shed light on this "secluded" sphere of women's lives. To some extent, we can observe these various stages primarily through the women's experiences as mothers. Women generally married late in their teens. The average woman, if she lived and remained married until her menopausal years, would have needed to have given birth to about six live children for society to reproduce itself. Some women died in childbirth, however, the marriages of others ended well before their childbearing years were over, and at least half of the females who reached menarche did not live to menopause. Even so, many women would have spent several years of their adult lives pregnant. It is no surprise, then, that nearly a dozen letters refer to pregnancy and childbirth.

An impending childbirth demanded advance preparations. In *P.Mich.* 8.508

Thaisarion requests radish oil, pointing out that she will need it when she gives birth. For what use? We are not told. In another letter (*SB* 5.7572) Thermouthas, who is seven months pregnant, mentions that she needs her servant to do the handiwork. While Thermouthas does not explicitly indicate that she needs her servant because of her pregnancy, it is probably safe to assume that this is the case. We do not know how far away Thermouthas was from her family, but we do discover from her letter that her father had visited (and had fallen ill). Furthermore, her husband, for whom she expresses deep affection, is in Philadelphia with her mother. There is no mention in her letter of anyone but her servant Rhodine helping the mother to be with her pregnancy.

Other letters dealing with childbirth, however, reveal that there was normally a considerable amount of assistance to the pregnant woman from family and friends. In a letter from the archive of the strategos Apollonios, the servant Teeus writes to her master that she desires to come upriver from Hermopolis to Heptakomia and stay with his wife, Aline, until she gives birth. In a similar letter (*BGU* 1.261), Thermouthas and Valeria postpone a trip until a certain Herois gives birth. Elsewhere (*P.Oxf.* 19) a mother wants her pregnant daughter brought to her, presumably so that she can assist her.

The dangers of childbearing were all too common in antiquity, although there is no evidence for the frequency of miscarriage, stillbirth, or death in childbirth. In *P.Fouad.* 75, we learn that Herennia died four days after she miscarried an eight-month fetus. A successful birth, however, would be followed by celebration. Furthermore, as one might expect, naming a newborn was a noteworthy event. In *P.Mil.* 2.84, a woman writes to someone who is probably a relative to let her know that the baby, since it is a girl, has been named after her. The relationship between the two women is unknown because of the fragmentary nature of the letter, but the sender writes that it would have been given her brother's name if it were male. In another letter (*P.Münch.* 3.57), a grandmother suggests that the parents name their new daughter Kleopatra.

REARING CHILDREN ᴄ∾

Once a child was born, the household's focus turned to child care. The surviving wet-nursing contracts from Roman Egypt mostly concern the rearing of slave children, who were, in many cases, abandoned babies picked up from the dung heaps. A few letters, however, refer also to the nursing of freeborn babies. In *P.Mich.* 3.202, Valeria and Thermouthas try to convince Thermoution to nurse a freeborn baby. They make a point of emphasizing the infant's non-slave status, advertising that Thermoution will both make higher wages and have greater fulfillment. A grandmother insists (*P.Lond.* 3.951 verso) that she does not want her daughter to nurse her newborn and tells her son-in-law to hire a nurse. As is not atypical in these letters, we are left to guess the reason for the woman's resolve that her daughter not nurse; in particular it is unclear whether in her circles it was thought preferable to leave the nursing of infants to servants and wet nurses.

Care and concern for children show up repeatedly in these letters. At least fifty of the women's letters contain greetings to and from children and of inquiries into their well-being. Taesis informs her husband (*P.Oxy.* 56.3860) that his "sweetest son December greets [him] and asks after [him] very frequently." Occasionally, the concern expressed in the letters stems from a child's illness. In *PSI* 3.177, a wife asks her husband to rush home because their son is sick. He hasn't been eating, and she fears that he may die. A woman might, of course, simply write to the recipient to keep an eye on the children. The landowner Diogenis (in *P.Mil.Vogl.* 2.77) instructs her caretaker to "watch the children" and then specifically to "Watch 'little' Isidora."

When children are mentioned in the main body of the letter, the topic mostly revolves around education. It appears that parents of the classes represented in these letters were quite concerned with their children's studies. Again the archive of Apollonios is of particular interest. In *P.Brem.* 63, Eudaimonis informs Aline that Heraidous is persevering in her studies. Likewise, in another letter from the same archive, Aline tells her husband that the children attend the lessons of a woman teacher. In another letter (*P.Oxy.* 6.930), a mother informs her son that she inquired after his teacher, who has since sailed away, in order to find out how her son was progressing. She writes that she learned from the teacher that her son is reading the sixth book of the *Iliad*, but she expresses concern that he (together with his attendant, the *paidagogos*) must now find a new teacher. Older children sometimes became their younger siblings' second mothers, as we see in *P.Athen.* 60. The writers instruct their younger sisters to light the lamp in the shrine, shake the pillows, and devote their attention to studying. It seems that their mother had been ill and the two young sisters were neglectful in their duties.

WEAVING AND OTHER
TEXTILE-RELATED ACTIVITY ᷇

The pursuit by far most frequently associated with women in antiquity was wool working, and in particular spinning and weaving. Wool working, as well as working with linen and cotton, does occur quite often in the letters, but perhaps not with the frequency that one might expect for a conventional women's pastime. In Roman Egypt weaving was as much a business enterprise as it was a private occupation. Commercially produced textiles were readily available and frequently purchased, at least in cities. In the letters, we observe that women in villages were likely to make requests for ready-made textiles from others who were either located in or traveling to towns. Nevertheless, from the letters we can substantiate the natural expectation that many women continued to spend a large amount of time with one or more of the many stages of clothing manufacture, suggesting that the long-standing cultural significance and tradition of wool working were still very much alive in Graeco-Roman Egypt. Considerations of economy may have joined ideology in encouraging home production of cloth.

The letters mention not only wool, the most widely used material, but also linen and cotton. Often these materials are requested, the writers simply mention that they made a piece of clothing out of a certain material, or prices are cited. Cotton occurs in only two letters. In the first, *P.Oxy.* 59.3991, the sender writes that her mother made a cotton tunic; in the second, *SB* 6.9026, there is a request for good cotton thread. Finally, linen is mentioned in three letters, which contain requests for linen cloth and yarn (*P.Rein.* 2.118; *P.Giss.* 68; and *BGU* 3.948).

The letters discuss several stages of textile production, such as cutting, dyeing, and weaving. Interestingly, we read very little in these letters about women spinning wool, the most "traditional" activity. One explanation for this absence might be that spinning was considered too mundane to warrant mention. There are, however, several letters with requests for wool yarn, which could indicate that spinning was too time consuming a task, and when spun wool was both available and not too costly the women would purchase it. Even if it was homespun, the women of these letters may well have had slave help with such tasks. All the same, several women do mention spinning in their letters. One letter, *SB* 14.11881, shows us a woman spinning flax in order to make clothing; Allous complains that she, "being a woman," is hard-pressed to support the orphaned children of her brother and asks for two pounds of tow so that she can spin it and make clothing for them.

Several letters refer to dyeing wool, but the women actually do the dyeing in only one of these. Senpikos tells her son that she will dye some wool (*SB* 5.7737). The other two letters (*P.Brem.* 63 and *BGU* 4.1205) refer to a professional dyer, male in both instances. In *P.Giss.* 20 (mentioned in the previous paragraph), Aline asks her husband what color to make his garment, suggesting that purple would be nice. Unfortunately, we cannot be certain whether Aline herself will dye it or have it dyed. A few letters mention the sending of dye. In *BGU* 6.1300, the letter's writer asks for dye to be sent to her. We might assume that she will dye the fabric or thread herself.

The cutting of fabric was another textile-related activity with which the women of these letters were involved. In *P.Rein.* 2.118, a daughter writes that she will cut the *kolobion*, a type of tunic, from the linen cloth that her mother will send to her. In *P.Tebt.* 2.413, Aphrodite informs the letter's addressee that Euphrosyne cut the *dalmatikon* (another type of tunic). Thermouthion writes in her letter to Isidoros that she had his tunic cut. It is interesting that while the cutting of garments is mentioned, none of the women reveal anything in their letters about stitching the cut pieces. In one letter (*P.Oxy.* 14.1679), Apia tells the addressee to receive from the seamstress various items of clothing. Discussion of embroidering is also scarce in the letters (see *P.Mey.* 22 and *P.Yale* 1.77).

Last, several letters demonstrate that at least some (and probably most) of these women wove. In *P.Oxy.* 56.3860, the wife informs her husband that she is weaving his cloak. Eudaimonis tells her daughter-in-law Aline (*P.Brem.* 63) that she began to weave the day after Aline left. In *BGU* 3.948, a mother asks her son to send linen thread so that she can make clothing. In *SB* 5.7572, a pregnant Thermouthas cannot do the work herself but mentions that she has set Rhodine (probably her servant) to the handiwork. Serapias informs her brother that his mother made the cotton tunic for him (*P.Oxy.* 59.3591).

Just as various foodstuffs were sent back and forth between the letters' senders and recipients, so were items related to wool working or other types of textile production. Many of these have already been mentioned. In *P.Oxy.* 31.2599, the female requests two weaver's combs. Taesis (*P.Oxy.* 56.3860) writes to her husband Tiro, who is away, perhaps on official business, informing him of the items she has received to date, and asks that he send purple dye or purple yarn among other things. In *P.Brem.* 59, a woman writes to Apollonios lamenting that she could only find inferior quality purple (dye) and that the weaving implements were bad also.

HOUSEHOLD MANAGEMENT ∿

Well-off ancient households generally included not only the nuclear family but extended family members and servants—mostly slaves, we must suppose, although status is not usually indicated explicitly. The household in an economic sense included the property, both productive assets and the home or homes. Household management, as a result, involved matters as diverse as sowing fields, dealing with tenants, purchasing land, selling animals, paying workers, cleaning the home, and of course the more traditionally recognized activities of weaving, child care, and food production.

Many letters exhibit evidence of women actively running the household. For example, in her husband's absence in the army, Apollonous takes over: "[T]he rental in kind and all the seed will be entirely available. And do not worry about the children: they are well and attend (the lessons of) a woman teacher. And with regard to your fields, I relieved your brother from 2 artabas of the rent; then I receive from him 8 artabas of wheat and 6 artabas of vegetable seed" (*P.Mich.* 8.464). Few letters involve women who are asking for help or having difficulties with the household. The fact that almost all of the letters concerning management are addressed to men suggests the familial context of such operations.

Women were also property owners in their own right. In Roman Egypt women may have been a fifth of the landowners, perhaps as many as a third in some localities. They oversaw the management of their own estates and gave orders to their caretakers. Seven letters (from five different female landowners) are identifiably addressed to such managers, conveying instructions regarding the maintenance of their properties. Klematia and Diogenis have been mentioned repeatedly in earlier chapters, but they are not alone. In *P.Oxy.* 14.1758 another Diogenis tells her manager to take care of unsettled business and keep a tenant away from fertilizer. Elsewhere (*PSI* 1.95), a landowner sends a letter to her manager to inquire whether or not he received wheat or a pledge and to find out what places are ready for sowing. Thais gives directions to her manager (*P.Oxy.* 6.932) about various agricultural matters, including measuring out grain for taxes and an order not to sell the piglets without her. Women also showed more direct action in estate management. In *P.Oxy.* 33.2680, Arsinoe informs her sister Sarapias that she will try to collect her rents if the roads are firm.

In some letters women give orders or make specific requests relating to the household to males who are not managerial employees but relatives. Their tone varies from insistent to inquisitive. One such example occurs in the letters from the Tasoucharion archive to Neilos, her "brother," who in this case is definitely not her husband but could be her brother or brother-in-law. In *BGU* 2.601, she tells him not to sell the grain. In *BGU* 2.602, she requests that he find out about an olive grove that she is considering purchasing. Last, in *P.Giss.* 97 she asks him to register some securities for a house in her son's name. Elsewhere (*BGU* 3.827) Zoe writes to inform her husband about some judicial matters that she is handling out of town in Pelusium and, in a frustrated tone stemming from his failure to reply to her letters, demands that he look after the house and shake out the wool and the clothing. In another letter (*BGU* 4.1097), a wife requests that her husband send lentils and radish oil and that he sow the allotment if it is inundated. Such instructions could be sent to women relatives, too, as happens in *P.Fay.* 127: Taorsenouphis instructs her mother to give a share of the crop and grapes to her sister.

By contrast, letters seeking advice or assistance, usually from a male, in the management of the household are fewer than might be expected. In *P.Oxy.* 48.3403, both the mother and the wife need money, the wife so that she can pay the wool workers. In her letter (*BGU* 3.822), Thermouthas asks her brother to write a letter about rent money that is owed by another woman. Areskousa, in another letter, writes to her brother in order to request cotton for his other brothers' clothes (SB 6.9026).

PUBLIC BUSINESS ∾

Household management sometimes brought women into contact with public officials, particularly to represent men of the family when these were away from home. Typically taxation or a liturgy was at stake. In *P. Mert.* 2.63, Herennia urges her father to pay a sum for the "Piety" of the temple of Souchos (apparently, a one-time tax), which "they (the collectors) are trying to collect from all directions." She writes that if he does not take care of it she will. In another letter (*O.Stras.* 788), Thaubastis urges father to come quickly because "they" are imposing an additional tax on her, which she refuses to pay. The urgency of her request to her father is conveyed by the repetition of the phrase "come quickly." The implicit threat was sometimes jail. In *P.Oxy.* 36.2789, Kleopatra asks her father to give a mason 5 artabas of barley because she is being harassed by the *dekaprotos* (a tax collector) and will be put in jail. In a second letter, *BGU* 16.2618, Tryphas reprimands her son regarding a fine he has failed to pay. She writes that the slaves are in jail and fears that they will die there. In addition, she is harassed daily by two *statores* (bailiffs) because of the money she owes. Finally, there is one example in these letters of a woman occupied with public officials not because of taxes but because of a theft. In *P.Brem.* 61 (Apollonios archive), a woman writes that she has been busy with the strategos confirming the contents of a stolen box.

WOMEN'S TRAVELS AND FREEDOM OF MOVEMENT ∾

The letters provide evidence for women's ability to travel in a fashion unparalleled in other sources. There are approximately forty letters that refer in some way to women traveling. Half of these do not supply a reason for the journey. The other half fall into three general categories: travel involving childbirth; travel involving estates; and family visits. The many mentions of travel in the archive of Apollonios involve several of these causes.

The first of these has already been mentioned. Women traveled both to give birth and to help with the childbirth of others. But travel was not always the best option for the mother to be. In *SB* 14.11580, the pregnant Didyme writes that, although she had prepared to travel home, she will remain in place for the birth of her child. Why, she does not say, but a certain Apollos had told her to go home to give birth, if she was well, but otherwise to write to him to come to her, leaving us only to surmise that she was not well enough to travel. Another letter depicts an instance in which the letter's sender postpones traveling until after someone's childbirth. In *BGU* 1.261, a group of no less than four women plan to travel to visit family, but only after a fifth woman gives birth.

Several letters reveal that these women were likely to travel in order to carry out the property management already discussed. Their travels between estates, or from estates for business trips to cities, testify to the women's high economic level. These women generally are property owners themselves. In *P.Oxy.* 14.1758, Diogenis, a landowner, gives orders regarding her property to her estate manager until she arrives to handle the business. We have already mentioned Arsinoe's offer in *P.Oxy.* 33.2680 to go and collect rents from her sister's tenant farmer. Arsinoe declares "if the roads are firm, I will go." Presumably she was traveling by donkey or cart. We hear in other letters mainly about river travel, but shorter distances could be traversed by donkey (*P.Oxf.* 19), camel (*O.Mon.Epiph.* 352 descr.; *O.Medin.HabuCopt.* 150), or horse (*BGU* 13.2350).

The other Diogenis, a female landowner from whom we have two letters, declares to her *phrontistes* that she is coming to the estate and wants everything in order. Her letters, found at Tebtunis, do not disclose any details about her journey, but she was going to her home in nearby Tali. Zoe, in *BGU* 3.827, who like Diogenis gives orders to the letter's recipient to look after her house, notes that she will leave Pelusium (where she is taking care of some business matters) soon.

Visits to family members, especially at holidays, offered another popular reason for traveling. In *SB* 12.10840, Mike is preparing to travel by boat in order to spend Lent and Easter with her mother. In *SB* 5.8027, a daughter tells her father not to bother to come up; instead, she will sail downriver to him, taking Persion with her. "The trouble indeed is not little," she cautions. A mother writes (*SB* 5.7737) to her son that she cannot come to him at the moment, because she must get her other son ready for his travels. From the tone of her letter, it seems she traveled to visit her son frequently. Another's travels could provide an opportunity for a female to come along. In *P.Mich.* 8.508, Thaisarion tells her "sister" that her mother can sail to her with Ammonios, who has sailed upriver with the prefect.

Travel was not without troubles. Intending to travel to Alexandria, Aphrodite (*BGU* 13.2350) had her foot trodden by a horse and was forced to delay her trip because of her injuries. Eutychis encountered one obstacle after another while en route to Oxyrhynchos (*P.Oxy.* 14.1773). There were, moreover, limitations on the freedom of women to travel. Not a single private letter explicitly mentions a female traveling by herself. A letter from Eutychis to her mother, however, hints at the possibility of women traveling alone. It conveys the burden of traveling by oneself when loaded with baggage; but does alone mean without servants? In *BGU* 1.261, it does seem that four women will be traveling as a group without any male escort. Thermouthas writes, "We [Thermouthas and Valeria] are praying to come to you; for it is necessary. We want to bring Demetrous to sail down with her mother." Evidence for two or more persons traveling together is common, with one individual's trip mentioned as an opportunity for another person to travel. This is not something limited to women, of course; there are many instances of males who join another person's travels. Convenience and safety must always have made it attractive to travel in company.

CHAPTER 10

Practical Help in Reading the Letters

A majority of the women's letters in this collection were identified as such because of the name of the author of the letter. A smaller group, in which the sender's name has been lost or too badly damaged for a full reading, was identified on the basis of feminine grammatical forms or other internal evidence such as terms of relationship. In Greek, women's names of normal declensions are clearly distinguishable by the presence of one of a number of word endings. In addition, there are a number of names distinguishable as feminine because of their Egyptian etymology, usually with prefixes such as Sen- (normally representing Egyptian "the daughter of") or Ta- ("the woman belonging to") attached to either the names of divinities or masculine names formed from divine names. With the arrival of Coptic and the increased tendency to drop Greek declensional endings from Egyptian names transcribed in Greek, the identification of names can become a bit more difficult. A newly popular repertory of biblical names (e.g., Maria, Mariam, and Martha) and saints' names (e.g., Thekla) is joined by names that can be identified as feminine by their Coptic etymology, including sometimes the feminine definite article at the beginning (e.g., Tegrape, "the [fem.] dove"; or Thello, "the [fem.] monk").

There are two important potential sources of confusion between masculine and feminine names. One is the existence of a few Egyptian names used for both men and women, such as Herieus. The other is a phonetic tendency in the Roman period to drop the omicron from the nominative of second-declension masculine names ending in "-ios" and of feminine names ending in "-ion". The problem can be acute with the masculine names in "-ios" because the result is a name ending in "-is" in the nominative, which is easily confused with the feminine third-declension nominative endings in "-is". As far as we know, we have not included any letters in which either of these uncertainties can affect identification, but we are conscious of having excluded some cases in which we could not determine gender.

In chapter 3 we discussed the relationship between names and cultural identity, noting that it is common for women to bear Egyptian names even in families in which the men have Greek names. A systematic inquiry into this question on the basis of private letters would need to take letters from men to women, and men to men, into account. But it is interesting that in our sample approximately 30 percent of the women authors of letters have Greek names that are not obviously theophoric (i.e., formed from a god's name) and about 6 percent are Roman. These figures are both somewhat higher than a gender-undifferentiated analysis of names at Karanis and somewhat lower than the (heavily male) nomenclature of the Greek-descended settler population in the Fayyum (cf. Bagnall 1997). Egyptian names and theophoric Greek names (mostly formed on the names of Egyptian divinities) total about 63 percent of the total, just under the comparable figure for men and women together for Karanis. Overall, the distribution appears to us to be very highly Greek, particularly when one bears in mind the tendency for women to have Egyptian names even in Greek-naming families.

KINSHIP TERMS ࿐

Kinship terms by definition imply family relationships, that is, relationships by blood or marriage. In official documents, contracts of marriage, and the like, they are to be taken literally. In letters, on the contrary, such terms are often used in an imprecise way, different from their lexical meaning; they may refer to relationships such as friendship or acquaintance with a senior or junior in age or rank. A gap between lexical meaning and usage of kinship terms also occurs in Greek literature and languages other than Greek (Dickey 1996: 61–90). In letters kinship words are extremely common, particularly in the initial address and the final salutations. It is necessary to evaluate their meaning afresh in every instance, and it is often impossible to reach definite conclusions. Difficulty also arises because writers did not always use personal pronouns consistently in letters, thus making it hard to define precise relationships. For example, when a woman refers to "my mother" in a letter to her husband, the use of this phrase rather than "our mother" does not automatically rule out the possibility that he was born of the same woman. Even when more than one letter sent by an individual is preserved or the writer is otherwise known, his or her precise relationship with other people mentioned in the letter is often unclear.

"Brother" (*adelphos*) is a particularly common term in the women's letters, which are addressed to men more frequently than women. It was used with various meanings and might refer to a sibling, a husband, or a sibling who also was the spouse of his sister, or it might indicate more distant relatives and even non-relatives, who could be friends, acquaintances, or business partners. This usage is also found in the Septuagint, the New Testament, and literature and documents in Latin and Egyptian. Determining the precise reference of this term is often hard. Sometimes there is no doubt that "brother" was used according to its lexical meaning, without other implications. The five letters that form the archive of Tasoucharion, for example, are all addressed to Neilos, who was this woman's sibling. If only *BGU* 2.601 were preserved, however, it would be difficult to determine the exact relationship between this man and woman. In this letter, Tasoucharion mentions many people whose relationship to her and the addressee is ambiguous, and in particular she greets a woman named Taonnophris as "sister." But the whole scenario is clarified by the other letters: Neilos was Tasoucharion's sibling, who was taking care of her business; Taonnophris was Tasoucharion's sister-in-law and Neilos's wife; and the two families had separate sets of children.

The practice of calling one's husband "brother" was almost universally accepted in Egypt, where the term "husband" or "partner in marriage" (*symbios*) was infrequently used. The two women who wrote *BGU* 3.827 and *P.Oslo* 3.159 to their respective "brothers" about various business matters also talk about family details. It is likely that they were addressing their spouses, but it cannot be determined whether the latter were also their siblings, as they sometimes were in this society, which practiced marriage between extremely close kin.

It has sometimes been claimed that in Egypt it was the existence of this practice that brought the extension of the term "brother" to indicate a husband not biologically related, but this is certainly untrue. Not only is this usage also attested in languages and countries that did not accept sibling marriage, but the custom of brother-sister marriage probably originated later than the habit of address of spouses in this fashion. It was common—representing perhaps a sixth of all marriages and more common in Arsinoe than elsewhere (Bagnall and Frier 1994: 127–34, with bibliography in n. 62)—only from the early Roman period to the beginning of the third century, when the extension of Roman citizenship to the entire population automatically made it illegal. We cannot say how far the practice persisted covertly after that point.

When women address letters to "brothers" who appear to be close kin, then, it is often very hard or impossible to reach a definite conclusion about the actual relationship, even when other texts regarding the same family are extant. A good case in point is the precise relationship of the strategos Apollonios and his wife Aline, who constantly addresses him as "brother." Was Eudaimonis the mother of both Apollonios and Aline? Probably she was not, but the evidence is not conclusive. As we have seen in the case of the archive of Tasoucharion, the term "sister" might indicate a sister-in-law as well as a sibling. Naturally, some confusion may arise when relationships among family members are uncertain. Like the term "brother," "sister" might also be used in reference to a nonrelative. This is clear, for instance, from *P.Mich.* 3.202. The young woman, Thermoution, whom Valeria and Thermouthas are trying to hire as the nurse for the latter's child, does not belong to their family, even though she is addressed as "sister." Thermoution's social and economic status appears to have been far below that of the women who are offering work to her.

"Mother" is another problematic kinship term that often occurs in the women's letters. It can be used according to its lexical meaning, but it can also indicate a mother-in-law or an older woman who was worthy of respect and affection. Ploutogenia writes a letter from Alexandria to a woman she calls "mother" in *P.Mich.* 3.221. The two women were certainly closely related, but it is not entirely clear whether Ploutogenia was addressing her biological mother or the mother of her husband, Paniskos.

We have seen that the mother of the strategos Apollonios was not necessarily or even probably the mother of Aline. Another woman in the archive, Soeris, addresses Aline as "daughter" (*P.Brem.* 64), but it is doubtful whether she was her biological mother either. Aline, moreover, writes a letter, *P.Giss.* 78, to a woman, Tetes, whom she calls "mother." The words she uses show that the two women had an affectionate relationship and that Tetes was also in close touch with Aline's daughter. In spite of that, however, Tetes was not a relative of Aline. She was probably a servant who had worked for Apollonios's family for a long time. The term "mother" in this case is indicative of her age and devotion and of the respect she had earned.

Last, two other kinship terms that may generate confusion in the women's letters and need not be taken at face value are *huios* and *teknon*. Their literal meaning is very close. *Huios* often appears in the initial address of a letter with the meaning "son," but the same person is then referred to in the body of the letter as *teknon*, a term that has the lexical meaning "child" and is gender neutral. Even though both terms are usually employed in addresses by the actual parents of the addressee, there are exceptions. The archive of Apollonios is again useful in pinpointing nuances in the meaning of kinship words. While the strategos is always addressed by his mother as "son" (*huios*), he is addressed in the same way in *P.Giss.* 68 by a woman, Arsis, who uses the same term to communicate to him the death of her "son" Chairemon. Thus, in the first instance Arsis refers by this term to a man who was her junior and whom she may have known for a long time because she worked in the family's weaving enterprise. In the second instance, however, Chairemon is properly addressed as "son" by his biological mother. This man was probably considerably older than Apollonios, as is shown by the fact that in another letter, *P.Giss.* 12, he addresses the strategos with the term *teknon*, which also alludes to a fairly close relationship between them.

As a rule the women's letters follow the same epistolary conventions for initial and final greetings as men's letters do. These formulaic expressions vary slightly from the Ptolemaic to the Byzantine periods. In Christian letters, for example, greetings are sent "in the Lord" or "in God." At the beginning of a letter, the greeting formula *chairein* is accompanied by the names of the sender and the recipient; these can stand alone, or together with terms of kinship and various adjectives indicating affection or respect. The adjective *idios* (her own) in *P.Oxy.* 6.932 and *P.Bad.* 2.35 refers to men who were women's employees, agents, and the like. In one letter, *P.Stras.* 8.772, *chairein* is supplanted by the recherché expression *eu prattein*, which is indicative of the education of this woman or of her scribe. Even more interesting is the case of another letter, *P.Grenf.* 1.53, in which the greeting expression is absent and is replaced by the simple indication that Artemis "writes" to her recipient, Sarapion, with whom she has a very difficult relationship. The idiom may be a translation of normal Egyptian phrasing at the start of letters. This letter, which also ends abruptly without salutations, is preceded and followed by a message from Artemis to her husband.

Greeting formulas are often followed by simple wishes for good health. Some of the Ptolemaic letters show greetings and the wish for health confined to one sentence. Occasionally a writer may feel the need to expand, wishing, for instance, as in *P.Oslo* 3.159, that "the best things in life" would fall upon the recipient or, as in *P.Neph.* 18, praying to the Lord that her letter will find the addressee "healthy and in good spirits." As the latter papyrus shows, a scribe's or a woman's respect for polite conventions generated these formulas. In *P.Neph.* 18, for example, the fervent initial prayer is in sharp contrast to the bitter feelings of the writer revealed in the course of the letter.

In all periods, the end of a letter was the place for salutations to relatives and friends and for the final farewell. Variations were few and rather insignificant. At the end of the Ptolemaic period, for instance, the final greeting was preceded by the expression "take care of yourself in order to be well," to which Isidora adds, in *BGU* 4.1204, "which is the most important thing." Similar expressions are found in *P.Oxy.Hels.* 45 (first century AD) and *P.Rein.* 2.18 (third century). Sometimes formulae seem to prevail, as in the short letter of Theano, who bids farewell to Dionysios and repeats her farewell immediately afterward (*P.Princ.* 2.67). Salutations to faraway people could be lengthy and detailed: a string of names of great significance for the people mentioned (and for those unmentioned). Sometimes a writer dispensed with these lists and mentioned people cumulatively ("everyone in the house"). Diogenis in *P.Oxy.* 14.1758 says it rather elegantly: "I greet all those you hold dear," a rather rare expression that was probably part of her personal lexicon.

Conventional references to an act of obeisance by the writer before a god or gods (*proskynema*) appear often in the initial part of letters of the Roman period (see Geraci 1971). The usage of the epistolary *proskynema* peaks in the second and third centuries and slowly disappears from the fourth century on, as Christianity becomes the dominant religion. A *proskynema* expression was already a conventional element in pharaonic letters, but this usage in Roman letters seems rather to be connected to pilgrimages to temples by visitors who left short inscriptions with their names and those of relatives and friends in order to attract a god's blessing. Performing an act of obeisance before a god and leaving a sign of it appears to have been an indigenous custom that the Greeks adopted.

Most letters—women's and men's—with the *proskynema* formula refer to an act of adoration before the god Sarapis and appear to have been sent from Alexandria. The provenance from this city has been hotly debated, with Wilcken (*Grundz.*, pp. 122–23) and Youtie (1978) in favor, and other scholars (most recently, Farid [1979]) objecting that shrines to Sarapis also existed in other parts of Egypt. The consensus now is that letters with the *proskynema* to Sarapis most likely did originate from Alexandria but that individual contrary cases are possible (see most recently *O.Claud.* 2, 65–68). In some of these letters, an Alexandrian provenance is clearly stated, as for instance in the letter of Serenilla, who feels lost in the city (*W.Chr.* 100), and in that of Isis, who writes after the four days' journey that took her to the capital. It should be noted that in the last two letters Sarapis is mentioned together with "the gods who share the temple," but it is uncertain whether this formula derived from an actual proskynema in a temple where the god was worshiped together with other gods.

Other epistolary acts of adoration are performed in the name of gods such as Zeus Kasios, Isis, Souchos, and Petesouchos or more generically in the name of the local gods or the gods of the country. In *BGU* 3.827, Zoe, who is in Pelusium, assures her recipient that she has performed an act of adoration for him before Zeus Kasios. It is likely that the formula she uses is not only a convention but refers to an actual visit to the temple of the god in this city. One wonders whether the same is true for Ptolema, who sends a letter to her mother (*P.Haun.* 2.18) from an undisclosed place; she writes a *proskynema* formula in the name of Isis in the middle of the letter rather than with the greetings. One letter, *P.Mich.* 8.473, mentions an act of adoration performed by the writer before "our lord Souchos." This was the crocodile god identified with the god Sobek, who was worshiped all along the Nile Valley but particularly in the Fayyum. It is uncertain where the woman writer resided at the moment, whether in her village of Tonis or somewhere else. Petesouchos was a form of Sobek adored in the Arsinoite, and the letter of Didymarion to Paniskos with a *proskynema* to this god was probably sent from this nome.

In conclusion, the letters that mention an act of obeisance before a god pose a question: did these women actually go to temples on behalf of faraway friends or were they simply using a formulaic expression? While it is sometimes possible to reach a conclusion, most of the time we are hampered by the limited evidence.

MONEY ∾

Because many letters deal with business matters and the management of family interests, sums of money are frequently mentioned. The monetary history of Egypt from early Hellenistic times to the early Arab period is complicated, but the essential points necessary to understand monetary references in the letters can be set out briefly. Ptolemaic Egypt used a monetary system borrowed from classical Greece, its principal unit the drachma. The drachma was initially a silver coin that represented a considerable amount of money—several days' wages for most workers. It was subdivided into six obols. Although Greek cities had sometimes minted obols (or their multiples) in silver, Ptolemaic Egypt mostly used bronze coins, which had a significant fiduciary element; that is, their nominal value exceeded the market value of the metal they contained. For reckoning very large sums, the talent, a unit of accounting amounting to 6,000 drachmas, was used.

Through a series of pressures and events still very much the subject of controversy, Ptolemaic currency came under pressure in the aftermath of the Fourth Syrian War (219–217 BC), and nominal prices of goods began to rise. Because of a shortage of coined silver, the bronze coinage began to play a larger role, and the relationship between silver and bronze changed. For the purposes of reading letters, the key point is that sums in drachmas after this time represent bronze drachmas, not silver, unless the contrary is made explicit. The ratio between them changed over time, but for most of the second and first centuries BC it was several hundred to one. Large nominal sums thus need conversion to be comparable to figures from the third century.

Although Ptolemaic bronze drachmas remained a unit of accounting in the very earliest part of the Roman period, the centuries from Augustus to Diocletian were essentially the era of a new "silver" drachma. In fact, the coinage was based on four-drachma coins (tetradrachms) of bronze with a small silver admixture. In the early Roman period a drachma was once again a significant sum—a good day's income—though perhaps only a fourth of what it had been worth under the earliest Ptolemies. Though there is some gentle drift in price levels, there was not a substantial price rise for most goods until the 160s, but a shortage of exactly dated documents with usable prices in the next few decades makes it hard to be sure how sudden the rise was. Nor is there general agreement about whether the rise in price levels was caused by a phenomenon akin to modern inflation or by a debasement of the imperial currency, something that did in fact take place in this period.

From the late second century until about 275 (or slightly later), the new price level remained roughly stable at something like twice the earlier Roman amounts. Then came a major upheaval, again not yet the subject of scholarly consensus, leading to price levels an entire order of magnitude higher than those seen up to that point. Once again the evidence for exactly what happened during the next quarter century is inadequate, but there was continued instability, probably the ultimate result of problems in the imperial finances. In the mid-290s, Diocletian ended Egypt's historically separate coinage and brought the province fully into the zone of standard Roman imperial coinage. A series of actions involving prices and currency left the price levels something like twice those of a quarter century earlier.

The next three-quarters of a century brought a series of devaluations and retariffings of the coinage, reflected in a staged series of jumps in price levels. The history of these changes is extremely complex, but an artaba of wheat, to use the single most important example, rose from a price in drachmas in three digits to a price in talents in three digits by the 360s—a rise of four orders of magnitude (see Bagnall 1985). A major currency "reform" in 351 provided the single largest point of change. During the same period, the gold solidus, minted from the reign of Constantine on at seventy-two to the Roman pound, occupied an ever more important role in larger transactions, with the now almost silver-free bronze currency requiring large volumes to make up any significant value. Although there were subsequent developments, the solidus and its fractions (one-third a tremissis, and one-twenty-fourth a carat) remained the units of account for most purposes until well after the Arab conquest, when the conquerors' dinar (the name itself derived from the Roman denarius) succeeded to the position of the solidus.

DATING ᠀

As was pointed out in chapter 6, most private letters from Hellenistic and Roman Egypt contain no date. The modern concern with the precise date of writing appears not to have been widely felt in this society. Perhaps in most cases the bearer of the letter could have told the recipient at least approximately when it was written. But the absence of exact dates is not uniform. A higher percentage of Ptolemaic letters than Roman ones have exact dates, in part because Zenon annotated letters with the exact date of receipt. Even if his correspondents took no pains with the date, this orderly filer wanted the information recorded. Some other Ptolemaic letters, including *UPZ* 1.159 and *P.Bad.* 4.48, also have dates given by the senders.

A considerable proportion of early Roman letters also has dates. These are most common in the letters from the Abusir el-Melek cartonnage in the Berlin collection, in the dossiers of Isidora to Asklepiades and of Athenodoros. Almost every letter in these groups has a date. *P.Wash.Univ.* 2.106, of the same period (18 BC) also is dated. There is also a considerable number of dated letters from the first century AD, with the last coming in 105 (*P.Mich.* 3.202). This pattern is not unique to women's letters but reflects habits found also in the larger body of letters by men. There is no obvious explanation for this history of changing habits.

These letters with exact dates are all dated according to regnal years. Under both the Ptolemies and the Romans, when a new ruler came to the throne, his (or her in some Ptolemaic cases) first year began immediately and lasted until the following Thoth 1 (New Year's Day), when year 2 began, no matter whether a few weeks or nearly twelve months had elapsed. (The Macedonian regnal years in use under the early Ptolemies worked differently, running for twelve months from the date of accession. Only in the Zenon letters do these come into question.) A year in which a regnal transition took place would thus be divided into parts with different numbering, and the known regnal years of all rulers add up to considerably more years than the actual number of elapsed calendar years.

More than 90 percent of all letters are lacking a precise date by regnal year (to which was usually added the month and day). In this collection we have assigned dates to these with varying degrees of exactness, in most cases following the editor's dating (the exceptions being mostly Coptic letters left undated by the editor). Sometimes the dates are based on a letter's belonging to an archive or dossier that can itself be given a fairly specific date. An example is the archive of Apollonios the strategos, where the letters can be assigned dates within a fairly narrow band, even though they do not themselves give precise dates. These assigned dates are based on the fact that Apollonios's archive contains documents that do have exact dates and that some events mentioned in the texts can be linked to historical happenings for which we have a reasonably well-established chronology.

More commonly, dates are assigned by editors on the basis of palaeography. Handwriting styles change over time, and by now, with some fifty thousand published papyri, papyrologists have a fair idea of how these changes correlate with the passage of time. These changing styles, however, are most precisely datable in the case of fully professional cursives, where we can be certain that the writer's skill is not concealing the underlying development of a writing style. As is discussed in chapter 6, few letters are written in such hands. More often they are written in an exaggeratedly clear semicursive that may be called a letter hand, intended to be legible to the recipient. These hands change less rapidly than fully cursive hands and are harder to pin down by date. Even more difficult are the handwritings of individuals whose education did not take them to a level of full fluency in handwriting. Particularly at the lower end of the spectrum of experience and competence, these hands, like those in elementary school exercises, remain relatively constant over long periods of time. All of these facts tend to reduce the precision of palaeography as a dating criterion, and many letters are dated only to a century or a span between centuries.

In some cases, additional precision can be added to dates by the use of internal evidence. For example, a letter writer who uses the name Aurelia before her given name is probably to be assigned to the period after AD 212, but perhaps not too long afterward, because once the novelty of acquiring Roman citizen status wore off Aurelius and Aurelia tend to be restricted to formal contexts in which an indication of status was necessary. As remarked earlier, the amounts of money mentioned in a letter can at times, particularly if we know what the money was for, help to give a sense of the date. Only within the fourth century, however, with its rapid monetary change, is such an indication likely to be more precise than palaeography. Occasionally the mention of a public office that did not come into being until a particular date, or that disappeared around a given time, can also provide information. But these cases are exceptions.

Letters

A. ARCHIVES AND DOSSIERS

I. LETTERS FROM THE ZENON ARCHIVE ॐ

Zenon son of Agreophon was an immigrant to Ptolemaic Egypt from Caunos, a city in ancient Caria, on the southwest coast of Asia Minor. The assemblage of papers of which he is the central figure is the largest papyrological archive known, with nearly two thousand texts. During the earlier part of his career, he was a business agent for Apollonios, the *dioiketes* (finance minister) of Ptolemy II Philadelphos. He spent a considerable period in Palestine and Syria, then in various locations in Egypt before being made in 256 BC the manager of the large estate in the Fayyum near Philadelphia that the king had given to Apollonios. In 248, under circumstances that remain only partly understood, he left Apollonios's service but remained in Philadelphia as a local notable. The archive includes numerous letters, but very few of them are from women, and women in general play a minor role in the documents of the archive, making up only 2 percent of the individuals mentioned in it. It is not even known if Zenon was married, and the documents reflect much more a male-oriented existence. The letters included in the present collection reflect mainly his role as the most important person in Philadelphia, looked to for resolving many problems.

P.Cair.Zen. 1.59028

Satyra to Zenon: a practical letter
258–257 BC (?)

LOCATION WRITTEN   Alexandria (?)
LOCATION OF ADDRESSEE   Philadelphia
LOCATION FOUND   Philadelphia

Greek

∽ ∽ ∽

Satyra to Zenon, greeting. While Apollonios gave orders to give us clothing, to me and my mother—you will also find the memorandum that Apollonios wrote about it—from that day we have received nothing. This is the second year already. It would be good for you to inquire and show Apollonios . . . to remember us, so that we may not be naked. And let him permit us to have this gift privately from you. Inquire also about our provisions. We got them in full only once, and this was what you ordered to give to us at the festival of Demeter. Please inquire also about these matters, if it pleases you too, as quickly as possible. Farewell.

(ADDRESS ON BACK): To Zenon.

(DOCKET): About Satyra, the little girl.

∽ ∽ ∽

THE LETTER IS WRITTEN in one hand of small size with the characters all separated. This hand is quite proficient and fluent in spite of the fact that the alignment leaves something to be desired and that letter size is not always consistent. The whole was probably not the work of Satyra.

The text shows a rather good command of Greek. The letter was eminently practical and went quickly to the point. The style suggests dictation.

Satyra was a harp player in the service of the dioiketes Apollonios. Two more letters in the archive that concern her (59059 and 59087) show that the requests about clothing allowance and wages that she addressed to Zenon in this letter were fulfilled.

LOCATION OF OBJECT
Cairo, Egyptian Museum, Cat. Gen. 59028. Plate XXIX in *P.Cair.Zen.* I.

BIBLIOGRAPHY
Edgar 1923: 190–91 (SB 3.6784); reprinted as *C.Ptol.Sklav.* 116. Translation in Rowlandson 1998: no. 77.

P.Cair.Zen. 3.59408

Note of Asklepias to Zenon
Third century BC

LOCATION WRITTEN   Unknown
LOCATION OF ADDRESSEE   Philadelphia
LOCATION FOUND   Philadelphia

Greek

∾ ∾ ∾

Note to Zenon from Asklepias. Please, with regard to the matter Eirenaios instructs you about, give me a traveling allowance, in order that I come upcountry to him and do not appear to neglect him. And he sent me a messenger bidding me. Therefore, what do you prescribe to me? Be well.

∾ ∾ ∾

A SHORT NOTE WRITTEN on a narrow strip of papyrus. This hand is quite practiced in spite of some unevenness. The letters are well formed and show occasional serifs.

Asklepias designates her message as a "memorandum." Epistolary conventions in fact are kept to a minimum at the beginning and at the end. The style is in keeping with the nature of the brief message.

The note of Asklepias conveys a curious impression due to some imbalance between her peremptory initial request, the "command" that she reveals that her husband sent Zenon, and the following explanations with the final question.

LOCATION OF OBJECT
Cairo, Egyptian Museum, Cat.Gen. 59408.

P.Col.Zen. 1.6

Simale to Zenon about her son
March 257 BC

LOCATION WRITTEN   Unknown
LOCATION OF ADDRESSEE   Berenikes Hormos
LOCATION FOUND   Philadelphia

Greek

Simale, the mother of Herophantos, to Zenon, greeting. Since I heard that
my boy had been mistreated and rather badly, I came to you and after
arriving I wanted to petition you about these matters. But when
Olympichos prevented me from seeing you, somehow I was brought in the
presence of my child and I found him lying down in a hardly laughable
state and seeing him was enough for me to grieve. But when Olympichos
arrived he said that by beating him rotten he would make him—or that he
had already made him—as someone who was already nearly decent. Thus I
beg and beseech you to concern yourself with these matters and to report to
Apollonios in which way my child has been continuously maltreated by
Olympichos as if he were responsible for his illness. For I, in addition to the
fact that I have received exactly nothing for a year already except for the
mna and 3 artabas of wheat since the month Dystros when Herophantos
has come to you—The boy himself tells me of the goodwill of Apollonios
and yourself that you keep on showing to him. I ask you, therefore, and beg
you that, if Apollonios has ordered to pay him anything, his wages be paid
to me. Rest assured that as soon as the god sets him free I shall bring him
back to you so that I may see you with regard to the rest. Learn the rest
from the person who brings you this letter, for he is not a stranger to us.
Farewell.

(ADDRESS AND DOCKET ON BACK): To Zenon.
From Simale the mother of Herophantos. Year 28, Peritios 6. In Berenikes
Hormos.

THE LETTER IS WRITTEN in a capable, fluent, and clear hand that is not completely even, of medium size with uniform characters and regular line spacing.
The writer leaves even margins on all sides. The scribe was probably a professional.

Orthography, morphology, and syntax are remarkably correct, and there is
a good variety of clauses, as in other Ptolemaic letters. Some unevenness can
be perceived only toward the end where a sentence is left unfinished.

This letter has many characteristics of a formal petition. In the first part, which is full of the pathetic and personal details so common in petitions, Simale informs him of the ill treatment that her son Herophantos was receiving at the hands of a certain Olympichos. The boy was in the retinue of Apollonios, but not everything is clear about this connection and the financial arrangements involved.

NOTE

Herophantos: Probably a minor, since his mother has a claim on the money he receives. Cf. contracts of apprenticeship.

LOCATION OF OBJECT

New York, Columbia University, Rare Book and Manuscript Library, Papyrus Collection, inv. 286.

Fig. 1. *P.Col.Zen.* 1.6. Simale to Zenon about her son. (New York, Columbia University, Rare Book and Manuscript Library, Papyrus Collection, inv. 286.)

P.Lond. 7.1976

Haynchis to Zenon: I need my daughter
253 BC

LOCATION WRITTEN   Unknown
LOCATION OF ADDRESSEE   Unknown
LOCATION FOUND   Philadelphia

Greek

Haynchis to Zenon, greeting. Taking beer from the large beer shop I dispose of 4 drachmas (worth) daily, and pay regularly. But Demetrios the vine dresser deceiving my daughter and taking her away keeps her in hiding, saying that he is going to live with her without me. But she was managing the store (with me) and supported me, since I am old. Now, therefore, I sustain loss since she is gone, and I myself do not have the necessities. But he also has another wife and children so that he cannot live with the woman he deceived. I ask you then to help me because of my old age and give her back to me. Farewell.

(DOCKET ON BACK): Year 32, Mecheir. Haynchis.

THE LETTER WAS WRITTEN by a professional. The writer used a thick pen and mostly separated letters but proceeded at a considerable speed and with a good rhythm.

This letter shows a good command of Greek in every respect, but the writer took down faithfully what Haynchis dictated, and the letter is not well structured. At the end details are added rather abruptly.

A petition in the form of a letter in which an old woman asks Zenon to return to her the daughter she needs to manage her affairs—specifically, a beer shop. The girl is squeezed between a married lover who supposedly deceived and snatched her and a mother who considers her personal property.

NOTE
without me: This could be taken literally as a spontaneous expression as Haynchis is dictating. She would not be able to live with the couple and stay with her daughter.

LOCATION OF OBJECT
London, British Library, Papyrus inv. 2660.

BIBLIOGRAPHY
Reprinted in Pestman 1994: no. 5; Clarysse and Vandorpe 1995: 97. Translation in Rowlandson 1998: no. 209.

P.Mich. 1.29

Senchons to Zenon about her donkey
July 256 BC

LOCATION WRITTEN Unknown
LOCATION OF ADDRESSEE Philadelphia
LOCATION FOUND Philadelphia

Greek

Senchons to Zenon, greeting. I petitioned you about my she-donkey that Nikias took. If you wrote to me about her, I would have sent her to you. If you think so, order (him) to return her in order that we may carry the hives into the pastures, so that they do not go to waste neither for you nor the king. And if you inquire about the matter, you will be persuaded that we are useful to you. And I will send you her foal. I ask you and beg you, therefore, not to put me aside (neglect me). I am a widow. Be well.

(ON BACK): Year 30, Pachons 2.

(DOCKET): Senchons about a donkey.

THE LETTER WAS WRITTEN by an Egyptian scribe with a brush so that occasionally some characters are unclear. The letters are large, mostly separated, and slightly bent to the right. The hand is proficient and not too slow.

The text consists of a series of short sentences, mainly in asyndeton. There are very few connective particles. Only the central part is syntactically more complex.

This letter is conceived in the form of a petition addressed to Zenon, who seems to have been directly involved with the beehives that Senchons was prevented from carrying into the fields because of a theft of a donkey. The final isolated detail of her state as a widow is meant to add some poignancy to her request.

NOTE
Senchons: The woman's name is Egyptian, written without the usual Greek ending.

LOCATION OF OBJECT
Ann Arbor, University of Michigan Library, Papyrus Collection, inv. 3198. Plate III in ed.prin.

BIBLIOGRAPHY
Text reprinted in White 1986: no. 20, with photo (upside down). On the Egyptian scribe, see Clarysse 1993: 195–99. On line 4, see *BL* 3.116.

SB 22.15276

Choirine to Zenon about weaving
Third century BC

LOCATION WRITTEN   Unknown
LOCATION OF ADDRESSEE   Philadelphia
LOCATION FOUND   Philadelphia

Greek

Choirine to Zenon . . . , greeting. Rest assured that the covering (?) . . .
drew . . . 3 staters with the yarns. Consider . . . for 6 months . . . for I am
distressed. Therefore, if you agree, half of the wool . . . consider . . . of the
young female slave to be given either food allowance or wool. She is naked
in fact . . . and will be even more so (?). I have nothing to rebuke her . . .
But you do not be neglectful of the slave. Farewell.

(ADDRESS): To Zenon.

(DOCKET): Choir(ine).

THE HAND IS RATHER competent but not as formal as in many letters of the
same archive. Letter size and line spacing vary.

Since the letter is fragmentary, it is difficult to form an opinion about the
writer's use of syntax. Morphology is correct.

The identity of Choirine is unclear. The aim of her letter is to keep Zenon
posted about some weaving that was done by a female slave. She reminds him
that the slave should be compensated since she had worked well.

LOCATION OF OBJECT
Florence, Biblioteca Medicea Laurenziana, PSI Inv. 371bis + 605. Plate of
371bis in ZPE 55 (1984), Taf. Va. Both fragments shown in G. Messeri Sa-
vorelli and R. Pintaudi, *I papiri dell'archivio di Zenon a Firenze* (*Pap.Flor.* 24,
1993), Tav. LXXIV.

BIBLIOGRAPHY
The fragment SB 16.13055 is described in *Pap.Lugd.Bat.* 20.75c. For the combination of the two fragments, see BL 10.217. Plate in *Pap.Flor.* 24, pl. 74.

2. OTHER PTOLEMAIC LETTERS

APF 41 (1995) 56–61

A dancer of Boubastis to her lord
Second or first century BC

LOCATION WRITTEN Unknown
LOCATION OF ADDRESSEE Unknown
LOCATION FOUND Karanis

Greek

∾ ∾ ∾

To my lord, from your *somphis* (dancer). I pray that all the gods may grant
you health and good fortune and even greater success with the kings. May
they give you favor, good appearance, success, and may the goddess
Boubastis give health . . .

∾ ∾ ∾

ONLY THE TOP PART of the letter survives. The hand is proficient but betrays
some irregularities.

What remains consists of formulaic expressions and pious wishes that are
usually found in Greek letters to high officials. The editors believe that such
formulas are rather Egyptian (or oriental). The writer may have belonged to
the Egyptian priestly milieu. Besides some common errors due to phonetic
spelling, there are two rarely used optatives.

NOTE
somphis: A Greek transcription of an Egyptian word. Boubastis was the cat
goddess of love, dancing, and music.

LOCATION OF OBJECT
Ann Arbor, University of Michigan, Papyrus Collection, inv. 4394a; plate 23
in edition.

BGU 6.1300

A shopping list of luxuries
Late third or early second century BC

LOCATION WRITTEN Unknown
LOCATION OF ADDRESSEE Unknown
LOCATION FOUND Probably Arsinoite nome

Greek

Tetos to her father, greetings. If you are well and things are otherwise according to your wish, it would be as we wish. I myself am well, and so are my mother and everyone in our household. When you sail upriver, please bring . . . and 2 shuttles, 2 medium-sized boxes and 3 smaller ones, 2 caskets, a case for alabaster ornaments, 2 tubes, 2 probes, an unguent box with a ring base and a Sikyonian goblet, 5 staters' weight of myrrh, 3 of nard oil, myrrh oil, oil for the girl for the head, . . . of purple and 2 rings, a golden mirrorbox, medium-white linen cloths with purple; and with respect to the slave girl, who was on the other side at Oxyrhyncha, take care that you manage matters concerning her securely and that nothing thus gets in your way. And bring up also 2 combs, 2 hairnets, 2 scarlet ones, 2 hair clasps, earrings (?) for the girl, a stater of sea-purple dye. Farewell. Year 12, Phamenoth 22.

WRITTEN IN A LARGE hand on a piece of papyrus used for an earlier text, which has been washed off.

The letter is well enough written, but as the larger part of it is essentially a shopping list, there is not much syntax to judge. Spelling is fairly good, but there are occasional phonetic interchanges.

Apart from one rather obscure passage concerning a slave girl, almost the entirety of this letter is a list of items Tetos wants her father to buy. Most of these are matters of clothing, cosmetics, and small containers for jewelry and cosmetics. The family is obviously very well off. Tetos does not trouble to varnish her list of requests with much in the way of news or even inquiry after her father's situation other than the perfunctory opening of the letter.

LOCATION OF OBJECT
Formerly Berlin, Staatliche Museen, Papyrussammlung, P. 11780; at present in Warsaw.

BIBLIOGRAPHY
Scholl 1990: 2.237, incorporating corrections in BL 2.2.32 and 6.16.

P.Bad. 4.48

Dionysia to Theon
127 BC

LOCATION WRITTEN   Probably Alexandria
LOCATION OF ADDRESSEE   Unknown
LOCATION FOUND   Hipponon (Herakleopolite nome)

Greek

∾ ∾ ∾

Dionysia to Theon her lord, greetings and health. I myself am well. I continually keep the best remembrance of you for all good, and I pray to the gods that I may receive you healthy in many ways, because you both rescued us from enemies and again left us and went away against enemies. Know then, as you gave instructions to carry out and sell the unnecessary goods, when I brought out the mattress, Neon laid hands on it in the agora, and with great violence seized it. It was judged for me that I had the right, since you were absent rather than present, to petition the city governor. But when (after he had done such awful things to me) he appeared with me, it was decided that it [the mattress] should be sealed up and lie in the *archeion* until you are present. For he said that you were not on military duty and I was not military household, but that you had sailed upriver because of work and you were not on royal orders. I have been anxious to no ordinary degree because Marsyas sent a letter, but you have not written anything to me. You will give me pleasure even now if you write back with news of yourself, so that I may be free from worry, please. Take care of yourself, so that I may embrace you in good health. Greet Marsyas and Ammonios. Aline and her children greet you. Farewell. Year 44, Phaophi 5. Above all, I bid you remember how you left me alone like the dogs, and you did not abide by what you exhorted. Even now, then, remember us.

(ADDRESS): Deliver to Theon from Dionysia.

∾ ∾ ∾

THE HAND IS GENERALLY careful and largely detached; it has enough style to be recognizable as of its period, but it shows signs of stress and unevenness. The greetings are added as an afterthought, perhaps after "farewell" had already been written, and they are tucked in awkwardly.

Despite a number of mechanical flaws scattered through the text, the writer's large vocabulary and complex syntax suggest overall someone with a good command of Greek. There are some phonetic spellings, an omitted syllable, some superfluous letters, and a remarkable (but not unique) middle of the verb "to be."

Dionysia writes to her husband Theon, who is upriver on military duty, seemingly in company with a comrade named Marsyas, who has unlike Theon written home. In Theon's absence, Dionysia has had a scuffle in the agora with one Neon, who beat her and seized some bedding she was trying to sell. Dionysia reproaches Theon in vigorous terms for the state in which she has been left, although—apart from the Neon altercation—she gives no details.

NOTES

mattress: *Enkoimetron*. The term can, however, refer to a piece of furniture rather than merely the bedding.

city governor: A chief judicial magistrate. The city is probably Alexandria.

archeion: Evidently here the seat of the city magistrates.

Farewell: Written in a somewhat exaggerated hand, which the editor thought might be a different hand, as indeed he thought the greetings all were; but it looks rather like the same writer trying to write in a different style.

LOCATION OF OBJECT

Heidelberg, Institut für Papyrologie, inv. G 603. Plates in *Propyläen Weltgeschichte* 3 (1962), after p. 584; Seider, *Paläographie der griech. Pap.* I, Tafel 10. Plate of back in Seider, *Paläographie* III, pp. 367–68.

BIBLIOGRAPHY

BL 2.2.176 (correction in line 12); BL 4.103 (translation of 13–14). For military and judicial aspects, see Kiessling 1927: 246–47; Wilcken 1927: 88–90; and *P.Ross.Georg.* 2, pp. 30–31.

P.Münch. 3.57

Grandmother suggests a name for a newborn girl
Second century BC

LOCATION WRITTEN   Unknown
LOCATION OF ADDRESSEE   Unknown
LOCATION FOUND   Unknown

Greek

∾ ∾ ∾

Mother NN to Ptollis, Nikandros, Lysimachos, Tryphaina, greetings. If you
are well, it would be as I pray to the gods to see you well. I received the
letter from you in which you inform me that you have given birth. I prayed
to the gods daily on your behalf. Now that you have escaped (from danger),
I shall pass my time in the greatest joy. I have sent you a flask full of oil and
. . . mnai of dried figs. Please empty the flask and send it back to me safely
because I need it here. Don't hesitate to name the little one Kleopatra, so
that your little daughter . . .

∾ ∾ ∾

THE LETTER IS WRITTEN on the back of what seems to be a business letter in
large detached letters penned along the fibers. Although reminiscent of
schoolhands, they are well formed and suggest at least a modicum of education.
This may (but need not) be the writer's own hand.

There are a number of phonetic spellings but only one significant lapse in
the Greek. The language is otherwise straightforward. The letter begins with
address to several children and the use of the plural, but it then shifts to focus
on the daughter who has given birth and to the use of the singular.

The interest of this letter comes from the comments of the mother about
her prayers for her daughter's safety in childbirth and her suggestion about
naming the child Kleopatra.

NOTES
Mother NN: The letter opens with the term of relationship rather than a
name, but it is quite likely that her name figured somewhere in the ten
letters or so following "mother."

flask: The Greek word is *phakos*, "lentil," used for a lentil-shaped flask used
to carry water or olive oil.

LOCATION OF OBJECT
Munich, Bayerische Staatsbibliothek, Papyrussammlung, Pap. graec. mon.
124. Plate in edition as Abb. 10.

BIBLIOGRAPHY

Rowlandson 1998: no. 225 (English translation); Llewelyn 1994: 57–58.

P.Petr. 3.42H (8)

In trouble with the king
Mid–third century BC

LOCATION WRITTEN   Unknown
LOCATION OF ADDRESSEE   Arsinoite nome
LOCATION FOUND   Arsinoite nome

Greek

Metrodora to Kleon, greetings . . . You have been urging me to come to you, and I would have left everything behind and come; but now I am in no small fear about how things will turn out for you and us. For the huntsmen who arrived early this morning reported to me what had happened to you, that the king treated you harshly when he came to the Lake . . .

FRAGMENTS OF AT LEAST six letters of Metrodora survive, but only this letter offers anything like connected sense.

The Greek is of excellent quality, idiomatic and stylish.

Kleon, the addressee, was an engineer in charge of the extensive land-reclamation works in the Fayyum undertaken under Ptolemy II. Metrodora, Kleon's wife, had been planning to come join him on site, which to her no doubt seemed like a frontier post, but now she hesitates on a report that the King is not happy with Kleon's work.

NOTES

us: The plural is used here, but not elsewhere in this fragment. It may include one or more children.

Lake: The name used for the Fayyum in the early Ptolemaic period. It referred to the large lake (Moeris) and its surrounding marshes.

LOCATION OF OBJECT
Dublin, Trinity College Library.

BIBLIOGRAPHY

Witkowski 1911: nos. 6 (the fragments labeled f) and 7 (a–e), Greek text with notes. Minor corrections in *BL* 1.381 and 2.2.111. A reedition by Bart Van Beek is forthcoming.

UPZ 1.59

Isias to Hephaistion: Time to come home!
168 BC

LOCATION WRITTEN   Unknown
LOCATION OF ADDRESSEE   Memphis, Sarapieion
LOCATION FOUND   Memphis, Sarapieion

Greek

Isias to her brother Hephaistion, greetings. If this letter finds you well and with other things going right, it would be as I continuously pray to the gods; and I myself am well, and the child, and all those in your household, who continually remember you. When I received your letter from Horos, in which you announce that you are in detention in the Sarapieion in Memphis, for the news that you are well I straightaway thanked the gods; but about your not coming home, when all the others who had been detained there have come, I am ill-pleased, because after having piloted myself and your child through such bad times and been driven to every extremity owing to the price of wheat, I thought that now at least, once you got home, I would enjoy some rest. But you have not even thought about coming home, nor given any regard to our situation, how I was in want of everything even while you were still here, not to mention this long lapse of time and such crises, during which you have sent us nothing. Moreover, since Horos, who delivered the letter, reported that you have been released from detention, I am thoroughly ill-pleased. Nonetheless, since your mother also is distressed, please both for her sake and for ours return to the city, if nothing more pressing holds you back. You will please me by taking care of your body so as to be healthy. (second hand) Farewell. (first hand) Year 2, Epeiph 30.

THE LETTER IS WRITTEN in a good, but largely detached, documentary hand, with only very limited ligaturing between letters. In several places, however, there are interlinear additions, including the entirety of line 6. "Farewell" should be in Isias's hand. *UPZ* 1.60, a letter from Hephaistion's brother Dionysios, was written on the same day and in much the same language, and probably the same writer produced both.

The Greek is fluent and has some claims to style, with complex constructions throughout. A fair number of corrections show both the care that was taken with the composition and the pains required to achieve this quality of language.

This letter belongs to the papers found in the Sarapieion of Memphis, probably along with those of Ptolemaios, the recluse whose archive from the reign of Ptolemy VI is one of the most important bodies of evidence for Egypt in this period. Hephaistion, like Ptolemaios, seems to have claimed that he could not leave the sanctuary because of an order of the god. Isias does not think much of this and supposes that Hephaistion's failure to come home is voluntary.

LOCATION OF OBJECT
London, British Library, Papyrus 42. Plates in *P.Lond.* Atlas I, pl. 17; Montevecchi, *La papirologia,* Tav. 18.

BIBLIOGRAPHY
Select Papyri 97; Cribiore 2001a: 91.

UPZ 1.148

A note about learning Egyptian
Second century BC

LOCATION WRITTEN Unknown
LOCATION OF ADDRESSEE Unknown
LOCATION FOUND Unknown

Greek

∿ ∿ ∿

Discovering that you are learning Egyptian letters, I was delighted for you and for myself, because now when you come to the city you will teach the slave boys in the establishment of Phalou... the enema doctor, and you will have a means of support for old age.

∿ ∿ ∿

THE HAND IS WELL made and clear, with serifs and other stylish traits.

The entirety of the letter is written in a single sentence, but with no opening greetings, no names, and no concluding greetings or wishes for health. The Greek is of a good standard, with correct spelling and a good vocabulary.

That the author is a woman we know from feminine participle and pronoun. Rémondon argued that this is a letter of wife to husband, rather than (as supposed by others) from mother to son. In any case, the writer is delighted that the recipient (male) is learning "Egyptian letters," by which Demotic must be meant, in order to teach slave boys in the establishment of an enema doctor. The slaves in question must be Greek speaking, learning Egyptian in order to master a specifically Egyptian medical skill taught in the native language; their masters will have wanted to exploit the increase in the slaves' commercial value that such training would generate.

LOCATION OF OBJECT
London, British Library, Papyrus 43. Plate in *P.Lond.* Atlas I, pl. 28.

BIBLIOGRAPHY
Rémondon 1964.

3. THE ISIDORA TO ASKLEPIADES DOSSIER ∾

The mummy cartonnage from which these papyri come was discovered early in the twentieth century by German excavators at Abusir el-Melek, ancient Bousiris, in the northern part of the Herakleopolite nome. The best-known part of the discovery was a body of documents from Alexandria, but that is only a small part of what the cemetery has yielded. In *BGU* 4, Wilhelm Schubart published as 1203–1209 a group of letters all (except perhaps one) addressed to a man named Asklepiades; he mentions two further letters too fragmentary to publish belonging to the same group, both of them from women (*BGU* 4, p. 347). An additional piece of the dossier was published in 1995 as *BGU* 16.2665. At least eleven letters were thus preserved in whole or in part.

There is no direct evidence for the place of writing, but the letters mention several places in the Herakleopolite nome and probably one or two places elsewhere. At least when *BGU* 4.1205 was written, Asklepiades seems to have been in Memphis, because the writer speaks of a third person's arriving in Memphis and getting a talking-to from Asklepiades. Some of the letters have both a date of writing and a date of receipt, varying apparently from a day to more than a week. It seems most probable that Asklepiades's correspondents were at various locations in the Herakleopolite, perhaps especially at Bousiris, and Asklepiades himself was in Memphis at least some of the time, some 80 to 100 km north of his correspondents. Asklepiades pasted the letters together into a roll after receipt, as the preserved juncture of two letters in *BGU* 4.1205 shows clearly.

The best-represented correspondent is Isidora, who refers to Asklepiades as her "brother." Various other brothers appear as well, but it remains unclear which of these are biological siblings and if any are married to one another. As normally in letters, no patronymics are given, and it is therefore impossible to identify the individuals confidently with anyone known from other texts. Nonetheless, there is a real possibility that Asklepiades is the same person as the strategos mentioned in the archive of Athenodoros (which also comes from Abusir cartonnage) and in some other documents a little later in the reign of Augustus. Certainly the family that produced this archive was wealthy and had wide landholdings.

BGU 4.1204

Isidora to Asklepiades: Reply to me quickly
28 BC

LOCATION WRITTEN   Probably Herakleopolite nome
LOCATION OF ADDRESSEE   Probably Memphis
LOCATION FOUND   Abusir el-Melek (Herakleopolite nome)

Greek

∾ ∾ ∾

Isidora to Asklepiades her brother, greetings and health always. I have enclosed under the same seal to you the letter to Paniskos. So send me the reply to everything quickly because the ship is departing. And continue to bear up bravely until it arrives, and take care of yourself so that you remain healthy, which is most important. Farewell. Year 3, Phaophi 5. Send the child's sleeping rug.

∾ ∾ ∾

THIS IS THE HAND of a scribe or a secretary, not Isidora, for whom see BGU 4.1205. It is a minute hand, fast and more ligatured than a standard letter hand.

The letter is written in good business Greek. Connective particles are used correctly and with a good sense of style.

The letter's contents are brief and allusive and take for granted earlier correspondence from which we would know what ship was meant, and whether it was traveling from Asklepiades to Isidora or from Isidora to some other destination.

NOTES
Paniskos: Called "brother" in BGU 4.1206.

until it arrives: Assuming that the boat is the subject; but it could also be Paniskos (as Olsson 1925 and White 1986 take it).

Year 3 [of Augustus], Phaophi 5: 3 October 28 BC in contemporary reckoning (Skeat 1993).

sleeping rug: Or mattress. In BGU 4.1205 Isidora says that its price was 120 drachmas, an enormous sum for a household object; it was perhaps a luxury model.

LOCATION OF OBJECT
Formerly Berlin, Staatliche Museen, Papyrussammlung, P. 13151; now in Cairo, Egyptian Museum, SR 2956.

BIBLIOGRAPHY

Olsson 1925: no. 2 (reprinted text with translation and commentary);
White 1986: no. 63 (text, translation, commentary).

BGU 4.1205, cols. ii–iii

Isidora to Asklepiades: instructions
28 BC

LOCATION WRITTEN   Probably Herakleopolite nome
LOCATION OF ADDRESSEE   Probably Memphis
LOCATION FOUND   Abusir el-Melek (Herakleopolite nome)

Greek

෴ ෴ ෴

(DOCKET): Received Year 3, Hathyr 8.

Isidora to Asklas her brother, greetings and health always, just as I pray. I
have received on the 27th the letters which you had written via —. It's
nice of you to try to make me responsible for the lentils and the peas. For
you are not even consistent with yourself, since you have written to
Paniskos that we sold (them). For we have not sold them; but do as you
wish. Only bear up bravely in the reckoning and in the collection, so that
when Paniskos arrives in Memphis you don't fall into difficulties. I sent you
the price of the bedding, 140 drachmas, but you should know, if you come,
who received it. It is not . . . Give Alexion the dyer on my account 100
drachmas for a bed rug for the child Artemas, solid, not empty. Do not
detain Achilleus, but give him the two boats because he is going to
Hermopolis; and take care of yourself, so that you may be well. Farewell.
Year 3, Phaophi 28.

෴ ෴ ෴

THIS TWO-COLUMN LETTER WAS preceded on the papyrus by another multi-
column letter, of which only traces of the end are preserved. This letter was
written by Isidora herself with detached characters that are uneven and sometimes retraced. The individual letters, however, are formed with a certain
elegance.

The Greek of the letter is vigorous and idiomatic but not very polished.
There are mistaken case forms here and there. The subjunctive form in line
17 has an unwanted temporal augment.

Fig. 2.   *BGU* 4.1205, cols. ii–iii. Isidora to Asklepiades: instructions. (Formerly Berlin, Staatliche Museen, Papyrussammlung, now Cairo, Egyptian Museum, SR 2957. Photograph courtesy of the Egyptian Museum, Cairo.)

The difficulties caused by Isidora's erratic Greek add to the problems of interpreting the letter. It concerns matters of business, including the sale of produce, the transfer of money, the ordering of bedding, and the provision of boats for a trip. Isidora does not hesitate to tell Asklepiades in brusque tones that he is wrong about this or that item.

NOTES

Asklas: A short form of Asklepiades.

on the 27th: Of Phaophi, the day before the letter is dated.

collection: Gk. *eisagoge*, which can refer to getting in a crop or to importing; it is not clear what is meant here.

bed rug: Cf. for the same word *P.Bad.* 4.48.

Hermopolis: It is unclear which of the places with this name is meant, but perhaps Hermopolis Magna is more likely than the village in the Arsinoite or the city in the delta.

LOCATION OF OBJECT

Formerly Berlin, Staatliche Museen, Papyrussammlung; now in Cairo, Egyptian Museum, SR 2957.

BIBLIOGRAPHY

Olsson 1925: no. 3 (text, translation, and commentary).

BGU 4.1206

Isidora to Asklepiades: instructions
28 BC

LOCATION WRITTEN   Probably Herakleopolite nome
LOCATION OF ADDRESSEE   Probably Memphis
LOCATION FOUND   Abusir el-Melek (Herakleopolite nome)

Greek

Isidora to Asklas her brother, greetings and health always as I pray. I have received what you had written. Our brother Paniskos has written that Noumenios has zealously sent Philon the *oikonomos* to him for the *dioikesis*. He has not yet indicated what has eventuated. Concerning Areios, Patrhimself is writing to him to get the wheat credited. You and Haramoites, bear up bravely in the collection of the price of the lentils and emmer. If anything else should occur, I will let you know; and take care of yourself, so that you may be well. Farewell. Year 3, Hathyr 6, early.

WRITTEN IN THE SAME hand as BGU 4.1205, probably that of Isidora. The difference with respect to the letter written on the right (1207) is striking. The characters are quite large, rigid, and detached. The writer visibly grows tired as the letter proceeds so that legibility is difficult toward the end.

Isidora again displays the linguistic characteristics found in BGU 4.1205. She carelessly omits syllables in two words and generally seems more abrupt than in the other letter.

The subjects at stake here are business matters as usual, including the collection of money from lentils and emmer wheat.

NOTES
dioikesis: Generally, financial administration.

oikonomos: This term is perhaps private rather than official.

LOCATION OF OBJECT
Berlin, Staatliche Museen, Papyrussammlung, P. 13152, col. i.

BIBLIOGRAPHY
Olsson 1925: no. 4 (text, translation, notes); White 1986: no. 64 (text, translation, notes).

BGU 4.1207

Isidora to Asklepiades: instructions
28 BC

LOCATION WRITTEN   Probably Herakleopolite nome
LOCATION OF ADDRESSEE   Probably Memphis
LOCATION FOUND   Abusir el-Melek (Herakleopolite nome)

Greek

(DOCKET): Received year 3, Hathyr 9, through Ptollion.

Isidora to Asklepiades her brother, greetings and health always . . . I have received what you had written. . . . red bedspreads . . . 3 sky-blue . . . , 2 mulberry-colored bedspreads. Concerning our brother Paniskos, Noumenios has zealously sent his brother Philon to him for the *dioikesis*. You and Haramoites, bear up bravely and collect the price of the lentils and emmer. Otherwise, take care of yourself, so that you may be well. Farewell. Year 3, Hathyr 3. If anything else happens, I will let you know if it seems necessary to go before I write (?). I have received 2,800 drachmas of silver by way of the agent, and Ptollion is bringing to you . . . If you send money, send along a twentieth.

(ADDRESS): To Asklepiades.

THE LETTER IS WRITTEN on a sheet glued to the right of BGU 4.1206, sent by Isidora to Asklepiades three days later. It seems that the letters were received in reverse order of sending. The writer of 1207 is quite experienced. The characters are small, fast, and ligatured.

The language of the letter is in line with that in the more professionally written letters of this group, with only relatively minor phonetic spellings and a correct use of connectives.

For the contents, see BGU 4.1206, from which this differs only slightly, mainly in the list of goods mentioned.

NOTES
brother Philon: "Brother" in such a context almost certainly means "colleague," and in BGU 4.1206 it is made explicit that Philon was an *oikonomos*.

dioikesis: Generally, financial administration.

2,800 drachmas: In silver, this is a very large sum of money at this period.

twentieth: The meaning of this request for an extra 5 percent is not clear.

LOCATION OF OBJECT
Berlin, Staatliche Museen, Papyrussammlung, P. 13152, col. ii.

BIBLIOGRAPHY
Olsson 1925: no. 5 (text, translation, notes); White 1986: no. 65 (text, translation, notes); cf. *BL* 2.2.25 (reading at the beginning of line 10).

BGU 16.2665

Tryphaina to Asklepiades about inundated land
28–27 BC

LOCATION WRITTEN   Probably Herakleopolite nome
LOCATION OF ADDRESSEE   Probably Memphis
LOCATION FOUND   Abusir el-Melek (Herakleopolite nome)

Greek

∾ ∾ ∾

Tryphaina to her son Asklepiades, greetings and health always. (I was happy?) receiving the letter from you on the 16th. If the *kleros* of Agelaos near Ogou has been only half inundated and so far that near Mouchis has not yet been flooded, I am ruined (?), and the money spent for the dikes of all of them. The things about which you wrote are more expensive here. The fatal (?) . . . and the price is not yet set. Two fine, red, beaten bed rugs and the child's . . . Don't forget . . . send. I sent the shoe for you back with Apollos. The thirty arouras near Nois have been inundated. Don't lease the allotment near Tale, but enjoy it there . . . Farewell. Year 3 of Caesar (?) . . .

∾ ∾ ∾

THE WRITER MAY BE either Tryphon or a scribe in the family employ. The hand is small, proficient, and betrays lots of confidence in writing. Speed is higher than in the average letter hand, but legibility is fairly good. Because of the bad condition of the papyrus it is impossible to determine whether the farewell and the date were written by the same writer.

Damage to the papyrus has made it more difficult than usual to follow the writer's sense, but much of the trouble comes from the informal syntax she uses, omitting verbs on occasion and disregarding cases of nouns.

The letter concerns, along with usual matters of getting and sending goods, the state of inundation of several parcels of land controlled by the family. So far the news seems not to have been good, although Tryphaina may of course be exaggerating.

fatal: It is hard to connect this to the rest of the context.

Year 3 of Caesar: The reading is very doubtful.

LOCATION OF OBJECT
Berlin, Staatliche Museen, Papyrussammlung, P. 25155. Photograph on microfiche 6 accompanying the volume.

4. FROM THE ATHENODOROS ARCHIVE ༦

This dossier was extracted from mummy cartonnage found early in the century at Abusir el-Melek, the ancient Busiris in the Herakleopolite nome. It is partly published in *BGU* 16, but the editor remarks that unpublished fragments remain. Athenodoros worked as an estate manager and minor official in the Herakleopolite in the late first century BC. At least some of his career was spent as a *phrontistes* (estate manager) for one Asklepiades, son of Dionysios, who seems to be the same man as the Asklepiades who was strategos of the Herakleopolite nome around 13/12 and continued to be an important landowner in that nome for about another decade. (See *BGU* 16.2601, 2605, 2662, and 2664 for details; he is probably also the man attested without titles in *BGU* 4.1197 and 1200.) It is possible that this is the same Asklepiades as the addressee of the letters in a dossier of family correspondence also from cartonnage at Abusir el-Melek (A3), but this cannot be demonstrated.

BGU 16.2617

Tryphas to Athenodoros about some goods
7 BC

LOCATION WRITTEN Unknown
LOCATION OF ADDRESSEE Unknown
LOCATION FOUND Abusir el-Melek (Herakleopolite nome)

Greek

∾ ∾ ∾

Tryphas to Athenodoros her son, many greetings and prosper always as I pray. I received what you sent, and I secured them by myself, forty tree trunks and one, and thirteen jars. Greet my lady daughters Tryphas and Artemis. Above all, take care of yourself so that you may be well, which is my greatest prayer with all the gods. Farewell. Year 23 of Caesar, Epeiph 17.

∾ ∾ ∾

THE HAND IS NEAT and practiced but not particularly attractive. At first glance one gets an impression of many ligatures, but close examination shows that these are in most cases connecting strokes that do not actually quite touch the next letter. The hand is the same throughout. It is not the same hand as BGU 16.2618, also from Tryphas, and in all likelihood neither is from her own hand. It is likely, however, that Tryphas penned the greetings.

The letter is simply expressed but contains a considerable number of minor errors reflecting pronunciation. There is a sign of oral dictation, perhaps a correction in afterthought, in the addition of "and one" after "forty tree trunks."

The writer is concerned to acknowledge safe receipt of some goods and to convey her best wishes to Athenodoros and to two "daughters," one of them named Tryphas and thus perhaps really her daughter, the other Artemis, who with Athenodoros is the recipient of 2618.

LOCATION OF OBJECT
Berlin, Staatliche Museen, Papyrussammlung, P. 25238. Photograph on microfiche in publication.

BGU 16.2618

Tryphas to Athenodoros about slaves
7 BC

LOCATION WRITTEN   Unknown
LOCATION OF ADDRESSEE   Unknown
LOCATION FOUND   Abusir el-Melek (Herakleopolite nome)

Greek

Tryphas to Athenodoros her son and Artemis her daughter, many greetings and good health always. Know that I have not received the wheat which you sent me; for I understood that it was not advantageous for me to receive it. So now give orders that it be sent. You did not pay the fine (?), nor is anyone able to free the slaves. Each day I am pestered by two *statores*, Sokrates and Elemon, because I am found owing. I have often written to you to see to the slaves. They will die in the jail. Please listen to me and lock up the grain and give nothing to anyone; for on the fifteenth it went up 3 obols, and they fear that it may become more expensive. Nardos and Nikas and all those in the household greet you. Take care of yourself so that you may be well. Farewell. Year 23 of Caesar, Pachon 15.

(ADDRESS): Deliver to Athenodoros my son.

THE HAND IS A practiced semicursive. It is not the same hand as 2617. Tryphas, however, probably wrote the greetings in her hand.

Apart from relatively minor orthographic details and a few omissions, the letter is accurately composed. This is a competent but unexceptional piece of business prose. It does, however, have a good vocabulary.

Tryphas writes to Athenodoros and Artemis, the latter perhaps Athenodoros's wife; the rest of the letter, however, is written in the second-person singular and evidently consists of instructions to Athenodoros. The main subjects are two slaves who are in jail for some reason, requiring Athenodoros to intervene and pay what is due; and the price of wheat, which has risen significantly and may go higher. Tryphas is concerned to see that the (probably substantial) supplies owned by the family are kept well protected.

NOTE
statores: Bailiffs, it seems.

LOCATION OF OBJECT
Berlin, Staatliche Museen, Papyrussammlung, P. 25245.

5. THE WOMEN OF THE FAMILY OF POMPEIUS ∾

This archive includes five letters written by Herennia and other women of her family to Pompeius. While it seems clear that Herennia was Pompeius's daughter, the relationships of Charitous and Heraklous with him are rather uncertain. In the editio princeps the editor of SB 9121 offered the hypothesis that the writer, Heraklous, was Pompeius's wife, since she bitterly complained to him about some trouble having to do with his estate. It is possible, however, that Heraklous was a relative of Pompeius but that Charitous was his wife. Both women apparently lived with him and took care of his business in his absence, but when Herennia writes to her father she sends her salutations only to Charitous. Thaubas may have been another daughter of Pompeius who lived away from him with her own family.

Pompeius lived in Arsinoe, the nome capital. Herennia lived at no great distance from him, maybe in the country, with her husband and children ("little" Pompeius, mentioned twice, may have been her son, and it is conceivable that Syrion was her husband). The last time she is mentioned she has just died, having given birth to a stillborn: it is Thaubas's letter that informs Pompeius of her death. In the two letters that Herennia sends she mentions not only domestic matters but also pressing affairs for her father. Charitous and Heraklous also seem to be concerned with more than the usual details regarding household management.

Both Thaubas and Charitous dictated their letters to scribes and did not add salutations in their hands. Since Heraklous's letter is mutilated at the end, it is impossible to know if she had subscribed. Herennia, however, was certainly fully literate. She seems to have written a letter in its entirety (P.Mert. 63) and subscribed another letter (SB 9122). It is conceivable that the second letter was also entirely penned by her: it may have been written at a later time when her handwriting had somewhat evolved.

P.Mert. 2.63

Herennia to Pompeius concerning a payment for "Piety"
AD 57

LOCATION WRITTEN   Probably Arsinoite nome
LOCATION OF ADDRESSEE   Unknown
LOCATION FOUND   Probably Arsinoite nome

Greek

Helenia [sic] to Pompeius her father, many greetings and continuing health. I have bought the olives for you. They are trying to collect from all directions for the "Piety" of the temple of Souchos, from everyone, even Romans and Alexandrians and settlers in the Arsinoite. They are trying to collect from Pompeius. I have not paid, on the grounds that I was expecting you to arrive today. Either take care of it yourself and do it, or if not, we'll pay it. And I received in good health the letter from Onomastos. We pray that all is well with you. So that you may <not> forget your children, receive another letter of Syrion your son. We greet you and Charitous and her children. And little Pompeius greets you. Year 4 of Nero Claudius Caesar Augustus Germanicus Imperator, Tybi 23.

(ADDRESS): Give to Pompeius her father from Helenia [sic] . . . to the father of Onomastos . . . to the house of Nemesous.

LETTERS ARE MAINLY DETACHED. Letter formation and size are irregular, and the lines of writing wander uncertainly across the sheet. Of the letters in this dossier, this one has the greatest chance of having been written by Herennia herself.

The spelling is phonetic enough to have drawn the editor's notice. Except for "and" connectives are largely absent, and the entire style is direct and lacking in literary graces.

The "piety" mentioned is probably an irregular levy for a special need of the temple of the crocodile god Sobek (Souchos). Pompeius seems not to be at any great distance from Herennia. Perhaps he was in the nome capital and Herennia in a country house.

NOTES
Piety: Gk. *eusebeia*. This is a short-form reference to payments made "in accordance with piety" or "on the basis of piety."

Romans, etc.: These three privileged groups are enumerated in a fashion suggesting that otherwise only undifferentiated Egyptians might have been subject to the *eusebeia* payment. Romans and Alexandrians were exempt from the poll tax; *katoikoi* (settlers) paid it at a reduced rate but were still legally Egyptians.

Syrion: A blank space of about two lines follows this statement before Herennia resumes the letter. It is not clear if Syrion was supposed to write in this space (perhaps only "farewell," which might have been effaced) or if his letter was on another sheet (in which case the blank is without explanation).

Tybi 23: 18 January 57.

LOCATION OF OBJECT
Dublin, Chester Beatty Library.

BIBLIOGRAPHY
White 1986: 141–42, no. 90.

Fig. 3. *P.Mert.* 2.63. Herennia to Pompeius concerning a payment for "Piety." (Dublin, Chester Beatty Library. Photograph © The Trustees of the Chester Beatty Library, Dublin.)

SB 6.9120

Charitous to Pompeius concerning his name unwritten in a register
Ca. AD 57

LOCATION WRITTEN   Unknown
LOCATION OF ADDRESSEE   Unknown
LOCATION FOUND   Probably Arsinoite nome

Greek

Charitous to Pompeius her brother, greetings. I want you to know that I took care of the matter about which you wrote me. I went to Zoilas the son of Argaios, and he went to the office of the *basilikos grammateus* and inspected and did not find your name written in the roll. So then come up to your home quite quickly. Greet the children of Herennia and Pompeius and Syrion and Thaisous and her children and her husband and all my friends. Farewell.

(ADDRESS): Deliver from Charitous to Pompeius her brother.

THE LETTER IS WRITTEN throughout in a single hand. The characters vary wildly in size in any part of the letter and are sometimes enlarged at the beginning of lines. Speed of execution varies considerably.

The Greek of this letter is very correct, apart from a few minor phonetic spellings. The author has used postpositive *oun*, iota adscript, and a relative clause correctly, suggesting a good level of education and experience in writing letters.

Apart from greetings, the letter's purpose is to communicate to Pompeius the results of a check of official records, carried out by a friend at Charitous's request. It appears that Pompeius was away from home. It is interesting that Charitous did not go herself but had an apparently unrelated friend go. This indirect consultation may have been intended to avoid arousing the curiosity of the *basilikos grammateus* about why a member of Pompeius's family wanted to look at the register in question.

NOTE
basilikos grammateus: The chief of the government record-keeping for the Herakleides division of the Arsinoite nome. That might suggest that the family's country holdings were in one of the villages of the Herakleides which yielded numbers of papyri, particularly Karanis and Philadelphia.

LOCATION OF OBJECT
Oslo, Universitetetsbiblioteket, inv. 1475.

BIBLIOGRAPHY

Eitrem and Amundsen 1951: 177–79; White 1986: 142–43, no. 91.

SB 6.9121

Heraklous to Pompeius about a woman harassing her
Ca. AD 57

LOCATION WRITTEN   Unknown
LOCATION OF ADDRESSEE   Unknown
LOCATION FOUND   Probably Arsinoite nome

Greek

Heraklous to Pompeius, greetings and continued health. Just as soon as the letter reaches you, come at once. Since Apeis died, Serapous does not stop disturbing me at home. Since then she harasses me, saying, "Produce the documents"—she stands there saying, "Two documents." I do not give them. Argyrios has completely confirmed us, saying, "You have not paid the sales tax." If the letter reaches you, come immediately. Otherwise, I'm leaving the house. If you don't come, I'm settling the house and coming to you, so that . . .

(ADDRESS): Only traces survive.

LARGE LETTERS MOSTLY SEPARATED or lightly connected and written slowly. They are the product of a skillful hand, but there is a bit of unevenness, and the lines go downward. The abbreviation of the initial greeting betrays the professional scribe. The letter is broken at the bottom, so we cannot tell if there were greetings in a second hand.

Although the spelling and syntax are no worse than average for letters, the letter has a disjointed feeling, the result of the vehemence and worry of the writer. Clauses tumble after one another, and there is a fair amount of repetition.

The letter concerns the aftermath of the death of Apeis, whose relationship to the other persons in the letter is not known. The difficulties probably concern his estate; at any rate, a woman named Serapous has been hounding Heraklous about it, demanding that she produce documents. Despite the assistance of one Argyrios, Heraklous is at her wits' end without Pompeius's help.

documents, sales tax: Probably the transfer of title to property, on which the *enkyklion* (sales tax) fell, was in question. Proof of payment of the sales tax on a piece of property was one way of showing presumptive ownership. The "you" who has not paid sales tax is then presumably Serapous, although it is not clear why the verb is plural. If this is correct, then she was probably herself brandishing documents and challenging Heraklous to produce documents to show that she was wrong.

Oslo, Universitetetsbiblioteket, inv. 1460.

BIBLIOGRAPHY

Eitrem and Amundsen 1951: 179–81; White 1986: 143–44, no. 92.

Fig. 4. *SB* 6.9121. Heraklous to Pompeius about a woman harassing her. (Oslo, Universitetetsbiblioteket, inv. 1460. Photograph courtesy of the University of Oslo Library.)

SB 6.9122

Herennia to Pompeius concerning goods
Ca. AD 57

LOCATION WRITTEN   Unknown
LOCATION OF ADDRESSEE   Unknown
LOCATION FOUND   Probably Arsinoite nome

Greek

〜 〜 〜

Herennia to Pompeius her [father], many greetings and continued health,
and I embrace my mother. I ask that you remind my father to buy a colored
himation suitable for a gentleman. Be satisfied . . . the price of the himation
. . . the Arsinoite. Don't forget to buy the . . . of pigment for Pration.
Receive two measures of lentils from Thaisous. And Antiphanes wrote me
that if . . . a sale there. I ask you to send me three staters (weight) of green
cloth for headbands. Little Pompeius greets you, his father and his mother.
Don't forget us. We greet your children and those in the house. (second
hand) Farewell. (first hand) Pharmouthi 6.

〜 〜 〜

THE HAND WAS DESCRIBED by the editor as an uneven "private hand." The
greeting at the end is written in a second hand, indicating that Herennia was
literate but dictated the body of the letter.

The scribe, however, is not a great deal more skilled than Herennia herself.
The spelling is very phonetic, but more importantly the composition of clauses
is ungainly. The letter is thus not only dictated but probably taken down pretty
much as it was spoken, with little attempt to tidy up the style.

This letter is concerned almost entirely with requests for goods, including
a cloak, some pigment, lentils, and green cloth, plus the usual greetings.

NOTE
his father and mother: Grandparents, in fact.

LOCATION OF OBJECT
Oslo, Universitetetsbiblioteket, inv. 1444.

BIBLIOGRAPHY
Eitrem and Amundsen 1951: 181–83.

Fig. 5. *SB* 6.9122. Herennia to Pompeius concerning goods. (Oslo, Universitetsbiblioteket, inv. 1444. Photograph courtesy of the University of Oslo Library.)

P.Fouad 75

Thaubas to her father Pompeius about the death of Herennia
AD 64

LOCATION WRITTEN   Unknown
LOCATION OF ADDRESSEE   Oxyrhyncha (Arsinoite)
LOCATION FOUND   Unknown

Greek

～ ～ ～

Thaubas to Pompeius her father, many greetings. When you receive my letter please come home at once, because your poor daughter Herennia has died, even though she had already come safely through a miscarriage on Phaophi ninth. For she gave birth to an eight-month child, dead, and lived on for four days, and after that she died and was given a funeral by us and her husband, as was right, and has been transported to Alabanthis. So if you come and wish you can see her. Alexandros greets you, as do his children. Farewell. Year 11 of Nero Claudius Caesar Augustus Germanicus Imperator, Phaophi 18.

(ADDRESS): To Oxyrhyncha, to the place called . . . , to Pompeius.

∾ ∾ ∾

THE HAND IS A well-trained, neat letter hand, with attempts at elegance but a tendency to run downhill. The greeting at the end appears to be in the same hand as the body of the letter, which is presumably written by a scribe.

The first half of the letter is composed with a good attempt at prose style. After the halfway point, the letter becomes a string of statements connected with "and" in a more typically paratactic structure; perhaps the scribe let up in his efforts to turn Thaubas's oral style into written prose.

This is a letter concerned solely with one important event in this family's life, the death of one of its members. Although Thaubas narrates the events in a straightforward fashion and without much comment, the adjective "poor" applied to Herennia lends a bit of overt feeling. Herennia survived a stillbirth by four days.

NOTES

Alabanthis: A village in the Herakleides district of the Arsinoite nome, on the south side of Lake Moeris.

see her: A clear statement of the fact that bodies were kept visible for some time after death.

Phaophi 18: 15 October, five days after Herennia's death.

Oxyrhyncha: A village in the Polemon district of the Arsinoite nome. Pompeius could probably have made the journey to Alabanthis in a day.

LOCATION OF OBJECT

Cairo, Egyptian Papyrological Society, inv. 171, now in Egyptian Museum, Journal d'Entrée 72112, SR 2787. Plate IXB in original edition.

BIBLIOGRAPHY

Youtie 1958: 374–76 = *Scriptiunculae* I 284–86 (*BL* 4.32; corrections to several lines); Coles, Geissen, and Koenen 1973: 239 (*BL* 7.57; correction to line 1); Hengstl 1978: 225–26, no. 90 (text using corrections in *BL* 4, German translation); Rowlandson 1998: 293–94, no. 228 (English translation).

6. THE TIBERIANUS ARCHIVE ∾

The Tiberianus archive includes both Greek and Latin letters. *P.Mich.* 8.465–466; 473–481, and 485–487 are in Greek. *P.Mich.* 8.467–472 and *ChLA* 5.299 are written in Latin. These papyri come from Karanis and refer to a military milieu. Claudius Tiberianus was a *speculator* and then a veteran, and his son Claudius Terentianus, who wrote the Latin letters, was enrolled in the *Classis Augusta Alexandrina* and then became a legionary. The letters of this archive illuminate in great detail the daily life of soldiers in the Trajanic period.

P.Mich. 8.473 and 474, which were probably sent by the same woman, Tabetheus, also mention vivid details of military life. Tabetheus, who together with another man is the only person in the archive who addresses Tiberianus as "brother," had a close relationship with him. Tiberianus's daughter lived with her, and she was also in touch with some of his sons. In her letters she mentions favors that she did for him in the hope of enrolling his help in a troublesome situation regarding her own son. Both letters appear to have been dictated to different scribes.

Tabetheus to Tiberianus about a murder committed by her son
Early second century AD

LOCATION WRITTEN Unknown
LOCATION OF ADDRESSEE Unknown
LOCATION FOUND Karanis

Greek

∾ ∾ ∾

Tabetheus to Claudius Tiberianus her brother very many greetings. Before
everything I pray that you are well and I make obeisance for you before our
lord Souchos. I was glad that you sent my son so that I could embrace him,
but you did not . . . him to the man. Saturnilus therefore has not found out
what I did for him. We have bought 3 mnas of linen and I sent them. Do
not blame me if you did not deliver (them) to the soldier Metellus; I would
like you to write about (this?) friend: Deliver them to him right away. I was
much annoyed. This year I was able to send you the garment; last year I did
not send it but I sent and sold them to Kabin the attendant. When we
went down from our home at Tonis and arrived at the guest's house of
Saturnilus, and I saw all our things untouched by the evil eye, I became of
the opinion that my own son should not trust Menas. And after he killed
him, he told me not to worry. I told Saturnilus, "I could not sleep worrying
that you cost me 1,200 drachmas damage." Let them go, as money spent for
my son. And I went down to Alexandria with my son. This is the reason
why folly got hold of him, because he did not approve that he (Menas)
consumed the monthly rations with the members of his family. If the god
wills and you receive the rations that I have made for you, do not . . . them
also. About last year's rations, I did not make them, . . . made them last
year. I sent them in Alexandria until the second shipment upriver. And he
was ill. I was anguished and distressed because of him, but I utterly rejoiced
that he remained alive. We cheered him up urging, "Have a taste of
Alexandria" but he says to us, "I do not want to." We thank the gods that
he is like you: Nobody can make fun of him. Salute all your people by
name. How much damage did I suffer last year because of Saturnilus; I
certainly did not owe anything but I suffered damage in everything.

(ADDRESS ON BACK): Give it to . . . Tiberianus from T(abetheus).

∾ ∾ ∾

THIS SCRIBE WAS PROBABLY at home with writing documents. His hand is clear
and very fluent and shows more ligatures than a usual letter hand.

Under the agitated dictation of Tabetheus, the scribe keeps on interrupting the flow of the letter. Overall there is a good variety of clauses that give the impression of a competent enough writer.

In spite of some obscure points, this letter presents a very eloquent portrait of the anguish of a mother because of a murder committed by her son and shows the close relationship she had with Claudius Tiberianus, who was probably in military service at the time. Closely related to Saturnilus's situation are the various attempts of Tabetheus to show Tiberianus that he is indebted to her because of the monthly rations and garments that she sends him and on account of some other business: she hopes that he can help her son.

NOTES

greetings: The initial abbreviation of *chairein* (greetings) is the work of a professional.

monthly rations: Contrary to the editor's statement, this term is not only used for the provisions sent by families to soldiers but also indicates the supplies that parents sent to students away from home.

LOCATION OF OBJECT

Ann Arbor, University of Michigan, Papyrus Collection, inv. 5501.

BIBLIOGRAPHY

On letters sent to Tiberianus, Bowersock 1971: 232–33. On the Latin letters, Cugusi 2002, II: 131–33 and nos. 141–48.

P.Mich. 8.474

Tabetheus (?) to Tiberianus
Early second century AD

LOCATION WRITTEN Unknown
LOCATION OF ADDRESSEE Unknown
LOCATION FOUND Karanis

Greek

∾ ∾ ∾

[Tabetheus to Claudius Tib]erianus her brother, many greetings . . . you arrived in Alexandria, I was very glad together with all my relatives . . . that you are coming immediately to us, since (your) son . . . waited for you when you were away until today. And until now . . . we wait for you together with the children. Therefore I am asking you to come to us . . . We will embrace you with the children if you come up . . . Your daughter Segathis is in my attendance: she is wise and . . . and she sent your son Isidoros to you in order to . . . your belts . . . the soldiers, for she follows after us lest she comes and . . . in the river, because I myself cannot leave the house . . . Isidoros salutes you and Segathis, and we salute . . . and the children. I received a letter from your son Claudius . . . as soon as you arrive . . . myself and Segathis to Alexandria . . . so far you did not agree yet to come.

∾ ∾ ∾

THIS IS THE PRODUCT of a professional scribe and shows more ligatures than a standard letter hand. Fluency and regularity combine with a decent legibility.

Since the style of the letter, with short phrases in asyndeton and some individual expressions, recalls that of P.Mich. 8.473, sent by Tabetheus but written by a different scribe, we should assume that the writing reproduces this woman's voice. The letter is fairly correct and mostly shows common phonetic errors.

This letter consists of an insistent invitation addressed by a woman—probably the Tabetheus of P.Mich. 8.473—to Tiberianus, who had just arrived in Alexandria to visit relatives who lived in a village nearby. Apparently a daughter of Tiberianus lived with Tabetheus, who also mentions two of his sons.

NOTE
Alexandria: According to P.Mich. 8.473, Tabetheus lived in Tonis, which was probably a village on the outskirts of Alexandria, presumably at the south of the city.

LOCATION OF OBJECT
Ann Arbor, University of Michigan Library, Papyrus Collection, inv. 5403; now in Cairo, Egyptian Museum.

7. WOMEN OF THE ARCHIVE OF APOLLONIOS THE STRATEGOS ∾

I n the second century AD the family of Apollonios belonged to the upper class of the Greek population of Hermopolis. When Apollonios was appointed strategos—head of the civil administration—of the district of Apollonopolites Heptakomia in Upper Egypt, he transferred there with part of his family, primarily his wife Aline and their smaller children. His oldest daughter Heraidous and his mother Eudaimonis remained in Hermopolis together with other relatives. Correspondence went back and forth between Hermopolis and Heptakomia. When Apollonios laid down his office in 120 he took with him all his private and official papers: these were found around Hermopolis, probably where one of the family's estates was located. Among these there are twenty-five letters of women who were related in some way to the strategos.

The office of strategos implied only civil duties, but the great Jewish revolt of the eastern provinces of the empire changed the situation to some degree: during the period of the revolt, which lasted in Egypt from 115 to 117, Apollonios also performed military service and took part in a battle. Many of the women's letters are therefore concerned with the dangers he was facing in the situation. Other letters mention an illness that was probably of some significance, considering that also male acquaintances and relatives manifested some preoccupation. Most letters are also concerned with relating about the welfare of relatives in Hermopolis and about practical problems, such as the management of a linen-weaving enterprise that belonged to the family, articles of clothing that Apollonios needed, and the construction of a mansion in the countryside of Hermopolis at the end of the Jewish Revolt.

While most of the women appearing in this archive are members of the upper class—Apollonios's relatives or acquaintances—others worked in the family's household or in the weaving enterprise. The most articulate apparently was the matriarch, Eudaimonis, who sent eleven letters: nine to her son Apollonios and two to her daughter-in-law Aline. Her letters are never conventional and commonplace: she always comes across as a strong personality, sure of herself and her bearing. Moreover, not only was she able to add personal greetings to her letters, but she probably wrote three of them in her hand. Even though only three of the letters of Aline are preserved, and the picture is less complete than for Eudaimonis, her letters show that she had received an education, used words that have a literary flavor, and wrote greetings in a minute and fluent hand. It is possible—but far from sure—that an intriguing letter, *P.Giss.* 79, was also written by her. Two more interesting letters, *P.Brem.* 61 and 64, were sent to Apollonios by women of the family, a sister of his and another relative whose identity is unsure. They both have all the impromptu characteristics of a modern telephone conversation.

Two women of the upper class who did not belong to the family circle are those who sent *P.Brem.* 59 and 62. The writer of the first letter, who added the greetings of her son, "the poet who played with his own lyre" may have made one of the few jokes appearing in the papyri. It is interesting that the writer of the second epistle, Philia, wrote to Apollonios without the mediation of a male relative. But it was not only women of high social status who kept a frequent correspondence. The letters of the archive of Apollonios also allow us to look at the writing habits of women of the lower classes. Two letters survive of a woman called Arsis, who worked in the family's weaving enterprise in the Hermopolite. Another woman who worked for Apollonios's family at a lower level than Arsis but had a closer relationship with some family members was Teeus, who sent three letters. She appears to have been a trusty servant who had been working for Eudaimonis for a long time and maybe had even raised Apollonios: it was with him that she had a personal, warm relationship. Finally another papyrus that was found in this archive is *P.Giss.* 81. It contains two letters, one by a woman, but the connection of the people mentioned in them with the strategos's family is obscure.

All these letters in Apollonios's archive show the existence of a group of women tied by strong bonds of love, friendship, loyalty, and social relationships. Separated by life circumstances and confronting worries caused by a war that raged with great ferocity, these women tried to overcome distances and reached out to loved ones through their correspondence.

P.Alex.Giss. 58

Eudaimonis to Apollonios concerning the Jewish Revolt
AD 116

LOCATION WRITTEN   Unknown
LOCATION OF ADDRESSEE   Unknown
LOCATION FOUND   Hermopolite nome

Greek

Eudaimonis to her son Apollonios, many greetings. Seeing the disturbances near us, I cannot endure and pray day and night all the gods and goddesses to watch you . . . please . . . behave yourself until the disturbances of this time are gone and you can meet us to console us. Do not delay in informing me about your well-being. (Young) Heraidous salutes you and . . .

(ADDRESS ON BACK): To Apollonios strategos of Heptakomia.

THIS LETTER IS WRITTEN in the round proficient hand of the scribe who also penned *P.Giss.* 19, sent by Aline. The characters, which are either separated or at least individually formed and linked lightly, show an elegant regularity and even some formality in occasional finials and bending of vertical strokes.

The text displays good observance of orthography, morphology, and syntax.

This letter was probably written in the first phase of the Jewish Revolt, since Eudaimonis refers to the "disturbances" as being still in progress in the Hermopolite. She manifests all her concern for the well-being of her son and advises him not to expose himself too much. Her granddaughter was still living with her.

NOTE
disturbances: The Jewish Revolt.

LOCATION OF OBJECT
Giessen, Universitätsbibliothek, Papyrussammlung, P.Giss.inv. 245.

BIBLIOGRAPHY
Hagedorn 2001: 148.

P.Brem. 61

A woman to Apollonios about a theft
First quarter of the second century AD

LOCATION WRITTEN Hermopolite nome
LOCATION OF ADDRESSEE Unknown
LOCATION FOUND Hermopolite nome

Greek

. . . to her brother Apollonios, many greetings. I salute you. From the day I departed from you and was in the Hermopolite, I have been busy with the strategos . . . the thieves wanted me to (confirm) the content of the box, swearing about its value. But I did not want to swear before (collecting) the money, knowing that without a threat from the strategos they do not . . . anything but . . . But how are you? I am distressed that you are ill again. Send me news about your well-being. Before all I regard your safety rather than all the things I seek after. I know how you value me and I often testify to all about what you have done for me. Greet Aline in a sisterly way (or: who is a sister to me) and mother Eudaimonis and your children free from harm. (second hand) I pray for your health. Pharmouthi 16.

(Postscript, first hand): You are not unaware that the fool is bothering me again and is such a fool because of his mother and because you are not here to shake out his foolishness. Take care, when I send you the children, Pausas and Kotteros, to advise them regarding that matter and to bring it to an end.

(ADDRESS ON BACK): To (Apollonios) strategos of Apollonopolite Heptakomia.

THIS PAPYRUS WAS INSCRIBED by five hands. It contains three letters sent to Apollonios, one by a woman who was a sister (or a close relative) of the strategos, the second by a close acquaintance, Chairas, and the third by his uncle Diskas. A secretary who wrote characters somewhat irregularly and mostly separated penned the first two letters. The woman added greetings to her letter in a large, oval, and formal hand reminiscent of a book hand with characters strictly separated. Chairas also added fast and fluent greetings to his letter. Diskas, however, penned his letter in its entirety in a small, fast, semicursive hand. It is possible that a fifth hand penned the address.

This letter is correct in every respect and shows a variety of clauses. The central question is colloquial. One can recover this woman's voice particularly in the postscript, where she spits out the words with many alliterations.

All three letters are concerned with an illness of Apollonios, who was in Heptakomia with his wife and mother. The most personal is the woman's letter: She probably took the initiative of writing to the strategos, while the two men may have simply taken advantage of the courier. The woman reveals that she had visited Apollonios but had discovered on her return that a theft had taken place in her house. It seems that after blurting out the whole affair, the woman felt somewhat guilty for not mentioning Apollonios's illness and tried to mend that. Her outspoken personality comes to the fore even more in the letter's postscript.

LOCATION OF OBJECT
Bremen, Staatsbibliothek, inv. 25.

BIBLIOGRAPHY
Cribiore 2001b: 235–36.

P.Brem. 63

Eudaimonis to Aline: family matters
July, AD 117

LOCATION WRITTEN   Hermopolite nome
LOCATION OF ADDRESSEE   Unknown
LOCATION FOUND   Hermopolite nome

Greek

~ ~ ~

Eudaimonis to her daughter Aline, greetings. Above all, I pray that you may give birth in good time, and that I shall receive news of a baby boy. You sailed away on the 29th and on the next day I finished drawing down (?the wool). I at last got the material from the dyer on the 10th of Epeiph. I am working with your slave girls as far as possible. I cannot find girls who can work with me, for they are all working for their own mistresses. Our workers marched through all the city eager for more money. Your sister Souerous gave birth. Teeus wrote me a letter thanking you so that I know, my lady, that my instructions will be valid, for she has left all her family to come with you. The little one sends you her greetings and is persevering with her studies. Rest assured that I shall not pay studious attention to God until I get my son back safe. Why did you send me 20 drachmae in my difficult situation? I already have the vision of being naked when winter starts. Farewell. Epeiph 22.

(Postscript): The wife of Eudemos has stuck by me and I am grateful to her for that.

(ADDRESS ON BACK): To her daughter Aline.

∾ ∾ ∾

THE POSTSCRIPT IN THE left margin was added after Eudaimonis wrote the date and salutations in her own smaller hand. The body of the letter is penned with medium-sized characters that are usually formed individually. Even though this hand looks proficient, it does not display the degree of penmanship that some other letters dictated by Eudaimonis show.

While this letter is written in rather correct Greek, one can perceive the effort of Eudaimonis in dictating it. The sentences are short and choppy and usually each one introduces a new thought. The syntax is rather simple.

Aline left Hermopolis a few weeks earlier to give birth to her new baby in Heptakomia, and Eudaimonis hopes she is going to have a baby boy. Eudaimonis shows the difficulties she had in finding slave girls to work with her in the family weaving enterprise and alludes to the labor unrest of their workers who requested higher wages. She reports that one of her daughters had a baby, and that the servant Teeus who had followed Aline had written to her and was grateful for the treatment she received. Apparently Heraidous was behaving well and was a diligent student. Eudaimonis reveals, however, that she herself was not going to behave well toward the gods until she had recovered her son.

NOTES

baby boy: Aline probably had at least two daughters. Cf. *P.Brem.* 65 where Wilcken supposed that "the other Eudaimonis" was a daughter of Aline. We do not know whether she had any sons.

studious attention to God: This letter reveals the peculiar character of the piety of Eudaimonis.

LOCATION OF OBJECT
Bremen, Staatsbibliothek, inv. 10.

BIBLIOGRAPHY
BL 5.19 (line 27); *BL* 8.68 and *BL* 9.39 (line 16). Cribiore 2001b: 231–33.

Fig. 6.   *P.Brem.* 63. Eudaimonis to Aline: family matters. (Bremen, Staatsbibliothek, inv. 10. Photograph courtesy of the Staats- und Universitätsbibliothek, Bremen.)

P.Brem. 64

Soeris to Aline: do not whine
First quarter of the second century AD

LOCATION WRITTEN   Probably Hermopolite nome
LOCATION OF ADDRESSEE   Unknown
LOCATION FOUND   Hermopolite nome

Greek

∾ ∾ ∾

Soeris to her daughter Aline, greetings. Before all I pray that you are well along with your brother Apollonios and your children free from the evil eye. Why are you writing to me "I am sick"? I was told that you are not ill: you make me so awfully worried. But see, I have been sick in my eyes for four months! You write to me about the half jars for my children, free from the evil eye . . . kept away from me . . . I shall give . . . bring to you. Why . . .

(ADDRESS ON FRONT): To her daughter Aline.

∾ ∾ ∾

WRITTEN ON THE BACK of a sheet of papyrus. The handwriting is proficient but not completely even.

The letter is written in colloquial Greek, with rather short and simple clauses, a few mistakes due to phonetic spelling, and one more serious error of conjugation.

This letter is like a telephone conversation, with questions and a spontaneous outpouring of feelings. Soeris may have belonged to Apollonios's family, as the use of the same name for a sister of Apollonios seems to indicate (cf. *P.Giss.* 21) or, less likely, may have been the mother of Aline. She certainly was on intimate terms with her since she accuses her of exaggerating the condition of her health. She felt entitled to be pitied for her own health problems.

NOTE
my children: The expression is dictated by affection, because Soeris was somehow related to them.

LOCATION OF OBJECT
Bremen, Staatsbibliothek, inv. 45.

BIBLIOGRAPHY
Cribiore 2001b: 225.

P.Flor. 3.332

Eudaimonis to Apollonios: family troubles
First quarter of the second century AD

LOCATION WRITTEN Hermopolite nome
LOCATION OF ADDRESSEE Heptakomia
LOCATION FOUND Hermopolite nome

Greek

Eudaimonis to her son Apollonios, greetings. You recall that two months ago today I set out to see the undisciplined Diskas, for he would not await your arrival. But now, together with some friends from the gymnasium he is planning to attack me, since you are away, in the belief that he will be able to gain his end unjustly. I have already done what was up to me and I have neither bathed nor worshiped the gods, in my fear for what hangs over you, if indeed it is impending. Let it therefore not remain impending, lest I too encounter trouble in the law courts. Before all I pray for your health and for that of my children and of their mother. Write to me constantly about your health so that I can have consolation for my trouble. Farewell, my lord. Phaophi 3.

(Postscript): At your wedding the wife of my brother Diskas brought me 100 drachmas. Since now her son Nilos is going to get married, it is right that we make a return gift, even if little disputes are between us.

(ADDRESS ON BACK): To her son Apollonios.

THE BODY OF THIS letter was written by a capable scribe, the same who wrote *P.Giss.* 21 and *P.Brem.* 63, all letters sent by Eudaimonis. The personal greetings of Eudaimonis are also fast and fluent.

This is a well-written letter in every respect: morphology, syntax, orthography, good use of particles, and sophisticated language. There are a variety of clauses and a long postscript. Some of the terms used are interesting.

This colorful letter, in which there are no allusions to the Jewish Revolt, mainly concerns a lawsuit brought against Apollonios by his uncle Diskas. Eudaimonis fears that in the absence of her son she will be implicated too, since in her view her brother plans to attack her together with some friends. She declares that she had done her part by refusing to bathe and make obeisance to the gods. The letter ends with proper expressions for good health. But in a postscript she reminds Apollonios that in spite of their grievances they have to send a suitable gift to Diskas's son for his wedding.

friends from the gymnasium: The adjective *gymnastikos* occurs only here in papyri. It could mean either "friends from the gymnasium" or "friends fond of athletics."

my children: Eudaimonis's phrase reflects affection for her grandchildren.

LOCATION OF OBJECT
Florence, Biblioteca Medicea Laurenziana, *P.Flor.* 332.

BIBLIOGRAPHY
Whitehorne 1994; BL 7.54 (line 26); Cribiore 2001b: 233–35.

Fig. 7. *P.Flor.* 3.332. Eudaimonis to Apollonios: family troubles. (Florence, Biblioteca Medicea Laurenziana, *P.Flor.* 332. Photograph courtesy of the Ministero per i Beni e le Attività Culturali. All further reproduction by any means is prohibited.)

P.Giss. 17

Teeus to Apollonios: we wish to fly to you
Early second century AD

LOCATION WRITTEN   Hermopolite nome
LOCATION OF ADDRESSEE   Heptakomia
LOCATION FOUND   Hermopolite nome

Greek

Teeus to Apollonios her lord many greetings. First of all I salute you, master, and I pray always for your health. I was in no little distress, lord, hearing that you had been ill, but thanks be to all the gods for they keep you free from harm. I beg you, lord, if you so wish, to send for us, else we die because we do not see you every day. Would that we were able to fly and come and embrace you, for we are anxious to follow you. So change your mind for us and send for us. Farewell lord . . . and everything is (well) with us. Epeiph 24.

(ADDRESS ON THE BACK): To the strategos Apollonios.

THE GENERAL IMPRESSION THAT this hand conveys is poor. The handwriting is rigid, and the characters are mostly separated. The ink dipping appears too frequent in parts. At times, however, this writer shows some ability and forms characters fluently.

The vocabulary is considerable and unusual and conveys an impression of urgency and affection. There are no phonetic mistakes. The syntax is remarkably correct and somewhat complex and shows some degree of education.

The same woman also sent *P.Giss.* 77 to Apollonios's wife Aline and *P.Alex.Giss.* 50 to the strategos; she is mentioned in *P.Giss.* 77, a letter from the strategos's mother. She was a servant in the household and was probably an old freedwoman who was on very familiar terms with the strategos. In this letter she shows her anguish for an illness of Apollonios, about which we are not informed. The strategos was far from home, either to discharge his duties in the district of Apollonopolites Heptakomia in Upper Egypt or on campaign during the Jewish War.

NOTE

change your mind: The meaning of *diallagethi* is ambiguous. It is translated as "be friends with me" in *Sel.Pap.* 115.

LOCATION OF OBJECT
Giessen, Universitätsbibliothek, Papyrussammlung, P.Giss.inv. 35.

Cribiore 2001b: 223 and 239.

Fig. 8. *P.Giss.* 17. Teeus to Apollonios: we wish to fly to you. (Giessen, Universitäts-bibliothek, Papyrussammlung, P.Giss.inv. 35. Photograph courtesy of Justus Liebig-Universitat, Universitätsbibliothek.)

P.Giss. 19

Aline to Apollonios, concerned for his absence
August or September, AD 115

LOCATION WRITTEN   Hermopolis
LOCATION OF ADDRESSEE   Heptakomia
LOCATION FOUND   Hermopolite nome

Greek

∾ ∾ ∾

Aline to her brother Apollonios many greetings. I am very worried for you on account of the things that people reported about what is happening and because you left me so suddenly. I take no pleasure in food and drink, but always stay awake day and night with only one thought, your safety. Only my father's care revives me, and by your safety I lay without eating on New Year's Day but my father came and forced me to eat. I beg you therefore to (look after) your safety and not to face danger alone without a guard. Do the same as the strategos here who puts the burden onto the magistrates . . . the name of my brother was posted . . .

(ADDRESS ON BACK): To Apollonios her brother.

∾ ∾ ∾

WRITTEN IN AN EXPERT, round letter hand. Interlinear space is regular, and the overall impression is of evenness and fluency. Aline, who was staying at the time with her own parents, apparently used a secretary who worked in Eudaimonis's house. The influence of this writer is also notable in the language.

This letter shows a sophisticated use of syntax and language. There is a considerable range of clauses that are employed with ability and variation. Some terms used are unusual or unique in the papyri.

Aline writes to her husband Apollonios revealing her anguish because of his sudden departure—probably to go back to the Apollonopolite district—on account of the outbreak of fighting in the Jewish War. News of the atrocities committed had reached her. She was staying at the time with her parents. As a rule, the office of strategos did not involve military service, and Aline begs her husband to shift dangerous duty on to his subordinates, as the strategos of the Hermopolite district was apparently doing. In the last fragmentary part of the letter, Aline also alludes to some danger that faced her brother, whose name had been posted.

NOTES
About the date, see Schwartz 1962.

New Year's Day: The Egyptian New Year, the first of the month Thoth.

day and night: About the expression used for staying awake day and night, cf. *P.Alex.Giss.* 58.4.

LOCATION OF OBJECT
Giessen, Universitätsbibliothek, Papyrussammlung, P.Giss.inv. 33.

BIBLIOGRAPHY
C.Pap.Jud. 436; *BL* 6.42 (lines 4–5); Cribiore 2001b: 226–27.

P.Giss. 20

Aline to Apollonios about building and a healing shrine
Ca. AD 117–118

LOCATION WRITTEN   Hermopolite nome
LOCATION OF ADDRESSEE   Unknown
LOCATION FOUND   Hermopolite nome

Greek

∾ ∾ ∾

Aline to Apollonios her brother, greetings. We give thanks to all the gods because of your safety . . . [long lacuna] You wrote about your health. . . . You are building . . . builders and carpenters . . . I am working at the wool as you wrote . . . tell me by letter which color pleases you or send me a small sample of it [or a little bit of wool]. If you want your light, white garment to fall down, give heed to the purple. I was given a response by the Dioscuri of your estate, and a shrine has been built for them. Areios the maker of votive limbs provides the service for them; he was saying, "If Apollonios writes to me about it, I will serve free of charge." You really ought to write him a couple of lines, in order for him to come forward promptly in a manner worthy of you and the gods. Your children are in good health and salute you. Write to us continuously about your health. Send what you have of Diskas . . .

(ADDRESS ON BACK): To Apollonios her brother.

∾ ∾ ∾

THE WRITING IS IN fast, comparatively small cursives, with more ligatures than in standard letter hands. It shows some unevenness.

The usual good command of Greek displayed in the letters from women belonging to Apollonios's family here is not accompanied by the choice vocabulary shown, for instance, in *P.Giss.* 19. The style and language suit practical purposes of communication. The letter shows a good variety of constructions and good orthography.

This is one of the late letters of the archive. Aline writes to her husband, who was back in Heptakomia after the conclusion of the Jewish War. She was in the Hermopolite to supervise some building work. Apollonios was having a grand house built in the countryside. Aline, moreover, had built a healing shrine to the Dioscuri, presumably for the local war wounded. The Areios mentioned, who volunteered to tend the sanctuary for free, perhaps hoped to sell his votives to the visitors. Aline gently advised her husband to get in touch with this man. In the meantime she was doing wool working.

NOTES

building: About the construction of Apollonios's house, see Husson 1983.

shrine: Further evidence of Aline's religiosity.

maker of votive limbs: A *koloplastes* was a manufacturer of artificial limbs to be used as votive offerings.

Diskas: Apollonios's uncle (see *P.Flor.* 3.332 and *P.Brem.* 61).

LOCATION OF OBJECT

Giessen, Universitätsbibliothek, Papyrussammlung, P.Giss.inv. 41.

BIBLIOGRAPHY

Husson 1983: 313–19; Hagedorn 2001: 149; *BL* 11.84; Whitehorne 1994; Cribiore 2001b: 227–29.

P.Giss. 21

Eudaimonis to Apollonios concerning garments
AD 115–117

LOCATION WRITTEN   Hermopolite nome
LOCATION OF ADDRESSEE   Heptakomia
LOCATION FOUND   Hermopolite nome

Greek

∽ ∽ ∽

Eudaimonis to Apollonios her son, many greetings. I much rejoiced when I heard that you are well, together with your sister Soeris. From the day you sent me word, I looked for the Laconian garment but I could not find any except for a worn out Attalian garment. You are aware that you gave half a pound and 2 drachmas of weight for the white gown on which account you spend one pound and a stater of weight. You are to buy and send it, in order that it can be sent to you in a hurry. I beg you to remain where you are in order not to grieve me . . . Salute your sister Aline. Soeris thanks you exceedingly and wrote me a letter about it. Young Heraidous salutes you and her mother. (second hand) Farewell, my son. Choiak 24.

(ADDRESS ON BACK): To Apollonios, strategos of the Apollonopolite.

∽ ∽ ∽

THIS LETTER, WHICH IS practically complete, was written by one hand for the main body, one for the salutations, and perhaps a different one for the address. The main hand is fluent and small without real ligatures and is only lengthening some strokes. It should be the hand of a secretary who was used to writing letters. The hand of Eudaimonis that shows in the salutations is smaller, fluent, and somewhat more cursive. Eudaimonis apparently also added an above the line remark.

Well written, with minor mistakes due to lack of sensitivity to aspiration. Even though it presents a variety of clauses, the overall structure is simple enough, since this was a practical, informative letter. The vocabulary is mainly colloquial and involves some words referring to garments that are not completely clear.

Eudaimonis writes to Apollonios who was in Heptakomia with Aline and their small children. His sister Soeris had joined them there. The initial allusion to Apollonios's good health may refer to a past illness of his, which is mentioned in other letters (see *P.Giss.* 17 and *P.Alex.Giss.* 50). This letter is mainly concerned with some garments that the strategos had requested to be sent to him. Eudaimonis reveals that she had trouble finding the garments in question and also complains that Apollonios had not sent her enough material. She also discloses her preoccupation with the situation caused by the eruption of the Jewish Revolt.

NOTE

"The Laconian" must be some kind of garment.

LOCATION OF OBJECT

Giessen, Universitätsbibliothek, Papyrussammlung, P.Giss.inv. 26.

BIBLIOGRAPHY

Hagedorn 2001: 149–50; Cribiore 2001b: 231 with plate, fig. 5.

P.Giss. 22

Eudaimonis to Apollonios
AD 117

LOCATION WRITTEN   Hermopolis
LOCATION OF ADDRESSEE   Heptakomia
LOCATION FOUND   Hermopolite nome

Greek

〰 〰 〰

Eudaimonis to her most distinguished son Apollonios, many greetings. First of all I pray to embrace you with good fortune, and to greet your sweetest person, now at last receiving a recompense for my piety, you free from harm and most blessed. This is all my prayer and concern. These things also please the gods . . .

(ADDRESS ON BACK): To Apollonios from (Eudaimonis).

〰 〰 〰

THIS LETTER SHOULD BE written in the same hand as P.Giss. 23 and 24, supposedly the hand of Eudaimonis. There is some ability in forming individual letters, but the general look is clumsy. Some letters are retraced and there are a few corrections.

The letter does not contain phonetic mistakes and shows correct observance of morphology and syntax. What is preserved shows rather simple constructions except for the long phrase in the central part. The last two sentences that start with the same word (*tauta*) have some rhetorical flavor.

Even though the connection of this letter with the Jewish Revolt is not completely secure, it is conceivable that it was written at the end of it, when

Apollonios returned safely from Memphis. Eudaimonis is anticipating with joy the moment when she will be able to embrace her son. The notion that it was her piety toward the gods that preserved him in that moment of danger fits well with this woman's pragmatic religiosity, which is also revealed by other letters.

LOCATION OF OBJECT
Giessen, Universitätsbibliothek, Papyrussammlung, P.Giss.inv. 97.

BIBLIOGRAPHY
Whitehorne 1994.

P.Giss. 23

Eudaimonis to Aline
First quarter of the second century AD

LOCATION WRITTEN   Hermopolite nome
LOCATION OF ADDRESSEE   Unknown
LOCATION FOUND   Hermopolite nome

Greek

∿ ∿ ∿

Eudaimonis to her daughter Aline, many greetings. I consider the most necessary of all my prayers that for your well-being and that of your brother Apollonios and your (children) free from harm. Afterward, thanks to god . . . the gods who . . . Aphrodite Tazbes . . . priesthood . . . Souerous and Heraidous salute you. Farewell . . .

(BACK): To Aline from Eudaimonis.

∿ ∿ ∿

AFTER THE FINAL SALUTATIONS the writer added a postscript that occupies the last line and part of the left margin. The large hand, probably Eudaimonis's, appears to be the same as those of P.Giss. 22 and 24: The individual letters are generally well shaped, but the overall look is untidy and unproficient. Clumsy and extensive cancellations contribute to the generally poor appearance.

What remains of this letter generally shows correct observance of syntax and morphology. There are a few minor mistakes due to phonetic spelling.

It is difficult to date this letter, since it seems to be unconnected with the Jewish Revolt. The most tantalizing part of the epistle was probably the middle one. Remarks about god, the gods, the goddess Aphrodite Tazbes, and a word for "priesthood" have perhaps to do with a local cult and would tell a lot about Eudaimonis's piety. The letter's postscript mentions the sending of certain items, also for Heraidous.

NOTE
Aphrodite Tazbes: This divinity is mentioned also in *P.Brem.* 23. In Heptakomia there was a processional avenue named after her.

LOCATION OF OBJECT
Giessen, Universitätsbibliothek, Papyrussammlung, P.Giss.inv. 96.

BIBLIOGRAPHY
Whitehorne 1994.

P.Giss. 24

Eudaimonis to Apollonios concerning the Jewish Revolt
June, AD 116

LOCATION WRITTEN   Hermopolis
LOCATION OF ADDRESSEE   Heptakomia
LOCATION FOUND   Hermopolite nome

Greek

ᔕ ᔕ ᔕ

. . . with the will of the gods and particularly of invincible Hermes they will never defeat you. For the rest, be well together with all yours. Heraidous, your daughter who is free from harm, salutes you. Epeiph 6.

(ADDRESS ON BACK): To Apollonios.

ᔕ ᔕ ᔕ

THE INDIVIDUAL LETTERS ARE not badly formed but the general impression that this hand conveys is of an "evolving" hand. The impression of clumsiness is reinforced by the fact that the writer used a thick pen and retraced and/or corrected some letters. This may represent the personal hand of Eudaimonis (cf. *P.Giss.* 22 and 23). The address in the back, however, is written by an expert hand in tall and narrow characters.

The little that remains is written correctly.

This letter was written by Eudaimonis to her son Apollonios from the Hermopolite during the course of the Jewish War. The strategos was probably still in Heptakomia with his family and not on campaign. The reference to "invincible Hermes" may mean that the Jewish forces had not yet achieved the crushing victory shown in *P.Brem.* 1. Heraidous, who greeted her father at the end, was staying with her grandmother, while Aline and the rest of the children were in Heptakomia.

NOTE
all yours: The phrase probably refers to relatives rather than to Apollonios's men (as in C.*Pap.Jud.*).

LOCATION OF OBJECT
Giessen, Universitätsbibliothek, Papyrussammlung, P.Giss.inv. 98.

BIBLIOGRAPHY
C.*Pap.Jud.* 437 (on the date).

Fig. 9.   *P.Giss.* 24. Eudaimonis to Apollonios concerning the Jewish Revolt. (Giessen, Universitätsbibliothek, Papyrussammlung, P.Giss.inv. 98. Photograph courtesy of Justus-Liebig-Universität, Universitätsbibliothek.)

P.Giss. 68

Arsis to Apollonios concerning the death of her son and business matters

First quarter of the second century AD

LOCATION WRITTEN   Unknown
LOCATION OF ADDRESSEE   Unknown
LOCATION FOUND   Hermopolite nome

Greek

Arsis to Apollonios her son greetings. It was my desire to salute you by letter, since you know what happened to my blessed son Chairemon, that the misfortune happened suddenly and he must have a second burial. I am writing to you on necessity. I do not have anyone but you besides god and I know the affection that you always had for him. I received news that the linen cloths are cheap where you are; therefore I bought there (an amount) for 300 drachmae but it is not enough. Please write to me to whom I should give these drachmae, plus 300 more, in order that (this person) takes them to you, since Phibas, his slave (?), is not familiar with the place and cannot come by himself and I cannot . . . [long lacuna] since it is necessary to buy the linen cloths. Farewell. Pachon 17.

(ADDRESS ON BACK): To Apollonios from Arsis the mother of Chairemon.

THIS LETTER IS WRITTEN slowly with very large characters that become smaller only toward the end. Even though some strokes are quivering and some are retraced, the hand shows some ability. The writer was probably left-handed since all the characters are bent backward. Arsis herself or one of her acquaintances penned this letter.

In terms of orthography, grammar, and syntax the letter is well written and employs a variety of clauses.

This letter is divided into two distinct parts. In the first Arsis—a woman who worked in the family's weaving enterprise—communicates to Apollonios the death of her son Chairemon and the fact that it was necessary to give him a second burial. She then proceeds to tell the strategos that she bought some cloths in Upper Egypt where he is and that she intends to buy some more but does not know to whom she should give the money to get it delivered to Apollonios.

NOTE

son: This term, used for younger addressees, sometimes only indicates a long acquaintance; see Dickey 1996: 64–72.

LOCATION OF OBJECT
Giessen, Universitätsbibliothek, Papyrussammlung, P.Giss.inv. 17.

BIBLIOGRAPHY
Cribiore 2001b: 238.

P.Giss. 77

Teeus to Aline thanking her
AD 116

LOCATION WRITTEN   Unknown
LOCATION OF ADDRESSEE   Unknown
LOCATION FOUND   Hermopolite nome

Greek

ᘓ ᘓ ᘓ

Teeus to Aline her lady, greetings. Before all Heraidous salutes you, and I salute all your (relatives). When they arrived here to us . . . then I knew that you sent me the dress. I will render thanks exceedingly for you to all the gods, because you clothed me. Would that . . . I could embrace you when you have a baby boy . . . so that it seems that I am with you and if you are going to give me something, a piece of garment . . . and send me what you have. Be well, lady. Hathyr 23.

(ADDRESS ON BACK): Give it to Aline.

ᘓ ᘓ ᘓ

THE BODY OF THE letter, the salutations, and the date are all in one hand, which is small, fluent, and clear with occasional irregularities.

This letter shows in general a good command of Greek. There are a lot of complex sentences with a variety of clauses. Particles are used correctly, and orthography is good.

The servant Teeus (cf. P.Giss. 17) writes to her lady Aline to thank her warmly about the gift of a tunic. Another piece of garment is mentioned toward the end. Teeus is in Hermopolis with Heraidous, while Aline is in Heptakomia with the rest of the family. Right at the start of the letter, Teeus puts the personal salutation to her mother from Heraidous. Since in another letter, P.Giss. 78, Aline apparently complained that her daughter had not saluted her, the opening of the present letter might be a response to that.

Giessen, Universitätsbibliothek, Papyrussammlung, P.Giss.inv. 14.

BIBLIOGRAPHY
BL 9.94 (line 11).

P.Giss. 78

Aline to Tetes: my daughter did not salute me
Early second century AD

LOCATION WRITTEN   Hermopolite nome
LOCATION OF ADDRESSEE   Hermopolis
LOCATION FOUND   Hermopolite nome

Greek

∽ ∽ ∽

Aline to her mother Tetes, greetings. You informed me about the sale of the garments. Please devote your energy to the rest. I know that . . . I was torn away from you, but it was of necessity, as you know and because of . . . My little Heraidous on writing to her father does not salute me and I wonder why. (second hand) I pray for your health.

(ADDRESS ON BACK): To mother Tetes.

∽ ∽ ∽

THE BODY OF THIS note was dictated, as the greetings written in a different hand show. The main hand is in fast cursives that are somewhat irregular and spiky. Aline writes her greetings. What remains shows fine and fluent characters of a smaller size than the rest.

This short and simple note shows a correct use of language in every respect. The instructions at the beginning are given in short sentences that become more complex as the note proceeds.

Aline writes to her old servant Tetes, probably from Heptakomia where she was with her husband and children except Heraidous. Tetes was probably working in the weaving enterprise that the family owned in the Hermopolite. Aline approves the sale of some garments and exhorts her to take care of other things. She is concerned about the fact that her daughter did not send greetings to her. It seems strange that Heraidous (probably a teenager) forgot to salute her mother. Was this a sign of some tension between the two?

LOCATION OF OBJECT
Giessen, Universitätsbibliothek, Papyrussammlung, P.Giss.inv. 11.

BIBLIOGRAPHY
BL 11.84; Cribiore 2001b: 227.

P.Giss. 79

A woman to her husband on economic matters
Ca. AD 120

LOCATION WRITTEN   Unknown
LOCATION OF ADDRESSEE   Unknown
LOCATION FOUND   Hermopolite nome

Greek

ᕦ ᕦ ᕦ

(col. ii) . . . if I could take hold of the management of our property, I would not hesitate, but in any case, as I am a woman, I exercise every care. So far Epaphroditos does not neglect anything but puts forth every effort for our sake and the sake of all your affairs. (col. iii) . . . so that he understands that you take care of everything. Just now the wine is very expensive, about three staters. Thus nobody is discouraged as to sell property. But if God allows a large yield next season, soon, because of what will be the low price of the produce, the landowners will be discouraged, so that we will be able to buy at a low price, as you wish. I am persuaded about the care that you are exercising . . . (col. iv) . . . Your brother Apollonios has brought from Alexandria your hooded cloaks that were well taken care of. I think that you should be friendly to all people as you were to the people from the district, so that we depart from them on good terms with friendship and without giving offense. Farewell, brother. Pauni 3.

ᕦ ᕦ ᕦ

TWO FRAGMENTS FROM A letter written all in one hand, salutations and date included, a small, clear hand slightly bent to the right that does not present real ligatures. The writer betrays an excellent familiarity with writing.

This letter is well written, with correct observance of orthography, morphology and syntax. There are no mistakes of phonetic spelling. A variety of clauses is used.

The letter was sent by a woman to a man who was probably her husband, giving advice to the man with regard to economic matters but with some humbleness ("since I am a woman"). A certain Epaphroditos was taking care of their affairs and, in her eyes, he was doing a good job. This letter refers to the years following the conclusion of the Jewish Revolt when after a while the price of agricultural produce became more stable: Since the wine was very expensive, prices for vineland were extremely high. This woman, therefore, advises her husband to wait for the next season before he buys land. Finally the woman offers her advice with regard to her husband's behavior, saying he should be nice to everybody. The identification of the writer with Aline is attractive, since the general tone and the advice given would fit well with the latter's personality, but much is unsure. The writer could well be a sister of Apollonios or another relative.

NOTES

I am a woman: Whitehorne accepts the identification of the writer as Aline.

next season: For agricultural difficulties in this period, see Schwartz 1962: 356–58.

LOCATION OF OBJECT

Giessen, Universitätsbibliothek, Papyrussammlung, P.Giss.inv. 74.

BIBLIOGRAPHY

Whitehorne 1994: 25; Cribiore 2001b: 236–37.

8. LETTERS FROM THE EASTERN DESERT ❧

The desert between the Nile Valley and the Red Sea is a large area mainly made up of stony terrain, much of it mountainous. In these mountains and the gully systems (wadis) running through them lay important resources, including gold and desirable building stone. On the Red Sea coast lay ports, particularly Berenike and Myos Hormos, from which and to which most of Rome's trade with India and East Africa sailed, and which also had close connections to the west and south coasts of Arabia. Both of these economic spheres were important to the imperial government, and particularly in the first two centuries of the Roman empire tremendous resources were put to work in the service of maintaining a network of roads, wells, and small forts through the desert. Many of the personnel in the desert stations were military, but there were civilians in various roles as well.

Thousands of letters written on potsherds (ostraca) have been discovered in several locations in the Eastern Desert, most of them found in the last couple of decades in excavations, but some found longer ago. The bulk of them are from men to men, for this was a very masculine environment; but the men in the desert received letters from women as well. Most of these letters are short and to the point, dealing with needs for supplies, but a few are more informative. Part of those printed here come from Wadi Fawakhir, a gold-mining area off the Wadi Hammamat, through which runs the road from Coptos in the Nile Valley to Myos Hormos on the coast. They were found in the course of mining explorations sixty years ago. The ostraca from the Florida collection, purchased on the antiquities market, come from one of the desert stations, as do the recently excavated ostraca from Maximianon.

BIFAO 94 (1994) 32–33, no. II (O.Max.inv. 279 + 467)

Sarapias to Ammonios
Second century AD

LOCATION WRITTEN   Eastern Desert (Philotera?)
LOCATION OF ADDRESSEE   Maximianon
LOCATION FOUND   Maximianon (al-Zarqa)

Greek

Sarapias to her father and lord Ammonios, many greetings. Before
everything I pray that you are well, and I make obeisance on your behalf
before the lady Philotera. I received from Nestereus 6 loaves of bread. If I
come to Myos Hormos, as I announced to you, I shall send you a jar of fish
sauce with the first donkeys. For I care as much about you as if you were my
own father. And if I find the linen for you I shall buy it. If you have a
drinking cup, send it to me. My brother salutes you.

(Postscripts): Don't forget to send me the scalpel. Receive 1 jar [and] write
to me about yourself. Greet Proklos.

THIS LETTER IS WRITTEN with considerable fluency at a rather fast pace and in
a different hand than the letter Sarapias sent at a later time. The writer was
very experienced and was probably a professional more at home with writing
documents.

The Greek is straightforward and colloquial, but somewhat abrupt. There
is one significant spelling lapse not explicable as a phonetic phenomenon,
and one correction.

This and the following letter were sent by Sarapias to a man she addresses
as father but who was, as this letter shows, not her actual father. He is presumably among the guards in the fort at Maximianon, one of the stations on
the road between Coptos and Myos Hormos. Her first letter indicates that she
is about to go to Myos Hormos, the largest port in this area; the second shows
that she has left Myos Hormos. The *proskynema* to Philotera suggests that in
both cases she may have been at the port bearing that name, the exact location
of which is unknown.

LOCATION OF OBJECT
Quft, Egypt, Supreme Council of Antiquities magazine.

BIFAO 94 (1994) 33–34, no. III (O.Max.inv. 267)

Sarapias to Ammonios
Second century AD

LOCATION WRITTEN   Eastern Desert (Philotera)
LOCATION OF ADDRESSEE   Maximianon
LOCATION FOUND   Maximianon (al-Zarqa)

Greek

ᴖ ᴖ ᴖ

Sarapias to Ammonios her father and lord, many greetings. I constantly pray that you are well, and I make obeisance on your behalf before Philotera. I left Myos Hormos quickly after giving birth. I have taken nothing from Myos Hormos. Recently I sent from Myos Hormos 4 drachmas in order that you bring me slices. Send me 1 small drinking cup . . . and send your daughter a small pillow. I have received 2 small loaves of bread. I pray for your health.

ᴖ ᴖ ᴖ

THE HAND IS NOT the same as in the other letter sent by Sarapias. This hand is stiff, upright, with letters all separated, but the overall look is regular enough. The writer was checking his or her speed, as the faster lines written in the margin show.

As in the first letter of this pair, the Greek is rather abrupt; here, in addition, a different scribe has written in an exceptionally phonetic orthography that inserts extra nasals at the end of several words, interchanges aspirated and unaspirated consonants, and seems to have a narrow repertory of vowel sounds capable of being represented in numerous ways.

See the preceding letter for the context. The most salient element of this letter is its mention of the writer's recently having given birth, but she says nothing about the child.

NOTE
slices: Usually referring to fish, which is unlikely to be traveling from Maximianon to the coast; perhaps meat?

LOCATION OF OBJECT
Quft, Egypt, Supreme Council of Antiquities magazine.

O. *Florida* 14

Maximo(u?)s to Tinarsieges, about childbirth
Second century AD

LOCATION WRITTEN   Unknown
LOCATION OF ADDRESSEE   Unknown
LOCATION FOUND   Eastern Desert

Greek

Maximos to Tinarsieges (her?) sister, many greetings and good health always. If you are coming to your days of giving birth, write to me so that I may come and perform your delivery, since I do not know your month. I wrote to you in advance for this reason, so that you might also act in advance and write to me so that I would come in the provisions boat, so that I too may remain with you and perform your delivery. For I advise you that I am intending to give birth at your house. If you don't send word to me, you do me no favor. I was going to send you jars for your delivery. I didn't send them for this reason, so that I might bring them when I come, along with two matia of lupines. The man who is bringing you the ostracon is returning to me. Do not neglect to write by way of him about the house-by-house census. They called your name and they did not call it again (?). I wrote to your brother upriver so that they might also submit your name inside in the [?]. I greet you and Kalleas and all those in the house by name. Send me leaves as for a small basket and I will make it for you . . . I pray for your health.

THE LETTER IS WRITTEN in an experienced letter hand and well disposed over the surface of a large ostracon. Letters are largely detached except in the farewell.

With the exception of some relatively minor phonetic spellings, there are few problems in the Greek. There are one or two places where the reading or meaning have still eluded all attempts to make them out. The overall style is unadorned but accurate.

The major subject of the letter is the writer's intention to come perform the delivery of Tinarsieges's baby and, it seems, be delivered of her own while there. The letter then turns to a problem in the census, the details of which are not entirely clear. The passages about delivering and being delivered point clearly to a woman as author, as does a feminine participle. But the sender's name is Maximos (i.e., Latin Maximus), clearly masculine. Various suggestions have been offered, including that "Maximus wrote the letter on behalf of his illiterate wife and that he inadvertently put his own name at the start instead of his wife's" (Thomas) and that Maximos is an error for Maximous, a feminine name not elsewhere attested (Van Rengen 1979).

NOTES

your month: Which month in her pregnancy, that is.

jars: Of wine.

house-by-house census: Conducted every fourteen years, the census required declarations from all heads of household. It seems to have been carried out in villages by visiting teams. From this text it appears that people were called up publicly by having their names announced.

LOCATION OF OBJECT

Tallahassee, Florida, Special Collections, Strozier Library, Florida State University, inv. 6. Plate in ed.prin., pl. 8.

BIBLIOGRAPHY

Thomas 1978: 144 (on line 9 and the problem of authorship); Van Rengen 1979: 332–33 (on the problem of authorship); Parsons 1985: 211 (several textual suggestions; *BL* 8.518–19).

Mother to son: you never write
First century AD

LOCATION WRITTEN   Berenike (?)
LOCATION OF ADDRESSEE   Unknown
LOCATION FOUND   Berenike (Red Sea coast)

Greek

∾ ∾ ∾

[Hikane] to Isidoros [her son, greetings. First of all] I thought it necessary, since the packet boat was putting out to sea, to write . . . me. I am in Berenike. I wrote you a letter [?but did not receive a] letter. Was it for this that I carried you for ten months and nursed you for three years, so that you would be incapable of remembering me by letter? And similarly you dismissed me through the Oasites . . . I didn't (do this to) you, but I left your brothers in Arabia . . . Egypt I might see your face and . . . my breath. Only I ask and beg and adjure you by the one whom you . . . and by the memory of the one who begot you, to sail away if you are well. I . . . Arabia and your sister who has arrived . . your aunt. I have saved myself . . . Your elder sister has departed and the younger one is present . . . I ask and beg you . . . For your brother . . . with the first winds, but he found some . . . and came to me in Berenike. Epaphras greets you warmly . . . and those who love us. [Year . . , month] 24.

(BACK): Deliver. Hikane to Isidoros her son, harborman.

∾ ∾ ∾

THIS IS A LARGE letter, written on a substantial sheet of papyrus. The overall impression is of a fairly good letter hand, with modest ligaturing and some fluctuation in letter size and shape. The lines, unsurprisingly for a letter this wide, waver somewhat. This is a good example of a private hand, Hikane's perhaps, or someone else who helped her.

Although there are slips of spelling and occasional mistakes in forms throughout the letter, the Greek is direct and vigorous, with good use of dependent clauses and occasional attempts at elegance. The fondness for putting possessive pronouns before the article-noun phrase is noteworthy.

Hikane writes from Berenike, the southernmost important Egyptian port on the Red Sea, which served as a major transit point for goods coming from and going to India. Her letter to her son states in extraordinarily pointed terms her vexation at his failure to write to her or come see her. Damage to the papyrus obscures the continuous flow of thought, but it appears that other members of the family are also in the region of the Red Sea and Arabia;

whether this term refers to the Arabian Peninsula or (as sometimes) to the land between the Nile and the Red Sea is not clear.

NOTE
Oasites: It is not clear if this refers to the inhabitants of one of the well-known Egyptian oases of the Western Desert or to those of some other place.

LOCATION OF OBJECT
Quft, Egypt, Supreme Council of Antiquities magazine.

9. THE DOSSIER OF EIRENE ❧

These three letters were written by the same person on the same day, and clearly all were dispatched together by way of a messenger named Kalokairos, perhaps a slave. Two of them are to the same couple, Taonnophris and Philon, one a letter of condolence, the other on business matters. The business letter gives orders for payment of a substantial sum of money to Parammon, and the third letter tells Parammon that he is to receive it along with some other goods.

P.Oxy. 1.115

Eirene to Taonnophris and Philon about a death
Second century AD

LOCATION WRITTEN Unknown
LOCATION OF ADDRESSEE Unknown
LOCATION FOUND Oxyrhynchos

Greek

Eirene to Taonnophris and Philon, be of good courage. I was as grieved and I wept over the fortunate one as I wept over Didymas, and I did everything that was fitting, and (so did) all my people, Epaphroditos and Thermouthion and Philion and Apollonios and Plantas. But all the same, one can do nothing in the face of such things. Therefore comfort one another. Farewell. Hathyr 30.

(ADDRESS): To Taonnophris and Philon.

THIS LETTER FORMS A group with P.Oxy. 1.116 and SB 20.15180, all from Eirene and all written in the same hand. The hand is practiced, well formed, and neat. Two of the three letters have significant corrections of errors; the present letter has some words written above the line.

The opening part of the letter reads somewhat jerkily and awkwardly, particularly before the "and" inserted between "I was grieved" and "I wept" was added; articulation consists of a series of "ands" until near the end. The platitudes of the last two sentences, however, are properly expressed, and the overall impression is one of a fairly well educated person writing under emotional stress. This characterization is confirmed by the other two letters from Eirene.

NOTES

be of good courage: Gk. *eupsuchein*, used in place of the usual *chairein* here. It is commonly used in epitaphs in bidding farewell to the deceased.

fortunate one: "Well fated," a euphemism meaning "deceased." The name of the deceased is not mentioned.

Hathyr 30: The same date as P.Oxy. 1.116, also written to the same two people, but on business matters, and as SB 20.15180.

LOCATION OF OBJECT

New Haven, Beinecke Rare Book and Manuscript Library, Yale University, Inv. 32.

BIBLIOGRAPHY

Chrest.Wilck. 479; Deissman 1923: 143 (with plate); White 1986: 115–16, no. 116; Rowlandson 1998: 341–42, no. 268; Chapa 1998: no. 2, with plate; Trapp 2003: no. 46. Plate also in J. Finegan, *Light from the Ancient Past* (Princeton 1959), pl. 137 (after p. 318); *BL* 2.2.93. Letters of condolence are discussed in detail in J. Chapa 1998; there is also a short treatment in Worp 1995: 149–54.

P.Oxy. 1.116

Eirene to Taonnophris and Philon
Second century AD

LOCATION WRITTEN   Unknown
LOCATION OF ADDRESSEE   Unknown
LOCATION FOUND   Oxyrhynchos

Greek

∾ ∾ ∾

Eirene to Taonnophris and Philon. I have given to Kalokairos for the account of Dionysios 340 drachmas, as he wrote to me to give him whatever he wanted. Please therefore give them to Parammon our workman, and if he has further need, furnish him whatever he wishes, and let him go quickly. I sent you by Kalokairos in my clothes case a measure of Ombitic dates and twenty-five pomegranates, under seal. Please send me two drachmas' worth of white loaves in it, as I have urgent need of them. I sent you through the same Kalokairos a box of very . . . grapes and a basket of fine dates, under seal. Farewell. Hathyr 30.

(ADDRESS): To Taonnophris and Philon.

∾ ∾ ∾

THE LETTER IS WRITTEN in the same handwriting as *P.Oxy.* 1.115 and *SB* 20.15180. There are no rewritings or corrections. The writer abbreviates several words in the second half of the letter and uses a sign for drachmas, confirming the impression of experience made by this group generally.

The language is straightforward and businesslike, using a genitive absolute properly in the first sentence and the connective *oun* in the second. The forms are throughout correct and the spelling good.

Eirene wrote two letters to the same couple on the same day. One was a letter of condolence (*P.Oxy.* 1.115), the other this letter about money and goods. The first matter concerns the sizable sum of 340 drachmas owed to "our workman" Parammon, who in turn receives SB 20.15180 informing him that Eirene has given instructions for him to be paid from cash given to Kalokairos, who is the bearer of the letters along with the money. Kalokairos is also bringing dates, pomegranates, and grapes, and Eirene asks for white loaves to be sent back to her via Kalokairos in the case in which she has sent the dates and pomegranates.

LOCATION OF OBJECT
Bristol, Percival Library, Clifton College.

BIBLIOGRAPHY
BL 1.316 (on line 19).

SB 20.15180
Eirene to Parammon
Second century AD

LOCATION WRITTEN   Unknown
LOCATION OF ADDRESSEE   Unknown
LOCATION FOUND   Oxyrhynchos

Greek

Eirene to Parammon, greeting. I wrote to Philon to give you 340 drachmas which I gave to Kalokairos, and whatever else you wish. So please receive from him also my clothes case, which I gave to Kalokairos, in which I wrote for two drachmas' worth of white loaves to be sent to me. And send the white loaves quickly to Philon, because I need them. Farewell. Hathyr 30.

WRITTEN IN THE SAME hand as P.Oxy. 1.115 and 116. The writer has made one interlinear correction and one more substantial alteration. The greeting and date are again in the same hand as the body of the letter.

The language is businesslike and unremarkable, but the correct usage of relative clauses and verbs confirms the impression given by Eirene's other letters of a solid command of business Greek.

For the contents, see P.Oxy. 1.116, the letter to Taonnophris and Philon on the same subject. Here, Eirene refers to that text as a letter to Philon only, no doubt because he was the member of the couple who would carry out her requests.

LOCATION OF OBJECT

Formerly Melbourne, Department of Classics, University of Melbourne, Papyrus 2; now lost.

BIBLIOGRAPHY

P.Oxy. 1.187 (description); Winkworth 1992: 85–87, with Tafel Ia; *BL* 11.235 (line 7).

10. THE DOSSIER OF TASOUCHARION ༄

This small archive includes five letters sent by Tasoucharion to her brother Neilos—*BGU* 601, 602, 714, 801, and *P.Giss.* 97. It is likely that in this case the term "brother" described an actual family relationship. Neilos was married to Taonnophris, who appears to be dead in *BGU* 801, one of the last letters of the archive. Tasoucharion herself was married, even though we do not know who her husband was. He might be one of the men whose names occur in the salutations in the letters. She had three children: Ptolemaios, Tiberinus, and Sarapion. Two letters, *BGU* 601 and 714, were sent from Alexandria, and in the letter of condolence, *BGU* 801, Tasoucharion says that she would like to go up-country to visit her brother in that trying circumstance, but she could not. Since all the letters were found in the Arsinoite, that is probably where Neilos resided. It is possible that Tasoucharion actually lived in Alexandria—or in its surroundings.

Of course this archive is also concerned with sending and receiving of supplies. But there is more than that. Tasoucharion appears to be a competent businesswoman. In *BGU* 602 she asks her brother to check on a certain olive grove of which she wanted to buy a share. *BGU* 601 and *P.Giss.* 97 are concerned with a house and securities for it. One may surmise that Tasoucharion was older than Neilos—or in any case more capable, and perhaps, more wealthy—since she appears to take many initiatives and to use him to check on business she would like to embark on.

Another characteristic of this dossier is that no two letters appear to be written by the same hand. This might be due to the fact that this woman moved around and thus had to use different scribes. It is also possible that she had several secretaries at her service, like the women of the Apollonios archive. She may have written in her hand one letter, *P.Giss.* 97, which is written in a somewhat shaky handwriting, particularly in the second part.

BGU 2.601

Tasoucharion to Neilos: business matters
Second century AD

LOCATION WRITTEN   Alexandria
LOCATION OF ADDRESSEE   Unknown
LOCATION FOUND   Arsinoite nome

Greek

Tasoucharion to Neilos her brother, many greetings. Before all I pray for
your health, and I make your obeisance before the lord Sarapis. Be informed
that I gave Ptolemaios deposits as security for the house in the Temple of
Demeter. So please write me about the house, what you did, and the deposit
of Sarapion . . . I gave to him. And write me about the registration. If you
are making my registration, please . . . write me as soon as possible, so that I
may get ready and sail upriver to you. And concerning the grain, do not sell
it. I greet my sister Taonnophris and the daughter of Bellaios. Didymos and
Heliodoros greet you. Ptolemaios and Tiberinus and Sarapion greet you. I
greet Sarapion son of Imouthes and his children and Somas and his
children and his wife, and Heron and Tabous and Ischyriaina. Satornilos
greets you. I pray for your health. Tasoucharion greets Pe- and her children.
Helene greets my mother warmly and her brothers. Chairemon greets you.

(ADDRESS): Deliver to Neilos from Tasoucharion his sister.

ALL THE LETTERS IN this dossier are in different hands. This letter is written
in a professional hand.

The letter is composed in a typical paratactic and colloquial style, with a
fair number of phonetic spellings. The writer loses her way in the syntax of
the greetings at the end, particularly writing nominatives where accusatives
are needed.

Apart from the extremely lengthy greetings, Tasoucharion is concerned
with several items of business, some of which she has carried out in Alexandria, others of which are in Neilos's hand in the Arsinoite. Lack of context
as usual wraps the transactions in a fog.

LOCATION OF OBJECT
Berlin, Staatliche Museen, Papyrussammlung, P. 6698.

BIBLIOGRAPHY
BL 1.55 and 2.2.19 (on line 16); 4.5 and 8.30 (on line 12); WB 2.78 s.v.
mesiton (on line 7); see Chapa 1998: 66–67.

BGU 2.602

Tasoucharion to Neilos: business matters
Second century AD

LOCATION WRITTEN   Unknown
LOCATION OF ADDRESSEE   Unknown
LOCATION FOUND   Arsinoite nome

Greek

Tasoucharion to Neilos her brother, many greetings. Before all I pray for your health. I want you to know that Souchas came to me saying, "Buy my share of the olive grove." Neilos gave me 4 mnas. Inquire about it and find out if it is "clean," and send me the copy of the same so that I may know what to do. I greet Serapion and his children and Heron and his children and Ammonous and her children and your wife and your child.

(ADDRESS): Deliver to Neilos from Tasoucharion the sister of Tasalos.

THE HAND IS NOT entirely proficient and is quite slow. The individual letters are well formed but are completely separated from each other and often lack in rhythm.

Given the different hands, it is not surprising that even Tasoucharion's name is written differently from the way it is in *BGU* 2.601. The language is otherwise similar with phonetic spellings throughout and the occasional loss of a declensional ending.

The Sarapis *proskynema* formula, present in *BGU* 2.601, is absent here, suggesting that the present letter may have been written somewhere other than Alexandria. But the omission may be without significance. Tasoucharion is again involved in various business transactions, evidently of some importance. Taonnophris is still alive in this letter (cf. section introduction).

LOCATION OF OBJECT
Berlin, Staatliche Museen, Papyrussammlung, P. 6699.

BIBLIOGRAPHY
Chapa 1998: 66.

BGU 3.714

Tasoucharion to Neilos
Second century AD

LOCATION WRITTEN   Alexandria
LOCATION OF ADDRESSEE   Unknown
LOCATION FOUND   Arsinoite nome

Greek

Tasoucharion to Neilos her brother, many greetings. Before everything I pray that you are well, and I make obeisance on your behalf before the lord Sarapis. I sent you by way of Kapanos . . . , and let me know if you received it or if you didn't receive it. The children greet you all individually, Ptolemaios, Tiberinus, Sarapion. Greet Taonnophris and your children, whom the evil eye does not touch, and Tabous with her husband and our father Heron and Peteeous and the children of Somas and Nestoriaina. Papa Satorneilos greets you, and let us know about your well-being. I pray for your health.

(ADDRESS): . . . from Tasoucharion.

"UNPRACTICED, THICK CURSIVE" WAS the editor's description of the hand.

The only noteworthy linguistic feature of this letter is the form of "greet" followed by a series of names and relationships in a mixture of cases, making it unclear if these people are to be greeted or are greeting Neilos. Most likely they are to be greeted.

The letter's provenance in Alexandria is indicated by the mention of obeisance before Sarapis. The business of the letter consists only of a damaged query about whether Neilos has received something that Tasoucharion sent him. Otherwise there is an extended series of greetings.

LOCATION OF OBJECT
Formerly Berlin, Staatliche Museen, Papyrussammlung, P. 8657; burned in Münster.

BIBLIOGRAPHY
BL 1.61 (on lines 5 and 7).

BGU 3.801

Tasoucharion to Neilos: condolences
Second century AD

LOCATION WRITTEN Unknown
LOCATION OF ADDRESSEE Unknown
LOCATION FOUND Arsinoite nome

Greek

∾ ∾ ∾

To Neilos her brother, from Tasoucharion. I was very sorry to hear about
Taonnophris. Bear it nobly, brother, for the sake of your children. And
except that my children are away, Ptolemais and Sarapion, I myself would
go upcountry. Receive from the man who is delivering this letter to you
dried fruits, 160 in number, and ten pinecones for the sacrifice for her.

(ADDRESS): Deliver to Neilos son (?) of Tasalos from Tasoucharion his sister.

∾ ∾ ∾

A LARGELY DETACHED HAND, but with ligatures. Some letters are remade, but
the individual letters are mostly not badly made. All the letters sent by Tasoucharion are in different hands.

The language of the letter is generally correct, but there are problems with
cases, most notably in the first word of the letter, where Neilos is in the
nominative rather than dative, and where the letter carrier is in the dative
rather than (like the definite article before the participle) in the genitive.

Taonnophris is mentioned (alive) in the three other Berlin texts, but evidently her death has been reported since they were written. Tasoucharion no
longer includes the formula of obeisance before Sarapis, but her statement
that she would go upcountry except for the absence of her children probably
indicates that she is still in Alexandria.

NOTE
pinecones: Burnt offerings in sacrifices. Cf. *P.Bour.* 23.

LOCATION OF OBJECT
Berlin, Staatliche Museen, Papyrussammlung, P. 8636.

BIBLIOGRAPHY
BL 1.68 (on lines 5 and 12); Chapa 1998: no. 3, with plate and corrections
in lines 4, 5, and 19.

P.Giss. 97

Tasoucharion to Neilos concerning securities
Second century AD

LOCATION WRITTEN   Unknown
LOCATION OF ADDRESSEE   Unknown
LOCATION FOUND   Arsinoite nome

Greek

Tasoucharion to Neilos her brother, many greetings. Before everything, I pray that you are well with all your people and I am also (well) with my children. The securities that I sent you through Louginianos please register them only in the name of Sarapion and inform me about it. Please send through the soldier Heraklinianos 2 jars of olives. Salute all the people of our family by name. I pray that you are well.

(ADDRESS ON BACK): Give it to Neilos from his sister Tasoucharion.

THE HAND OF THIS letter is different from those of the other letters of this archive. In the first part it is rather competent: a common letter hand even though not particularly attractive and regular. In the second part, the hand seems to degenerate: it is much more developed horizontally and flattened. The editor distinguished two different hands but it is probably only one, the hand of a person (perhaps Tasoucharion herself) for whom writing was not a daily concern.

The spelling is mostly phonetic, and there are orthographic mistakes. There is also an error of agreement.

This letter is probably connected with BGU 601 and the securities for a certain house. The Sarapion who made a deposit according to that letter is probably the same appearing in this. Tasoucharion also asks her brother to send her some olives.

NOTE
Sarapion: Tasoucharion's son of this name, referred to in BGU 601, 714 and 801, is probably not the person alluded to here.

LOCATION OF OBJECT
Giessen, Universitätsbibliothek, Papyrussammlung, P.Giss.inv. 38.

Fig. 10. *P.Giss.* 97. Tasoucharion to Neilos concerning securities. (Giessen, Universitätsbibliothek, Papyrussammlung, P.Giss.inv. 38. Photograph courtesy of Justus-Liebig-Universität, Universitätsbibliothek.)

11. THE DOSSIER OF DIOGENIS ᢒ

These two letters sent by Diogenis are part of a large archive of the papers concerning Kronion and members of his family (collected in *P.Kronion*). One of the letters sent by Diogenis (*P.Mil.Vogl.* 76) is addressed to Kronion son of Kronion, who was *phrontistes* (manager) of the property she had in the countryside of Tebtunis. It is possible that the addressee of *P.Mil.Vogl.* 77 was the same Kronion.

Diogenis appears as the daughter of Lysimachos in *P.Kron.* 16, a contract written in AD 138, in which her age is given as forty-five. From her two letters it seems that her relatives and "little" Isidora, who might have been her daughter, lived in the country, while she was somewhere else, perhaps in Arsinoe. This woman, coming from a property-owning family, shows a strong personality when she gives Kronion a series of peremptory commands.

P.Mil.Vogl. 2.76

Diogenis to Kronion concerning her arrival
Second century AD

LOCATION WRITTEN   Unknown
LOCATION OF ADDRESSEE   Tebtunis (?)
LOCATION FOUND   Tebtunis

Greek

∾ ∾ ∾

Diogenis to her dearest Kronion, greeting. Be expecting me when I come up to you at Tali. But I pray that once I am there I will not find you at fault in anything: I hope that none of these things will happen. My brother Lourios will communicate to you everything concerning me.

(second hand) I hope that you are well. Salute all my relatives and Isidora, and let her go to a woman teacher.

(first hand) If Didymas opposes the payment to Lourios, produce my box, and send his documents under seal. Epeiph 20. But if you also have need of him for the *artabia* or something else, go to him and he will do everything.

(ADDRESS ON BACK): . . . from Diogenis.

∾ ∾ ∾

LONG AND NARROW PAPYRUS apparently written by two hands. Presumably Diogenis herself added the salutations. Then she dictated a postscript to the scribe, who added the final date. After that Diogenis dictated a second postscript. The main hand is attractive, fluent, and proficient. The second hand should be that of Diogenis, a fast hand inclined to the right. It is interesting that the formulaic part of this postscript is faster than the end, which introduces a new thought.

The style is emphatic and brusque with twice the direct object beginning a clause and the verb postponed until the end. The text mainly consists of commands in the imperative. Apparently this scribe takes down faithfully Diogenis's words without many embellishments and a minimum of connectives. The text is fairly correct.

Diogenis, who plans to visit her *phrontistes* Kronion, sends him a series of peremptory commands in advance. She seems a bit in a hurry as she dictates this letter. The fact that she asks Kronion to salute her own relatives possibly means that he was on close terms with her and them.

NOTES
Talei: A village in the Arsinoite not far from Tebtunis.

Isidora: Perhaps the young girl mentioned in *P.Mil.Vogl.* 77.

artabia: A land tax of one artaba per aroura.

BIBLIOGRAPHY
D. Foraboschi, *P.Kron.* 16, p. 36 (important corrections to the text; reported in *BL* 6.85); *BL* 7.118 (another textual correction). We also owe some readings to G. M. Parássoglou. For the business activities of Diogenis, cf. *P.Mil.Vogl.* 6.297 and 298.

Fig. 11. *P.Mil.Vogl.* 2.76. Diogenis to Kronion concerning her arrival. (Milan, Istituto di Papirologia, Università degli Studi, inv. 41. Photograph courtesy of Istituto di Papirologia, Università degli Studi di Milano.)

P.Mil.Vogl. 2.77

Diogenis to Kronion on business matters
Second century AD

LOCATION WRITTEN Unknown
LOCATION OF ADDRESSEE Unknown
LOCATION FOUND Tebtunis

Greek

. . . him at this time . . . and sell the wheat necessary and collect the bronze at your house while I come, because I need it. Go to Myrtale and ask her for the money. If she does not want to give it to you, lock her up. See that I do not come and find the wall built up. And make the exedra ready and let the dining room be paved, according to the arrangement Aphys wants; shake out the woollen cloths and the clothes and watch (plu.) the children and things at home. Watch "little" Isidora. I pray that you are well. Pachon 25.

(Postscript): . . . but the keys . . . I arrive; it will be your concern that I arrive.

(ADDRESS ON BACK): . . . .Dioge(nis).

THE MAIN HAND IS experienced. It is clear, with only a few ligatures. Salutation and date are by a different hand, probably that of Diogenis. The letters are smaller and faster. The postscript may have been written by the main hand: a thicker pen was responsible for some unevenness.

The letter is a series of injunctions in the imperative with a few dependent clauses. The orthography and syntax of the letter are correct. There is only one word spelled phonetically and a superfluous iota adscript.

The name of the addressee is not preserved. It could possibly be the same Kronion to whom P.Mil.Vogl. 76 is addressed. It appears that Diogenis is about to arrive, as in that letter. The commands she gives mix property management, a certain affair having to do with copper, the possibility of locking up a woman if she refuses to give it, and household chores.

NOTE
shake out: For a similar injunction to shake out clothes, directed to a man, cf. the letter of Zoe to Apollinarios, BGU 3.827.

LOCATION OF OBJECT
Milan, Istituto di Papirologia, Università degli Studi, inv. 42.

BIBLIOGRAPHY
See BL 7.118 (correction to the text).

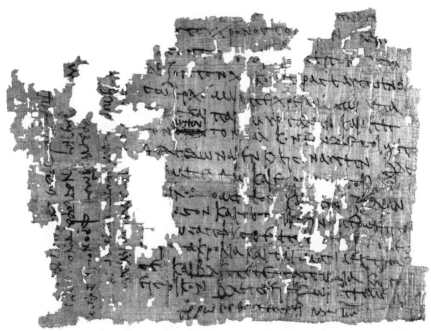

Fig. 12. *P.Mil.Vogl.* 2.77. Diogenis to Kronion on business matters. (Milan, Istituto di Papirologia, Università degli Studi, inv. 42. Photograph courtesy of the Istituto di Papirologia, Università degli Studi di Milano.)

12. THE DOSSIER OF THERMOUTHAS ❧

This dossier includes two letters written by Thermouthas to her "brother" Apolinarios. As usual, their family relationship is not entirely clear. Apolinarios was away and Thermouthas reported to him on a number of matters. She planned to go visit him with a whole group of women. Both letters, and particularly BGU 1.261, give a vivid picture of a world of women, who gave birth, traveled, took loans, and, like unrepentant Taesis, refused to pay money that was due.

Thermouthas perhaps wrote BGU 1.261 in her own hand but had recourse to a scribe for the second letter.

BGU 1.261

Thermouthas (and Valeria) to Apolinarios about travel and money
Second–third century AD

LOCATION WRITTEN   Unknown
LOCATION OF ADDRESSEE   Unknown
LOCATION FOUND   Arsinoite nome

Greek

Thermouthas to Apolinarios her brother, many greetings. I want you to know, I and Valeria, if Herois gives birth, we are praying to come to you; for it is necessary. We want to bring Demetrous to sail down with her mother. You write to me, "Take care of Zoidous." We do not see that she has done anything; she has nothing in view except the interest on the money which you gave her. You gave ten staters to the tax collectors of Kerkesoucha; and as to what you said to me about Taesis, I received nothing from her. Didymarion will testify to you that Taesis said, "I'm not giving anything to Thermouthas," because Zoidous said "Don't give her (anything)." You and your sister know that you wrote to Heras . . . so that he might serve us. We thank him. Longinia greets you; she (Valeria?) greets you and Zoidas her sister. We greet Serenos. Herois and all those in the household greet you individually. Farewell.

(ADDRESS): Deliver to Apolinarios from Valeria and Thermouthas.

THIS IS THE HAND of an unpracticed writer, Thermouthas's or someone else who helped her. It shows bad alignment, difficulty in controlling ink flow, and low speed. The final farewell is in larger and a bit smoother characters.

The writer's use of Greek is colloquial and wastes no words. Spelling is frequently phonetic and occasionally unclear. Thematic forms of *didomi* appear.

Apart from greetings, the letter has two subjects. One is the hope of Thermouthas and Valeria to sail downriver to Apolinarios once Herois (who is in their household) has given birth, along with another couple of women. Presumably they want to be present for the birth. There is no sign that any men are expected to be part of the women's party. The rest of the letter is devoted to some financial matters, involving a loan and a tax payment.

NOTE

Thermouthas: The letter is written in her name, but she quickly associates Valeria with herself and the address even puts Valeria's name first among the senders. The unspecified subject of "greets" in line 29 may be Valeria.

LOCATION OF OBJECT

Berlin, Staatliche Museen, Papyrussammlung, P. 1837.

BIBLIOGRAPHY

BL 1.34 (on lines 1, 9, 11, 14, 21, and 23); rejecting 5.10 (on line 9).

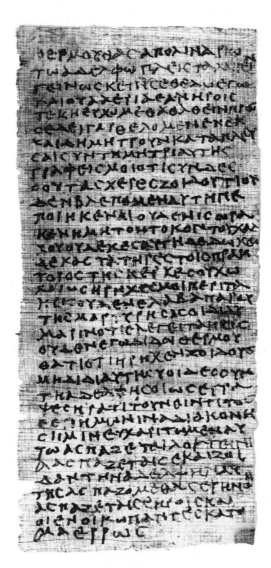

Fig. 13. *BGU* 1.261. Thermouthas (and Valeria) to Apolinarios about travel and money. (Berlin, Staatliche Museen, Papyrussammlung, P. 1837. Photograph courtesy of the Staatliche Museen zu Berlin, Preussischer Kulturbesitz; Ägyptisches Museum und Papyrussammlung. Photo M. Büsing.)

BGU 3.822

Thermouthas to Apolinarios
Second–third century AD

LOCATION WRITTEN   Unknown
LOCATION OF ADDRESSEE   Unknown
LOCATION FOUND   Arsinoite nome

Greek

Thermoutas [*sic*] to Apolinarios her brother, greetings. I want you to know, don't be concerned about the taxes in grain. I found a farmer to take them; but who is supplying the seed? And concerning the reckoning for your property, your sister received six artabas besides seed. Write to Koupaneous about the house, for Taesis is saying, "I'm not paying the rent." For she owes me money for the rent, and she is reproaching your sister about the wall (?), because you are not collecting the rent from the woman who is living in your house. So that we also may find an appropriate occasion to speak to her, write a letter for Koupaneous to Taesis, so that he may find some appropriate opportunity to speak to her. Koupaneous greets you warmly; Valeria greets Zois. Greet Serenos. Herois greets you, and Demetrous and all those who love you greet you. I pray for your health.

(Back): And if you think it proper, send me blank papyrus, so that we may be able to write a letter. Hermias is bringing you the . . . about Kastor, about the . . .

(ADDRESS): Deliver to Apolinarios from Thermouthas his sister.

THE HAND IS CLEAR, legible, and graceful, with some letters separated and others that are lightly connected. The fluency, rhythm, and layout betray an expert writer. The address is in larger characters, occasionally provided with finials.

There are many phonetic spellings in this letter. More interesting are an interrogative for relative, an active form of a deponent verb, and a subjunctive where an infinitive would have been expected.

This letter covers a variety of business matters. In Apolinarios's absence, Thermouthas has taken care of the grain taxes through a tenant. The major issue about which she is concerned, however, is rent on their house, where a disagreement has arisen. Taesis's refusal to pay also appears in *BGU* 1.261.

LOCATION OF OBJECT

Berlin, Staatliche Museen, Papyrussammlung, P. 7146.

BIBLIOGRAPHY

BL 1.69 (about the hand and date, and on lines 14, 20, and 27); 3.14 (on lines 20ff.). Unpublished corrections by G.M. Parássoglou also included.

13. DIDYME AND THE SISTERS ✑

These two letters have given rise to considerable speculation about the milieu in which they were produced. Particularly important has been the question whether "sisters" and "brothers" in these texts are to be taken as normal kinship terms (even if not meant literally in the biological sense) or as references to common membership in Christian communities, particularly of a monastic sort. That they come from a Christian milieu is clear enough, and the plural forms in the opening are not paralleled elsewhere in family letters. See Emmet 1984 and Elm 1994: 236–44 for discussion, the latter coming down in favor of a monastic source: "While caution is advisable, the evidence favours a community of women and men who are not relatives and are united by other than business interests alone: at the very least by their shared Christianity, but perhaps by ascetic principles as well. . . . For the present this somewhat vague conclusion has to suffice, but the two papyri have presented us with a potential model of ascetic life for women, aspects of which might reappear in literary sources."

P.Oxy. 14.1774

Didyme and the sisters to Atienatia
Early fourth century AD

LOCATION WRITTEN Unknown
LOCATION OF ADDRESSEE Unknown
LOCATION FOUND Oxyrhynchos

Greek

∼ ∼ ∼

To my lady sister Atienatia, Didyme and the sisters (send) greetings in the
Lord. First of all it is necessary to greet you, praying that you are well. Write
to us, my lady, concerning your health and whatever orders you need, with
full liberty. Let us know if you received your orders. There is a balance with
us from the money of your orders, I believe, of 1,300 denarii. Canopic cakes
received for you from them will be dispatched. Greet my blessed lady sister
Asous and her mother and . . .

(ADDRESS): To my lady sister Atienatia, Didyme with the sisters.

∼ ∼ ∼

THIS LETTER IS COMPLETE except at the bottom. The hand is slow, with mostly
detached letters but a few ligatures. The individual letters are well formed and
not without style.

The language of the letter is straightforward and simple. Phonetic spellings
are numerous but unremarkable. The use of "in the Lord" with *k(uri)o* abbreviated in the manner of Christian texts shows that the author is a Christian.

This letter is one of two from Didyme and the sisters, the other being SB
8.9746, which is written to another woman (Sophias). The mention of "the
sisters" in both texts has led to considerable debate about the possibility that
Didyme was the head of a group of female Christian ascetics (see Elm 1994:
236–37, 241–44, with bibliography; Wipsyzcka 2002a). In the present text,
the only persons mentioned are female, but this is not the case in SB 9746.
These women have been described as engaged in business, but the activities
at stake—getting and sending produce, foods, and clothing—do not differ
materially from those of ordinary family letters.

NOTE
denarii: The usage of this Roman currency term is a sign of the fourth-century
date; the sum is equal to 5,200 drachmas.

LOCATION OF OBJECT
Berkeley, Bade Museum, Pacific School of Religion, inv. P. 4.

BIBLIOGRAPHY
Ghedini 1923: no. 17; Naldini 1998, no. 37.

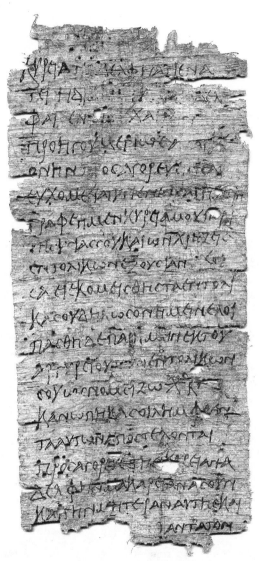

Fig. 14. *P.Oxy.* 14.1774. Didyme and the sisters to Atienatia. (Berkeley, Bade Museum, Pacific School of Religion, inv. P. 4. Photograph courtesy of the Bade Museum, Pacific School of Religion.)

SB 8.9746 = SB 3.7243

Didyme and the sisters to Sophias
Fourth century AD

LOCATION WRITTEN Unknown
LOCATION OF ADDRESSEE Unknown
LOCATION FOUND Unknown

Greek

∾ ∾ ∾

[To] my beloved [lady] sister, [Didyme and] the sisters, greetings in the Lord.
First of all we think it necessary to salute you. We received from brother
Piperas (or the brother of Piperas) the provisions for the voyage . . . her
until she comes home to us. But they are being made. We also received
from other people for her 7 double knidia and a coarse sack of sour grapes.
If we find (someone) we will also send you through this person both the
sack and the knidia we have found. We have not yet received the rest. And
be eager (to tell us) what you want so that we may send it through
acquaintances. I wish you to know about the cloth that you sent to Loukilos
that I sent you 2 pairs of sandals of the same value, which were bought
directly from the weavers for 4 talents (?) but that you did not mention to
me in writing, and through the sailor Sipharos son of Plou. . . (?) for the
bride of Pansophios (? or daughter-in-law of Pansophion) a large ostrich egg
and a small basket containing Syrian palm dates, but you did not write
about them. Salute the most beloved Didyme and the dearest Favorinus.
The implements of the most beloved Didyme were found in the sack of the
wool of Severus. The lady and the other lady Valeriane salute you and those
of the circle of Philosophos, Loukila and Pansophion. Salute the excellent
Bikeutia (and ask whether) she received from Aionios the head cover and
the 2 canopic cakes. And salute everyone, Italia, Theodora. Farewell in the
Lord, may the Lord preserve you for us.

(ADDRESS ON BACK): To the lady sister Sophias, Didyme and the sisters.

∾ ∾ ∾

THE HAND IS VERY similar to that of P.Oxy. 14.1774, written by the same
person. This letter is written throughout in one hand with fluency and regularity. The characters are relatively small, but legibility is excellent because of
the absence of ligatures: some characters merely touch. The address is written
in much larger letters with some attempts at style.

Besides some mistakes due to phonetic spelling and a few other orthographic errors, the text is rather correct. The sentences are short and simple,
without connective particles, but there are a few relative clauses.

The sender is the same Didyme who wrote *P.Oxy.* 14.1774. The addressee, however, is different, and none of the people mentioned is common to both letters. The letter mostly concerns the sending and receiving of supplies of various kinds (note the large ostrich egg) and the provisions for the trip of some woman. It is clear that letters went back and forth from sender and addressee.

NOTES

lady sister: The editor restored the name of Sophias in the lacuna in line 1, but restoring [*kuria m]ou* provides a more normal formula.

2 sandals: This presumably refers as usual to 2 pairs of sandals. The price points to a fourth-century date.

LOCATION OF OBJECT

Berlin, Staatliche Museen, Papyrussammlung, P. 13897.

BIBLIOGRAPHY

Text, translation, and commentary in Naldini 1998, no. 36. See most recently Gonis 1997a: 143–44, for important corrections (see *BL* 11.209–10). Discussion in Elm 1994: 236–37, 241–44 and Wipszycka 2002a.

Aegyptus 66 (1986) 190–91 (P.Alex.inv. 675)

Two women write to a clergyman
Eighth century AD

LOCATION WRITTEN Unknown
LOCATION OF ADDRESSEE Unknown
LOCATION FOUND Unknown

Coptic

❧ ❧ ❧

I, Tmmatoi the humblest, your mother, and Tenbora, write to their lord
father: Before the matter, we greet you with all my heart and all my soul,
and we embrace the dust of your feet; and Theodore and Ama Heu embrace
you warmly. I heard that you were ill, and my heart was distressed. Look
now, send your news to me, or else I am greatly afflicted. May the Lord bless
you. You are in need because of your illness. . . . because it is God who sent
you to them as a helper and as rescuer. Now, your servant came to us
yesterday, and he informed us that the matter concerning which we
beseeched you, about Konstantinos, he informed us that you were so kind as
to embrace him. May God grant him the means to serve you and find your
blessing. We beseech . . . your mercy upon him, and inform us and all the
brothers. <All the brothers> embrace you warmly and . . . because they
heard that you were ill. And our sister Eudokia greets you. May the Lord
. . . you and establish you upon your throne in peace; for all of us are
awaiting you as you received . . . all of them to give them food in its season,
and with him destroying all your enemies under your feet. Farewell in the
Lord, my beloved father and son. The Holy Trinity.

(ADDRESS): Give to my beloved father and son the Papas from his humblest
mother.

❧ ❧ ❧

THE WRITER WAS ABLE to produce a rather extensive text with little discomfort,
but the overall appearance of the script leaves much to be desired. Alignment
is faulty, some letters are retraced and corrected, and the pace is rather slow.

Apart from some phonetic variation, the letter is fluently written. There is one apparent omission by haplography. A couple of biblical paraphrases help lend an air of learning to the composition.

Most of the letter is devoted to expression of concern about a reported illness of the recipient, who is addressed as papas and may well be a bishop. The authors—mostly writing in the plural, but sometimes the singular—ask for news. There are also references to other matters previously treated in correspondence and thus not explained here; it looks as if Konstantinos had been placed in some sort of position with the addressee through the women's intervention.

NOTES

food in its season: An allusion to Psalm 144.15.

destroying all your enemies under your feet: Cf. Psalm 109.1 and 1 Corinthians 15.5.

LOCATION OF OBJECT

Alexandria, Graeco-Roman Museum, inv. 675.

BIBLIOGRAPHY

Bagnall, Cribiore, and Renner, forthcoming (new edition).

O.Brit.Mus.Copt. add. 23

Maria the nun to Kyriakos the anchorite
Sixth–eighth century AD

LOCATION WRITTEN Unknown
LOCATION OF ADDRESSEE Unknown
LOCATION FOUND Unknown

Coptic

Give it to my holy father and the true worshiper of God, Apa Kyriakos the anchorite, from Maria the nun, the sinner. Before the word of my insignificance, I embrace the footstool of the feet of your holy paternity. Be so kind as to remember me in your prayers, that God give me the way to walk on the rock to him . . . time . . . very much in my sins, and send your blessing to me that I may place it in my home and it may be for me a beautiful fragrance of my soul and I may see it in my house and it may urge me toward the good. Be so kind as to pray God for this little orphan, for his father is dead and has left him to me, for he . . . spirit of God . . . greatly.

OSTRACON; THIS IS A fast, small hand, capable of producing an extensive text. It is not the same hand that wrote another ostracon by the same nun Maria.

The letter is written in a straightforward style, with standard spelling.

Maria, who is also known from *O.Brit.Mus.Copt.* 53,6, asks Apa Kyriakos for his blessing and his prayers on behalf of an orphan left in her care. The reference to her house and to her care of the boy suggest that she lives in her own residence rather than as part of a cenobitic community.

LOCATION OF OBJECT
London, British Museum, Department of Egyptian Antiquities, ostracon 21297.

O.CrumST 233

Sarah to Ezekiel announcing a death
Sixth–eighth century AD

LOCATION WRITTEN Unknown
LOCATION OF ADDRESSEE Unknown
LOCATION FOUND Unknown

Coptic

This humblest Sarah writes to her lord father Ezekiel. Now, I inform you
that Paulos died. Although you were protecting him and my children, he
still died. Look, your charity is poured out upon them until now. I inform
you concerning this man that he seized me for a debt. He said, "What did
you pay again . . . ?" Now, be so kind . . . my priests . . . go to the . . .

OSTRACON; NO DESCRIPTION OF the hand.

There are many supralinear corrections to the text, and the spelling is very
phonetic. The style is simple and paratactic.

Sarah informs Ezekiel of the death of Paul. The point of the clause following is not entirely clear; is Sarah reproaching Ezekiel (if you had protected
him, he wouldn't have died), consoling him (despite your protection, he died),
or even flattering him (Paulos died [but] if you had protected him together
with my brothers, he would not have died—presumably Sarah's brothers are
indeed being protected by Ezekiel)? The discussion then shifts to a debt, before
the ostracon loses its lower right corner and the text becomes discontinuous.

LOCATION OF OBJECT
Former collection of Colin Campbell; present whereabouts unknown.

O.CrumVC 70

Rebecca to Apa Elias about an offering
Sixth–eighth century AD

LOCATION WRITTEN   Unknown
LOCATION OF ADDRESSEE   Unknown
LOCATION FOUND   Unknown

Coptic

∽ ∽ ∽

Rebecca, daughter of Papas, writes to my beloved holy father Apa Elias the priest. Be so kind, seeing that at the time when I came to the community, we entrusted certain goods to Maria, your sister, and Pkounthos went and took them, and I said to him, "Give me something, that I may give it for the offering of my father." And he said to me, "There is a censer there, that I did not take; go and take it." Be so kind, therefore, as to say to your sister to give it to me, and I will sell it and bring an offering for my parents. Farewell in the lord. Forgive me for not having found papyrus.

∽ ∽ ∽

OSTRACON. NO DESCRIPTION OF the hand.

Rebecca, a nun, writes to a priest about her wish for some funds for an offering on behalf of the salvation of her parents. She had evidently turned her property over to Maria, the "sister" of the priest, at the time of her entry into monastic life, and wants to retrieve one item from those goods in order to sell it to raise cash.

LOCATION OF OBJECT
Oxford, Bodleian Library, Coptic ostracon, inv. 503; now in Ashmolean Museum.

O.CrumVC 92

Tshemshai to a holy man
Sixth–eighth century AD

LOCATION WRITTEN   Unknown
LOCATION OF ADDRESSEE   Unknown
LOCATION FOUND   Unknown

Coptic

∾ ∾ ∾

I, Tshemshai, the mother of Lazarus the carpenter, greet your holy
fatherliness. Be so kind as to cause your life-giving word to reach me. For
the mother of the little girl has carried off all that she had and has not
given her anything. Moreover they are detaining me, that I should swear on
her behalf. Be so kind as to send David the *lashane*, that he may take the
girl's belongings; for she is an orphan. He will not turn you down. Do not
forget Lazarus, for he is your son. For it is you who has pity on the orphans.

∾ ∾ ∾

OSTRACON; NO DESCRIPTION OF hand.

The writer asks an unnamed man, probably a prominent monk, to intervene with the local headman on her behalf in a dispute over the carrying off
of some property. The case is referred to in a fashion suggesting that the holy
man already knew the parties and something of the situation.

NOTE
lashane: Village headman.

LOCATION OF OBJECT
Oxford, Bodleian Library, Coptic ostracon inv. 468; now in Ashmolean Museum.

P.Herm. 17

Leuchis asks Apa John to get the Goths out of her house
Ca. AD 380

LOCATION WRITTEN Unknown
LOCATION OF ADDRESSEE Lykopolis
LOCATION FOUND Probably Lykopolis

Greek

To my lord the pious Apa John, Leuchis daughter of Malamos. Your goodness embraces all those without resources; and let your mercy extend to me too, lord. After God, I await your help, that you ask the tribune of the Goths to remove them from my house, since I am a widow woman. My lord, do it for God's sake.

THE WRITING IS DESCRIBED by the editor as "a large, sloping hand."

The letter is simple and short, but it shows signs of rhetorical formulae and literary pretensions. Coexisting with these are many vowel interchanges and some strikingly mistaken case forms (accusative for nominative, for example), which suggest that the person who wrote this had a rather uneven education.

Apa John, the recipient of this letter, is probably to be identified as the famous anchoritic monk of that name known from Palladius's *Lausiac History*. Several other letters, in Greek and in Coptic, belong to the same dossier. His prestige allowed him to intervene with civil and military officials, and Leuchis asks him to get a military tribune of the Goths to remove "them" from her house. The Greek form is feminine, but no group of women has been mentioned earlier in the letter, and it is likely that "them" in fact refers to Gothic soldiers who had been billeted in her house. The housing of soldiers in the houses of ordinary civilians was an old and much-resented practice. Leuchis justifies her request on the grounds that she is a widow.

LOCATION OF OBJECT
Manchester, John Rylands University Library, *P.Herm.* 17.

BIBLIOGRAPHY
French translation in Rémondon 1972: 266; discussed in Zuckerman 1995: 188–89, which redates it to the fourth century.

P.Lond. 6.1926

Valeria to the monk Papnouthis
Ca. AD 340–350

LOCATION WRITTEN   Unknown
LOCATION OF ADDRESSEE   Herakleopolite nome (?)
LOCATION FOUND   Herakleopolite nome (?)

Greek

To Apa Papnouthis the most honored and Christ-bearing and adorned with
every virtue, (from) Valeria, greetings in Christ. I ask and beg you, most
honored father, to ask for me a kindness from Christ and that I may obtain
healing. I believe that in this way I may obtain healing through your
prayers, for revelations of ascetics and worshipers are manifested. For I am
afflicted by a great disease of terrible shortage of breath. I have believed and
believe that if you pray on my behalf I will receive healing. I beg of God, I
beg also of you, remember me in your holy prayer. Even if in body I have
not come to your feet, in the spirit I have come to your feet. I greet my
daughters, and remember them in your holy prayer, Bassiane and Theoklia.
My husband greets you greatly, and pray for him. My whole house also
greets you. I pray for your health, most honored father.

(ADDRESS): To the most honored father Apa Papnouthis from his daughter
Valeria.

THIS HAND SHOWS ALL the features of a good letter hand and even exhibits a
certain grace. In spite of the fact that the letters are all separated, the writer
did not proceed too slowly.

The editor described the orthography and grammar of this letter as the
poorest of the dossier of letters addressed to Papnouthis. Certainly the grammar is colloquial and the orthography rich in vowel interchanges. But in these
respects it is similar to many private letters, and by the standards of these
letters it is hardly among the most uneducated.

The letter is a good specimen of a letter addressed by a layperson to a well-
known ascetic, asking for prayer for healing of a medical condition. Other
letters of this sort can be found in this dossier and in the Nepheros archive.

NOTES
Papnouthis: Probably a holy man at a monastery located on the edge of the
Herakleopolite and Kynopolite nomes.

his daughter: Meant spiritually.

London, British Library, Papyrus inv. 2494.

BIBLIOGRAPHY
Tibiletti 1979: no. 28 (text, Italian translation); Rowlandson 1998: no. 67
(English translation). Cf. BL 9.149 (on the translation of lines 19–20; not
adopted here). In line 6 we translate G. M. Parássoglou's *benefikion*.

P.Nag Hamm. 72

Proteria asks two monks for chaff
Mid–fourth century AD

LOCATION WRITTEN Unknown
LOCATION OF ADDRESSEE Unknown
LOCATION FOUND Probably lesser Diospolite nome

Greek

∿ ∿ ∿

To Sansnos and Psatos, monks, (from) Proteria, greetings. If it is possible
where you are to seek out a little chaff for the maintenance of my donkeys,
(please do so), because they are short of it and I do not find it here to
purchase. If you find it, send to me about the price, how much it is per
wagonload of chaff, and so that the boat may come . . . (so that I may
express) to you the utmost gratitude. (breaks off)

(ADDRESS): Proteria to Sansnos and Psatos.

∿ ∿ ∿

THIS LETTER IS WRITTEN in a flowing, ligatured hand characteristic of experienced writers of the period. There are several minor corrections and two
instances of final nu represented by a line over the preceding vowel.

The language of the letter is straightforward and unadorned. Spelling is
somewhat but not notably phonetic.

Proteria is concerned entirely about getting chaff for her donkeys, and she
seeks the help of two monks in the matter. These monks lived in the heartland
of Pachomian monasticism, and the letters probably date from the 340s or
shortly before, but it is not certain that the present text in fact comes from a
Pachomian monastery.

Cairo, Coptic Museum, Nag Hammadi Codex 7.12c. Plate in *The Facsimile Edition of the Nag Hammadi Codices: Cartonnage* (Leiden 1979).

P.Neph. 18

Taouak to Eudaimon and Apia
Mid–fourth century AD

LOCATION WRITTEN   Unknown
LOCATION OF ADDRESSEE   Unknown
LOCATION FOUND   Probably Herakleopolite nome (monastery of Hathor?)

Greek

༄ ༄ ༄

To my lord brother Eudaimon and my beloved sister Apia your wife, Taouak, greetings in the Lord. Before all else I pray in my prayers that you receive my letter (?) healthy and in good spirits in the Lord. I am writing this for the second time to you about the one aroura. For as you see me in such a state, and this . . . because you have right now 6 artabas from my supply, even though you know the price of the wheat, (and) that I am a woman, I cannot buy (it). Nor on the other hand did you write, "We don't want the aroura." . . . take it myself or give it to Erisia (?), and what I gave through you, you ought to send me by yourself, the six artabas, or whatever . . . If you rob me, let me know and you will see before God. For we are God's treasure. I greet all yours by name, and Poueris greets all of you. Farewell.

(ADDRESS): To my lord brother Eudaimon . . .

༄ ༄ ༄

A TYPICAL FOURTH-CENTURY LETTER hand, largely ligatured but not especially fast. Although not elegant, the hand is competent and experienced. The writer uses a Christian style of abbreviation of sacred names in one or two places.

Along with normal phonetic spellings, the writer struggles occasionally with correct expression. More seriously still, a number of constructions are awkward, incomplete, or ungrammatical.

Despite the usual framework of warm opening and closing greetings, the body of this letter deals in acrimonious terms with a business matter, involving an aroura of land and six artabas of wheat. Clearly she expected Eudaimon and Apia to have delivered to her the wheat, which she says they owe her. Taouak's statement that she is a woman and cannot buy (presumably wheat) is remarkable; the context is not clear enough for us to know exactly what she means. That there was no legal or social prohibition on her doing so, we can see from many other texts. It is possible that she is a female monastic and in that state is not allowed to engage in worldly business transactions, but this is only speculation.

NOTE

God's treasure: It is not clear to whom the plural "we" refers, nor exactly what the claim to be God's treasure (or treasury) means. It suggests, however, that Taouak was part of a religious group with claims of sanctity that she expected Eudaimon and Apia to treat seriously.

LOCATION OF OBJECT

Trier, Universitätsbibliothek, Universität Trier, inv. S. 73–5; plate in edition, Tafel 14,2.

SB 18.13612

A mother to Apa John
Fourth century AD

LOCATION WRITTEN Unknown
LOCATION OF ADDRESSEE Lykopolis
LOCATION FOUND Unknown

Greek

To my lord father benefactor Apa John, the mother of Philadelphos the monk. After providence you pity and save all those who take refuge in you. Have pity on me too for the sake of my son the monk; for Theognostos the *exactor* both myself the widow and the orphans . . .

(ADDRESS OR DOCKET ON THE BACK): Request of the mother (of Philadelphos).

THE HAND IS LARGE, clear, and inclined to the right. Even though there is some variation in letter size, it is rather competent and not too slow.

The text is correct in every respect and shows a good command of Greek. It presents a most unusual feature in a non-literary text: some punctuation marks. Together with the indications given by the hand, these facts point to the work of an accomplished writer.

This is a petition couched in the form of a letter that a widow addresses to Apa John, a monk who appears in other papyri. It seems to refer to some prevarication committed by a tax-collecting official (*exactor*), but the details are lost. This woman asks the favor in the name of her son, who was a monk.

NOTE
Apa John: The famous anchorite whose archive includes *P.Herm.* 7–10.

LOCATION OF OBJECT
London, British Library, Papyrus 1014.

BIBLIOGRAPHY
Described in *P.Lond.* 3, p. lii, no. 1014. See *BL* 10.221 on the connection to Apa John. About *apotaktikoi*, the most detailed study is Wipszycka 1975: 632–34. There is some uncertainty about the precise meaning of the term *apotaktikos*. In *P.Oxy.* 46.3312, the view is taken that they were coenobitic monks, but in *P.Oxy.* 3203 the opposite view is maintained. In *P.Herm.Rees* 7–10, Apa John is described as an *apotaktikos* and an anchorite at the same time. See the bibliography in Bagnall 2001 [2002].

SB 20.15192

To some monks
Fifth or sixth century AD

LOCATION WRITTEN   Unknown
LOCATION OF ADDRESSEE   Unknown
LOCATION FOUND   Unknown

Greek

To the most pious and holy monks, Kyra, greetings in the Lord. I am writing to beseech and remind you—for it becomes your piousness to do yourselves what pleases God—as you are supplicated and sworn by the mysteries of the Christ that are celebrated in these holy days. Do not be neglectful of myself, but unremittingly look upon and pray for myself so that we will give thanks to the Lord to the fullest. Farewell, most pious ones.

THE COMPETENCE OF THE writer of this letter shows in the ability to maintain a steady flow of ink and in the evenness and rhythm of the whole. Legibility is very good because of the large letter size and because most characters are either separated or lightly linked.

The competence in the Greek also betrays the professional. Besides a few common mistakes due to phonetic spelling, this letter is written correctly.

Kyra addresses a supplication to some monks during what appears to be a Christian festival, perhaps Easter.

NOTE

monks: A community of monks seems to be addressed but no further details are provided.

LOCATION OF OBJECT

Heidelberg, Institut für Papyrologie, inv. G 3850. Plate IV in ZPE 94 (1992).

15. THE ARCHIVE OF PAPNOUTHIS
AND DOROTHEOS ∾

The three letters printed here are part of an archive, most of which was published as *P.Oxy.* 48.3384–3429, with a few other pieces published elsewhere. These two brothers resided in Oxyrhynchos but traveled extensively in the countryside as part of their work collecting taxes and managing estates for wealthy Oxyrhynchite landowners. Their period of activity extended from the early 340s until at least the 370s, but documents from the archive are spread very unevenly through this period.

The archive shows graphically how private landowners, in seeking to discharge their responsibilities as short-term civic officials with tax-collection duties, hired business agents to take on their obligations. The practice not only saved a great deal of work; it seems also to have helped limit their liability for failure to collect the full amount, because the agents are seen in many cases advancing the amount of taxes due, then collecting it from villagers. No doubt the agents in ordinary circumstances made a good profit for assuming this risk and for mediating between the gold currency demanded by the government and the bronze coins paid by the farmers.

The persons in the archive are all, as far as we find any information, Christians. The brothers' mother Maria bears a specifically Christian name.

P.Oxy. 48.3403

Maria to her son Papnouthis about money
Mid–fourth century AD

LOCATION WRITTEN   Unknown
LOCATION OF ADDRESSEE   Unknown
LOCATION FOUND   Oxyrhynchos

Greek

～ ～ ～

To my lord son Papnouthis, his mother Maria, many greetings. You have
again been persisting in your neglect and did not send me word about the
matters about which I instructed you. Please therefore send me the money.
Your wife also says herself that you are to send her money for the wages of
the wool workers, so do not be neglectful, quickly send them. Hurry to
write us about the work. I pray for your health for many years.

(ADDRESS): Unread traces.

～ ～ ～

THE WRITER USES A fluent cursive hand, but the editor rightly complains that
it is "crabbed and difficult to decipher." The greetings at the end are in the
same hand as the body of the letter. Overall the hand is (despite crabbedness)
a scribal hand of considerable rapidity.

As a composition the letter is neither colloquial nor literary. Spelling errors
are minor orthographic deviations. Sentences are mostly a bit abrupt, but there
are dependent clauses throughout and even a case of repeated definite article
in "your neglect." Overall the impression is of a pretty competent business
writer.

The contents are almost entirely complaints from Maria that Papnouthis
has not sent the money he was supposed to send her; for that matter, he was
supposed to send money to his wife, too, to cover the wages of wool workers
who presumably were employed by the family. (Maria is also writing on behalf
of Papnouthis's wife.) The absence of the usual wishes for good health is
striking; so too is the perennial shortage of cash.

LOCATION OF OBJECT
Oxford, Papyrology Rooms, Sackler Library.

BIBLIOGRAPHY
Rowlandson 1998: 243–44, no. 180(a).

P.Oxy. 48.3406

Klematia to Papnouthis
Mid–fourth century AD

LOCATION WRITTEN   Unknown
LOCATION OF ADDRESSEE   Unknown
LOCATION FOUND   Oxyrhynchos

Greek

From Klematia, landlady, to Papnouthis, caretaker at Sadalou, greetings.
Measure out six artabas of wheat and lentils into the boat of Pagas so that
we may have them here, and help Pagas so that we may have the extra
payments of the vintage there, and try and bring wool up with the boat,
and do not be neglectful because of the baked brick. And collect from
Paumis the two jars of honey because of the festival, and the honey cakes,
and from Pagas the wool.

(ADDRESS): Unreadable traces.

EXCEPT FOR SMALL MARGINS at top and left, the entire sheet is filled with this
letter, written "with a thick pen and rather smeared," as the editor noted.
Although there is some attempt at connecting letters, it is superficial. The
hand is extremely uneven in size and shape of letters, layout and spacing. It
is an awkward specimen in practically every respect.

In just sixty words there are fifteen corrections or errors, not only phonetic
spellings. The sentences have no articulation except "and" and "so that." One
notes also "try to bring" expressed with two consecutive imperatives, a vac-
illation between singular and plural forms of the verbs, and an omitted direct
object. The overall effect is very striking—rough, oral, and strongly colloquial.

The content of the letter is a series of instructions about various matters,
including sending foodstuffs, drink, and wool from the estate's unit at Sadalou
to wherever the estate owner was, perhaps in Oxyrhynchos. Transportation is
to be by boat. Klematia's interest extends to every detail.

LOCATION OF OBJECT
Oxford, Papyrology Rooms, Sackler Library.

BIBLIOGRAPHY
Rowlandson 1998: 243–44, no. 180(b).

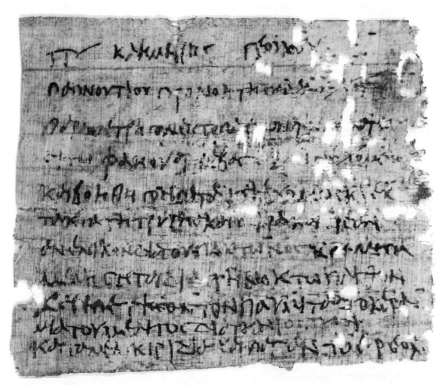

Fig. 15. *P.Oxy.* 48.3406. Klematia to Papnouthis. (Oxford, Papyrology Rooms, Sackler Library. Photograph courtesy of the Egypt Exploration Society.)

P.Oxy. 48.3407

The landlady (Klematia) to Papnouthis and Hatres
Mid–fourth century AD

LOCATION WRITTEN   Unknown
LOCATION OF ADDRESSEE   Unknown
LOCATION FOUND   Oxyrhynchos

Greek

From the landlady to Papnouthis, caretaker, and Hatres, overseer, greetings. Make haste to send out the bull driver together with the bullocks and their yoke and ropes today to our farmstead Akindynou for the hauling of rock of my lord brothers Nepotianos and Diogenes. You know yourselves that they are not strangers. But by all means today, since they have agreed to take them [the rock] away on Sunday, that is, tomorrow the 11th. Therefore, brothers, do not decide to delay and let the work of the men be hindered, and you would bring me no little outrage. Concerning the wheel, you can handle the matter. Tomorrow our brother Lucius is coming to you.

(ADDRESS): Unreadable traces.

THE ENTIRE LETTER IS written in one hand, a characteristic cursive of its period, a good, standard business hand at home in a business letter.

The text is "from the landlady," i.e., the heading omits her name as if written by someone else on her behalf, just as the handwriting would suggest. The writer uses a range of connectives with some sophistication, and the occasional instances of "and" never open new instructions. This is high-quality business prose.

This letter also comes from the Archive of Papnouthis and Dorotheos. Like *P.Oxy.* 48.3806, it is a letter from the landlady, but in this case evidently composed and written by an agent who does not even mention Klematia's name. Papnouthis and Hatres are ordered to lend a team of bulls with their driver to help two men haul rocks. They are called "brothers," but so are the addressees of this note, who are employees. Nepotianos and Diogenes, however, are clearly more important to Klematia, and she is eager to oblige them.

NOTES
Akindynou: "Of Akindynos," an *epoikion* named after an individual, probably a former owner.

brothers: In both cases probably not to be taken in a familial sense but a collegial one.

Sunday: The Lord's Day (*kyriake hemera*).

LOCATION OF OBJECT
Oxford, Papyrology Rooms, Sackler Library.

16. COPTIC LETTERS FROM KELLIS ๑

The large village of Kellis was one of the most important centers of the Dakhla Oasis, called the Mothite nome in the fourth century. Excavations of its ruins (modern Ismant el-Kharab) since the mid-1980s have revealed an important temple complex, several early Christian churches, and large domestic complexes, consisting of sprawling houses that probably accommodated a number of families. Several of these houses have yielded considerable numbers of papyrus documents and letters. House 3, the source of two of the four letters published here, was particularly rich in private letters, many of which have language marking them unmistakably as the products of members of the Manichaean movement, a dualistic sect that represented itself as a truer form of Christianity than that embodied in the Catholic Church. Members of these families traveled frequently to the Nile Valley and had property interests there. The letters found at Kellis were probably for the most part written in the valley on such travels, but some may have been written more locally. It is striking that the limited body of Coptic letters published so far has yielded five from women, whereas the Greek letters from Kellis are all written by men. The Coptic letters are also remarkable as the earliest body of Coptic correspondence not coming from a monastic milieu. They show a high level of education and an easy command of Greek, in which opening and closing greetings are often written, and from which much vocabulary is borrowed. They can be dated to the third quarter of the fourth century because of the dated Greek documents found with them.

P.Kell.Copt. 11

A mother to her son
Probably before AD 355

LOCATION WRITTEN Unknown
LOCATION OF ADDRESSEE Kellis
LOCATION FOUND Kellis

Coptic

∾ ∾ ∾

To my lord son Psenamounis, your mother Tsemnouthes . . . whose image I
pray all the time to greet in my house another time. Your father greets you
warmly together with your sister Tsemnouthes and all your children, each
by name. Do not concern yourself . . . they have imposed 6 grammata upon
you, you and your brother. They have released your father because he has
become an important (or old) man. But nevertheless your father is
convinced that they have been satisfied with you . . . to send another
solidus to us . . . we did not find anyone there . . . If a man should come,
you should quickly send . . . demand for the solidus 6 myriads, a solidus, a
myriad of bronze, 1500 . . . Shai greets you. He says, "If the affair is
protracted, write to me and I shall come to you myself." We were not
ascribed to carry anything to bring to you. Farewell.

(ADDRESS ON THE BACK): To my lord son Psenamoun, Tsemnouthes your
mother.

∾ ∾ ∾

THE CHARACTERS ARE ROUND, almost all separated, and formed with care.
Finials and roundels often decorate the vertical strokes. Alignment, however,
leaves something to be desired, and the whole appears a bit too crowded.

The text of the letter is in Coptic, but the address, the first lines, and the
final "farewell" are written in Greek. The letter is correctly phrased and employs an elaborate style.

The main purpose of this letter of Tsemnouthes to her son is to communicate the imposition of some fine or tax on him and his brother. She also
mentions sums of money, but much is obscure because of the lacunose state
of the text.

NOTE
6 grammata: Probably a tax or fine.

LOCATION OF OBJECT
Dakhleh Oasis Project magazine, inv. A/2/101 + 102; plate 4 in the edition.

P.Kell.Copt. 42

A mother and a sister write to Paulos
AD 355–380

LOCATION WRITTEN   Unknown
LOCATION OF ADDRESSEE   Kellis
LOCATION FOUND   Kellis

Coptic

My beloved son, who is greatly honored by me, Paulos. I, your mother
Louiapshai and your sister Maria are writing to you in the Lord, greetings.
Before everything we greet you warmly, praying God every hour that he will
guard you for us for a long time until we greet you another time and our joy
will be complete. What therefore are these things that you are doing, since
you do not send a letter to us at all, so that we might receive . . .

THE LETTER IS WRITTEN on both sides of a wooden board that already had two
holes drilled into it and a crack. The hand is a bit coarse but experienced and
employs a thick pen.

The language is formal. According to the editor, the prayer it contains is
similar to prayers found in the Kellis Manichaean letters.

It is unclear whether the board is complete or not. The text, in any case,
consists only of greetings and of the common complaint of not receiving
correspondence.

LOCATION OF OBJECT
Dakhleh Oasis Project magazine, inv. A/5/108 + 102; plate 34 in the edition.

P.Kell.Copt. 43

Tehat to her son
Ca. AD 355

LOCATION WRITTEN   Unknown
LOCATION OF ADDRESSEE   Kellis
LOCATION FOUND   Kellis

Coptic

I, your mother Tehat, greet my son . . . Put your hands on a pack animal
and send . . . this is the time therefore, send a pot . . . to these orphans, for
you sent . . . Have pity for them and set up pots for them, for they do not
have father or mother. Until you know, the baked loaves . . . every widow
eats . . . Who is it that bears their care and their worry . . . do some other
ones for them. I sent the letter to you through Tiberius . . . he did not give
it to you. Live and be well for a long time.

(Back): I have given to brother Timotheos son of Tiberius an oil flask with
a chous of oil to bring it to you, and a letter of father Leporios that had the
inscription from my name. But when you receive them, give them back of
necessity, as father Leporios wrote to you. Chrestos, son of Sophos, to whom
you have given the small oil flask, can show you the things there . . . and
there the small oil flask that was given to him, because again I wrote to
them that it should be given. I brother Leporios greet you my brother
warmly and ask you, father . . . to write back to me about everything. I
Makarios greet my lord brother warmly.

(ADDRESS): To my lord son Psenpsais (?), your mother . . .

THE WRITER OF THE Coptic text on the front—maybe Tehat herself—had been
exposed to a good amount of writing but never achieved fluency and rhythm.
The text appears crowded, some strokes are retraced, there is excessively frequent ink dipping, and the number of ligatures is very limited. The writer of
the Greek text was more capable, wrote faster, and achieved a good fluency.

   The Coptic text is so poorly preserved that it is difficult to have a fair idea
of the competence of the writer. The Greek text observes grammar and syntax
accurately. The clauses are connected smoothly.

   The Coptic text mainly regards charitable work that Tehat would like her
son to do to help some orphans and widows. According to her, a previous
letter that she had sent him was not delivered. Tehat may have also dictated
the Greek text, which concerns an oil flask and a letter of a certain father
Leporios, who sends his greetings.

Tehat: The woman who sends this letter may be the same who was the recipient of other letters and perhaps wrote *P.Kell.Copt.* 50.

Dakhleh Oasis Project magazine, inv. P61DD; plate 35 in the edition.

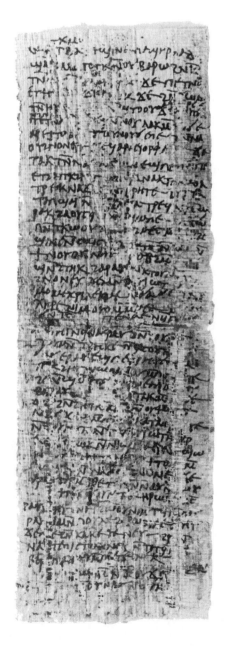

Fig. 16. *P.Kell.Copt.* 43. Tehat to her son.
(Dakhleh Oasis Project magazine, inv.
P61DD. Photograph reproduced courtesy
of Colin A. Hope on behalf of the
Dakhleh Oasis Project.)

P.Kell.Copt. 50

Tehat (?) to her son
Ca. AD 355

LOCATION WRITTEN   Unknown
LOCATION OF ADDRESSEE   Kellis
LOCATION FOUND   Kellis

Coptic

∾ ∾ ∾

. . . first of all I greet you warmly and I pray God for your health night and day, you and your brothers and your mother. Now then, beloved son, all the things I am asking you, do not neglect them until I reach you. I know in fact that you will be wearied because you are alone. Everyone is wearied until he can rest. Now if you can bear, you will rest more. Take care of the camel and do not neglect to demand your allowance. Do not let the son of Prememouris ridicule you. He says, "I gave your allowance to your father." I did not receive anything from you since I left you except a chous of barley; I took it from the girl. The small boy (?) leave him since you did not demand anything. The man from Mut, pay your account with him and with the man from Trimithis. In the meantime, do not neglect anything until I come: in fact I will not delay without you, the time to send someone. Write to me about your health and do not let anyone talk you out of giving me the piece of writing for who is he? Only take care of your house until I come. Do not let them know at all that I am away from them, for we labored I myself and Hatre since we left. His camel stayed (?) and the Libyan stayed. We were not assigned to take anything although we paid freight and what is upon them, 300 to the border. We labored until we were assigned to go to the warehouses as they were empty. Tryphane greets you, and Shoi and Loudon . . . Timotheos son of Toni. Ask from him also the 54 talents . . . written this letter from the warehouses. If he should pay you do not give him his surety, for I have another account with him. Ask from Horion the other 1200 . . . son of Apollodoros . . . ask from someone also the 5 chous of barley (?) so that if I come to Kellis I may send (a letter) and thank. Let him ask from them and also from Timotheos son of Toni . . . Live and be well in the Lord, beloved.

∾ ∾ ∾

THE HAND IS FAST, competent, but not completely regular. There are corrections and additions written over the line. The sender may have been the same woman, Tehat, who wrote *P.Kell.Copt.* 43, but the two letters were penned by different writers.

The letter appears to have been written with competence in a style that is mostly oral and not too elaborate. The language stands out among the other Coptic letters from Kellis, which mostly use southern Coptic linguistic varieties not based on Sahidic. This letter, however, is closer to Sahidic and to what may be called an "early Theban dialect" in many features.

The attribution of this letter to Tehat rests on the mention of people who appear in other letters concerning her and particularly on the lines "I and Hatre." Hatre was Tehat's husband or son, and he was running with her the family business of tailoring garments. This letter mainly concerns a series of pressing exhortations to a son to take care of various financial matters, while he waits for the writer's arrival.

NOTES

mother: The identity of the mother mentioned in line 4 is unsure. On the hypothesis that Tehat wrote this letter, she would be another relative or a respected old acquaintance.

allowance: The word used is *annona*, probably not in this context the tax known as *annona militaris*.

LOCATION OF OBJECT

Dakhleh Oasis Project magazine, inv. P85E; plate 42 in edition.

BGU 3.948

Kophaëna to Theodoulos
Fourth–fifth century AD

LOCATION WRITTEN Unknown
LOCATION OF ADDRESSEE Unknown
LOCATION FOUND Herakleopolis

Greek

∾ ∾ ∾

To my son Theodoulos from your mother Kophaëna, and Zenon, greetings.
Before everything I pray to almighty God that you are well with respect to
your health and safety. I want you to know what the steward told you, that
"Your mother, your mother Kophaëna, is ill," look, for thirteen months and
you have not even tried to write me a letter, because you know that I have
treated you better than (my other sons?), and you have not tried, hearing
that I am ill, you have not tried to send anything to me, not even
something short. So please send me ten pounds of woolen yarn, and I'll
make clothing for you, as far as I am able, because I have nothing to make
for you. Please send me a little supply of grain, and I'll send you a little . . .
Your nurse greets you, and I Kophaëna and your son Zenon and your sister
Kyrilla and her children. Please then, my son Theodoulos, buy for me 6
pounds of black wool, so that I may make a hooded cloak for myself, and I
will send you the money for the money you spend on it. I pray for your
health for a long time.

(ADDRESS): Deliver this to Theodoulos from Kophaëna.

∾ ∾ ∾

WILCKEN DESCRIBED THE HANDWRITING as a "large, thick half-uncial." Above
the text, written three times stands the Christian symbol chi-mu-gamma, and
at the end there is a chi-rho monogram.

The colloquial language, with a strongly oral tinge, has provided much
employment for philologists.

Kophaëna writes to her son to complain of his neglect. For thirteen months she has been sick, and he has not written even once. From the greetings it is evident that she is surrounded by other family; she is in no danger of dying of want. She takes advantage of the guilt she is piling on Theodoulos to ask him for various goods, especially wool that she can use to make clothing for him, naturally.

NOTE

your mother: The words are written twice, the first time with omission of the second eta. Neither instance is crossed out, but it is possible that the writer intended deletion of the misspelled one.

LOCATION OF OBJECT

The papyrus was destroyed when the ship carrying it burned in the harbor of Hamburg.

BIBLIOGRAPHY

Ghedini 1923, no. 44; O'Callaghan 1963, no. 1; Naldini 1998, no. 93; *BL* 3.15 (on lines 13, 14, and 20); 7.16 (on line 15); 8.37 (on line 4).

CPR 14.53

Letter of the early Arab period
Seventh–eighth century AD

LOCATION WRITTEN   Unknown
LOCATION OF ADDRESSEE   Unknown
LOCATION FOUND   Unknown

Greek

〜 〜 〜

We have received with eagerness the letter from my God-protected master,
and on learning from it of your good health and well-being we gave the
customary praise to the kind, benevolent God . . . with us, but according to
the multitude of his mercies . . . in the matter of the nurse, for God has
helped us also in this matter and . . . Concerning the matters of which he
spoke to us in private and in confidence, Marcus did not . . . he knew
exactly what to say to us about the whys and wherefores of our debts . . . he
darkened our reasoning, since he was unable to instruct us as he ought.
Would our lord be so good, after reading the letter, if you may . . .
something through him, to send us a complete reply, how we may act in
accord with your will. For it is much better . . . rather than in want. We
have also heard concerning the . . . accounts against you. If this is true, may
your God-protected master examine . . . large imposts of that which is
falsely assessed against you . . . to the one ordering, saying to him that if
these were true . . . against you. We did not receive the pepper . . .

(ADDRESS): To my God-protected master and brother in God (papyrus breaks
off).

〜 〜 〜

THE HAND IS A large, neat, professional semicursive of a type found in Greek
and Coptic hands of the period; there are a number of lectional signs, including breathings and an accent. The writers clearly had access to a first-class
scribe.

The Greek is also highly professional, although the loss of the left side and
bottom of the papyrus makes some of the constructions unclear to us. Apart
from a few iotacisms, the orthography and syntax are irreproachable.

Enough is preserved to show that most of the letter has to do with some
financial obligations, both those of the writers and of the recipient. The tone
of the letter is very polite, supportive and noncontentious, but the authors
clearly want precision about just what is expected of them.

NOTES
we: That the subject is feminine is deduced from the feminine participle at
the end of line 1. This plural form coexists with the use of "my" in the

address and greeting. In all likelihood the author is reflecting both herself and the larger group on behalf of which she is writing.

multitude of his mercies: Evidently a reminiscence of one or more passages in the scriptures.

LOCATION OF OBJECT
Vienna, Österreichische Nationalbibliothek, Papyrussammlung, inv. G 19780. Plates 47–48 in edition.

BIBLIOGRAPHY
Cf. *BL* 9.77 (restoration of line 4); Papathomas 1995: 154 (noted *BL* 10.57) (on the construction of lines 8–9).

P.Col. 10.290

Tegrape, etc., write to the family
Fifth–sixth century AD

LOCATION WRITTEN   Unknown
LOCATION OF ADDRESSEE   Unknown
LOCATION FOUND   Unknown

Greek

∽ ∽ ∽

(Front): To my truly most admirable brothers my master Petros and Elias (and Maria?), Paladia and wife Tegrape and Elias, greetings. Above all I thank God concerning your . . . my lord son Petros. Since you left me, I am getting along with your (?) . . . . and up till today I stayed with her, and I do not leave her. (traces)

(Back): And I Tegrape have written to my brothers Elias and Petros and Maria. I thank brothers Petros and Elias. Therefore (?) ask the landlord to deliver the wine to us . . . Since you left here, I am alone for a year, we have received nothing. You sent two cog wheels and one *sphairion*; I gave them for . . . ; bring another one here and the things there . . .

∽ ∽ ∽

THE MAIN HAND IS a fairly rounded cursive hand, insouciant and uneven. There are diaereses on initial iota and upsilon (for eta), and there is an abbreviation stroke.

There are numerous phonetic spellings throughout. The failure to use case endings consistently in personal names makes it somewhat uncertain just who are the addressees and who the senders.

This papyrus preserves part of a letter from a woman, or women, to several persons, at least some of whom are members of her family. It appears that Tegrape ("the dove") is the principal author, even though other names are included with hers in the greetings. The front concentrates upon the relationship between the author and another woman, and the back upon economic matters, as the author requests that her brothers intervene with a landholder concerning the delivery of wine, and complains of other difficulties.

NOTES

wife Tegrape: Probably Petros's wife, but this is only one of the things left unclear by the string of names with haphazard use of case endings.

Maria: It is not certain whether the author has forgotten to include Maria among the addressees or among the senders. The reappearance of the name among the addressees in line 11 suggests the former, and we have so interpreted it.

cog wheel: From the saqiya gear drive, which was frequently used throughout Egypt in this period to power irrigation devices of several types.

sphairion: The meaning of the word here is unknown.

LOCATION OF OBJECT

New York, Columbia University Libraries, Rare Book and Manuscript Library, inv. 48. Plates 47–48 in the edition.

P.Grenf. 1.61

Maria to her master
Sixth century AD

LOCATION WRITTEN Unknown
LOCATION OF ADDRESSEE Unknown
LOCATION FOUND Arsinoite nome

Greek

∾ ∾ ∾

To the dearest master of my soul and lord most honorable in everything
Maria salutes you, the nurse of your children, and to the lady of my eyes,
my lady Maria, and to my beautiful son Chryses, it is your nurse who salutes
you. Before everything I am sending prayers and supplications up to my
God and Christ our savior to always maintain you in good health and good
spirit. You wished to show me, my lady . . .

(Back): . . . is fine so far and will preserve us all. Give it to the master of my
soul . . .

∾ ∾ ∾

WRITTEN IN THE SAME hand throughout. The lines are wavering, and the
characters are stilted, completely separated, and of varying size. This hand is
strictly bilinear and is closer to a literary hand than to the flowing documentary hands of this period.

Most of the preserved letter consists of a long address and wish for health
expressed in the elaborate style of the period. There is a perceptible similarity
with Coptic letters. Connectives are kept to a minimum; there are some phonetic spellings.

The servant Maria writes to her master and his children whom she raised
(or to their mother and one son). The main purpose of the letter is lost.

NOTE
nurse: The term "mama" seems to designate here a slave or servant who raised
the children of the addressee.

LOCATION OF OBJECT
Oxford, Bodleian Library, Ms Gr class e.43 (P).

BIBLIOGRAPHY
On lines 11 and 13, see *BL* 1.184.

To Apa Heraklammon
Fifth or sixth century AD

LOCATION WRITTEN Unknown
LOCATION OF ADDRESSEE Unknown
LOCATION FOUND Unknown

Greek

∾ ∾ ∾

. . . to be in good health and. . . . (receive) my greeting . . . your holiness,
which punishment the abbess . . . because I am much tormented. The eyes
of evil people do not allow one to look up. Therefore I beg (you): pray for
me, so that God may now become reconciled and I can escape the snares of
evil people. I mean, this happened to me because . . . Therefore, I beg you
also even now: Pray for me, because I am badly tormented also about the
holy sacrifice. Do not neglect to write to us about your health . . . about us.
I am acquainted with your religiousness. (Since I had) ready a little cheese,
I sent it through . . . the one who is bringing you this letter and a little
dessert . . .

(ADDRESS ON BACK): . . . to apa Heraklammon . . .

∾ ∾ ∾

WRITTEN BY A PROFESSIONAL scribe with relatively small letters and restrained
use of flourishes. The hand is very competent and maintains throughout an
even letter size, interlinear space, and flow of ink.

The competence of the hand is correlated with a good command of Greek
in spite of a few phonetic mistakes and some obscurity in the central part.
Connectives are employed throughout. It is difficult to be sure how much the
writer elaborated on the woman's dictated text.

Much is unsure about the identity of the woman writer and of Apa Heraklammon and about the nature of their relationship (private, official?). This
woman seems to have been part of a religious group. While she sometimes
uses plural pronouns, in general she employs striking expressions to refer to
her personal torment with respect to an obscure circumstance.

NOTE
holy sacrifice: *Hagia prosphora.* It stands here in the accusative after "I am
afflicted," and the syntax is unclear. The reference is presumably to the Eu-
charist.

LOCATION OF OBJECT
Cologne, Institut für Altertumskunde, Papyrussammlung, inv. 5850. Pl. XVII
in the edition.

P.Oxy. 67.4629

Letter to a countess
Sixth–seventh century AD

LOCATION WRITTEN Unknown
LOCATION OF ADDRESSEE Probably Oxyrhynchos
LOCATION FOUND Oxyrhynchos

Greek

First of all I greet my sweetest mother many times, along with my entire household. Concerning the boat of the lord John, I often sent to him and he gave me no answer. So, I ask your Motherhood—see, I have sent Eutychios the black man to you—at all costs, as you would do your own business, do also mine. Concerning the one solidus' worth of honey, get it through Paneous (alias? the son of?) Peuar. Concerning the two solidi which are owing (?), collect them from Ammon the son of Carus, and concerning the two mnai of wool, please seek them from Limenios and send them to me. Write to me about your health and that of the lord Sarapion and the lord Martyrios. I send many greetings.

(ADDRESS): Deliver to the most . . . lady countess, from the lady (?) . . .

THE HAND IS, AS the editor remarks, "a large, sloping and almost unligatured script" resembling a book hand, but not as formal and with occasional irregularities.

The letter is composed of a series of matters of business, strung together as usual, but with an attempt to provide connective particles and not without some flair. Spelling is mostly standard, but there is one colloquial form.

The writer responds to questions she has been asked by the Countess about a series of matters and asks her to take care of some business of hers. The sums of money involved, for example a solidus' worth of honey, point to the milieu of wealth.

NOTE
countess: As the editor remarks, the title *kometissa* (probably the wife of a *komes*) is otherwise attested only in the literary sources.

LOCATION OF OBJECT
Oxford, Papyrology Rooms, Sackler Library.

BIBLIOGRAPHY
Beaucamp 1990–92, II: 311–12.

SB 5.8092

Chrysaris to Leontios about recovering her money
Fifth century AD

LOCATION WRITTEN Unknown
LOCATION OF ADDRESSEE Unknown
LOCATION FOUND Arsinoe (?)

Greek

To my lord brother Leontios, Chrysaris, the daughter of Ambrosios, greeting. Be aware that I learned that you have been living in Narmouthis quite some time ago, and I did not want to come there to you because of the ejectment, even though I could also take with me Elias the baker who is my dependent and could collect from you. And many times the same Elias told me, "I'm also going to get letters from the bishop or the vicarius to the councillors if they are going to collect from you." And I did not want to for God's sake, lest you suffer ejectment. Please therefore send me the 2 solidi. If you want me to come there, write back to me, and I will come to you. If again you want to send me the half, 8,000 talents?, send it immediately, and the balance within a few days. I pray for your health for a long time, my lord.

(ADDRESS): Deliver to Leontios the cumin seller from Chrysaris daughter of Ambrosios.

WRITTEN IN A PROFICIENT, fast hand that becomes even faster toward the end. The writer uses many ligatures and does not strive after clarity and legibility. Note the professional abbreviation of *chairein*.

This letter shows a good command of Greek even though the style is not formal. The sentences are long and well articulated, and morphology is usually correct. The phonetic mistakes are many but rather commonplace.

Chrysaris writes to Leontios, who owes her some money and probably re-settled in Narmouthis because of that. She reveals that she could have pursued him there with the help of one of her relatives but that she chose not to do so and wants to know what is the best course to recover her money.

LOCATION OF OBJECT
Lund, University Library, plate in *P.Lund.* 2.

BIBLIOGRAPHY
P.Lund. 2.5; BL 7.198.

SB 14.11492

To her brother Philoxenos
Sixth century AD

LOCATION WRITTEN Unknown
LOCATION OF ADDRESSEE Unknown
LOCATION FOUND Unknown

Greek

I have taken the liberty (?) to write to your fraternity with respect to the purchase in advance so that you would please purchase in advance (?) wool for the value of one tremis for me. And when the lady Patricia needed a solidus' worth of wool, I heard her tell Apa Romanus, "Go to Terythis," and I asked her to let me go with him when he was going, and she remembered and let me go with Apa Romanus. And when we arrived there we did not find any ready, but they gave us a time on the following day to deliver it to him. Since therefore I too need a tremissis' worth of wool and they agreed with me to bring me my own tremissis' worth, please let your fraternity send me a tremissis from there lest I would be found doing otherwise to the people of Terythis, and with God's help when I come to the city I am going to render an account to my master. Please receive 6 melons from the letter carrier free of charge. Do not neglect to send me a reply. I salute you warmly and I make obeisance to my brother. Do not take . . . the fact that I write to you as a brother because I write to you as a master. Greet warmly our common sister Theodote and particularly your lady mother. Send me the little one and take care . . .

(ADDRESS ON BACK): Deliver to my sweetest brother Philoxenos . . . from brother Hyacinthos.

FLOWING, PROFESSIONAL HAND WITH harmony and style. The lines are evenly spaced. The address is in the same larger hand with letters entirely separated for the sake of clarity.

The letter shows a good command of Greek. The vocabulary is learned. The sentences are long and elaborate, with a frequent use of the genitive absolute and the articular infinitive. Occasionally a colloquial, oral style prevails. Morphology leaves something to be desired even though sometimes it is difficult to distinguish a morphological error from an orthographic variation. The latter are particularly numerous and consist of many vowel and consonant interchanges.

This letter is written by a woman to a certain Philoxenos whom she calls brother. The two of them seem to have a sister in common but not a mother.

It is interesting that the writer is concerned about the propriety of addressing him as "brother" since she seems to have a rather formal relationship with him. The letter concerns the purchase of some wool. The writer would like Philoxenos to lend her some money that she promises to repay to him.

LOCATION OF OBJECT
Ann Arbor, University of Michigan Library, Papyrus collection, inv. 497.

SB 14.12085

Alexandra to her father Eutropios
Fifth century AD

LOCATION WRITTEN   Unknown
LOCATION OF ADDRESSEE   Unknown
LOCATION FOUND   Unknown

Greek

Alexandra to Eutropios, my master, ever most esteemed and respected father. When the brother of Annianos (brother Annianos, my brother Annianos?) went to Tophos and sold the wine, I told him about the solidi according to what you told me, that they should be sent to Alexandria and he said that you wrote to him to take them with him. Be aware that I troubled Heraklios together with Annianos but he has not given me anything. About the storehouse, Kopres tried in any way to prevent the storehouse from being opened, and I and my brother Theopemptos tried in any way to have it opened. We made Alphios give 500 pounds . . .

THE HAND IS FLUENT and proficient, with a strong sense of style and a remarkable rhythm. The letters are comparatively small, but some of them are enlarged for the sake of elegance.

Besides the customary phonetic mistakes and the use of double conjunctions, the letter is well written.

When Alexandra writes to her father to report to him about family affairs, she seems capable of managing the situation . . . and her two brothers. It is impossible to know what kind of storehouse she is talking about.

NOTE
Tophos: The location of this place is unknown.

LOCATION OF OBJECT

Ann Arbor, University of Michigan Library, Papyrus collection, inv. 1044.

SB 18.13762

Phoibasia to the banker Agapetos
Sixth or seventh century AD

LOCATION WRITTEN   Unknown
LOCATION OF ADDRESSEE   Alexandria
LOCATION FOUND   Unknown

Greek

∾ ∾ ∾

I have already written to your lordship through the courier of the imperial
service and when the courier came back but did not bring me a letter, we
were all very discouraged, as the Lord knows. Then the courier interrogated
by me about the reply said, "I received a letter for the curator and I found
him at the Perone and right away he dismissed me. But your letter I gave it
to NN the soldier of the imperial service so that he would deliver it to the
lord Agapetos." I do not know whether you received it or not, only that we
were (all) discouraged. Now that the ecclesiastic courier Johannes is coming
down with a letter from the bishop, I thought it was necessary to write
through him and greet your lordship. I inform you, as I have also written in
that letter, that, as your lordship enjoined to me to lay down the planks and
to lay on top a wall of 1 cubit, so the mason did and built 4 rows (of bricks)
for the wall; but before he put the ceiling, the most holy bishop sent
(people) and stopped the construction, not only but he threw down the 4
rows (of bricks) that I laid down for the wall. While at first he was coming
there every day and checked through the gate and said to the mason, "Do
your work fast," as soon as I gave the wages he had the whole construction
thrown down. I sent a letter to him saying, "I am going to write to him,"
and he responded, "If you wish, write, for I do not pay attention to him and
I pushed (it) down; this is not my concern." But we were all worried that,
now that the construction had been overturned, something might happen
to you. Your lordship was requested—as I also asked in person—to send me
a little mushroom and the small (jar of) oil and the garum in the omphalos
bottle, so that you send me, because I am busy with the wedding of your
servant. Tell Sinouthios the slave to send me the knives that he stole for
. . . your answer, since when I am coming I hope to take his small vessel as
it is.

You were requested (to send) the embroideries for the hooded cloak, because the ones it has are small . . . We all pray to embrace you in person . . . and your servant Ioustos and Viktor your (pl.) servant [greet] you warmly. I myself, Phoibasia your servant hope to embrace you shortly in Alexandria, (second hand) because of what I suffered. (first hand) Kyra the bride greets you warmly. Viktor the slave greets you and the others of his (family) Viktor and Sinouthios. I the young Anastasios, your servant, utterly pray for your health so that . . . God gives us the most love and to my insignificance . . . The son of the blessed Damianos . . . and offer you thanks . . . of the . . . fame, intact because of you, amen.

(ADDRESS ON BACK): To my master in all the most illustrious . . . overseer . . . Agapetos banker.

THIS LETTER WAS CERTAINLY dictated to a scribe. The hand is typical of this period. It is very fluent, fast, bent to the right, and does not show much concern for legibility. An addition was made by a second hand, which is capable but slower, less fluent, and less ligatured. This might represent Phoibasia's hand.

The scribe who penned this had a very good command of Greek. The sentences are long and elaborate, and the whole letter is overall correct. A few errors such as occasional lack of augment or the few nonstandard spellings do not impair the general impression of expertise. The continuous switching between second-person singular and plural is a sign of dictation, as well as occasional repetitions.

Phoibasia writes a long and interesting letter to the banker Agapetos who was probably her husband. She relates at first about the difficulties encountered in delivering a letter to him. Next she informs him about a certain construction that the local bishop approved at first but had taken down later. The last part of this letter is occupied with household requests and business and salutations from people whose relationship with Agapetos is unclear.

NOTES

curator: Nothing is known about the identity and prerogatives of this curator.

Perone: Apparently a neighborhood of Alexandria.

mushroom: Most mushrooms in the Amanita family are highly poisonous; the very few edible species are far from choice food.

LOCATION OF OBJECT

Florence, Biblioteca Medicea Laurenziana, inv. PL I/3. Plate in *Tyche* 1 (1986), plates 27 and 28.

SB 20.14226

Therpe to her father concerning a feast
Fourth–fifth century AD

LOCATION WRITTEN   Unknown
LOCATION OF ADDRESSEE   Unknown
LOCATION FOUND   Unknown

Greek

To the master of my soul truly the most esteemed, my father Theon,
Therpe. Before everything I pray God the Almighty about your health. As
you informed me about the linen cloths we found 15 pounds in the
presence of my father Sarapion . . . Inform me so that I receive the leg
ornaments so that I can wear them at the feast, because mine broke. Don't I
deserve the cakes and the spiced wine of the Kalends? You did not send me
anything, not even a bit of money for the feast. Send D . . . so that she
makes my *himation*. Do not forget to send the ornaments. I pray for your
health for a long time, lord father.

(ADDRESS ON BACK): To the master of my soul, my father Theon, Therpe.

A PRACTICED HAND THAT is reasonably clear in spite of the numerous ligatures.
Two-thirds of the letter are written in a comparably small hand with lines
crowded together. Afterward the writer considerably enlarges both letter size
and interlinear spaces.

   In spite of a few orthographic mistakes, the writer correctly observes morphology and syntax. Connective particles, however, are not used, and the
Greek is a bit stilted with short and simple phrases.

   The sender of this amusing letter sounds young and immature. The letter
is whiny and full of requests. Therpe immediately tells her father about something he was interested in but proceeds then to list all her complaints. Her
pressing concern is a feast to celebrate the New Year.

NOTES
leg ornaments: *Periskelidia* were metal bindings worn by women over the
knee.

feast: Probably that celebrated on the first of Thoth.

himation: A woman's outer garment.

LOCATION OF OBJECT

Vienna, Österreichische Nationalbibliothek, Papyrussammlung, inv. G
25982 + 28579.

BIBLIOGRAPHY

BL 11.228 (discussion in Bagnall 1997).

18. CORRESPONDENCE OF BISHOP PISENTIUS ～

These interrelated groups of letters (A18–A20) all come from the west bank of the Nile opposite Thebes, modern Luxor, and concern the last years of Roman rule and the early decades of Arab rule in Egypt, from the end of the sixth to the second half of the seventh century. Jeme, the central place, was a large village rather than a city, but by this period it was probably the most important village in the area, referred to in Greek texts as the Memnoneia, the region around the statues of the New Kingdom pharaoh Amenhotep III called the Colossi of Memnon. More importantly for us, it has left to us a remarkable quantity of material in various languages, some of it excavated scientifically, some looted. The environment was bilingual, but the bulk of the surviving documentation is in Coptic, and it is clear that this was the primary language of everyday use.

To the north of Jeme, in the foothills, were a number of monasteries, including two excavated with some care. The best known of these are the Monastery of Epiphanius and the Monastery of Phoibammon, both of which also produced abundant textual finds. The monasteries were closely connected to Jeme, and there was constant interaction between the village and the monasteries, including movement of people and goods between them. We see a particularly striking pattern of reliance by male monks on goods and services provided by their female relatives outside the monastic world. (See Wilfong 2002: 110–12; and MacCoull (1998) [2000], for the Monastery of Epiphanius.)

Pisentius (born 569) was bishop of Coptos, on the opposite bank of the Nile to the north of Luxor, from 599–632. He came from the region of Jeme, had part of his monastic formation in the local monasteries of Phoibammon and Epiphanius, and remained close to his home region. When the Sassanian Persians invaded Egypt, Pisentius fled to the mountains above Jeme and waited out their occupation (619–629) there, returning to Coptos only for his last days. He was well known in Jeme and constantly consulted by men and women of that area on a host of matters; the letters included here, found apparently in his West Bank refuge, show part of the range of matters attested in his correspondence. After his death he was the subject of a biography and widespread reverence.

O.CrumST 360

The mother of Paniskos writes to Bishop Pisentius
Sixth–eighth century AD

LOCATION WRITTEN   Unknown
LOCATION OF ADDRESSEE   Thebes, Monastery of Epiphanius
LOCATION FOUND   Thebes, Monastery of Epiphanius

Coptic

∽ ∽ ∽

I,——, the mother of little Paniskos, greet her beloved father Apa Pesynte.
I write asking you to be so kind as to ask God that he grant (?) that I lift up
my eye, because it is ruined. Be so kind, if God grants, to send to me,
otherwise sending to me. For I am a weak person in poverty. I, Daniel, write
greeting Apa Pesynthios and and all the monks by name, from least to
greatest. Farewell in the lord.

∽ ∽ ∽

OSTRACON; NO DESCRIPTION OF the hand.

The addressee is evidently the head of a monastery, and it seems likely that
this is indeed the well-known bishop of this name. The writer asks for his
intercessory prayers on behalf of her eyes, but the expression of her wishes is
very obscure.

NOTE
Daniel: He presumably wrote on behalf of the woman, as no change of hand
is indicated. It is all the more striking that he spells the recipient's name
Pesynte when writing for her, Pesynthios (a Greek form) when writing on his
own behalf.

LOCATION OF OBJECT
Formerly collection of Walter Crum; now Oxford, Ashmolean Museum, Bodleian Coptic Inscr. 249a–d.

P.Pisentius 28

Two seamstresses write to the bishop
First half of the seventh century AD

LOCATION WRITTEN   Unknown
LOCATION OF ADDRESSEE   Koptos
LOCATION FOUND   Koptos or the Theban region

Coptic

Before everything we embrace and greet the footstool of the feet of our lord
father who is honored in every way. Since your holy fatherly lordship sent
wheat south to us, i.e., 6 artabas, we have acted in accordance with your
instruction. Be so kind as to pray for us and for your holy prayers to be on
our behalf. If you wish us to bind the girls to do the work—and our lord
father orders us to bind them to carry the cross without stopping—be so
kind, then, lord, as to give us the work. For indeed you have mercy on us
on every occasion and you do it for us also. Now, we are your servants
Tsheere and Koshe.

Look, I have sent two tunics with sleeves and two coverings to your holy
fatherly lordship. If they please you, be so kind to me—me, Koshe—as to
take them. For you know that I am very distressed concerning my
handicrafts. Now as for the two hoods which I will make, I shall send them
to you also, and they will come with the tunics. Now, as for the five tunics,
I sent them to your holy paternal lordship, I—your servant Tsheere, that
is—(the tunics being) four sack tunics and one secular tunic. Be so kind,
then, my lord father, as to be merciful to me, because I am distressed and I
am (troubled?) concerning the wool which I received, because . . .

(ADDRESS): (To) our lord the truly Christ-bearing father, Apa Pesynthios the
bishop, (from) his humblest servants.

A FAST HAND, inclined to the right. The lines are crowded, and there are a
few clumsy erasures, but the handwriting is generally proficient on both sides.

The tone of supplication and respect in this letter makes it difficult to be
certain how far their relationship with the bishop rested on explicit agree-
ments for work and how far the two women worked on a speculative basis.
But it is clear that they were periodically paid for their work. The letter comes
from both Tsheere ("the daughter") and Koshe ("Nubian"), but much is written in the first-person singular and both women include individual remarks
as well as their joint requests.

LOCATION OF OBJECT
Paris, Louvre, R. 79.

BIBLIOGRAPHY
Wilfong 2002: 41–42, based on a transcription by Crum.

SB Kopt. 1.295
A widow's petition
Ca. AD 630

LOCATION WRITTEN Jeme
LOCATION OF ADDRESSEE Thebes, Monastery of Epiphanius
LOCATION FOUND Thebes, Monastery of Epiphanius

Coptic

First I embrace the sweetness of the holy feet of your truly God-loving fatherliness, which intercedes for us before God; and you are the one who beseeches God for the entire people and whom God has appointed true high priest to make petition for the whole people before God; and you are our patron who intercedes for us before God and men. I am this wretched one, miserable beyond (all) men on earth, and greatly weighed down with grief and sadness, and heartbroken for my husband who is dead, and for my son whom the Persians beat (?) . . . and my cattle which the Persians carried off.

Now, I beg you of your holy fatherliness to send and bring the headman of Jeme and Amos, and ask them to leave me in my house and not to have me wander abroad. For they said to me, "You are liable for the field." The son, also, whom I had was heartbroken and took to flight. And also the pair of cattle which were left from the Persians—the moneylender came forth and carried them off and sold them on account of his loan which I borrowed for the tax. Be so kind to me as for me to be settled in my house.

(ADDRESS): Give it to my lord father the holy [bishop] Pesente, from this poor wretched wife of the deceased Pesente.

A LARGE OSTRACON OF limestone written on both sides and on the bottom edge, in a clear, well-formed, detached hand.

The author, who does not give her name, is a widow, who has lost her cattle to the Persian invaders (619–629), and whose son has fled. She appeals to Pesente, who is almost certainly the bishop, to intervene with the authorities in Jeme to keep her from losing her house, evidently in foreclosure for unpaid taxes on a field of hers.

NOTE
liable for the field: Liable for the taxes or other obligations due on the property.

LOCATION OF OBJECT
Cairo, Coptic Museum, inv. 4326. Plates I–II in *Bulletin de la Société d'Archéologie Copte* 10 (1944), before p. 177.

BIBLIOGRAPHY
First published in Drescher 1944: 91–96, plus plates I–II before p. 177, with translation and commentary; Wilfong 2002: 84.

O.Medin.HabuCopt. 143

Nonna to Paul

Sixth–eighth century AD

LOCATION WRITTEN Unknown
LOCATION OF ADDRESSEE Unknown
LOCATION FOUND Jeme

Coptic

∾ ∾ ∾

I, Nonna, write greeting Paulos son of Moses, saying: Pisrael came last year and took your cattle and was begged and gave them to you again, now remit the piece of flax to us for them, lest Pisrael come and take them again. Now look, I have written and have testified to you; send me the answer. Farewell.

∾ ∾ ∾

OSTRACON. AN EXPERIENCED HAND, which writes relatively fast but with few ligatures. It becomes slightly more cursive toward the end.

The context of this note is unknown to us, but Nonna is concerned that there will be a repetition of an incident of the previous year, when Pisrael seized some cattle, evidently against some debt owed him.

LOCATION OF OBJECT
Formerly Chicago, University of Chicago, Oriental Institute, MH 1299, now in Cairo, Egyptian Museum.

20. COPTIC LETTERS FROM THE MONASTERY OF EPIPHANIUS

O.Mon.Epiph. 170

Maria and Susanna to Panachora

Sixth–eighth century AD

LOCATION WRITTEN Unknown

LOCATION OF ADDRESSEE Unknown

LOCATION FOUND Thebes, Monastery of Epiphanius

Coptic

[---] we will repay to you.

I, Maria, write to Panachora: Be so good as to let your compassion reach me and send me a . . . , for my heart has flown forth. For the barbarians have carried off the father and have carried off the son . . . me the (news?); for they have slain . . . my heart has flown forth. If . . . to me, and my heart is at rest. . . . I do obeisance unto your holiness.

I, Susanna, . . . write and do obeisance at the footprints of the feet of your holiness. Be so good . . . my son . . . dead.

THIS PECULIAR OSTRACON CARRIES the ending of a letter and two more letters by two women. It is certain that three hands were at work. The hands of the women's letters are different, which might lead one to think that they penned them personally. Both hands are competent and fluent. The first is a typical Coptic hand, with round letters all separated. The second hand is more flattened and is developed horizontally.

Even in its fragmentary state, this sherd with two letters conveys something of the disastrous state of the writers, whose menfolk have been carried off, and perhaps killed, by "the barbarians." This reference is most probably to the Persian occupation of 619–629. Unfortunately it is not clear what, apart from prayers, the women are asking for.

LOCATION OF OBJECT

New York, Metropolitan Museum of Art, accession 12.180.151.

BIBLIOGRAPHY
Wilfong 2002: 84.

O.Mon.Epiph. 177

Prisoners ask for help
Sixth–eighth century AD

LOCATION WRITTEN Unknown
LOCATION OF ADDRESSEE Unknown
LOCATION FOUND Thebes, Monastery of Epiphanius

Coptic

༄ ༄ ༄

. . . we were at pains and wrote to you and you have forgotten us in the
captivity where we are, while they hung us up backward and took our
breath out (of our bodies), and you did not visit us. For we gave our life for
you; look you have forgotten us. Don't trust the men, lest they kill us. For
as the Lord lives, if you don't reach us today with the money, there will be
no life left in us. Send the rations for us to the jailer and give loaves and
. . . Then don't fail to see that they reach us today; otherwise, as the Lord
lives, we will take six soldiers and come north and will hand you over and
all your affairs, until they are paid.

(ADDRESS): Give it to Pesenthios and Papnoute, from . . . she and Thekla.
Pay the wage of . . . who shall bring this potsherd to you.

༄ ༄ ༄

OSTRACON, BROKEN AT THE top. This hand appears proficient on both sides.
On the bottom half of the recto, however, the letters are much more crowded
and irregular, as if the writer had not planned to use the reverse and was afraid
to run out of space.

This remarkable Coptic letter, postage to be paid by the recipients, comes
from Thekla and a fellow prisoner, whose name is partly lost (and sex inde-
terminable), to two men, Pesenthios and Papnoute. They complain of torture
and of being short of food (which prisoners had to provide for themselves);
they ask for the recipients to send food immediately, claiming that they are
on the verge of death from starvation. Then they threaten, rather oddly, to
come with six soldiers and seize the two men with all their possessions. How
they will accomplish this is not evident.

New York, Metropolitan Museum of Art, accession 12.180.228.

O.Mon.Epiph. 194

Esther asks a holy man for help
Sixth–eighth century AD

LOCATION WRITTEN Unknown
LOCATION OF ADDRESSEE Unknown
LOCATION FOUND Thebes, Monastery of Epiphanius

Coptic

∾ ∾ ∾

I, Esther your servant, write and do obeisance to my father. Be so kind as to instruct me . . . I bear my children . . . they die. Perhaps (I) do something unfitting. Be so kind as to send me a rule whereby I may walk; for my soul is grieved . . . at the time . . .

∾ ∾ ∾

OSTRACON. FLUENT, SLANTED HAND that writes, with considerable expertise, mostly detached letters.

Damage at right makes it difficult at times to be certain of the meaning and thus of the correctness of the preserved portions of the text. There is perhaps a slip, but spelling is generally good.

Esther's letter is damaged at right, but the main point seems clear: her children have all died young. She supposes that she is unwittingly the cause of these disasters and asks the recipient for a "rule" or commandment, which is presumably intended to avert the death of future offspring.

LOCATION OF OBJECT
Cairo, formerly Egyptian Museum, Journal d'entrée 44674.151, now in the Coptic Museum 4530/151.

Eudoxia to Pson the anchorite, in search of forgiveness
Sixth–eighth century AD

LOCATION WRITTEN Unknown
LOCATION OF ADDRESSEE Unknown
LOCATION FOUND Thebes, Monastery of Epiphanius

Coptic

~ ~ ~

Before all things I salute the footstool of your feet. Be so kind, then, I
entreat and beseech you, my holy father, to entreat God on my behalf, that
he may be merciful to me and forgive me my sins. For I have sinned against
him and he will not bring the enemy away from me. For my iniquities and
my sins are very, very many, and they are heavy on me, and he has given
me into the hand of my enemies. Have pity, then, and entreat God for me,
that I may cease from this scourge that is upon me. My holy father, don't
delay in entreating God for me; for it is you who entreat him on behalf of
the whole world. Farewell in the Lord, my beloved holy and revered father,
Apa Pson the anchorite. I, this sinner Eudoxia, whose sins are very many.
Have pity, then, and help me.

~ ~ ~

OSTRACON. THIS WRITER SEEMS to have taken down faithfully the repetitious
words of beseeching Eudoxia without having the time to phrase a more com-
pact text. His small, separated letters show the remarkable evenness that is a
mark of a professional.

The Coptic of the letter is straightforward and mainly correct, although
the whole composition lacks skill in articulating clauses.

Eudoxia somewhat repetitiously asks Apa Pson to intercede with God on
her behalf. She is clearly suffering from a severe "scourge," presumably an
illness, which she attributes to her sins.

LOCATION OF OBJECT
New York, Metropolitan Museum of Art, accession 12.180.85.

O.Mon.Epiph. 300

Thello asks for help with an unpaid debt
Mid- to late 620s AD

LOCATION WRITTEN Unknown
LOCATION OF ADDRESSEE Unknown
LOCATION FOUND Thebes, Monastery of Epiphanius

Coptic

. . . your [father]liness (?), and I embrace the prints of the feet of your God-lovingness, my lord father. I, this servant (and) widow, Thello, (widow) of the deceased Peter, son of Plos, in the congregation of Ptene, inform your paternity—for it is you whom God has appointed to inquire concerning the affairs of the poor—for before the Persians came south, my deceased husband gave some grain to the priest of Apa Shenetom and Sakau, (son) of Joui, and they sowed it in the plain. They have not paid me anything for it until now. And look, I have paid them many a visit, saying "Write me (a note) for it, until the place is at peace and you can pay me a little yearly." They went to law, one with another, and it was decided that each one should write down his share. Look . . .

OSTRACON. THIS HAND IS reasonably capable but has an uneven look, mainly because of the frequent ink dipping. The writer was very familiar with the pen but was not a first-rate professional.

The author is a widow in a community not far from the monastery. Her late husband had lent seed grain to two local men, which they have not paid back, evidently as a result of the local disturbances produced by the Persian invasion. Indeed, the two borrowers have fallen out over their respective shares of the debt, but that case has been settled. Still, nothing has been paid, and they have not even drawn up new loan notes in favor of Thello.

NOTE
Apa Shenetom: A church named after a local martyr.

LOCATION OF OBJECT
New York, Metropolitan Museum of Art, accession 14.1.166.

BIBLIOGRAPHY
Wilfong 2002: 84.

O.Mon.Epiph. 336

Koletjeu to Epiphanius
First half of the seventh century AD

LOCATION WRITTEN Unknown
LOCATION OF ADDRESSEE Unknown
LOCATION FOUND Thebes, Monastery of Epiphanius

Coptic

Since you came yesterday (?) and said, "I will not leave until you have received the wine," look, here now is the wine. I have received it from Sarapion's son. He has not . . . except (?) one. Look, the solidus (worth) of wine I collected, (but) I have not found a man to whom to sell it so far. If I sell it, I will bring up the solidus. Be so good and for God's sake be diligent to go with Constantine to the dwelling of Apa David and ask him concerning his property; for he and his children have been robbed, and he does not know it. For they have carried off his cloak and his orphan children. Now if you are at home, for God's sake do not put off going with him and inquiring well of him, so that I may give you thanks. If you have ground grain, send to me and I will fetch his grindstone and come up.

(ADDRESS): Give it to my beloved son Epiphanius, from Koletjeu, his mother. I, Apa Iohannes, greet your paternity. Be so good as to pray for me. Send me a "seal" for my children.

OSTRACON, WRITTEN IN A practiced, semicursive hand, which is probably that of Apa Iohannes, who adds his greetings at the end. The first half of this ostracon shows that Apa Iohannes was capable of writing an elegant and flowing text with letters well spaced out. In the rest, however, the hand becomes faster and a bit irregular, probably for lack of space.

There are nonstandard forms suggesting the spoken dialect of the region.

Koletjeu (Koloje) refers to herself as Epiphanius's mother, and perhaps this is to be taken at face value, for she certainly speaks to him in a more directive and less wheedling tone than most of his correspondents. She is concerned about the sale of a quantity of wine, but even more about a robbery that has happened to Apa David, apparently without his knowledge; she asks Epiphanius to look into the matter and take care of him.

NOTES

his orphan children: It is not clear if it is the children themselves who have been carried off or their clothing.

"seal": The meaning is uncertain: possibly an amulet, or perhaps eucharistic bread.

LOCATION OF OBJECT
New York, Metropolitan Museum of Art, accession 14.1.91.

BIBLIOGRAPHY
Wilfong 2002: 111.

Fig. 17.   *O.Mon.Epiph.* 336. Koletjeu to Epiphanius. (New York, Metropolitan Museum of Art, accession 14.1.91. Photograph courtesy of the Metropolitan Museum of Art, Museum Excavations, 1913–1914. Rogers Fund, 1914 [14.1.91].)

O.Mon.Epiph. 386

Two women write Moses
Sixth–eighth century AD

LOCATION WRITTEN   Unknown
LOCATION OF ADDRESSEE   Unknown
LOCATION FOUND   Thebes, Monastery of Epiphanius

Coptic

∽ ∽ ∽

I, Tatre and Katharon, write to Moses, the humblest and God-loving. I greet
you as a brother. I beg you to write a portion upon the canon and send it to
us. I, Tatre, write with my own hand. Be so kind as to pray for me; I am a
sinner.

∽ ∽ ∽

OSTRACON. THIS IS THE hand of Tatre, as she indicates. The characters are
rigid and strictly separated overall but her performance visibly improves as she
proceeds. In the first few lines corrections and insertions above the line ham-
per the reading.

Tatre writes this letter to Moses in her own hand, as she proudly records;
although she includes Katharon in the initial salutation, practically every form
in the letter is singular, right from the "I" at the start. There are a couple of
significant misspellings.

Wilfong has suggested that the women who wrote this letter were female
monks, even though they do not explicitly identify themselves as such. They
ask for a portion of an ecclesiastical canon to be written out for them.

NOTE
humblest: An epithet (Gk. *elachistos*) that people usually use of themselves,
not of others. The editor comments, "Women seem apt to misuse such epi-
thets."

LOCATION OF THE OBJECT
Cairo, formerly Egyptian Museum, Journal d'entrée 46304.36, now in the
Coptic Museum, 4531/36.

P.Mon.Epiph. 433

Tagape to ?Epiphanius about the Persians
Early 620s AD

LOCATION WRITTEN   Unknown
LOCATION OF ADDRESSEE   Unknown
LOCATION FOUND   Thebes, Monastery of Epiphanius

Coptic

I embrace [? your holy fatherliness who is honored] in every way. In the
matter of the youth, be so kind . . . pray for him. Look . . . bring the vessels
. . . quickly. Then pray for me that God may take those trials from me. Be
so kind, as regards the lying words that . . . God, thou knowest; and I say
within my soul, while I [. . . and] I will depart and leave the matter to you,
until your fatherliness [. . . But] if you want me to remain, I will remain. If
the district (?) gets stability, be [so kind . . .] send the end (of the matter)
to your servant, that I may go . . . to your lordship. I will entreat your
[paternity . . . ?to send me] instruction in the matter of the Persians, for
they will be coming south, and I will give [. . . Pi]shenai and Toumrout.
Farewell in the lord.

(ADDRESS): [Give it to my beloved?] holy father, from Tagape his servant.

WRITTEN IN A GOOD professional cursive hand, presumably by a scribe.

After several more personal matters, Tagape may allude to the present lack
of stability in the area, and clearly refers to the expectation of the Persians'
imminent arrival.

LOCATION OF OBJECT
New York, Metropolitan Museum of Art, accession 12.180.318.

Fig. 18. *P.Mon.Epiph.* 433. Tagape to ?Epiphanius about the Persians. (New York, Metropolitan Museum of Art, accession 12.180.318. Photograph courtesy of the Metropolitan Museum of Art, Museum Excavations, 1911–1912. Rogers Fund, 1912 [12.180.318].)

These two letters, in the same hand, were both probably addressed by the same woman, Christophoria, to the same man, Count Menas. From internal evidence one can say that she was writing from a monastery (called by the Greek word *topos*), of which she was probably the head, to a Count (Gk. *komes*) named Menas, whose family was responsible for significant gifts to establish and support the monastery. These letters are part of a batch of papyri from Hermopolis (mod. Ashmunein). On the other side of *P.Lond.Copt.* 1105 is a later letter, this one from Menas to a servant, who is severely reprimanded (*P.Lond.Copt.* 1113); it is perhaps a copy kept by Menas. That text, in turn, was written in the same hand as a letter addressed to another count concerning the irrigation of vineyards and a debt due from the writer (*P.Lond.Copt.* 1115). *P.Lond.Copt.* 1114 is also in the same hand, apparently another letter addressed to a count. It is clear that the entire find probably came from a wealthy household.

P.Lond.Copt. 1104

Christophoria to the count Menas
Sixth–eighth century AD

LOCATION WRITTEN Unknown
LOCATION OF ADDRESSEE Unknown
LOCATION FOUND Hermopolis

Coptic

God will convince your filial lordship that, excepting the concern for your body, we have now no other care more pleasant than to see you almost daily and to know of your good health. For besides the care of our sins and the establishment of your body, we have no object at all for which to pray. Now, though our difficulties and the cares which at present are spread upon us are very great, we have cast all behind us because of your great suffering, which is a burden upon us, even as if our eye were diseased. Inform us then, in your honored letters, whether you are better or how you fare. For our heart is daily disturbed on your account. Believe that my humility and your humble adorers all the brethren do daily pray for your health. And as to the only matter about which we sent, (it is) that you should tell us how you do, and, if God has given grace that you should be able to rise, we desire to see you, that our grief may be changed to joy. For the Word that was made flesh and bade the paralytic, "Take up thy bed and walk," may he heal your body, that you may go on from strength to strength; and may his help from henceforth strengthen you. Farewell in the power of the Holy Trinity.

(ADDRESS): The glorious beloved lord and son, the Christ-loving count Menas, (from) Christophoria the humblest.

WRITTEN COMPETENTLY IN AN upright hand with letters all separated. Occasionally some unevenness is noticeable.

This letter consists entirely of Christophoria's expression of her concern, along with that of the community of which she is part, for the health of the addressee, who has been suffering from a serious illness.

LOCATION OF OBJECT
London, British Library, Department of Oriental Manuscripts, Or. 6075.

P.Lond.Copt. 1105

Christophoria writes with good wishes
Sixth–eighth century AD

LOCATION WRITTEN Unknown
LOCATION OF ADDRESSEE Unknown
LOCATION FOUND Hermopolis

Coptic

Before the words of our humility we embrace and greet your beloved, filial,
honored lordship. Also a host of years again for the new year, with the lord
Christ granting you a lot of trouble-free and distress-free life, and causing
your days to be to you like those of heaven, and that you may see the
children of your children turning to you until generations upon generations,
your great love much accepted because of your philanthropy, which you do
along with your house. For since this monastery has been established
through God and the assistance of your good benevolent disposition, Christ
has accepted it of you. May the Lord repay well to you ten thousand times
in this world and that which is to come. We greet warmly our beloved
daughter Kyra and the little children . . . particularly your Eukleia . . . us
face to face (?) . . . we repay our debt with every zeal. Farewell in the Lord.

(ADDRESS): To our glorious beloved lord . . . Christophoria.

WRITTEN COMPETENTLY IN AN upright hand with letters all separated. Occasionally some unevenness is noticeable.

Christophoria writes to the patron of the monastery (*topos*), of which she
is apparently head. The contents are mainly occupied with good wishes.

LOCATION OF OBJECT
London, British Library, Department of Oriental Manuscripts, Or. 6076.

B. THEMES AND TOPICS

1. FAMILY MATTERS AND HEALTH ∾

BGU 2.380

A mother writes to her son
Third century AD (after 212)

LOCATION WRITTEN   Unknown
LOCATION OF ADDRESSEE   Unknown
LOCATION FOUND   Arsinoite nome

Greek

∾ ∾ ∾

His mother to Hegelochos her son, greetings. Setting off at a late hour to
Serapion the veteran, I inquired about your well-being and that of your
children. And he told me that your foot is hurting from a splinter, and I was
worried that you were excessively slow; and when I said to Serapion that
"I'm coming with you," he said to me nothing too much was troubling you.
If you know yourself that anything is bothering you, write to me, and I'll
come down, I'll travel with whomever I find. Don't forget, child, write me
concerning your health, as knowing fear about a child. Your children greet
you. Aurelius Ptoleminos to his father, greetings. Persuade Dionysios.
Farewell, child (?).

∾ ∾ ∾

THE WRITER, WHO HAD obvious difficulties with penmanship, tried hard to
produce an acceptable letter. The individual letter shapes are a bit elaborate
and formed with an attempt at elegance, but the lack of regular writing practice shows in the somewhat wobbly lines and in the retracing of strokes. At
the end the writer shows that he or she had reached the limit of what he or
she could produce.

The language is marked by striking phonetic spellings, rather beyond the usual run, and an exceptionally oral style, switching in and out of direct discourse. It would be easy to form the impression of a poorly educated writer. But there is also some unusual vocabulary, and we even find attempts to introduce connectives. This might be a rare piece of autograph writing by someone normally accustomed to using an amanuensis.

The letter is entirely devoted to the mother's worries about her son's health. His foot has been injured by a splinter (or thorn), and she is concerned that some other malady (we may suppose an infection) has overtaken him. It is noteworthy that the mother's informant is a veteran, and that she is prepared to travel with him or anyone else she finds. The fact that the grandmother is taking care of the children and that their mother is nowhere mentioned suggests that Hegelochos's wife may have died, or perhaps that the marriage ended in divorce.

NOTES

His mother: She does not give her name, rather unusually.

Aurelius Ptoleminos: This seems to be the son's message, written in the same hand as the rest of the letter. What follows, however, is obscure.

LOCATION OF OBJECT

Berlin, Staatliche Museen, Papyrussammlung, P. 7108 verso.

BIBLIOGRAPHY

BL 1.42 (on lines 1, 5, 10, 15, 24); Schubart 1923: 93 no. 66; Hohlwein 1927: 16ff.

Fig. 19. *BGU* 2.380. A mother writes to her son. (Berlin, Staatliche Museen, Papyrussammlung, P. 7108 verso. Photograph courtesy of the Staatliche Museen zu Berlin, Preussischer Kulturbesitz, Ägyptisches Museum und Papyrussammlung. Photo M. Büsing.)

P.Bour. 25

Tare to her aunt Horeina
Fourth century AD

LOCATION WRITTEN Apamea in Syria
LOCATION OF ADDRESSEE Koptos
LOCATION FOUND Unknown

Greek

To my lady and longed for aunt, Tare daughter of your sister Allous, greeting in God. Before all I pray God that you receive my letter in good health and in good spirit. This is my prayer. Be informed, my lady, that my mother, your sister, has died during the Paschal feast. When I had my mother with me, she was all my family. Since the time when she died, I remained alone, without anyone in a foreign place. Remember then, aunt, as if my mother were still alive, to send me (news) if you find someone. Salute all our family. May the lord keep you in good health for a long peaceful time, my lady.

(ADDRESS ON BACK): Give the letter to Horeina sister of Apollonios of Koptos from Tare daughter of her sister from Apamea.

THE HAND USES LETTERS all separated and inclined to the right. Letter size varies and occasionally becomes very small. The writer in any case seems quite competent.

The letter reveals a good command of Greek and the ability to use it for rhetorical purposes. The writer uses connective particles throughout, a choice vocabulary, and a relatively complex syntax. Phonetic mistakes are few and commonplace.

Tare writes from Syria to her aunt who lives in Koptos. Her letter, the principal aim of which is to announce the death of her mother, also reveals that she did not have other relatives living with her. Without doubting the overall sincerity of the message, it seems clear that the scribe who took down the text was familiar with the topos of death (and life) in a foreign land.

LOCATION OF OBJECT
Paris, Université de Paris-Sorbonne, Institut de Papyrologie, P.Bour.inv. 53.
Plate III in the edition.

BIBLIOGRAPHY
Complete bibliography in Naldini 1998: no. 78.

P.Col. 8.215

Apollonous to Thermouthas
First–second century AD

LOCATION WRITTEN   Unknown
LOCATION OF ADDRESSEE   Philadelphia
LOCATION FOUND   Philadelphia

Greek

Apollonous to Thermouthas her mother, many greetings. Before all things
we pray that you are in good health, along with Apollonarion. I want you
to know that I heard from those who have come to me that you have been
ill; but I was glad to hear that you have gotten better. I ask you earnestly
and beg you, take care of yourself and also of the little girl, so that you may
get through the winter, so that we may find you in good health. We are also
all well. And concerning the Syrian woman, up to now nothing bad. I ask
you if you hear about Thermouthas, send me word. I ask you—it isn't a big
deal—if you find anyone coming down, send me word concerning your
health and the little girl's. I ask you and beg, if it is possible, for you to see
the little girl three times a day. Think that I am near you. I will send you
the earring now, for mine hasn't been made yet. If Esas the son of
Thermouthas finds you a (good) price, sell (it). Also pay us a visit. Receive
from . . .ktor a *salotion*, in which there are twelve dried fish and twenty-two
sesame cakes for the little girl, and give them to her one by one. Gaius send
you his best regards, and Thermouthas, and Isidoros, and Diogenas, and we
greet Apollonarion. We send regards to Ammia and her child. All send
regards to you. Farewell. I send regards to Hera and her children. Tybi 3.

(ADDRESS): Deliver to Philadelphia to Thermouthas.

THE ENTIRE LETTER IS written in the same hand, although the first two lines
are written with a thicker pen point and too much ink. The hand is not a
beginner's, but it is uneven and a bit too detached to be called fluent. There
are several corrections.

The spelling is phonetic to a high degree; unaccented syllables are omitted,
most notably in the writer's name, which is spelled Aplonous. The style is
repetitive and paratactic, with hardly any connectives.

The bulk of the letter is devoted to concerns about the health of the
recipient and particularly of a little girl who has been ill. There are also the
usual notes about goods being sent and goods to be bought. Gonis (2003) has
suggested that Apollonous here is the same as the sender of *P.Mich.* 8.464

(Apollonous to Julius Terentianus); if this is correct, the letter may have been written at Karanis.

NOTE

three times a day: It is not evident whether the frequency requested by Apollonous is the result of the girl's age, an illness, or some other cause unknown to us.

LOCATION OF OBJECT
New York, Columbia University Libraries, Rare Book and Manuscript Library, inv. 318.

BIBLIOGRAPHY
Classical Philology 30 (1935) 143–47 (SB 5.7660); cf. Hombert 1935: 405; Wilcken 1937: 83; Gonis 1997a, 2003.

Fig. 20.   *P.Col.* 8.215. Apollonous to Thermouthas. (New York, Columbia University Libraries, Rare Book and Manuscript Library, inv. 318.)

P.Haun. 2.18

Ptolema to her mother Chenatymis
Third century AD

LOCATION WRITTEN   Unknown
LOCATION OF ADDRESSEE   Unknown
LOCATION FOUND   Unknown (Arsinoite nome?)

Greek

❧ ❧ ❧

Ptolema to Chenatymis her mother, greetings. Before everything I pray that you are well and I embrace you. I want to know, I thank my father for what <he has done> for the seemliness of his people, fittingly for him and the fortune of his whole house; and I make obeisance before the lady Isis. Know that he made me free, wherefore you too should thank him very much. I have received 3 white loaves and fish from Onnophris from Psya. Receive for now from Achilletos (?) son of Ptollarion, 4 leavened loaves. Greet my sister and let me know if she has given birth and what has been born. I pray for your health. I pray for your health. Tybi 21.

(ADDRESS): Deliver from Ptolema to Chenatymis her mother.

❧ ❧ ❧

THE HAND IS A "medium-sized, practised cursive," as the editor describes it, faster and more ligatured than a typical letter hand. The editor thinks that the letter was dictated to a scribe, perhaps because the quality of the handwriting is not matched by that of the Greek.

The Greek is mediocre, not so much because of spelling as because of the loose, paratactic structure, coupled with some incorrect forms. One critical clause seems to have been bungled beyond confident recovery by the omission of a verb.

Ptolema's letter covers a number of subjects, including the receipt of goods, the usual wishes for health, and the expected birth of a child to Ptolema's sister. But the main purpose is to tell Chenatymis how grateful Ptolema is, and Chenatymis should be, to her father, because he has made her *eleuthera,* free. As the editor remarks, one possibility is that we should take this literally: her biological father has manumitted her. Another is that we should take *eleuthera* in its common meaning of "wife," that is, a woman married with the appropriate formalities. In either case we might expect more details, but we do not get any.

NOTES

what <he has done>: The dependent clause seems to be missing a verb, but what we print here is only an attempt to suggest what Ptolema may have intended.

Psya: A place in the Arsinoite nome, probably in the Herakleides division.

LOCATION OF OBJECT
Copenhagen, University of Copenhagen, Institute of Classics, inv. 100.
Plate VI in the edition.

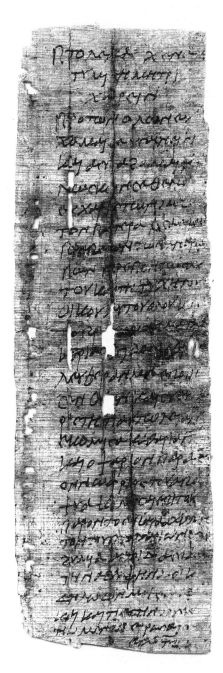

Fig. 21. *P.Haun.* 2.18. Ptolema to her mother Chenatymis. (Copenhagen, University of Copenhagen, Institute of Classics, inv. 100. Photo Adam Bülow-Jacobsen.)

P.Lond. 3.951 verso (p. 213)

To a son-in-law: get a nurse for the baby
Second half of the third century AD

LOCATION WRITTEN   Unknown
LOCATION OF ADDRESSEE   Unknown
LOCATION FOUND   Unknown

Greek

... after she died, they sailed downriver. I hear that you are compelling her to nurse. If she wants, let the infant have a nurse, for I do not permit my daughter to nurse. I greet warmly my sweetest daughter Apollonia and Euphrosyne. I greet Pinna. Your brother Besas greets you warmly, and Syros and his wife (also greet you). Do all you can to come for the Calends, as you wrote.

(ADDRESS): To Rufinus.

THE EDITOR CALLS THE hand "a large, rough, semi-uncial hand," but despite some irregularities and an upward slope it has style (including serifs) and is the work of an experienced writer. It may be the product of someone used to writing fast who is deliberately slowing down for the occasion.

The Greek is correct and characteristic of good letter writing, with one colloquial formation in the last sentence. There is no concluding wish for health.

The name of the writer is lost, and nothing in the remaining text tells us whether the writer was the father-in-law or mother-in-law of the addressee. Wilcken, admitting that he was reading between the lines, opted for the mother-in-law. The writer tells the recipient that she or he does not approve of having the new mother nurse the child; hire a nurse, if nursing is needed. We have included the letter because it is interesting enough for the way of life of women of the wealthier classes that the doubt about authorship deserves to be resolved in favor of inclusion.

NOTE
Calends: Probably refers to the 1 January celebration of the Roman New Year.

LOCATION OF OBJECT
London, British Library, Papyrus 951 (verso). Plate in *P.Lond.* Atlas III, pl. 58.

BIBLIOGRAPHY

Wilcken, *Chrestomathie* 483 (revised text); Hengstl 1978: 189–90, no. 76 (text, German translation, extensive bibliography on wet nursing); *CPGr.* 1, App. B.5 (pp. 198–99) (text, Italian translation). Cf. also *BL* 4.44 and 9.136 on line 9.

P.Mert. 2.82

Nike to Berenike
Late second century AD

LOCATION WRITTEN Unknown
LOCATION OF ADDRESSEE Unknown
LOCATION FOUND Unknown

Greek

Nike to Berenike her lady sister, many greetings. Before all I pray that you are well, and I constantly perform your obeisance before the gods here, praying that you may have life's good things. I wrote you, lady sister, two other times besides this, and perhaps they were not delivered to you. And you wrote to me, "You did not write to me even once." Was I so boorish as not to write you? For we write each time, and perhaps they don't deliver it to you. I am very unwell, whether because of the air I do not know. If I recover, with the gods' help I'll write to you. Greet my mother Athenais and our brother Achillion and everyone by name. I, Sarapammon, greet you, and Hieratike greets you. I pray to the gods that you are well, lady sister.

(ADDRESS): Deliver to Berenike from Nike her sister.

THE WRITER USES A practiced letter hand, with at the start some attempt at the elegance of the chancery style. Because the writer adds his own greeting near the end of the letter, we know his name, Sarapammon. The closing greeting is written in a slightly faster hand, but it is not obviously that of a different writer.

   Sarapammon's Greek is generally confident and good. Spelling errors are few, but there is one apparent omission of a syllable. Connective particles are used conscientiously if not with much flair. One forms the impression that

Sarapammon was doing his best to transform the dictated text into his concept of good letter Greek, even if he could not help the repetitiousness of the contents.

Much of the letter is devoted to trading reproaches over not having written back to previous letters, and as usual there are wishes for health and greetings. The most striking item is Nike's note that she has been unwell and is uncertain whether to attribute her illness to the *aer*, which can refer to what we call air or to the weather or climate. Without knowing the time of year we cannot speculate on the possible influence of the Egyptian seasons.

LOCATION OF OBJECT

Dublin, Chester Beatty Library.

BIBLIOGRAPHY

Turner 1960: 216 (correction to line 16); Youtie 1964: 22–25 = *Scriptiunculae* II 1008–11 (reedition; extensive corrections registered in *BL* 5.67).

P.Mich. 8.510

Taeis( ) to her son
Second or third century AD

LOCATION WRITTEN Apate (Red Sea coast?)
LOCATION OF ADDRESSEE Karanis (?)
LOCATION FOUND Karanis

Greek

༄ ༄ ༄

Taeis . . . to her (son) and lord, many greetings. Before everything I pray for
your health and happiness . . . if you sold . . . of the father . . . brother
Sempronius . . . drachma . . . I got the little papyrus that you told me that I
should receive from . . . my son, write to me about your well-being. I
cannot tell you [long lacuna] of Nemesos because a great plague has been in
Alexandria. As you steered me when you were beside me, again you steer
me now that you are away. I would like you to know that we are fertilizing
the date palms in Apate. If Taseus listens to me, she will receive from me a
basket . . . I fulfilled all the public dues thanks to you. The small papyrus
that you said that I should not give, I did not give it to anyone. You will
give it yourself, I said. I have not found anyone by me among the friends
. . . 3 worthy garments . . . you receive (?) a return gift . . . Nepotianus . . .
4 choes every day . . . Serenus . . . (in the margin) . . . to his mother
because she is worried about him. Your sister and her children salute you.

༄ ༄ ༄

THIS HAND IS VERY clear and attractive with well-spaced lines. The writer was
a professional scribe or secretary.

The letter shows a decent command of Greek in spite of some orthographic
errors and nonstandard spelling of words.

One of the reasons why this woman writes to her son is to remind him
that she has recovered a certain small papyrus but she has not given it to
anybody: the matter is mentioned twice. She also mentions the plague that
ravaged in Egypt in the second and third centuries. She is grateful to her son
because of his assistance, and she keeps him abreast about things at home.

LOCATION OF OBJECT
Ann Arbor, University of Michigan Library, Papyrus Collection, inv. 5404;
now in Cairo, Egyptian Museum.

Isidora to Sarapias on family matters
Third century AD

LOCATION WRITTEN   Alexandria
LOCATION OF ADDRESSEE   Karanis
LOCATION FOUND   Karanis

Greek

∾ ∾ ∾

Isidora to Sarapias her daughter many greetings. Before everything I pray for
your health and that of people in your family and I make obeisance before
the lord Sarapis for you and your son. You know that I am disheartened
because of your brother. I did not receive his *deposita* because I was ill: They
have (certain) days for receiving them. About what you have told me,
"Send a chiton for the little girl," I will send it if I find someone
trustworthy. And with the gods' will I will come to join you. If I have
something, it is yours and your brother's. I heard that you have developed a
disagreement with your husband because of your father. He has not
remained beside me because it is winter. If I come up, I will steer him again.
I am waiting (to see) whether Apollos will soon serve in the army: whether
he is enlisted or not I must come upcountry. Write to me about your well-
being in a hurry. If you want to write a letter, together with Serenus the
brother of Scambys I await for his obeisance at the bay of Sarapis. Salute
the father of the children and the children. Salute Thausarion. Salute your
children. Salute Peeous and Pemes. Onnophris, do not make me blame you
because you're on bad terms with her. Apollos salutes you and your
children.

(ADDRESS ON BACK): give it to Onnophris the priest . . . from Apollos son of
Salibotas.

∾ ∾ ∾

THIS LETTER WAS WRITTEN with a thick pen by a proficient and elegant hand.
About half of the letter is written slowly in a large, upright hand, but the last
ten lines are smaller in size, slightly bent to the right, and written faster. The
same hand wrote the address in clear, fully detached characters.

The letter, which presents a variety of syntactical constructions, shows a
number of iotacisms, lack of sensitivity to vowel quantity, and, more importantly, difficulty in conjugating verbs.

It is winter, and Isidora is in Alexandria. Her daughter to whom she writes
is in Karanis with her family and apparently with Isidora's husband whose
presence has caused some family disagreement. One of her sons has probably
died in military service and another is thinking of enlisting in the army. Isidora

is staying in the house of someone and gives a full address. She is planning to reach her family soon.

Sarapis: Isidora makes obeisance only for Sarapias and her son. But Sarapias had other children, and a little girl is mentioned. Were the other children only females?

deposita: Savings by soldiers.

winter: The reason why Isidora's husband did not remain in Alexandria in winter is obscure.

Apollos: The editor thinks that Isidora's son Apollos has yet to arrive, but this seems unlikely: he salutes people in the letter and his name is given as the sender.

LOCATION OF OBJECT
Ann Arbor, University of Michigan Library, Papyrus Collection, inv. 5805. Plate VIII in ed.prin.

BIBLIOGRAPHY
Cf. *BL* 7.112. On the address of this letter and other addresses of the same type, see Llewelyn 1994: 71–78, particularly 74.

P.Mil. 2.84

Giving a daughter a name
Fourth century AD

LOCATION WRITTEN   Unknown
LOCATION OF ADDRESSEE   Unknown
LOCATION FOUND   Unknown

Greek

∾ ∾ ∾

. . . (I hope that) I find (you and) your husband in good spirits. Andrias and
Nikias greet you, and also little Lampadis. If I had happened to give birth to
a male, I would have given it my brother's name. But now since it is female,
it has been called by your name. I also greet the wife of the *optio* . . . (in the
margin) . . . they banned the . . .

∾ ∾ ∾

THE HAND IS A fluent letter hand of its period, with hints of chancery style,
evidently a professional product.

The orthography of the letter shows the usual characteristics of the period:
Iotacism, third declension accusative in nu, omicron/omega interchange. Still,
the overall impression is one of the ability to write fairly complex constructions.

This letter was taken by its editor and others to have been written by a
woman, but it was instead taken to be the work of a man in the translation
of Hanson and van Minnen published in Rowlandson 1998: no. 226. As the
author's name is lost and there are no gendered forms preserved, this view is
presumably based on the verb *gennesai*, which they render "engender." But
the meaning "give birth to" is also well attested. If we take "my brother" to
refer to the writer's husband, as it so often does, the probability shifts to a
female author. The mention of the *optio* may indicate that we are in military
circles here and perhaps that the naming has taken place in the husband's
absence.

NOTE
optio: A military staff officer.

LOCATION OF OBJECT
Milan, Università Cattolica del Sacro Cuore, Istituto di Papirologia, inv. 49.
Plate in *Aegyptus* 33 (1953).

BIBLIOGRAPHY
Published by Traversa 1953: 64, with facsimile. Reprinted as SB 6.9441. Comments by Hombert 1954: 329, used for reedition in *P.Mil.* 1. Corrections by
D. Hagedorn and J. Bingen in *BL* 6.77. Translation in Rowlandson 1998: 292
no. 226.

P.Oxf. 19

Serapias to Herminos her son
Third century AD (after 208)

LOCATION WRITTEN   Unknown
LOCATION OF ADDRESSEE   Unknown
LOCATION FOUND   Unknown (Arsinoite nome?)

Greek

Serapias to Herminos her son, greetings. At my request, do me the favor of bringing my daughter so that she may give birth, so that I may be grateful to you, by Mesore 1. Do not be worried about the charges for the donkey (?), so that I may be your friend.

THE HAND IS A rough, elementary one, and letter size is very uneven.

The Greek of the letter is as rough as the handwriting, not just a phonetic witness to pronunciation. There are several subordinate clauses, but also several signs of the author's struggle with the language.

This brief note has one purpose, namely, to get Herminos to bring the writer's daughter to her for the delivery of her child. The use of "my daughter" and the lack of seeming connection between Herminos and the pregnant woman suggest that "son" here is not to be taken literally.

NOTES

give birth: For other references to travel to give birth, see chapter 9.

Mesore 1: The placement of this phrase is as awkward in the Greek as in the translation, but it probably goes back to "bring."

donkey: One might also read "wine" here; that would require an abrupt change of topic, but these occur often.

LOCATION OF OBJECT
Oxford, Bodleian Library, Ms. Gr. Class. f 105 (P). Plate in edition, pl. IX.

BIBLIOGRAPHY
Correction to line 5 by Cl. Préaux in *BL* 3.102, commenting also on the spelling ("une prononciation grecque moderne").

P.Oxy. 7.1067

Helene to Petechon about the burial and estate of a brother
Third century AD

LOCATION WRITTEN Unknown
LOCATION OF ADDRESSEE Unknown
LOCATION FOUND Oxyrhynchos

Greek

Helene to Petechon her brother, greetings. You acted badly in not coming
on account of your brother. You let him not take care of his burial. Know
then that a strange woman inherited from him. So go to Theon and tell
him about his storeroom that his storeroom has been sealed up although he
owes nothing, and tell Petechon the son of Polydeukes that "If you are
going to come, come; for Dioskoros is carrying out the liturgy on your
behalf. If you know that you are not going to come, send me your brother
Kastor." I pray for your health.

And I, Alexandros, your father, greet you warmly. Buy me fish from the sea,
and send it by way of a trustworthy man . . .

THE ENTIRE LETTER IS written in a single semicursive hand, including the
greeting and the following lines in which Alexandros, the father of the writer
and recipient, adds a request in his own voice. As the papyrus breaks off before
the end, we do not know if the father added further greetings, and if so whether
it was in a different hand. It is possible, but not likely, that Alexandros wrote
the entire letter.

The language is forceful and direct, with a minimal (but repetitive) use of
linking particles and conjunctions.

NOTES
burial: The translation given here is literal, but it is not clear who the first
"him" can be, or if there is a case error of some sort.

strange woman: Gk. *allotrian*, a woman from outside the family.

Kastor: If the family terms are to be taken literally, Polydeukes had sons
named Kastor, Dioskoros, and Petechon. Kastor, Polydeukes, and Dioskoros
often appear together in families and may indicate twins.

LOCATION OF OBJECT
Toledo, Ohio, Toledo Museum of Art.

BIBLIOGRAPHY
Transl. Schubart 1923: no. 59. BL 8.240 (restoration of 30).

P.Oxy. 10.1299

Slaughtering the pigs and salting the fish
Fourth century AD

LOCATION WRITTEN   Unknown
LOCATION OF ADDRESSEE   Unknown
LOCATION FOUND   Oxyrhynchos

Greek

To my lord son Ision from Psais and Syra, many greetings. Before all else I pray to the lord God for your health and prosperity; Thonis your brother sends you many salutations. Next, since the New Year we have been very ill, but we give thanks to God that we have recovered; and up to the present time we have not killed the pigs. We are expecting you to come. You know that on your account we have not salted any fish, but we salted this year, and, if possible, I will prepare it for your coming. Do as I told you about the. . . of knives and the pepper. Your brothers Horion and Heraiskos salute you, An. . .n and her children salute you, Tachosis and her husband salute you, Triadelphos and his wife and children salute you. I salute Kamokos and his household, I salute Hepsates and his wife with their children, I salute Hatres, Pseke and all our friends by name. I pray for your long-continued health. Hathyr 10.

(ADDRESS): Deliver to Ision . . . from his parents Syra and Psais.

THIS IS A FLUENT and proficient letter hand. It is large and clear with ligatures kept to a minimum. The opening and the final salutations in two lines betray some elegance. The same hand writes the whole letter in an identical style, including final greeting and date.

The letter is correctly written only in the formulaic parts; the rest contains every kind of error. It was dictated to a scribe. Even though both husband and wife sent it, Syra's voice emerges.

Naldini included this letter from a couple to their son (probably to be taken literally) in his corpus of Christian letters, on the basis of the reference to "the lord God." In this interpretation he assigned a nontechnical meaning to *ethukamen* (line 7), which could be understood as "we have sacrificed" (as the original editors did) but which Naldini translates simply as "we have killed." For Christian pig slaughtering see also *P.Oxy.* 56.3866.3, where the term is *choirothusia*, literally "pig sacrifice."

LOCATION OF OBJECT
Northwood, Middlesex, Merchant Taylors' School.

BIBLIOGRAPHY
Naldini 1998: 301–3, no. 76.

P.Oxy. 42.3059
Didyme to Apollonios, affectionately
Second century AD

LOCATION WRITTEN   Unknown
LOCATION OF ADDRESSEE   Unknown
LOCATION FOUND   Oxyrhynchos

Greek

∾ ∾ ∾

Didyme to Apollonios her brother and sun, greetings. Know that I am not seeing the sun because you are out of my sight; for I have no other sun but you. I am grateful to Theonas your brother. Receive what I sent to your father as from Theon the son of Athenaios, the friend . . .

∾ ∾ ∾

THE HANDWRITING IS LARGELY detached, with some use of spaces between words. Letters are well made, with perhaps attempts at elegance; the line level, by contrast, wanders a bit. There are no corrections and no blunders. This is a good letter hand.

The style of expression is notably more literate than most letters, with an indirect statement using the participle, an articular infinitive as object of prep-osition, good use of connectives, and above all the extraordinary expression of affection which occupies most of the surviving papyrus. The pretensions of language thus match those of handwriting.

LOCATION OF OBJECT
Oxford, Papyrology Rooms, Sackler Library.

P.Petaus 29

Didymarion to Paniskos
Late second–early third century AD

LOCATION WRITTEN   Probably Arsinoite nome
LOCATION OF ADDRESSEE   Alexandria
LOCATION FOUND   Probably Arsinoite nome

Greek

Didymarion to Paniskos the most honored, greetings. Before everything I pray that you are well, and I perform your obeisance before the lord Petesouchos. I was very glad to hear that you and your children were safe and what has happened has been wiped away. I want you to know that my daughter is very much bothered by your mother. For she wrote to me, saying, "If she spends another month with me like this, I'll throw myself into the sea." I'm writing to you now since you're like a father to them. Look, what is the truth? So far she did not blame your brother, but I say this so that he may not treat her badly. Greet Harpalinos warmly, and Herais and your children and all your people by name. (Second hand) I pray for your health.

(ADDRESS): Deliver to Alexandria to Paniskos the cavalryman, from Didymarion.

THIS WRITER WAS ABLE to form individual characters rather competently but could not produce an entirely satisfying text. The hand is roughly bilinear and writes with separated letters. The final salutations are written in a slightly different hand but it cannot be entirely ruled out that the writer was the same.

The Greek is straightforward but contains a rare word or two. The orthography includes a number of phonetic spellings but is otherwise unremarkable.

The recipient was a cavalryman, thus a member of a relatively privileged unit in the Roman army. At the moment of writing, he was in Alexandria, and we do not know how this letter happened to be found in the Arsinoite (never sent? brought back?). The daughter whose irritation with Paniskos's mother is so vividly reported was probably also in Alexandria, to judge from her threat to throw herself into the sea, and Paniskos is thus in a good position to check into the situation.

NOTES
most honored: This would normally suggest that we are not dealing with a letter inside a family circle. Here, however, we may have one of the rare examples where *timiotatos* is used in a family setting.

Petesouchos: A crocodile god honored in the Arsinoite nome, which is thus probably the origin of the text (purchased together with Arsinoite papyri).

LOCATION OF OBJECT
Cologne, Institut für Altertumskunde, Papyrussammlung, inv. 323.

P.Rain.Cent. 70

An unexpected sorrow
Third century AD

LOCATION WRITTEN   Unknown
LOCATION OF ADDRESSEE   Hermopolis (?)
LOCATION FOUND   Hermopolis

Greek

∽ ∽ ∽

. . . For, remembering the extreme and unexpected misfortune, I can't sleep even briefly. But you yourself are also a support in it for me, and I am all inflamed in myself, being unable to come to you and lament and weep with you. For perhaps I could have been relieved. I also asked . . . to permit . . . to you . . .

∽ ∽ ∽

THIS FRAGMENT, BROKEN AT top and bottom, is written in a clear, upright letter hand with some flair.

The letter displays in relatively few sentences a considerable vocabulary and some sophistication of construction; the Greek is entirely correct.

That both writer and recipient were women emerges from the feminine forms used, but their names are lost. It is hard to say if this was originally itself intended as a letter of consolation or, perhaps more likely, as a reply to one. It is unusual in its explicit emotionality.

LOCATION OF OBJECT
Berlin, Staatliche Museen, Papyrussammlung, P. 21 964. Plate in edition, Taf. 73.

BIBLIOGRAPHY
Chapa 1998: 87–91 with plate and corrections (lines 7, 8, and 14).

Fig. 22.   *P.Rain.Cent.* 70. An unexpected sorrow. (Berlin, Staatliche Museen, Papyrussammlung, P. 21 964. Photograph courtesy of the Staatliche Museen zu Berlin, Preussischer Kulturbesitz; Ägyptisches Museum und Papyrussammlung. Photo M. Büsing.)

Antonia to her father about a disagreement with her husband
Second century AD

LOCATION WRITTEN   Koptos
LOCATION OF ADDRESSEE   Oxyrhynchos
LOCATION FOUND   Probably Oxyrhynchos

Greek

∾ ∾ ∾

Antonia to Pro. . .ios her father and lord, many greetings. Before all I pray that you are healthy and fortunate, along with my brothers, free from the evil eye, and all our folks. I was going to write to you another time, but Aspasiotes (?) did not let me. Just now when I am writing to you, he is not in Koptos. So I ask you, my lord father, do not be distressed. For I know that you have done all these things to persuade me, and I am very grateful to you. Since the time you have written these things to him, he has stopped being with me. So I ask you, my lord father, and beg you, if you wish, <not?> to try again to persuade me any more. For I know that you want to persuade me about everything, and to inform me well . . . that I may embrace you again . . . and I may revive again . . .

(Fragment B): . . . I greet my lords and brothers, free from the evil eye, by name, and my mother Prokope and her children and all those in the house by name. Kasyllas greets all of you, and his father and Kasyllous and her children and Thais and her daughter and Isidora. I pray that you are well and healthy and more fortunate for many years. Phamenoth 20.

(ADDRESS): Deliver to Oxyrhynchos to . . . her father.

∾ ∾ ∾

WRITTEN ACCORDING TO THE editor in large uncials with a thick pen. The papyrus had earlier been used for another text, which has been washed off. The editor, pointing out that the concluding greeting is written in the same hand as the rest, suggests that Antonia wrote the entire letter; but he also notes the possibility that the entirety was written by someone else. The text itself, however, gives good grounds for supposing that Antonia wrote it herself.

The Greek corresponds to the handwriting: "Extraordinarily vulgar," as the editor put it. The usual vowel interchanges occur throughout, and final nu is dropped several times. Against these may be put the concerted attempt to connect sentences properly and a respectable command of the use of tenses.

Wilcken interpreted this as the letter of an unhappily married woman to her father. Her husband has prevented her from writing to him hitherto, and only his absence from Koptos now has made it possible for her to write. The father had written a stiff letter to the husband, who in consequence has stopped sleeping with her. Now the father is trying to persuade Antonia to leave her husband, but she does not want to and asks her father to stop trying to persuade her. But, Wilcken concludes, this novel might read quite differently if only the text "<not> to try" were better preserved. The placement of "not" inside brackets reflects the uncertainty of the translation.

LOCATION OF OBJECT
Würzburg, Universitätsbibliothek, inv. 2.

PSI 3.177

Isidora to Hermias
Second–third century AD

LOCATION WRITTEN   Unknown
LOCATION OF ADDRESSEE   Oxyrhynchos (?)
LOCATION FOUND   Oxyrhynchos

Greek

Isidora to Hermias her lord brother, very many greetings. Do everything you can to put everything off and come tomorrow; the child (?) is sick. He has become thin, and for 6 days he hasn't eaten. Come here lest he die while you're not here. Be aware that if he dies in your absence, watch out lest Hephaistion find that I've hung myself. . . .

THE LETTER IS WRITTEN on the back of a text in Demotic. The thick pen used by the writer is responsible for the stiff look of the whole. The hand is not completely regular but shows a definite competence. There are very few ligatures and some variation in letter size.

The Greek of the letter is direct and somewhat colloquial, with some phonetic spellings. Overall, however, it is clear as far as it is preserved.

Isidora is afraid that her child is about to die, and she asks Hermias, presumably her husband, to come home at once. She suggests the extremity of her own mental state by warning—how hyperbolically we cannot say—that she might commit suicide if the child dies and Hermias is not there to support her. The letter is evidence against the notion that high child mortality led to a lack of "emotional investment" in young children.

The text continues for another half-dozen lines, of which only the beginnings are preserved, not enough for translation. There are further references to coming and to eating.

child: *P[ai]dion*. Only part of the supposed pi is preserved, and it is very doubtful. The traces of the letter look more like delta, lambda, or even chi, but the first two do not suggest any plausible restorations and chi offers only *ch[oiri]dion*, "piglet" (suggested by G. Parássoglou), which would hardly seem to fit the dramatic language following unless it is a pet name.

LOCATION OF OBJECT
Florence, Biblioteca Medicea Laurenziana, *PSI* 177.

BIBLIOGRAPHY
Textual corrections (lines 4, 6, 9) in *BL* 1.392, 6.173.

SB 3.6264

A woman to Kopres, blaming her daughter-in-law
Second century AD

LOCATION WRITTEN Unknown
LOCATION OF ADDRESSEE Unknown
LOCATION FOUND Probably Arsinoite nome

Greek

To Kopres, greeting. I know your quick temper, but your wife inflames you
when she says every hour that I do not give you anything. When you came
up, I gave you small coins because I received some grain; but this month I
could not find (anything) to give you. I am keeping nothing back from you
because I trust you in everything. Your wife says in fact, "She does not trust
you" . . . (in the left margin) Nobody can love you, for she shapes you
according to her advantage (?) . . .

THE HAND IS CAPABLE and fluent. It was probably not that of the woman in
question but that of someone accustomed to writing documents.

It is very likely that the scribe preserved this woman's words in their entirety. The letter is a spontaneous outpouring of indignant phrases connected
by an excessive number of particles. Orthography is generally observed. The
vocabulary is graphic and personal.

The general tone of this letter suggests that the writer was the mother of
Kopres. In replying to her son, who had complained of being treated unjustly,
this woman puts the blame entirely on her daughter-in-law. The letter is vivid
and somewhat amusing. The editor called it "A Woman's Tongue."

NOTE
When you came up: The editor supposes that *anerchomenos* in lines 8–9 is a
masculine used instead of a feminine, thus referring to the writer. It is probably
better to refer it to Kopres and suppose an error in case.

LOCATION OF OBJECT
London, British Library, Papyrus inv. 1920.

SB 5.7572

Thermouthas to her mother Valerias about her pregnancy
Early second century AD

LOCATION WRITTEN   Unknown
LOCATION OF ADDRESSEE   Unknown
LOCATION FOUND   Philadelphia

Greek

~ ~ ~

Thermouthas to Valerias her mother, very many greetings and always good
health. I received from Valerius the basket with 20 pairs of wheat cakes and
10 pairs of loaves. Send me the blankets at the current price, and nice wool,
4 fleeces. Give these to Valerius. And at the moment I am 7 months
pregnant. And I salute Artemis and little Nikarous and Valerius my lord—I
long for him in my mind—and Dionysia and Demetrous many times and
little Taesis many times and everyone in the house. And how is my father?
Please, send me news because he was ill when he left me. I salute nurse.
Rodine salutes you. I have set her to the handiwork; again I need her, but I
am happy. Phaophi 8.

(ADDRESS ON BACK): Deliver to Philadelphia to Valerias, my mother.

~ ~ ~

THIS VERY INEXPERIENCED HAND could be that of Thermouthas herself. It is a
round, strictly bilinear hand that stands out because of its size. The writer had
difficulty maintaining the lines straight and controlling the ink's flow. The
letters are rigid and "multistroke," and their inclination varies.

Orthography and syntax of the text are in correlation with its clumsy hand.
The letter consists of a string of finite clauses connected by "and". Only once
is a causal clause used. The writer does not employ connective particles. There
are iotacisms and other phonetic errors.

Besides the usual mention of items dispatched and requested and the sending of greetings to various people, this letter contains the news that the woman
writer is pregnant and happy about it. Thermouthas's husband, for whom she
has an unusual display of affection, is in Philadelphia where her mother lives.
Rodine was probably a servant and not her daughter, as the editor supposed.

LOCATION OF OBJECT
Ann Arbor, University of Michigan Library, Papyrus Collection, inv. 188.

BIBLIOGRAPHY
Photo in Rowlandson 1998: 285, pl. 30.

SB 14.11580

Didyme to Thesis
Second century AD, after 138

LOCATION WRITTEN   Unknown
LOCATION OF ADDRESSEE   Unknown
LOCATION FOUND   Theban region

Greek

Didyme to Thesis, greeting. I had prepared myself for coming. Apollos himself told me as he was leaving, "If you are well go to your home to give birth; if you want, write to me and I will come." The bearer of this ostracon told me, "Remain there."

OSTRACON WRITTEN WITH A thick pen. The letters, which are inclined to the right, are all separated and do not show any ligatures. The hand is informal but rather fluent.

This note consists of a series of clauses without any connective particles. The style is mostly oral, and the note ends rather abruptly. The editor produced a normalized version because of the large quantity and variety of errors due to phonetic spelling.

This short note is of uncertain interpretation, mainly because it is unclear how to punctuate it. In writing to Thesis, who may have been her mother, Didyme reports different advice from Apollos and from another man in order to justify the fact that she is waiting to give birth away from home. It is uncertain whether Apollos was her husband, who had to leave for business, or another relative.

LOCATION OF OBJECT
Amiens, private collection of M. Pezin. Plate in ZPE 21 (1976), Taf. Va.

BIBLIOGRAPHY
The whole archive of ostraca to which this piece belongs is supposed to be dated after 138: BL 9.274.

SB 16.12326

Heliodora to her mother Isidora on troubles brought by her daughter
Late third century AD

LOCATION WRITTEN   Unknown
LOCATION OF ADDRESSEE   Unknown
LOCATION FOUND   Unknown

Greek

Heliodora to my mother, many greetings. I am strongly embittered toward you because you did not even deem me worthy of receiving news through a letter of yours. From the time when I went away from you, many troubles have been inflicted upon me by my daughter. See how much she provoked to anger the landlord and his neighbors and then was vexed at him. She stripped me of everything and got hold of my gold jewels and my earrings and gave me a (worn) tunic so that . . . Invoke the god for me so that he would pity me. Do everything to send my brother to me. I am going to Senepta with Hermous. Do not send me . . . . : what I have is enough for me. Salute all my brothers and the people who love you. I pray for your health.

(ADDRESS ON BACK): To my mother Isidora.

THIS IS THE FLUENT hand of a professional. It is clear in spite of some ligatures and is comparatively faster than most letter hands.

This letter is well written with rather correct morphology and syntax and only occasional phonetic mistakes. Connective particles, however, are few, and usually thoughts are expressed in a simple way. The vocabulary is unusual and probably represents this woman's lexicon.

Three generations of women appear in this letter. Heliodora writes to her mother mainly to complain about her own daughter's behavior. She also manifests her annoyance at her mother's failure to correspond with her. She is invoking the presence of one of her brothers, maybe in the hope of salvaging a situation that she may exaggerate.

Ann Arbor, University of Michigan Library, Papyrus Collection, inv. 1363.

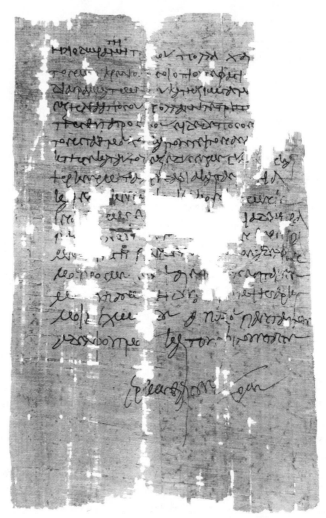

Fig. 23. SB 16.12326. Heliodora to her mother Isidora on troubles brought by her daughter. (Ann Arbor, University of Michigan Library, Papyrus Collection, inv. 1363.)

Plousia to her brother Syros concerning his coming
Second century AD

LOCATION WRITTEN Alexandria
LOCATION OF ADDRESSEE Unknown
LOCATION FOUND Unknown

Greek

∾ ∾ ∾

Plousia to Syros her brother, greeting. I make obeisance for you before the lord Sarapis and the gods who are in the same temple. Learning that you are well, I thanked all the gods. You will say to Par. . . "We did everything so that the person who carries this letter might have his livelihood until you come to us." But if you decide not to come, send us signs because we waited during the strife . . . of the things of the storeroom and knowing for sure that you are well I will be free from worry. And moreover, I am also asking you this, brother . . .

(ADDRESS ON BACK): Deliver to Syros from (Plousia).

∾ ∾ ∾

THE LETTER IS WRITTEN proficiently even though the writer had some occasional problems in controlling the ink flow, particularly at the beginning. The letters are mostly separated, and the lines are well spaced. The whole conveys a sense of rhythm and proportion.

The letter is well written in every respect and observes correct orthography, morphology, and syntax. Phonetic mistakes are also very few.

In writing to her "brother," Plousia mainly entrusts to him a message for someone else that contains an intriguing reference to a *polemos* (strife). This could indicate anti-Jewish riots under Flaccus or later conflicts that ravaged Alexandria.

LOCATION OF OBJECT
Ann Arbor, University of Michigan Library, Papyrus Collection, inv. 1622.

W.Chr. 100

Serenilla to her father Sokrates
Second–third century AD

LOCATION WRITTEN Alexandria
LOCATION OF ADDRESSEE Unknown
LOCATION FOUND Arsinoite nome

Greek

Serenilla to Sokrates her father, many greetings. Before all, I pray that you are well, and I make your obeisance each day before our lord Sarapis and the gods who share the temple. I want you to know that I am alone. Keep in mind, "My daughter is in Alexandria," so that I may know that I have a father, so that they may not see me as someone without parents. And the man bringing you the letter, give him another concerning your health. And I greet my mother and my brothers and Sempronius and his people.

(ADDRESS ON BACK): Deliver it to Sokrates son of Skiphas from his daughter Serenilla through her brother Sarapammon.

IT IS POSSIBLE—ALBEIT NOT certain—that Serenilla wrote this letter herself. This letter's hand betrays all the usual uncertainties facing someone who was not writing on a daily basis: varying letter size, corrections, irregular ink dipping, and some degeneration toward the end. Occasional multistroke letters show that the writer was getting tired.

The letter contains the usual phonetic spellings, particularly iotacisms. Otherwise it is written in standard epistolary formulas, except for the central section.

Serenilla is at pains to point out that she is alone in Alexandria and to ask her parents to keep her in mind, thinking that to the outside world she looks like an orphan. It is curious that she refers to the person bringing the letter in impersonal terms, but the address identifies the bearer as her brother Sarapammon. Even if "brother" is not to be taken literally, it may indicate that the letter was written before Serenilla knew who would deliver it.

NOTE

Sarapis: This phrase is in many letters the sole evidence for having been written in Alexandria. Here we have explicit indication of Alexandrian origin immediately afterward in the letter.

LOCATION OF OBJECT

Berlin, Staatliche Museen, Papyrussammlung, inv. 6901.

BIBLIOGRAPHY

BGU 2.385; Schubart 1923: no. 74.

W.Chr. 499

Senpamonthes to Pamonthes about her mother's mummy
Second–third century AD

LOCATION WRITTEN   Unknown
LOCATION OF ADDRESSEE   Unknown
LOCATION FOUND   Unknown

Greek

Senpamonthes to Pamonthes her brother, greetings. I sent you the body of Senyris my mother, prepared for burial, with a tag around the neck, through Gales father of Hierax in his private boat, the shipping costs having been paid in full by me. There is an identification mark on the mummy: a linen shroud is on the outside, rose-colored, with her name written on the abdomen. I pray for your health, brother. Year 3, Thoth 11.

(ADDRESS): To Pamonthes son of Moros from Senpamonthes his sister.

THE HAND IS A well-formed semicursive. The greeting at the end is written in the same hand but more rapidly. This was a practiced writer, who wrote the body in a letter hand for the sake of intelligibility for the reader, not because of inability to write yet more cursively.

The language is fluent but not terribly graceful, with the entirety of the content expressed in two complex sentences. The writer was not, however, a master of the Greek system of case endings, and there are several blunders. The second sentence seems to end with an awkward construction most charitably seen as an accusative absolute.

Senpamonthes tells Pamonthes that her mother's body has had its proper funerary preparation, has had a mummy label attached (thousands of these survive, made of wood), and has been shipped by a friend's private boat. Pamonthes will be able to identify the body by the rose-colored cloth in which it is wrapped, with her name on it. The letter is important evidence for the way the funerary practices of Egypt worked in this period and helps to illuminate the use of mummy labels.

NOTE

my mother: This may mean that she was not also Pamonthes's mother (in which case "brother" is probably not to be taken literally and may indicate that he is Senpamonthes's husband), but that is not a necessary inference, as use of the pronouns is not always consistent.

LOCATION OF OBJECT

Paris, Bibliothèque Nationale, *P.Paris* 18bis.

BIBLIOGRAPHY

P.Paris 18b, with pl. XXII; reedited as *W.Chr.* 499 (on the original). Reprinted in *Pap.Lugd.Bat.* 19, pp. 230–31 (on the basis of the plate). Translation and plate in Borg 1998: 11, with Abb. 11.

2. BUSINESS MATTERS

P.Bad. 2.35

Johanna to Epagathos, full of reproaches
AD 87

LOCATION WRITTEN   Unknown
LOCATION OF ADDRESSEE   Ptolemais Hermeiou
LOCATION FOUND   Unknown

Greek

∾ ∾ ∾

Johanna to Epagathos her own, many greetings. You acted badly in changing and going back on your agreement which acknowledged me as the owner of 20 drachmas and the interest. Let me have the principal. I am astonished that you have become faithless. Do not compel me, then, . . . This is a sign of unkindness. You will also tell Taesis, "Don't you wish yet to include Epagathos as a free man?" Concerning Pheragathos, let him not neglect, if he can, to bring us both (his?) son and . . . Know that Elpis has not yet been found . . . Come with Taesis without anger, if she comes up. Don't neglect to bring me the other . . . Know that . . . is paying 1 drachma and Anthousa – obols, like Taesis. Know that I have not received the bronze from Prosdokimos. Bring us doums. Pheragathos and Taesis and Lysis greet you. Anthousa greets you. Greet Philadelphos and all his people. Farewell. Above all, take care of yourself so that you may be well.

Year 7 of Emperor Caesar Domitian Augustus Germanicus, Choiak 19.

(ADDRESS): To Ptolemais Hermeiou. Give to the —phylax for delivery to Epagathos.

∾ ∾ ∾

THE WRITER FORMS LETTERS with difficulty, one stroke at a time. Letter shapes are irregular, and the lines wobble up and down. The awkwardness of the handwriting combines with relatively modest damage to the surface and the author's less than flawless Greek to make understanding difficult in a number of passages.

The language of the letter is generally very abrupt, and it is at times hard to follow whatever flow of thought connects the sentences. The spelling is largely phonetic, with a large ration of interchange of o-sounds, many iotacisms, and the like. The writer's vocabulary, however, is extensive.

The writer's interest seems above all concentrated on Epagathos's reneging in a loan transaction, which he seems to have carried out in his name but with a side agreement acknowledging that it was with her money. Now he insists it is all his, and she asks at least to recover the principal.

NOTES

tell Taesis: We take what follows as direct discourse, quoting what Epagathos is to say to Taesis on Johanna's behalf. It is not clear if Epagathos has not yet been manumitted or if there is some reason that he is not being treated as such.

Ptolemais Hermeiou: A Greek city in the Thebaid, not far from Panopolis, founded by Ptolemy I.

LOCATION OF OBJECT
Heidelberg, Institut für Papyrologie, inv. 81.

BIBLIOGRAPHY
Olsson 1925: no. 51 (Greek text, translation, notes); C.Pap.Jud. 2.424 (Greek text, translation, notes). Cf. BL 2.2.174, 3.255, 4.103, 6.33 with various notes on the text, esp. from S. Kapsomenos.

Fig. 24. P.Bad. 2.35. Johanna to Epagathos, full of reproaches. (Heidelberg, Institut für Papyrologie, inv. 81. Photograph courtesy of Papyrussammlung des Instituts für Papyrologie der Universität Heidelberg.)

P.Mert. 1.32

Allous to Morion about land
Early fourth century AD

LOCATION WRITTEN Unknown
LOCATION OF ADDRESSEE Unknown
LOCATION FOUND Unknown

Greek

ↄ ↄ ↄ

Allous to Morion, greeting. Up to today I have, with the help of your mother, fulfilled the pledges on your behalf. If then you wish to make sure of buying it, give an installment to Libike (or the Libyan woman) through her servants. And copies of the securities have been made for you. So if you don't return, you're going to complain. For there are certain people who have been after the place.

ↄ ↄ ↄ

THE HAND IS A fluent semicursive, probably professional.

The style is colloquial and direct; spelling is very phonetic. The writer certainly had not had any extensive training in classical orthography.

The contents are an urgent matter of confidential business. A piece of land is for sale, and handling the transaction seems to be in Allous's hands. The details are unclear, both because of ambiguity in Allous's writing and because information known to both of them was, as usual, omitted. What is clear is that if Morion does not get the needed cash to Allous quickly, other interested buyers will snap up the property. Perhaps a deposit had been paid to hold an option on the property for a time. Morion's mother, thus probably Allous's mother-in-law, was also helping her. It is possible that the two women were on the country estate, near which the property in question was located, and Morion in the city. The close suggests that Morion's presence will be needed to complete the deal.

LOCATION OF OBJECT
Dublin, Chester Beatty Library.

P.Mich. 3.221

Ploutogenia to her mother concerning financial matters
Ca. AD 296

LOCATION WRITTEN   Alexandria
LOCATION OF ADDRESSEE   Unknown
LOCATION FOUND   Philadelphia

Greek

Ploutogenia to my mother, many greetings. Before everything I pray that
you are in good health before the Lord God. It is 8 months already since I
came to Alexandria but you did not write to me a single letter. Again you
do not treat me like your daughter (but) like your enemy. The bronze
vessels that you have by you, give them to Atas and then get them back
from the same Atas full. And write to me how much money you received
from Koupineris and do not be neglectful. Take care of the irrigation
machine and of your cattle, do not be idle and do not wish to trouble . . . If
your daughter is going to get married, write to me and I come. I salute you
and your children. I also salute those who love us each by name. I pray that
you are well always.

(ADDRESS ON BACK): Give it to my mother from her daughter Ploutogenia.

THE LETTER WAS WRITTEN by a professional scribe who was familiar with the
chancery style. The characters are upright, show a good number of ligatures,
but are remarkably clear. Even though the chancery style is not present in all
its formality, the hand is quite stylized.

The letter mostly consists of commands in the imperative, besides a relative
and a conditional clause. Connective particles are very few. The scribe took
down what this woman told him without much reworking.

The letter is part of the Paniskos archive. Ploutogenia is in Alexandria and
writes to her mother with regard to some financial matter and things concerning the household. The initial complaint about not receiving letters is
much more than a formulaic expression and leads to accusations that her
mother does not treat her well. There is no mention of Ploutogenia's husband
and daughter. Like other letters in this archive, this shows that this woman
was strong and somewhat independent.

NOTES
Lord God: In line 3 Ploutogenia uses the Christian formula. Her husband
Paniskos, who does the same in *P.Mich.* 3.216 and 219, employs a pagan
formula in *P.Mich.* 3.214.

your daughter: It is peculiar that Ploutogenia calls those who were presumably her sister and siblings "your daughter, your children." Did her mother remarry?

bronze vessels . . . full: The meaning may be "get them all back" rather than "get them back filled."

LOCATION OF OBJECT
Ann Arbor, University of Michigan Library, Papyrus Collection, inv. 1362.

BIBLIOGRAPHY
BL 6.81. For the archive of Paniskos, to which this text belongs, see Winter 1927: 73–74 and plate XXVI. Text reprinted as M. Naldini 1998: 121–23 no. 17.

P.Oxy. 1.114

Eunoia about pawned goods
Second–third century AD

LOCATION WRITTEN   Unknown
LOCATION OF ADDRESSEE   Unknown
LOCATION FOUND   Oxyrhynchos

Greek

∾ ∾ ∾

. . . Now take care of redeeming my goods deposited with Sarapion. They are pledged for 2 mnas. I have paid the interest up to Epeiph at the rate of a stater per mna. An incense-colored Dalmatian hooded cloak, an onyx-colored Dalmatian hooded cloak, a tunic and a white hooded cape with true purple border, a striped facecloth of Laconian type, a garment of purple linen, 2 armlets, a necklace, a coverlet, a (statue of) Aphrodite, a cup, a large tin flask and a wine jar. At Onetor's, get the 2 bracelets. They are pledged for eight "hands" since last Tybi at the rate of a stater per mna. If the money is not sufficient because of the carelessness of our lady Theagenis, if then the money is not sufficient, sell the armlets to make up the money. Greet Aia and Eutychia warmly. I pray for your health. And Alexandra. Xanthilla greets Aia and all her people.

(ADDRESS): . . . from Eunoia.

∾ ∾ ∾

THIS LETTER, OF WHICH the beginning is lost, is written in well-formed letters slanting to the right, which give the impression of fluency. Most of the letters are detached except for some superficial ligatures: a typical letter hand. The close and added final greetings are in the same hand as the body of the letter, but slightly faster and less neat. There are two corrections, a letter overwritten and a syllable written too soon and canceled.

The language is simple and blunt, a series of instructions with no flourishes. Connective particles are absent except for the *oun* used to emphasize the repetition of the phrase "if the money is not sufficient." The list of goods at Sarapion's is simply given, outside any sentence structure. The overall effect is thus jerky. Spelling and syntax, however, are generally good, and use of the verb forms shows some sophistication.

Eunoia writes to a correspondent, presumably in Oxyrhynchos. Except for the greetings at the end, the entire contents concern goods pawned at two pawnshops. The goods are all luxury garments, metal vessels, and jewelry; one lot is worth two hundred drachmas, perhaps half a year's income or more for most people. The interest rate is 48 percent, four times the legal maximum on loans of money.

NOTES

Aphrodite: See Burkhalter 1990: 51–60. The statue is presumably made out of metal rather than terracotta.

eight hands: The meaning of the expression is unknown. An error for "mnas" is possible, but the amount would be very large.

And Alexandra: Another greeting, added as an afterthought, as is the following sentence.

LOCATION OF OBJECT

Windsor, England, Eton College Library, Myers Museum inv. ECM 2197.

BIBLIOGRAPHY

BL 1.316 (line 7); *BL* 2.2.93 (same correction). Translations in *Sel.Pap.* 1.131; Rowlandson 1998: 257–59, no. 191.

P.Oxy. 6.932

Thais to Tigrios on business
Late second or early third century AD

LOCATION WRITTEN Unknown
LOCATION OF ADDRESSEE Unknown
LOCATION FOUND Oxyrhynchos

Greek

Thais to her Tigrios, greetings. I wrote to Apolinarios to come to Petne so
that he might measure out (the wheat?). Apolinarios will tell you how the
deposits and the taxes (stand); the name (is to be) whatever he tells you. If
you come, release six artabas of vegetable seed to the sacks under seal, so
that they may be ready, and if you can come up to check the donkey (do
so). Sarapodora and Sabinos greet you. Don't sell the piglets without me.
Farewell.

THIS BUSINESS LETTER IS written in a slanting and semiligatured hand with
pretensions to elegance. If not professional in the sense of being the product
of someone who earned a living by writing, it is nonetheless of the quality
one finds in teachers' models. The writer uses abbreviation several times, twice
to end a line neatly; diaeresis appears a half-dozen times.

The language of the letter is entirely lacking in elegance. Although it is
orthographically accurate apart from iotacism, it is extremely abrupt and at
various points omits a direct object, a verb, and the apodosis of a conditional
sentence. The overall impression is of a skilled writer taking down exactly
what is being said, rendering it faithfully but not attempting to redraft it.

Thais writes to a member of her staff about various matters of estate business. She is perhaps writing from a country estate at Petne to an agent currently in Oxyrhynchos but evidently likely to be traveling to properties outside
it. The third person mentioned, Apolinarios, is probably also a steward of
some sort. The tenor of the letter is that of a well-to-do landowner.

NOTES
her Tigrios: Gk. *idios*, for Latin *suus*, used of dependents in business letters
(see Cuvigny 2002: 148).

Petne: A village northeast of Oxyrhynchos, on the Nile side of the nome.

measure out: The absence of an object suggests that the year's main
payment of taxes after harvest is intended—a substantial task for a large
landowner.

name: Tax receipts were drawn up for credit to a "name" or account. One household might deal with multiple names because property belonged to one or another member of the family. Apolinarios is to determine which account a payment is to be credited to.

release: The text is brief to the point of obscurity, but Thais probably means that the seed is to be released from storage into sacks for transport.

LOCATION OF OBJECT
Urbana, University of Illinois, inv. GP 932.

BIBLIOGRAPHY
Rowlandson 1998: 236–37, no. 173(a) (translation).

P.Oxy. 14.1765

Kousenna to Apammon
Third century AD

LOCATION WRITTEN   Unknown
LOCATION OF ADDRESSEE   Unknown
LOCATION FOUND   Oxyrhynchos

Greek

Kousenna to Apammon the *tarsikarios*, greetings. Eight letters to you, and not once did you deign to write to me about what you received. Because of this I did not send you the second (shipment). Hurry even now to write me so that I may send you the remainder. I am sending back to you again the three staters which you sent me. For if you don't send me the whole, send me the remnants. I greet Syra and Silvanus your son and the priestess with your children, Syra. To you the *tarsikarios*: if you find anyone, send me Silvanus. Receive with the letter sixty fava beans and 4 pieces of papyrus for the head, and you and the priestess apportion (them).

(ADDRESS): From Kousenna to Apammon the *tarsikarios*.

A COMPLETE LETTER, WRITTEN in a slanting hand, which tends to run uphill to the right. The letters are partially ligatured and well practiced if a bit awkward at times.

The text is an odd combination of graceless but colloquial directness and occasional sophistication. The writer uses crasis and connectives, but writes a definite article in place of relative in 10. There are several corrections sprinkled through the letter. The use of diacritics combined with the particles and a good vocabulary suggests an educated person, but the level of carelessness is considerable.

The writer's exasperation at writing her ninth letter to Apammon, a weaver of Tarsus cloth, is palpable. She had sent him a shipment of something, whether raw materials or something unrelated (food?) cannot be said. But because of his failure to acknowledge receipt, she has held back the second batch. The remainder, apart from greetings, concerns the repayment of money (12 drachmas), a request to Apammon that he send Silvanus, and (as an afterthought on the back) the information that with the letter were going some fava beans and some papyrus.

NOTES

tarsikarios: A specialized weaver in a particular type of cloth associated with the Cilician city of Tarsus.

fava beans: Probably the pods are meant; otherwise the number seems too small to concern oneself with.

pieces of papyrus: Gk. *chartarion,* here probably referring to pieces used to wrap unguents for anointing the head.

LOCATION OF OBJECT
Wellesley, Mass., Wellesley College Library.

P.Oxy. 33.2680

Arsinoe to Sarapias
Second–third century AD

LOCATION WRITTEN Unknown
LOCATION OF ADDRESSEE Unknown
LOCATION FOUND Oxyrhynchos

Greek

Arsinoe to Sarapias her sister, greetings. Since Achillas was sailing downstream, I thought it necessary to greet you in writing. Concerning the matter that you wrote me was finished, please give it to Achillas my brother so that he may bring it to me. Receive from the same Achillas a jar of pickle . . . If the roads are firm, I shall go at once to your tenant and ask him for your rents—if indeed he will give them to me; for you should have sent me a letter for him. All the same, if instead you wrote to him in advance to give them to me, I shall go off and collect them. Greet Polykrates and all your people. Poleta and Demetrous greet you. If you want anything sent to you, write me and I will send it immediately to you. I topped up the jar of pickle because it had sunk. The bottom layers are better than the top ones. Farewell. Choiak 27.

(ADDRESS): From Arsinoe to Sarapias the wife of Polykrates.

THE LETTER IS WRITTEN in a well-made, partly ligatured hand. The hand of the subscription is more rapid than that of the text. The main hand may be that of a secretary or of a skilled family member, and the subscription that of Arsinoe.

The language is as stylish as the hand, with just two orthographic errors, an appropriate use of particles, complex sentence structure, and a good vocabulary. The use of verb tenses is precise and educated.

The bulk of the letter consists of the usual requests and dispatches and greetings. But the middle is devoted to a striking statement that Arsinoe will go collect Sarapias's rents from her tenant, or at least will try to; she gently reproaches Sarapias for not having given her a written authorization to show the farmer. But she then suggests that perhaps Sarapias has written directly to the tenant. We thus get a notable picture of Arsinoe's willingness to travel and to act as a rent collector, as well as a suggestion that the tenant is capable of reading or having read to him a letter from the landowner.

LOCATION OF OBJECT
Oxford, Papyrology Rooms, Sackler Library.

BIBLIOGRAPHY
Rowlandson 1998: 235–36, no. 172.

PSI 9.1080
Diogenis to Alexandros
Third century AD (?)

LOCATION WRITTEN   Unknown
LOCATION OF ADDRESSEE   Oxyrhynchos (?)
LOCATION FOUND   Oxyrhynchos

Greek

Diogenis to Alexandros her brother, greetings. As you instructed Taamois about a house for us to move into, we found one which we shall let go before we move over to Agathinos. The house is by the Ision, next to the house of Claudianus . . . We are moving there in Phamenoth. I want you to know that I received from Bottos a hundred and twenty drachmas. I sent you . . . of purple dye by Sarapiakos. The letter which you forwarded to me to deliver to Bolphios, I have delivered. Many greetings to little Theon. Eight toys have been brought for him by the woman whom you told me to greet, and I have forwarded these to you . . .

(ADDRESS): To Aurelius Alexandros. To Bolphios . . .

THE WRITER WAS A professional used to writing documents. This hand is relatively fast and bent to the right and shows a good number of ligatures that alter the letter shapes. The overall appearance is attractive and stylized.

Apart from minor spelling variations, the letter is written in reasonably correct Greek, with some attempt to avoid abrupt transitions.

The contents are a typical mixture of news and greetings; most interesting is the information about house hunting.

NOTE
Aurelius Alexandros: The presence of Aurelius indicates a date after 212.

LOCATION OF OBJECT
Florence, Biblioteca Medicea Laurenziana, *PSI* 1080.

BIBLIOGRAPHY
Text and English translation at *Sel.Pap.* 1.132. For the address cf. *BL* 10.246.

SB 14.11588

Aria to her son Dorotheos
Late fourth century AD

LOCATION WRITTEN   Unknown
LOCATION OF ADDRESSEE   Unknown
LOCATION FOUND   Unknown

Greek

My lord son . . . Aria his mother, greetings. First of all, I pray to the divine Providence before God that my letter is given to you as you are healthy and prosperous. And I wish you to know that of the 1,000 myriads (of denarii) I did not get anything from . . . nianos except the 500 myriads in Alexandria. And as you said to get the 200 myriads from the apprentice of Ameinias, I did not find him. And about the 500 myriads, would you get them and send them? You know where I got them. And I went to the bleacher for the 3 and 1/2 pounds. And as you said, "Go to my sister Maria and she will give them to you," I went and she gave me nothing. So, what does go right for me? So know this too, know that the orphan child is in my house and I also need to spend for myself. And about the two and a half pounds—2 1/2—I owe nothing except the pay for the bleacher. But if I owe something, I pay with this stuff of mine. And in fact I have sold the same linen stuff at 10 myriads per pound. I am amazed how you neglect me. I salute you all each by name.

(Back): NN and all of us each by name salute you.

(ADDRESS): Deliver to Dorotheos son of Philippos from his mother Aria.

THIS HAND GIVES AN impression of clumsiness, but the letters are well formed, and the writer was able to pen a long text with relative ease. Some letters, however, are retraced, and there is a general lack of rhythm and proportion. The hand becomes worse toward the end. The lines all slope downward.

This letter shows a rather simple syntax, consisting of a series of short clauses joined by *kai*. The style is often oral and spontaneous and contains direct speech and questions. The orthography leaves much to be desired.

This letter comes from a Christian milieu. The impression that it conveys is that either Aria was encountering lots of mishaps or she was very prone to complaining. The series of setbacks that she recounts one after the other, capped by the presence of an orphan child in her house and compounded with her desire to show her son that she is following his instructions and pays all her debts, has its humorous sides. Since she is actually rendering a careful account of her financial problems, she was probably handling family finances.

While she accuses her son of neglecting her, she makes sure to disclose to him that she is in need of money for herself.

LOCATION OF OBJECT
Ann Arbor, University of Michigan Library, Papyrus Collection, inv. 337.

SB 16.12981
Isis to her brother Serapion
Second–third century AD

LOCATION WRITTEN   Unknown
LOCATION OF ADDRESSEE   Unknown
LOCATION FOUND   Unknown

Greek

∾ ∾ ∾

Isis to Serapion her brother, many greetings. I make obeisance for you every day before the local gods. (Know) from me that Philon did not (give me) a single artab of wheat . . . 20 drachmas (or: that owing 1 artab of wheat, he [someone] . . . 20 drachmas) and know that it is all right. Send me for the expense . . . I sail up to you. Come to us as soon as possible. I gave 12 drachmas for fodder. Salute warmly your father. Your son salutes you warmly and also (your) mother and my mother and sister . . .

(ADDRESS ON BACK): Give it to Serapion from (Isis).

∾ ∾ ∾

APPARENTLY SERAPION REUSED THE back of the letter sent by Isis. This is an "evolving" hand. The letters, which are separated, are jerky and rigid even though they are not badly formed individually and even aim at some elegance. The inexperienced writer got tired toward the end, and the letters became larger.

A quick and practical letter expressed with simple and short phrases with no connective particles. The writer was familiar with Greek and did not use too many phonetic spellings but was interested only in efficient, unadorned prose.

There is nothing compelling in the letter to make one view "brother" Serapion as the "partner or friend" of Isis, as the editor suggests. He may easily have been her husband who was paying a visit to his father and maybe discharging some business. Isis was home with other relatives and kept him informed about the state of their affairs.

LOCATION OF OBJECT
Ann Arbor, University of Michigan Library, Papyrus Collection, inv. 1026.

BIBLIOGRAPHY
For the date, see *BL* 10.217, arguing that because of the high price of the wheat the letter should be dated to 191–192, 194–198, or 205–209.

3. LEGAL MATTERS

BGU 3.827

Zoe to Apollinarios: financial and judicial matters
Second–third century AD

LOCATION WRITTEN   Pelusium
LOCATION OF ADDRESSEE   Unknown
LOCATION FOUND   Arsinoite nome

Greek

Zoe to Apollinarios her brother, greetings. (I make) obeisance on your
behalf before Zeus Kasios. I want you to know, that I found the wife of
Acharis and I gave her all the written material; and I am waiting to receive
my own and to set out—and the unsettled business of Gemellos, so that I
may collect (them). I found (her) with her guardian, but they say that . . .
through the epistrategos, because you can . . . from the epistrategos and
write me. There is not yet any money with the guardian. If I see that
nothing has happened, I am leaving. Look now, this is the third letter I'm
writing you. Look after my house, shake out the wool and the clothing. I've
been sick since I arrived in Pelusium. Serenos greets you; Petronius and his
sister and Hermione greet you. Greet Charitous and her sister-in-law.
(second hand) Farewell. (first hand) Phaophi 14.

(ADDRESS): Deliver to Apollinarios from Petronius the *dromadarius*, from
Pelusium.

IN SPITE OF THE editor's claim that the handwriting of this letter is unpracticed,
the writer seems capable enough. The thick pen he used is mostly responsible
for the uneven and coarse overall look. The final greetings and the date are
supposedly by a second hand, but it is not sure whether the writer is the same.

The language of the letter is colloquial, with numerous phonetic spellings.
The writer omits the verb in the *proskynema* sentence and uses the wrong case
with *meta* ("with") on two occasions.

Zoe is in Pelusium, where she has fallen sick. Nonetheless she is actively pursuing some financial and judicial business, part of which concerns a woman. It is interesting both that Zoe takes such an active role and that the other woman's *kyrios* (guardian, often seen as a pure formality) is so directly involved with the woman's money. Here, as so often, "brother" in the address may indicate that Apollinarios is Zoe's husband.

NOTES

Zeus Kasios: The local god of Pelusium.

Petronius the *dromadarius*: He may have written the body of the letter and the address for Zoe. The title indicates that he was a soldier riding a one-humped camel, probably involved in patrolling the desert roads east of Pelusium.

LOCATION OF OBJECT

Berlin, Staatliche Museen, Papyrussammlung, P. 7150.

BIBLIOGRAPHY

BL 1.70 (on lines 1 and 30); 7.15 (on line 18).

To Sarapion
Ca. AD 41–67

LOCATION WRITTEN Unknown
LOCATION OF ADDRESSEE Unknown
LOCATION FOUND Unknown

Greek

. . . I therefore write to you so that you may be informed. But we have not yet done anything. If our opponent goes up, keep an eye on him. For I am afraid that he may give up, for he is disgusted. Concerning Sarapas my son, he has not stayed with me at all, but went off to the camp to join the army. You did not do well counselling him to join the army. For when I said to him not to join, he said to me, "My father said to me to join the army." Concerning Epaphroditos, he is here with me. Please—I have lentils in the middle house, send this to me and a chous of radish oil, so that I may have monthly provisions here. For I'm not disturbed, but remain of good courage. And if the allotment is inundated, hurry and sow it well. I informed you about the crops . . . a letter to the prefect . . . us, so that it may be paid to the treasury and the balance given for seed.

Year .. of Claudius Caesar Augustus Germanicus Imperator, Mesore 22.

(Back): Greet your mother and Demetrios and his children. Greet . . . his mother and Dionysia and her children and . . . and her mother.

(ADDRESS): — of Demetrios, to Sarapion her father.

THE TEXT IS WRITTEN competently in a large hand that is not particularly attractive. The letters are mostly separated, well formed, and slightly bent to the right, which is indicative of a relative speed of execution. The hand is probably the same throughout.

The language of the letter is straightforward, competent business prose, with a few connectives and some dependent clauses, but otherwise little adornment. There are a few phonetic spellings and some omissions and corrections, but overall the impression is one of competence. There are several oral turns of phrase among the constructions.

The writer deals with various sorts of business, reproaching Sarapion strongly for what she sees as bad advice to Sarapas.

NOTES
give up: It is not evident why the writer should worry about an opponent's giving up.

treasury: The granary which held public grain.

The date is 15 August of a year between 41 and 67, cf. *BL* 11.24 (it would be possible to restore Nero before Claudius).

LOCATION OF OBJECT
Berlin, Staatliche Museen, Papyrussammlung, P. 11050.

BIBLIOGRAPHY
Olsson 1925: no. 38 (text, translation, and notes, with a correction to line 16); cf. *BL* 1.97 (various corrections); 8.40 (about the date formula).

Fig. 25. *BGU* 4.1097. To Sarapion. (Berlin, Staatliche Museen, Papyrussammlung, P. 11050. Photograph courtesy of the Staatliche Museen zu Berlin, Preussischer Kulturbesitz, Ägyptisches Museum und Papyrussammlung. Photo M. Büsing.)

O.Crum 133

Thanasia tries to resolve a debt
Sixth–eighth century AD

LOCATION WRITTEN   Unknown
LOCATION OF ADDRESSEE   Unknown
LOCATION FOUND   Unknown

Coptic

∾ ∾ ∾

Thanasia writes to her lord the priest Apa Ananias and Apa Bartholomaios.
Be so kind, since I left the village, three years ago now, the village scribe
said to me, "Go north." I went. It happened that I came over to the village
because I was in the vicinity. Now then, he has arrived. Be so kind as to ask
him, "Why do you detain her?" Indeed, he said, "I wanted the deed of the
house." I drew up the deed (?), but he did not take it, nor did he dissolve
the surety. Be so kind as to ask and beg him about me. Indeed, I have paid
except for a —. I gave it to you. Good health in the Lord, Ananias and
Bartholomaios.

∾ ∾ ∾

OSTRACON; NO DESCRIPTION OF the handwriting is available.

The style of the letter is very oral, with clauses strung together as the writer
narrates the events that have led her to write. The spelling is generally good.

The precise events behind this letter are unclear, but it looks as if Thanasia
(a short form of Athanasia) was either indebted to an unnamed person or was
surety for someone else's debt, which has caused her continuing problems even
though, she says, she has already paid almost everything. She asks the priests
for their help in resolving the dispute.

LOCATION OF OBJECT
Formerly collection of Lady Longmore; present location unknown.

O. *Theb* D14 (p. 62)

A Demotic letter
AD 92–93

LOCATION WRITTEN   Unknown
LOCATION OF ADDRESSEE   Unknown
LOCATION FOUND   Thebes

Demotic

Senbouchis the daughter of Senchonsis (?) greets —— the son of Phthoumonthes here before Amon the great god, who shall cause [me to see] thy face in all prosperity (?) before everything [on earth]. There is nothing to reproach me with up to today (?). I . . . I pray you to let them send . . . southward on account of what has happened (?). I am in trouble (?) [with regard to?] Psenchonsis son of Teos (?). Give . . . here to the 'ysh-priest (?); inquire in [every ?] place (?) . . . Written in the 12th year of Domitian . . .

OSTRACON, BROKEN AT LEFT with the ends of lines (Demotic is written from right to left).

The large number of question marks in the translation reflects the editor's uncertainty about the correct interpretation of some elements of the letter. The opening greeting conveys the sense that the Greek *proskynema* formulas do, mentioning the local god. This woman appears to be defending herself against some charge in the next sentence, but later admits that a dispute has arisen on another front and appears to be asking for something, perhaps money to help her discharge a debt.

LOCATION OF OBJECT
Toronto, Royal Ontario Museum.

BIBLIOGRAPHY
Plate in original edition, pl. VII.

O.Vind.Copt. 257 = O.CrumST 378

Taouaou complains about pigeon taking
Sixth–eighth century AD

LOCATION WRITTEN   Unknown
LOCATION OF ADDRESSEE   Unknown
LOCATION FOUND   Unknown

Coptic

I, Taouaou the daughter of Joachim, write to my father Zacharias: At the
time when Joachim came to settle, he received a pair of coverlets and a
half-trimesion from Georgios. He deposited the . . . as a pledge with him.
Well, for two years he caught pigeons (there?). The first year, he caught 60
pair (?), the second year he caught 70 pair. He filled a . . . I don't know
how many he took. The third year, which is the current one, he came and
took 10 pair. Be so kind as to ask him (?). If he does not . . . , let him
divide it with me, for I need it for my work.

THE HAND IS FAIRLY capable but gives a general impression of roughness, which
is caused by a few corrections and ink smudges.

The text is difficult to understand, as there are not only nonstandard spellings but several words the identification and meaning of which are unclear.
The gist seems to be that Georgios has been taking doves from a ground given
in pledge by the writer's father Joachim. It is not clear whether he has left or
died.

NOTE

settle: The verb here is uncertain, and the editors have been unsure about the
meaning. It may refer to migration, but "come to an end" in the sense of "die"
is also possible.

LOCATION OF OBJECT
Vienna, Österreichische Nationalbibliothek, Papyrussammlung, inv. KO 592.

O.Vind.Copt. 258

A woman to a cleric, about a date palm
Sixth–eighth century AD

LOCATION WRITTEN   Unknown
LOCATION OF ADDRESSEE   Unknown
LOCATION FOUND   Unknown

Coptic

First I embrace and kiss the sandals of the feet of your holy and in every
way respected lordship. Anoup came south and spoke to your lordship about
a small date palm, which he has planted on my property. Certainly either
he told you the truth or he told you lies. There is no lie in great men,
especially you, you the father of all of us, and every man in the entire
village knows the affair of that place, that it is mine. I brought in the priest
and the great men of the village. When I made them a testimony against
him, he said, "I will take it away." . . . Then he sent me . . . lawsuit with
me, as it was going to go . . . But what (decision) your lordship is going to
send us, I will not be disobedient to you. Farewell in the lord, our holy,
respected, Christ-loving father, (from) your sinful servant woman.

PROFICIENT HAND WITH SOME irregularities probably caused by the rough surface.

The Coptic is straightforward, with a few dialect forms.

The writer, whose female identity is explicit in her self-identification at
the end, writes to a senior cleric (perhaps a bishop), about a legal matter in
which she is embroiled, a palm tree planted by another person on her property.
Anoup, her opponent, has already appealed to the cleric; our writer promises
to obey his decision but makes it clear that she believes the village is on her
side in the matter.

LOCATION OF OBJECT
Vienna, Österreichische Nationalbibliothek, Papyrussammlung, inv. KO 693.

P.Gen. 1.74

Herais to Agrippinus
AD 139–145

LOCATION WRITTEN   Unknown
LOCATION OF ADDRESSEE   Unknown
LOCATION FOUND   Unknown

Greek

Herais to Agrippinus her son, many greetings. Before everything I pray that you are well and progressing. You should know, son, that I and Dioskoros have gone off to the strategos with Asklas, who was saying, "I got a petition of the iuridicus." And we didn't get any petition at all. Therefore please take a copy, seal it and deposit it in a jar, and give it to my brother or to Julianus or to Valerius Rufus. And what you can send, write it in a letter, seal it, and send it. We have to wait in the city for another ten days. The strategos heard us and I told him not to approach the . . . , neither him nor anyone else. For Antoninus was in the city with us. And he helped us greatly, also for what concerns Apolinarius, both before the centurion and before the strategos. You should be very thankful to him [Antoninus] now (?). And bring a bottle of oil from Serenus my brother and four large loaves. Herais and Thermouthis and Herais greet you . . .

THE HAND IS SEMICURSIVE and quite experienced. The writer, who was probably at home with writing documents, could easily go much faster but tried to produce a legible text. There are, however, more ligatures than in a standard letter hand.

This letter strings together a series of statements only loosely integrated with one another. Syntax and spelling are generally good, with the exception of a faulty case in one participle and a few orthographic irregularities.

This letter belongs to a dossier concerning the trial of Drusilla. Herais is the widow of Gaius Julius Agrippianus, who lent some money to Valerius Apolinarius, the husband of Drusilla, and seized some land after the money was not reimbursed. After the death of her husband, Drusilla kept on trying to recuperate her land and, since Agrippianus had died, she attacked his son Agrippinus. Herais represented her son, because he was too young. In this letter, she asks him to give her a copy of a certain petition.

LOCATION OF OBJECT
Geneva, Bibliothèque publique et universitaire, P.Gen. inv. 130bis.

BIBLIOGRAPHY

BL 1.167 (corrections to several lines). Reedited by P. Schubert and I. Jornot, *P.Gen.* I, 2d ed. (2002): 216–20. On this papyrus and the whole affair, see Schubert 2000.

P.Hamb. 1.86

Ptolema to Antas
Second century AD

LOCATION WRITTEN Unknown
LOCATION OF ADDRESSEE Unknown
LOCATION FOUND Arsinoite nome

Greek

Ptolema to Antas her brother, greetings. You write to Longinus (?) to expect the prefect. Look, the prefect went upriver. If you extricate yourself safely, come quickly before the prefect, so that if we can we have the boy examined. All the fields are in good condition. The southern basin of the 17 (arouras) has been sold for the cattle. Your cattle ate one aroura and went to Pansoue. Everything there has been released for the cattle. The west of the vegetable field was released for hay cutting. We sold the hay in the allotments, except for six basins on the east, for 112 dr. Hay is very cheap. Three arouras were bought for you though Vetranius for hay at 130 dr., and have been sold also through him for the use of sheep for 68 dr. Longinus greets you, and Sarapion and all those in the house. Vibius went to Psenyris to sell the grain. All your people are well. Farewell. Mecheir 30.

WRITTEN FAST IN A SMALL, experienced hand with some ligatures. The scribe was used to penning documents and does not seem too concerned with legibility.

The Greek is direct and lacking in any literary pretension. There are one or two rare usages and a curious form. The use of abbreviations is extensive enough to suggest a practiced writer.

Two major areas of concern appear in this letter. One is a desire to take advantage of the prefect's presence on his annual tour of the country to get a boy examined by him. The *epikrisis* was a scrutiny of qualifications for some privileged status. Antas may have been a soldier or veteran, but it is impossible to say if it was the military connection or metropolitan status that was at stake here. The remainder of the letter has to do with agricultural operations. It is obvious that the scale of the family's holdings was considerable.

NOTES
Pansoue: Probably the Arsinoite village attested in late papyri as Panse.

Psenyris: An important Arsinoite village.

LOCATION OF OBJECT
Hamburg, Staats- und Universitätsbibliothek, inv. 289.

BIBLIOGRAPHY
Translation in *Sel.Pap.* 1.119; cf. also *BL* 7.66 and 8.146 on the interpretation.

P.Lond. 3.988 (p. 243)

Lucia to Casullas
Third century AD

LOCATION WRITTEN Unknown
LOCATION OF ADDRESSEE Unknown
LOCATION FOUND Unknown

Greek

Lucia to Casullas her brother, many greetings. You write to me, "Register the documents of Pais." How can I, when you have them? So send them to me. Asklepiades came and we submitted enough before the prefect. So send me urgently . . . the official notification. Look, you were unwilling to arrange it, so we left for important business. So send me the documents at once, for he has his own. Take care not to neglect it. I pray for your health.

(ADDRESS): Deliver to Casullas from Lucia his sister.

THE WRITER WAS AT home with writing documents and wrote rather fast, slowing down only occasionally. The overall look, however, is uneven because of letters that were corrected or retraced.

The letter is extremely abrupt, even peremptory, although a few connectives are sprinkled through it. There are a few orthographic deviations, one supralinear correction, and a colloquial expression ("How can I, when you have them?").

Casullas has told Lucia to register some documents, forgetting that he had them. She scolds him for this, mentioning in passing a submission to the prefect and a trip on urgent business.

NOTES

documents: The use of "register" suggests that these are likely to have been deeds concerning property.

his own: Perhaps referring to Asklepiades.

LOCATION OF OBJECT
London, British Library, Papyrus 988.

BIBLIOGRAPHY
Corrections in *BL* 1.293 (lines 4, 7, and 8, and the date) and 6.63 (line 13).

P.Mert. 2.83

Taos and Thermouthion to Agathopous
Late second century AD

LOCATION WRITTEN   Unknown
LOCATION OF ADDRESSEE   Unknown
LOCATION FOUND   Unknown

Greek

Taos to Agathopous his dearest, greetings. I want you to know that Taharmiusis has summoned us—me and Seias and Faustion and the wool seller and his wife. They said that I especially attacked her along with you and an assistant when she was banqueting, and that we took gold things from her—as she says. Please then take care for me, as you have done also for the others—not just because the affair is yours, but also because I am relying on you not to bother me (to go) to Alexandria. I also had your son write to you about me, and likewise again the wool seller to write to you in his letter. Greet your daughter Arsous and Besas and Heraklas and all those who love you. Apollos my son greets you and all your people. Thermouthion says, "Lysanias said to me, 'Bring money, so that I may take it to him.'" But she didn't give it. If you want me to give it, write to me and I will send whatever you need to you through your brother if he leaves in Phamenoth. So as soon as you get this letter, write back to us, to me and Thermouthion—to me, so that I may know what care you are taking for me, to Thermouthion, so that you won't fail to get whatever you need. She greets you and all yours. (traces of concluding salutation)

(ADDRESS): Deliver to Agathopous from Thermouthion.

THE HAND IS A neat semicursive, with somewhat more ligaturing than one normally finds in letter hands. The writer is very experienced. Diaeresis occurs on upsilon and iota quite frequently.

The language of the letter is confident, correct, and idiomatic, although with rather more energy than style. The writer made two corrections.

The main substance of the letter concerns a supposed assault of which Taos and several other people have been accused. As the editor notes, although Taos can be either masculine or feminine, it seems that here he is a man. Part of the way through the letter, however, Taos first quotes Thermouthion, then asks Agathopous to write back to both of them. Thermouthion appears to be his wife. Thermouthion's concerns involve a payment of money. The address on the back indicates only Thermouthion as the sender, a fact which led the editor to suggest that Thermouthion wrote the letter on behalf of an illiterate husband, "although in that event his wife displays a surprisingly high standard of literacy." It is more likely that a trained scribe wrote the letter on behalf of Taos.

NOTES

gold things: Gk. *chrysia*, which could mean gold coins but could also be a general term; jewelry might be more obviously in view to be snatched during an assault.

take care: "Care" here renders the Gk. *phrontis*, which the editor translated "consideration." Presumably Taos is asking for some particular sort of intervention, for which this word is probably a euphemism.

she didn't give: The writer first put "I didn't give," as if continuing to quote Thermouthion.

Phamenoth: February–March.

LOCATION OF OBJECT

Dublin, Chester Beatty Library. Plate XXXI in the edition.

BIBLIOGRAPHY

Text reprinted as *Papyrological Primer*, 4th ed., no. 81. Corrections to lines 18 and 22 in *BL* 5.67 and 7.105.

P.Mich. 8.507

Artemis to Socrates about a legal representative
Second or third century AD

LOCATION WRITTEN   Probably Alexandria
LOCATION OF ADDRESSEE   Karanis (?)
LOCATION FOUND   Karanis

Greek

∾ ∾ ∾

Artemis to Socrates, greeting. Before everything, I pray for your health. I
arrived in the city on the 9th. I ask you, if you can, send me one of your
people because I need him to be my legal representative, since it is not
possible that a woman goes to law without a legal representative. Be certain
that if you help the affair will be successful. Let him come quickly; rest
assured that if I suffer damage you are going to suffer damage too, but if we
gain, the affair (or the profit) is yours. We salute your mother Thatres and
Achilles and Sarapion and Ptolemaios and Kastor and Tasoucharion. I pray
for your health.

(ADDRESS ON BACK): Give it . . . . from Harpakysis.

∾ ∾ ∾

THE HANDWRITING IS NOT completely regular but nevertheless the hand of a
professional. The writer maintained throughout tight interlinear spaces even
though a third of the papyrus was left unwritten.

The syntax of this letter with its good variety of clauses seems to indicate
a capable writer. Spelling, however, leaves much to be desired. Note the nominative instead of dative in the address and a verb used twice in the active
instead of the passive.

Artemis has arrived for some legal business, presumably in Alexandria.
Even though she seems to be accompanied by someone—she switches from
the first singular to the plural pronoun—she needs a legal representative and
asks Socrates for one. She reminds him quite abruptly that they are in a certain
affair together, and he owes her some help.

NOTE
Harpakysis: The editor thinks that the Harpakysis who appears in the address
may have been Artemis's host. In this case, a response would be sent to his
address. It is also possible that he wrote the letter for this woman.

LOCATION OF OBJECT
Formerly Ann Arbor, University of Michigan Library, Papyrus Collection, inv.
4726; now in Cairo, Egyptian Museum.

P.Oxy. 56.3855

Thermouthion to Isidoros
Ca. AD 280–281

LOCATION WRITTEN Unknown
LOCATION OF ADDRESSEE Unknown
LOCATION FOUND Oxyrhynchos

Greek

Thermouthion to Isidoros her brother, many greetings. I had your tunic cut.
Ammonios did not give the wheat, saying "I am giving two artabas."
Investigate about the business that you know about. If you learn that the
governor is coming out, come here, but if not write me quickly. Buy me the
things I wrote you about before. Write a petition about the matter you
know and send it off, and let the subscription to the petition be brought to
me. I said that you have full authority in the matter. Taesis greets you, and
(my/your?) son Kopreas. Amois greets you. Everybody greets you
individually.

(ADDRESS): Deliver (?) to Isidoros from Thermouthion.

THE LETTER'S HAND IS semidetached. Some letters have serifs and resemble
chancery hands, although this impression diminishes as the letter proceeds.
There is no farewell at the end, and it is likely that the damage to the papyrus
at the bottom has carried it away.

There are some phonetic spellings, the late Greek forms -*is*, -*in* for -*ios*,
-*ion*, and a couple of minor corrections. Sentences are short and abrupt, with
no connective particles and a series of instructions given without much soft-
ening.

Thermouthion's abruptness and rapidity are matched by her deliberate obscurity, which may be the result of haste, of desire to conceal her business
from prying eyes, or of a combination of these. The governor's (*hegemon's*)
possible visit is mentioned, and Thermouthion instructs Isidoros to write a
petition and send the results to her. But we are left in the dark about its
subject ("the matter you know"). From her remark that Isidoros has full authority to act, we may suppose that it concerned Thermouthion's property.

LOCATION OF OBJECT
Oxford, Papyrology Rooms, Sackler Library.

P.Ryl.Copt. 310

A widow's lament
Fourth or fifth century AD

LOCATION WRITTEN   Unknown
LOCATION OF ADDRESSEE   Unknown
LOCATION FOUND   Upper Egypt

Coptic

∾ ∾ ∾

. . . price and he . . . Thereafter that . . . sent his mother and she brought
southward the rest of what remained. And afterward that merchant also
went north and constrained him and delivered him to a magistrate, a *papa*
(?), and he . . . him, saying "He is my debtor for 170,000 talents." And he
shut him up and maltreated him, until, against his will, he wrote (a
document giving) him his children. He delivered me to the . . . of
Antinoopolis; and he . . . to demand of me, and he let me go. Now
therefore . . . me to (?) . . . and Taese. Neither have I eaten from them nor
have I drunk from them; and I am a widow for twelve years now, since I . . .

∾ ∾ ∾

THE SCRIPT IS A fine, regular majuscule with a literary appearance. This is the
work of someone familiar with writing literary texts. The hand shows some
finials and thickening of some strokes. It uses a thick pen. The hand is round,
almost bilinear, with well-proportioned letters and a good control of the ink
flow.

This fragmentary letter (or petition?) describes the actions of a merchant
against his debtor, including forcing him to hand over his children as collateral
for a debt, a phenomenon found elsewhere. The precise connection of all this
to the writer, who has been a widow for twelve years, is not clear; unless the
narrative concerns events long ago, presumably the beleaguered debtor is not
her husband nor the children hers.

LOCATION OF OBJECT
Manchester, John Rylands University Library, Coptic papyrus 310. Plate I in
the edition.

P.Wash.Univ. 2.106

Dionysia to Panechotes about judicial business
18 BC

LOCATION WRITTEN Unknown
LOCATION OF ADDRESSEE Oxyrhynchos (?)
LOCATION FOUND Oxyrhynchos

Greek

Dionysia to Panechotes her brother, many greetings and good health always. I am very thankful to you, because you heard that builders repaired my house. You did not send me word or remembrance or a sheet of unwritten papyrus. So write me a letter and send it. Moreover I ask you to give testimony through the strategos to him, before Pedo sails up and I with my people sail down and present my suit against him. I ask you not to neglect this and to send me word as quickly as possible. Greet Athenis and Ptolla and Harasis and all those in the household. Ventidius greets you warmly, and so do Helene and Outidion and all those in the household. So don't be neglectful about the matter, until we come to you. Farewell. Year 12 of Caesar, Tybi 18.

(ADDRESS): Deliver to Panechotes.

THE WRITER MAKES LARGE, detached, widely spaced letters, in lines a bit farther apart than usual that waver across the sheet. Letters are of very uneven darkness, showing a frequent and not very skilled handling of the pen and ink. All the same, the writer is by no means entirely unskilled, and there is some attempt at shaping individual letters.

The bulk of the spelling variants are normal phonetic ones (iotacisms, interchange of o-vowels, e/ai exchange, etc.). There is also an article used in place of a relative pronoun.

After a variant of the usual complaint about not having heard from the other, Dionysia goes on to deal with a pending court case. The Pedo mentioned is L. Antonius Pedo, prefect of Egypt, evidently sailing upriver from Alexandria as part of his judicial tour of Egypt (the *conventus*). Dionysia is planning to sail downriver from wherever she is; Pedo's tour thus presumably was not going to reach her hometown. Although Dionysia needs Panechotes's testimony, it seems clear that she is the principal litigant and that she will act herself rather than through an intermediary.

NOTE

to him, against him: The person is not specified, presumably being well known to both parties. It seems unlikely that the first can refer to the strategos.

St. Louis, Washington University Library, inv. 444. Plate XXX in original edition.

BIBLIOGRAPHY

Clarysse 1990: 104–5 (on lines 8–9) (*BL* 9.373).

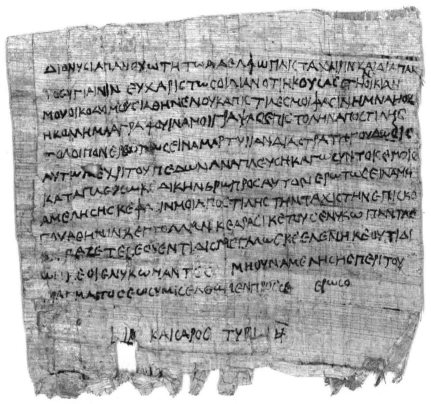

Fig. 26. *P.Wash.Univ.* 2.106. Dionysia to Panechotes about judicial business. (St. Louis, Washington University Library, inv. 444. Photograph courtesy of the Washington University Libraries, Special Collections.)

O.Bodl.dem. 399

Tachib writes about plants
First or second century AD (?)

LOCATION WRITTEN   Apollonopolis Heptakomia
LOCATION OF ADDRESSEE   Thebes (?)
LOCATION FOUND   Thebes (?)

Demotic

❧ ❧ ❧

Tachib daughter of Osoroueris: I have caused a bundle of grapevines to be brought to Osoroueris. Let the ring be sent later, but have a seedling sent to me (now) for the expense. Send me a message; come to Qus. Written.

❧ ❧ ❧

OSTRACON WRITTEN IN A clear Demotic hand of the Roman period.
    The letter is a fairly typical message about the sending and receiving of goods, mainly plants in this case.

NOTE
Qus: The Egyptian name of Apollonopolis (Parva) or Heptakomia.

LOCATION OF OBJECT
Oxford, Bodleian Library, Demotic ostracon, inv. 399; now in the Ashmolean Museum.

O.Vind.Copt. 181

Tsanna to her son Lot
Sixth–eighth century AD

LOCATION WRITTEN Unknown
LOCATION OF ADDRESSEE Unknown
LOCATION FOUND Unknown

Coptic

Tsanna writes greeting her beloved son Lot. Give the vessels which you and Kyriakos have. He said, "I'm not giving to you." He gave them and received interest for them. He said, "If you demand it and he comes south, I'm not giving it to you." If he spends another five years, he has no claim (?). Be so kind as to give the *sharmchach*. Look for them. Look, Tebiou took her sack of barley for the barley which you are surety for. Be so kind if you encounter him, to give the . . .

WRITTEN ON THE SIDES and bottom of a pot. The hand is proficient. It slopes to the right and is moderately fast in spite of the fact that the letters are mostly separated. Some unevenness is probably due to the writing material.

Tsanna writes in a cryptic fashion about matters no doubt clear to the recipient. We do not know who "he" in the third sentence is, nor exactly what is going on. It looks as if most of the letter deals with loans.

NOTE
sharmchach: An otherwise unknown word; it is in the plural.

LOCATION OF OBJECT
Vienna, Österreichische Nationalbibliothek, Papyrussammlung, inv. KO 340.

P.Benaki 4

Mother to son
Fourth century AD

LOCATION WRITTEN   Unknown
LOCATION OF ADDRESSEE   Unknown
LOCATION FOUND   Arsinoite nome

Greek

To my most holy lord son . . . With God's help, I have come back quickly for your sake. I have sent you a basket of parsley roots, a basket of shoots (?) and a basket of some small raisins. Wash them and put them outside in the sun, wherever possible. Then put them into a funnel and two Knidian jars, and, when you have them ground into flour, let me know by letter. I have not sent you anything else, in case you travel down. I shall write you about a few other matters: I have sent you . . . Write and tell me what you receive . . . , because I have heard that you have received . . . because I came to see you.

ON THE BACK IS a letter from a son to his mother, evidently a reply to this letter, written across the fibers. The hand is largely detached, with letters of uneven size, not a practiced hand but not an absolute beginner's either.

The writer's spelling is very phonetic, going beyond simple interchanges in representing the sounds. Nasal sounds at the end of words, and sometimes in the middle, are frequently omitted; lambda and rho are interchanged.

In neither letter does the writer identify herself or himself by name, nor is either recipient given a name; only relationships are mentioned (and these, the editor suggests, may be spiritual rather than biological). The presence of Christian phraseology and abbreviations in the son's reply establishes the Christian identity of the parties; this coupled with the fourth-century date causes the editor to speculate that the letters predate Constantine. That does not seem a necessary inference, as the authorities could no doubt have established the parties' identity if necessary. The "son" may well have held a high church position, to judge from the epithet "most holy" applied to him.

LOCATION OF OBJECT
Athens, Benaki Museum, inv. 614A.

P.Bour. 23

Thermouthis to Agrippinus
Second century AD

LOCATION WRITTEN   Unknown
LOCATION OF ADDRESSEE   Unknown
LOCATION FOUND   Unknown

Greek

Thermouthis to Agrippinus her brother, many greetings. Before everything I pray for your health. Be aware that Phaesis went to Karanis with Saturnilus. Please, brother, also buy me 2 pounds of unguent—for I also wrote to Julianus to buy 2 more himself—and 10 pinecones. But send them right away—you know what oppresses (worries) me—otherwise I was not going to write to you. Salute all your people. I pray for your health.

(ADDRESS ON BACK): To Julius Agrippinus from his sister Thermouthis.

WRITTEN THROUGHOUT IN A proficient, upright hand that emphasizes the vertical strokes. While the hand proceeds slowly at times, making very clear and detached letters, in other parts the pace quickens and the ligatures multiply.

The letter is written rather correctly besides the usual iotacisms and phonetic spellings. The style of writing, however, is largely oral. Thermouthis's voice is evident in the asides that interrupt the flow of the writing.

This letter seems to be concerned with things that Thermouthis needed for a burial. She asked not only Agrippinus but another man, too, to procure them for her in a hurry.

NOTE
pinecones: On their use for funerary practices, cf. *BGU* 3.801.

LOCATION OF OBJECT
Paris, Université de Paris-Sorbonne, Institut de Papyrologie, P.Bour. inv. 50.

BIBLIOGRAPHY
Several corrections to the text in *BL* 3.31–32.

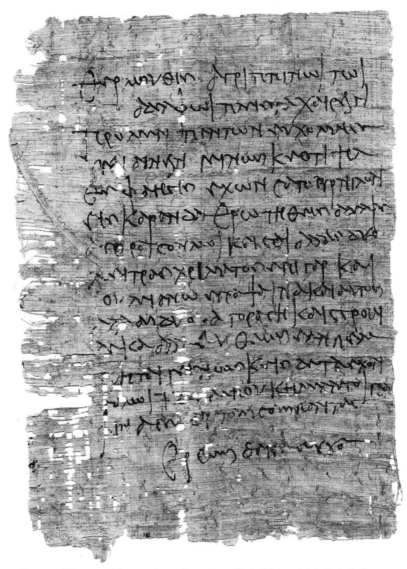

Fig. 27. *P.Bour.* 23. Thermouthis to Agrippinus. (Paris, Université de Paris-Sorbonne, Institut de Papyrologie, P.Bour. inv. 50.)

P.Fay. 127

Taorsenouphis to Ision her mother
Second or third century AD

LOCATION WRITTEN   Probably Alexandria
LOCATION OF ADDRESSEE   Bacchias
LOCATION FOUND   Bacchias

Greek

〜 〜 〜

Taorsenouphis to Ision her mother, many greetings. Before everything I pray
that you are well, and I make obeisance for you before the lord Sarapis.
Please give your [or our] share of the crop from the vineyard to my sister,
and a bunch of grapes. I sent you three pairs of bowls, 1 for you and 1 for
Petesouchos and 1 for the sons-in-law of your sister, and a little cup for
little Theonas, and another for the daughter of your sister. And if you
receive lentils, send them to me by Katoitos.

(ADDRESS): Deliver to the mother of Taorsenouphis.

〜 〜 〜

AN EXPERIENCED HAND WITH characters all detached. The writer was probably
struggling to maintain a low speed.

The spelling is free from many of the usual phonetic spellings of the period,
but there are some more interesting ones. The syntax is straightforward and
unadorned, hardly more than a series of instructions and notices.

As usual, it is likely that the *proskynema* formula before Sarapis indicates
an Alexandrian origin. That is perhaps also reflected in the fact that Taorsenouphis sends craft goods rather than food to her mother, but hopes for lentils
in return and gives instructions about the wine harvest.

LOCATION OF OBJECT
Cairo, Egyptian Museum, Cat. Gen. 10243, Journal d'Entrée 31667, SR 2001.

P.Hamb. 2.192

Demetria to Apia
First half of third century AD

LOCATION WRITTEN Antinoopolis
LOCATION OF ADDRESSEE Unknown
LOCATION FOUND Unknown

Greek

Demetria to Apia her sweetest sister, greetings. As soon as I arrived at
Antinoopolis, I did not neglect your instruction, but right away, before the
freight was loaded, I bought it. But the damned skipper left without any
reason, and I seemed to be sluggish even though I was not to blame. Now
that I have found someone going up to you, I have sent you oil worthy of
you. I want you to know that it is expensive, and I barely got a chous for 18
drachmas; but it's worthy of you. I will also send you the upper garment for
the festival. Greet my most honored Helene warmly, and Nike and Rhodine
and Attous. And you remember the purple. I pray that you are well, dearest
sister. Farewell.

(ADDRESS): To Apia from Demetria.

THE OPENING OF THE letter is written very fluently and shows the writer's
ability. In the rest, however, this hand strives for clarity, producing characters
that are printlike and strictly separated. The result is a bit clumsy, particularly
in the central part, and alignment leaves something to be desired.

The composition is as professional as the hand, despite a slip here and
there, most striking a superfluous iota on the name of the sender right at the
start. There is not much ornament, but the vocabulary is ample.

The professionalism of the writing corresponds well to the obviously mon-
eyed milieu these women belong to: only the best will do. Presumably wherever Apia lives (evidently upriver from Antinoopolis) good olive oil is scarce,
and Antinoopolis as a Hellenic city will have offered a good place to buy it.

NOTES
expensive: Except for one outlier, this price seems to be toward the high
end of the known spectrum for any period up to 275.

upper garment: *Aliklion*, from Lat. *alicula*; cf. *P.Col.* 10.279.2n.

LOCATION OF OBJECT
Hamburg, Staats- und Universitätsbibliothek, inv. 404.

BIBLIOGRAPHY

Hengstl 1978: 223–25, no. 89 (incorporating suggestions for interpretation in *BL* 4.38).

P.Oslo 2.52

Zenarion to her brother Theon
Second century AD

LOCATION WRITTEN   Unknown
LOCATION OF ADDRESSEE   Unknown
LOCATION FOUND   Unknown

Greek

Zenarion to Theon her brother, greeting. Before everything I pray for your health. I (received) 7 cheeses and the pilot (said) that they were eaten by mice . . . Since you wrote that you did not receive neither the . . . nor the cheeses whole . . . [long lacuna] . . . be at hand because there is need of him. He writes blaming me . . . Urge Serenus to come forth quickly because we need him and if Serenus comes let him rise up. I salute (you and) your mother and the . . . and Homonoia and Demetrion. Agathous and Eisarous and . . . salute you. I pray for your health.

(ADDRESS ON BACK): To Theon from Zenarion.

THIS IS THE PRODUCT of a first-class professional who produced an attractive and legible text. There are finials at the end of some vertical strokes. The characters in the initial salutation are greatly enlarged.

The text is remarkably correct, and there are no phonetic spellings. The impression that the syntax is relatively simple derives from the letter's fragmentary state. There are causal clauses and an articular infinitive. Connective particles, however, are entirely lacking.

What remains of this letter concerns spoiled cheeses that were sent to Zenarion by boat, and a certain Serenus whose arrival is expected impatiently for some reason that escapes us.

NOTE

eaten by mice: This is the only occurrence in Greek of the adjective *muobrotos*.

Oslo, Universitetetsbiblioteket.

BIBLIOGRAPHY
On various restorations, particularly in lines 17–18, see *BL* 2.2.212; *BL* 3.123.
On the back, see *BL* 7.124.

P.Oxy. 2.300

Indike to Thaisous
Late first century AD

LOCATION WRITTEN Unknown
LOCATION OF ADDRESSEE Unknown
LOCATION FOUND Oxyrhynchos

Greek

∾ ∾ ∾

Indike to Thaisous her lady, greeting. I sent you by way of the camel driver Taurinos the "breadbox," concerning which please let me know by return that you received it. Greet lord Theon and Nikoboulos and Dioskoros and Theon and Hermokles, who are free from the evil eye. Longinos greets you. Farewell. Germanik( ) 2.

(ADDRESS): To the gymnasium, to Theon son of Nikoboulos, the oil supplier.

∾ ∾ ∾

UNFORTUNATELY, THE EDITOR GIVES no description of the handwriting; the location of the original papyrus is not known and no photograph is extant.

The letter, though brief, shows a good standard of language, with a nicely turned relative clause using an aorist participle. Apart from iotacisms, there is one phonetic spelling.

The contents are simple, notification of dispatch of a *panarion*, a request to be notified on its arrival, and greetings to family members, including probably the recipient's husband, father-in-law, and children.

NOTE
oil supplier: Probably it was a salaried post in charge of the oil supply in the gymnasium, a critical function. It is interesting that the letter is to be delivered to Theon, who must be Thaisous's husband, at work rather than at home.

No record of current whereabouts nor of distribution by the Egypt Exploration Society.

BIBLIOGRAPHY

Olsson 1925: no. 78; White 1986: 93, no. 94.

P.Oxy. 6.963
Ophelia to Theanous about a chair
Second or third century AD

LOCATION WRITTEN   Unknown
LOCATION OF ADDRESSEE   Unknown
LOCATION FOUND   Oxyrhynchos

Greek

Ophelia to Theanous her mother, greetings. I greet you, mother, wishing to catch sight of you already through this letter. I am grateful to you, mother, for your concern for the chair; I received it. You are acting in character, dearest mother, in taking care . . . If you send instructions . . .

(ADDRESS): to Theanous her mother.

THE HAND IS A fluent, neat letter hand with limited ligaturing. There are no corrections or remade letters apparent.

The language of the letter is straightforward and correct, with a good use of connectives and tenses and a respectable vocabulary; only a tendency to repetition mars the crispness of the formulation. The repeated use of "mother" is particularly striking.

This is a thank-you letter for a chair, presumably an armchair of some substance (despite the diminutive). The tone is rather emotive by the standards of papyrus letters: "Mommy dearest, it's just like you!"

NOTE
chair: Gk. *kathedrarion*, a word attested only here. It is the diminutive of *kathedra*, the term for a throne or a teacher's chair.

LOCATION OF OBJECT
Toledo, Ohio, Toledo Museum of Art.

P.Oxy. 10.1291

Zois to Ischyrion about bread
November, AD 30

LOCATION WRITTEN   Unknown
LOCATION OF ADDRESSEE   Unknown
LOCATION FOUND   Oxyrhynchos

Greek

Zois to Ischyrion her brother, greetings. No one brought me a letter about
the loaves of bread, but look, if you send a letter by Kollouthos, an artaba
will come to you immediately. If you wish to depart to Alexandria, Apollos
son of Theon is going tomorrow. Farewell. Year 17 of Tiberius Caesar
Augustus, New Augustus 29.

(ADDRESS): To Ischyrion.

THE HANDWRITING IS SEMILIGATURED and characteristic of the period. The
letters are generally well formed, the letter well laid out. The pen seems to
have been dipped into the ink relatively frequently. There are a couple of
remade or corrected letters.

The composition is punchy and vivid rather than subtle; no time is wasted
on greetings and the like. Iotacisms are common, rho is written instead of
lambda in one word, the accusative of Alexandria lacks its nu—all rather
colloquial features. The false iota adscript on *artabe*, by contrast, is a bit of
misplaced pretension to precision.

Zois apparently knows that Ischyrion is likely to need an artaba of bread,
but in the absence of a specific request she has held off acting. She is presumably close to Oxyrhynchos, as she expects Ischyrion to have the letter before
the next day.

NOTE
New Augustus: The month of Neos Sebastos (= Hathyr, November-Decem-
ber).

LOCATION OF OBJECT
Cairo, Egyptian Museum, Journal d'Entrée 47466; SR 1024.

BIBLIOGRAPHY
Olsson 1925: no. 20.

P.Oxy. 22.2353

Sinthonis to Harpochras
AD 32

LOCATION WRITTEN   Unknown
LOCATION OF ADDRESSEE   Unknown
LOCATION FOUND   Oxyrhynchos

Greek

Sinthonis to Harpochras her son, very many greetings and continual health. We are babbling, what you say and what I say. Didymas says, "If he saw that you intend to hand the slave over to me, make Harpochras himself grow his hair long with you for ten years." He should not go off for the money. His son Eros has brought me two hundred drachmas, and has got a note for a hundred drachmas from the man from Memphis, which he intends to spend on the festival. Your brother has sent a letter from Koptos: "Send the letter to my brother Harpochras." We have not opened it. We don't know what is written there. If you want something, write; if loaves or wheat, write. If you want to allow not to kill the pig until he comes, write. If you want to kill this pig, write. If your sister goes to her mother, take nothing from her, and fare well. Farewell.

(ADDRESS): Deliver from Sinthonis to Harpochras her son.

SINTHONIS'S VOICE CAN BE heard in this letter. She either dictated it word for word or wrote in the heat of the moment. The letter is written fairly correctly but consists of thoughts piled in a disorderly way. There are a few colloquial expressions.

The editor complained about the obscurity of this letter, but subsequent interpretation has clarified its syntax and structure, if not all of its references. The matters of the slave, the letter, and the pig are all characteristic examples of subjects understood by the writer and recipient, but not fully by us.

LOCATION OF OBJECT
Oxford, Papyrology Rooms, Sackler Library.

BIBLIOGRAPHY
Grassi 1956:204–5, improves the interpretation of the letter.

P. Tebt. 2.413

Aphrodite to Arsinoe
Second or third century AD

LOCATION WRITTEN Unknown
LOCATION OF ADDRESSEE Tebtunis (?)
LOCATION FOUND Tebtunis

Greek

Aphrodite to Arsinoe her lady, many greetings. I make obeisance on your behalf before the local gods every day, praying for your health. I restored at once to the (wife) of Mamertinus the thing you sent, and Serenion received the papyrus sealed. Do not think, lady, that I have neglected your instructions. Euphrosyne, after she cut the dalmatikon, . . . Isidoros. And receive through Artes also the carryall and four wraps and four Puteolans and one jar (?) and 5 reeds of thread; it was agreed with you to send these from her wages. I received the birdcage from Didymos. We are behindhand in sending you letters because of having no . . . Ambrosia and . . . and Athenodoros and Thermouthis and their household greet you, and all your friends greet those who love you.

(ADDRESS): Deliver from Aphrodite to her mistress.

THE HAND IS DETACHED and uneven in size. Some letters are overinked. The lines are wobbly and trend a bit down to the right. The entire letter is written in a single hand.

The spelling and syllabication leave much to be desired. Letters are omitted on numerous occasions, even entire syllables. Aphrodite's own name is spelled Aphodite in the letter, Apodite in the address. At least once a word is divided so that only its last letter appears on the next line.

The writer addresses the recipient as *kyria*, "lady" or "mistress." She reports on the carrying out of various instructions. It may be that Aphrodite is in fact a slave; the name was common in the slave population. There are some difficulties in understanding what she says, partly because of her spelling but partly because of the rarity of some of the items that she mentions.

NOTES

behindhand in sending: Note that an anticipated regular flow of missives must stand behind this plurality of letters not sent.

friends: The form is feminine.

LOCATION OF OBJECT
Berkeley, University of California, Bancroft Library.

BIBLIOGRAPHY
BL 1.428 (on lines 8, 10).

P.Tebt. 2.414

Thenpetsokis to Thenapynchis
Second century AD

LOCATION WRITTEN   Unknown
LOCATION OF ADDRESSEE   Unknown
LOCATION FOUND   Tebtunis

Greek

Thenpetsokis to Thenapynchis her sister, warmest greetings. Before all I
pray that you are well, and your children and Pasis the *koryphos*. I sent you
through Protas 50 dried figs. I would have sent them to you long since
except that I have been ill; but if I get well I will send a cup of orris root for
your daughter. Give Tephersais the loom and the pallet and the bundle (?)
of the reeds for weaving and the saddle (?) and the mortar and the two
kneading troughs and the boxes with papyrus packets and the little chest
and the cup and the lamp stand and the basket with its contents at the
bottom and the feeding bottle (?) and the big case. Kotos will give you the
box for Tephersais which I lent him, for it does not belong to the brother of
your mother. I greet you and your brothers (greet you). Let the daughter of
Kephalas also give the measure to Tephersais, let her sell it, and let her send
the money to me, since I am coming. I greet Aphrodite our mother. The
trough belongs to Agathangelos, to be given to the children. Tell the wife
of the tinsmith Ameimon about your son, "Give the wooden stool and the
wall cabinet and the little lamp."

(Top margin): Receive 50 dried figs from Tephersais.

(ADDRESS): Deliver to Thenapynchis the wife of the potter.

THIS TEXT IS WRITTEN in a typical letter hand, with neat, mainly detached
letters and a few ligatures. The lines of writing slope up to the right to varying
degrees. The same hand has written the entire letter.

 The spelling is phonetic, the syllabic division almost nonexistent. At times
the spelling is so nonstandard that it is impossible to be certain what word is

meant. But there are also signs of an education somewhat beyond the basics. The contrast between the quality of the hand and the pervasiveness of difficulty in writing is very unusual and suggests a learning disability.

This is almost a pure type of the letter about goods, full of information about things being sent and instructions about what to do with various objects. Many of the words used are rare or even unique. Rarely, the social context can be partly described, because the recipient is identified as a potter's wife, and one of the people mentioned in the letter is a tinsmith's wife. This village letter thus comes from an artisanal level, even if we do not know Thenpetsokis's own station. It is interesting that Thenpetsokis refers to two women only by their relationships (to men), not by name.

NOTES

koryphos: The meaning is uncertain and much debated. On one etymology it would mean approximately "virgin fucker" (see Lukaszewicz 1992: 43–46). This seems, even if a nickname, unlikely in a letter like this, however, and (given the writer's difficulties) it may be more likely that it is a nonstandard form of *koryphaios*, a priestly rank (see W.Chr. 76).

orris root: Extracted from the rhizome of three species of iris, orris root has a variety of uses, including mixing into washing water to impart a fresh smell to linens. The reference here, however, is likely to be to one of the medicinal uses, as it is a diuretic, emetic, and cathartic, and useful in cases of chronic diarrhea.

papyrus packets: *Chartaria*, probably referring to papyrus as a wrapping material for unguents, cf. *P.Oxy.* 14.1765.

wall cabinet: *Thyrion* is a diminutive of *thyris*, which can refer either to a window or to a wall niche, sometimes outfitted with cabinetry. It is not certain which meaning is intended here. Cf. Husson 1983: 109–18.

Thenpetsokis: She just might be the woman who submitted the census declaration *P.Tebt.* 2.480 (published in full in *Aegyptus* 72 [1992] 79–82), of AD 203.

LOCATION OF OBJECT

Berkeley, University of California, Bancroft Library.

P.Yale 1.77

Eirene to Epaphrys
Early to mid–first century AD

LOCATION WRITTEN   Perhaps Small Oasis
LOCATION OF ADDRESSEE   Oxyrhynchos (?)
LOCATION FOUND   Probably Oxyrhynchos

Greek

Eirene to Epaphrys her brother, warmest greetings. Before all I greet you greatly with all your family. Next I ask you, brother, do not be neglectful about the bracelet. As I informed you, it is to be of a gold piece (?), for a hand of a mature woman. As for those of the younger girl, let them be as if to fit the arm of Matrous, at a weight of two gold pieces, as I informed you in another letter. By the other delivery . . . (at the weight) of three gold pieces, since hers is going to another use. Receive from Petechon 1 m(—?) of wild stavesacre, which Diogas indicated that he (?) had sent (back of papyrus) to Zoilas by way of Hermodoros. You will please tell Zoilas that, as I informed you, I did not find an opportunity to give (it) to Hermodoros. I gave to Petechon both a design (?) and a new sack, for you to give the wool for it (to him), if you think it best. Moreover, come to me to the Oasis, so that you don't reach me after the annual accounting. Let (them) know in Oxyrhynchos if the matter of the house is finished. Farewell. Thoth 10.

(ADDRESS): From Eirene to Epaphrod(itos) her brother.

THE HAND, ALTHOUGH A bit ungainly and marked by a number of slips and corrections, has some sense of style but is perhaps a little below average for letters. Whether Eirene wrote the letter herself or dictated it cannot be said.

The language is vivid and oral and the orthography by no means bad for a letter, although there are many small mistakes. The most important slip comes right at the start, when the author gives her name in the genitive rather than the nominative.

The first half of the letter is largely concerned with the making of a bracelet for an adult woman. It remains difficult to be sure how to punctuate some of this section and thus to understand precisely what the writer is ordering. Eirene proceeds to indicate that it is to be for the arm of a mature woman. The second part of the letter concerns a delivery which could not be completed in the manner originally expected and so has been carried out by an alternative courier. This section is followed by some instructions concerning the recipient's possible journey to the Oasis.

Epaphrys is a short form of Epaphroditos (the name abbreviated in the address on the back).

two gold pieces: The Greek is unclear here. This may indicate their weight (each). A bracelet of 2 *chrysoi* would weigh 13.45 grams.

stavesacre (wild astaphis): A tall annual grown for its seeds, which contain a high percentage of alkaloids and are used for externally applied vermicides, particularly against body lice.

design (?): Gk. *eidos*, the sense of which here is uncertain. If it refers back to the previous sentence, it could denote the stavesacre; if it introduces a new thought, with the sense "also," then in connection with a weaving project it is more likely to refer to a drawing or cartoon of the design supposed to be woven.

LOCATION OF OBJECT

New Haven, Beinecke Rare Book and Manuscript Library, Yale University, inv. 115.

BIBLIOGRAPHY

Bagnall 1999: 109–17 (revised text, translation, commentary).

PSI 9.1082

Palladis to her husband concerning some garments
Fourth century AD (?)

LOCATION WRITTEN Unknown
LOCATION OF ADDRESSEE Oxyrhynchos (?)
LOCATION FOUND Oxyrhynchos

Greek

∾ ∾ ∾

To my lord brother Amm. . . , Palladis sends many greetings. I want you to
know, my lord brother, that I was sending Eutychios to you, having found
an opportunity for the ferry. But your brother said that if he wanted he
would send for him. So if you see fit, send for him. I want to serve you more
than myself. Already I sent to you three times on his account. I want you to
know that I sent you the hooded mantle and the woolen tunic with a white
embroidered shawl via the sailors of the ferry, wrapped up in your bath
towel. Ortos and Severus and Chrysos took them; he has put them in the
hands of the three. He handed them over. Concerning the orders for
payment, if I collect them again from others, I'll write to you. If they luckily
come to you, let me know . . .

∾ ∾ ∾

THE CROWDED LINES, THE difficulty in maintaining an even ink flow, the os-
cillating alignment, and the slow speed make this hand appear worse than it
actually is. The writer was certainly not a professional but was familiar with
writing relatively long texts. Whether this was Palladis herself or whether she
dictated a disjointed and repetitious text to someone else is impossible to
know.

The language is marked by a high incidence of phonetic spellings and
errors. In fact, there is little here that is any more obscure than the typical
letter, with its allusive mention of goods and business.

Palladis is concerned to transmit news about the sending of Eutychios (a
slave of theirs?) and some items of clothing. Before the papyrus breaks off,
Palladis moves on to financial matters.

LOCATION OF OBJECT
Florence, Biblioteca Medicea Laurenziana, PSI 1082.

BIBLIOGRAPHY
For the reading of line 12, see BL 6.184.

PSI 14.1418

Lysistrate to Germania
Third century AD

LOCATION WRITTEN Probably Alexandria
LOCATION OF ADDRESSEE Oxyrhynchos (?)
LOCATION FOUND Oxyrhynchos

Greek

Lysistrate to Germania her daughter, greetings. Before everything I pray that
you are well, and I make obeisance on your behalf before the lord Sarapis
and the gods who share the temple. I want you to know that I took care of
the flasks, but I don't have anyone to transport them. If you have someone
reliable who can get them, send him to me. I instructed your brother Kai. . .
that if he could find someone able (to transport them) he should send him
to me. I also want you to know that the woolen yarn . . . is expensive . . .

THIS WRITER COULD WRITE long texts with little discomfort and good results
but without achieving much elegance. The letters are all separated and their
inclination varies. The writing speed is not uniform.

The Greek is straightforward, with ordinary iotacisms but little else to
distinguish it from the ordinary, either for good or ill.

Most of the letter is concerned with finding someone to carry some flasks
(*lagynia*) from Lysistrate to Germania. Just before the letter breaks off, it turns
to woolen yarn, apparently with a complaint about the cost.

LOCATION OF OBJECT
Florence, Istituto Papirologico G. Vitelli, *PSI* 1418.

SB 5.7743

Claudia Dionysia to her brother Tiron concerning provisions and money
First century AD

LOCATION WRITTEN   Unknown
LOCATION OF ADDRESSEE   Unknown
LOCATION FOUND   Unknown

Greek

Claudia Dionysia to Tiron her lord brother, greeting. I am writing to you now as I have not been feeling well because of my usual illness from the 17th of the month of Tybi until today. Therefore I was not able to send you anything until now. If you receive from Hyperephanos—the friend of Ptolemaios, the son of our father Matrinus—my letter and a jar of *pyren* (aromatic herb?) and a jar of *alix* (rice wheat) and baskets of dainties inscribed with your name, let me know. Send me news constantly about your health and about what you want henceforth. Please, brother, send me in a hurry as allowance through an order for payment the money that you can collect from my revenues. Greet your sister together with our (your?) children and all the people of your family. Everyone salutes you. (second hand) I pray for your health, my lord brother, with all the household. Mecheir 10.

(ADDRESS ON BACK): Deliver to Tiron from Claudia Dionysia.

A HAND WITH SEPARATED characters that are almost strictly bilinear and deco-rated by serifs. The writer strives (but not always successfully) to produce an attractive text and uses a line filler to end a line harmoniously. Dionysia writes the final salutations with a thick pen. Her hand is a bit coarse and shows letters not completely separated and cursive epsilon.

The text conveys the impression of a good knowledge of Greek even though clauses are juxtaposed without connectives. The syntax is simple but correct. There are no orthographic errors, not even those due to phonetic spelling, and the vocabulary is appropriate. It is noteworthy that the verb stands at the end of many sentences. Some influence from Latin?

The letter is about the dispatching of provisions and a request for money from this woman's revenues. Everything else is uncertain, including the relationship of Claudia Dionysia and her "brother" and the nature of her "usual" illness.

LOCATION OF OBJECT
Cairo, Institut français d'archéologie orientale, inv. 120.

SB 14.11585

Thermouthis to Nemesion
AD 59

LOCATION WRITTEN   Unknown
LOCATION OF ADDRESSEE   Philadelphia
LOCATION FOUND   Philadelphia

Greek

Thermouthis to Nemesion, greeting. I would like you to know that Lucius has come. With regard to his tunic of thick sackcloth that you have in the city, bring it, if you come down. The hood, he has it here. I gave it to him before on his word alone, so that he might have it until you come down. And with regard to the wages of the shepherds he said, "I am sending a soldier . . . immediately—he says—to seize the shepherds' belongings that remain." Our mattress he has not given (me): "Bring my old one," he says. And with regard to the shovel he says that you asked them 3 staters per shovel. Farewell. Year 5 of Nero, Epeiph 13.

(ADDRESS ON BACK): Deliver to Nemesion.

THE HAND SHOWS A limited degree of competence but does not write too slowly. The characters are mostly separated but not badly formed, and some of them show an initial transition toward cursive forms. Alignment leaves much to be desired as do rhythm and overall look of the text. The writer—Thermouthis perhaps—was able to write with some confidence.

Even though orthography is particularly faulty and prompted the editor to produce a corrected version, the overall knowledge of Greek that this letter reveals is not elementary. There is a variety of subordinate clauses. The use of direct discourse and the frequent repetition of *legei* (says) confer much vividness to the text.

When Thermouthis writes to her husband, she is only concerned with the efficiency of her message: greetings and final salutations are reduced to a minimum. In her husband's absence, she takes care of his affairs. The letter is primarily concerned with the needs and actions of Lucius, a business associate of Nemesion.

NOTE

Part of the archive of Nemesion, tax collector of Philadelphia. That he was Thermouthis's husband is confirmed by a tax receipt, BGU 7.1614A.

LOCATION OF OBJECT
Ann Arbor, University of Michigan Library, Papyrus Collection, P.Corn. inv. I 11. Plate 41 in Rowlandson 1998.

BIBLIOGRAPHY
Translation in Rowlandson 1998: no. 259.

5. WORK: AGRICULTURE

P.Col. 8.212

Apollonous to Kolulis about a waterwheel
February, AD 49

LOCATION WRITTEN Unknown
LOCATION OF ADDRESSEE Unknown
LOCATION FOUND Unknown

Greek

Apollonous to Kolulis her brother, many greetings. As soon as you receive the letter, go to the wheel and pull down the whole wall and move the machinery to the . . . place. As for the rest, take care to keep well. Ninth year of Tiberius [Claudius] Caesar Augustus Germanicus Imperator, Mecheir 17th, *dies Augustus*.

THE HAND APPEARS A practiced semicursive, and yet it is possible to see how it was made one stroke at a time; the writer may have been an experienced professional deliberately writing slowly. The letter is in the same hand throughout.

The letter is a bit abrupt and peremptory in style but correct and businesslike. The writer has corrected the end of a line to avoid an incorrect syllabic division. The absence of any greetings and the professionalism of the writing suggest a scribe.

This letter is strikingly lacking in any personal greetings or sense of connection, and it is possible that "brother" here does not denote a family relationship at all but is a business agent. Cf. *P.Oxy.* 36.2789, where Moros the "brother" of the writer is identified in another letter as a mason.

NOTES
wheel: Presumably the *saqiya*, the animal-driven compartmented waterwheel used for raising water to garden land, which was usually walled. This is one of the oldest mentions of such a wheel.

dies Augustus: This is here the birthday of Britannicus, the son of Claudius and Messalina.

LOCATION OF OBJECT
New York, Columbia University Libraries, Rare Book and Manuscript Library, inv. 493.

BIBLIOGRAPHY
Gonis 1997a: 139, note 13; cf. Wilcken 1937: 82–83.

P.Mich. 8.464

Apollonous to Julius Terentianus: the children go to school
March, AD 99

LOCATION WRITTEN   Unknown
LOCATION OF ADDRESSEE   Unknown
LOCATION FOUND   Karanis

Greek

෴ ෴ ෴

Apollonous to Terentianus her brother, greetings and, before all, good health. I wish you to know that since I wrote to you beforehand about my affairs, well, then . . . that the rental in kind and all the seed will be entirely available. And do not worry about the children: they are well and attend (the lessons of) a woman teacher. And with regard to your fields, I relieved your brother from 2 artabas of the rent; well, then, I receive from him 8 artabas of wheat and 6 artabas of vegetable seed. And do not worry about us and take care of yourself. I was informed by Thermouthas that you procured yourself a pair of belts and I was very glad. And with regard to the olive groves, they bear good fruit so far. And with the gods' will come to us if you can. And I wish you to be healthy and your children salute you and all your people. Farewell. Year 2 of the emperor Caesar Nerva Trajan Augustus Germanicus, Phamenoth (?) 20.

(ADDRESS ON BACK): Deliver it to Julius Terentianus soldier.

෴ ෴ ෴

ACCORDING TO THE EDITION, this is a proficient letter hand.

The letter mostly consists of a series of clauses connected paratactically and of some exhortations in the imperative. It is rather correct besides the usual nonstandard phonetic spelling.

Apollonous writes to Julius Terentianus, a soldier away in service, who was probably her husband. In his absence, she is capably managing their affairs and reporting to him by letter. This letter is full of positive news with regard to the productivity of their fields and olive groves. As Apollonous reassures her husband about the well-being of their children, she provides an intriguing detail: The children are following the lessons of a woman teacher. It is also interesting that apparently another woman informed Apollonous that Terentianus had gotten himself a pair of belts (?). This Apollonous may also be the author of *P.Col.* 8.215 (so Gonis 2003).

NOTE

attend the lessons of a teacher: Cf. *PSI* 1.94. About women teachers and the terms *deskale* and *deskalos*, see Cribiore 1996: 22–24. Considering the status of this family, this teacher must have taught reading and writing.

LOCATION OF OBJECT

Cairo, Egyptian Museum, Michigan inv. 6001.

BIBLIOGRAPHY

White 1986: no. 101; *BL* 8.214 (line 3); Gonis 2003.

P.Oxy. 14.1758

Diogenis to Didymas about agricultural work
Second century AD

LOCATION WRITTEN   Alexandria
LOCATION OF ADDRESSEE   Unknown
LOCATION FOUND   Oxyrhynchos

Greek

Diogenis to her most esteemed Didymas, greetings. Before everything I pray that you are well, with your children whom the evil eye does not touch, and I make your obeisance before the great Sarapis, praying for the best for you and all your household. Please sequester the fertilizer which my tenant Hatres dug up from my fields, and do not permit him to pile it up until I arrive. Also take care of handling the other unsettled business I have with you, so that I may not become an object of contempt because of my negligence. I greet all those you hold dear.

(ADDRESS): Deliver to Didymas (papyrus breaks off).

THE HANDWRITING IS A fluent cursive, not quite as rapid as it looks at first glance, with breaks mainly between syllables. There are a few corrected letters, but the whole is unmistakably the work of an experienced and competent writer.

The language of the letter is businesslike and unadorned, with a certain abruptness. The vocabulary, however, is extensive, with unusual words. The overall tone is that of an educated woman writing to a not wholly satisfactory employee in some irritation, probably using a scribe used to writing business documents and letters.

The main object of this letter is an order to Didymas to stop Hatres, Diogenis's tenant, from using a quantity of fertilizer that he has dug on her land, until Diogenis can arrive and direct matters to her liking. She also nudges Didymas to take care of other unfinished business for the sake of her reputation. Didymas is perhaps a local estate manager or steward of Diogenis in charge of her Oxyrhynchite holdings.

NOTES

Sarapis: References to making obeisance before Sarapis indicate Alexandria as the place of writing.

fertilizer: Gk. *chous*, the exact meaning of which is not certain. It may refer to well-aged manure. See *P.Col.* 10.273.11, note.

Dallas, Bridwell Library, Perkins School of Theology, Southern Methodist University.

P.Ryl. 2.243

Demarion and Eirene to their steward about lack of water
Second century AD

LOCATION WRITTEN   Unknown
LOCATION OF ADDRESSEE   Unknown
LOCATION FOUND   Unknown

Greek

Demarion and Eirene to their dearest Syros, many greetings. We know that you are distressed about the deficiency of water; this has happened not only to us but to many, and we know that nothing has occurred through any fault of yours. Even now we know your zeal and attentiveness to the work of the allotment, and we hope that with god's help the field has been sown. Put down to our account everything you expend on the cultivation of the allotment. Receive from Ninnaros for Eirene's account the share belonging to her, and similarly from Hatres for Demarion's account the share belonging to her. We pray for your health.

(ADDRESS): To Syros from Eirene and Demarion.

THIS IS THE WORK of a professional: text and handwriting are at the same level. The hand is round, flattened and clear but shows more ligatures than the usual letter hand. It is rather fast but the writer often tries to slow down.

This is generally a good piece of business prose, with extensive use of participial phrases and a relative clause. There are a couple of corrections and one duplicated syllable; spelling is generally good.

This letter is clearly written in response to one from Syros, the women's steward. Syros has reported on a lack of water, whether the result of a low Nile or of a problem with the distribution system is hard to say. The remark that this has happened to many suggests that a low Nile is at fault. The authors are at pains to assure Syros that they know that this is not his fault, and that his qualities are as appreciated as always.

LOCATION OF OBJECT
Manchester, John Rylands University Library, *P.Ryl.* 243.

6. WORK: WEAVING AND CLOTHES MAKING

P.Oxy. 14.1679

Apia to Serapias about clothing
Third century AD

LOCATION WRITTEN Unknown
LOCATION OF ADDRESSEE Unknown
LOCATION FOUND Oxyrhynchos

Greek

Apia to Serapias her lady mother, greetings. I greet you warmly, lady,
praying for the best for you. Receive from the seamstress, my lady, the
saffron-colored clothes of your daughter, a tunic and a . . . , and a tunic for
Heraklammon. I think that you will recognize which are those of your
daughter, for I rolled them up with one another. The seamstress will
transmit to you verbally what I told her, for I am writing this to you very
late. Agathos is coming to you perhaps on the ninth to bring you some
things for the festival. So, lady, do not be in suspense, we are fine. Serenos
your son greets you warmly, and Lucius and Techosis and the children and
Taamois and all our people. I greet your people. I greet warmly Loukammon
my brother, whom I beg to write to us if he received his tunic from Leukos,
since Beryllos forgot to take it. I greet warmly Alexandros and Kyrillous. I
pray for your health.

(ADDRESS): To Serapias her mother, (from) Apia.

THE CHARACTERS ARE DETACHED except for some connecting strokes. The
strokes are of normal weight, and the lines are well laid out. There are, however, many remade letters and a too frequent dipping of the pen into the ink,
as well as some corrections. A single hand has written the whole letter. It is
somewhat similar to the handwriting of Aurelia Charite (see plates V and
XXX in P.Charite).

There are ten corrections in the text, mostly rewritings and insertions, in
twenty-nine lines. Actual blunders in the final version, however, are few, and

these mostly phonetic banalities (vowel interchanges). There is a relative clause and occasionally an interesting word order. The basic connectives are found. The overall impression is of tolerable fluency and grace.

This letter was written to be carried by a seamstress who was also bringing some items of clothing, and it is, apart from the usual greetings, mainly occupied with a list of the garments to be expected. The writer informs us that the letter itself was written at the last minute before the departure of the seamstress.

LOCATION OF OBJECT
High Wycombe, Bucks, England, Wycombe Abbey School.

BIBLIOGRAPHY
P.Mich. 8.501.15n. (*BL* 3.139), on the reading in lines 6–7.

P.Oxy. 31.2593

Apollonia to Philetos and Herakleides about woolen materials
Second century AD

LOCATION WRITTEN   Unknown
LOCATION OF ADDRESSEE   Unknown
LOCATION FOUND   Oxyrhynchos

Greek

❧ ❧ ❧

Apollonia to Philetos, greetings. I greet you warmly, and Herakleides, and I sent you by way of Onnophris the younger the yarn for the outfit of Herakleides: 7 mnai of woof at a weight of [.] staters, making 110 reels; and warp from Lykopolis weighing 90 staters, that is 75 balls. The price of these is: for the warp, at twenty-one drachmas for 30 staters weight, total 63 dr.; the price of the wool of the woof is 36 dr. 30 staters' weight has already been spun for one stater, and I gave 4 dr. from my own funds for the expense of preparation of a weight of 10 staters of wool. I gave out to be spun three mnai at the rate of an obol for a stater's weight, making 17 dr. 5 ob., and I spun the remaining four mnai and put into them a colored black thread; from them put three mnai into the cloak of the outfit. We greet you warmly. Farewell. The warp has been soaked here at my place. (second hand) Year [. .], Thoth.

(ADDRESS): Deliver to Philetos for Herakleides.

❧ ❧ ❧

THE LETTERS ARE ALMOST wholly detached. The characters are sometimes a bit awkward but mostly well made. There are a couple of corrections. The writer of the body of the letter gives the impression of being a private person with adequate experience and a decent command of the script but probably not used to writing a great deal. The second hand may be that of Apollonia.

The letter's text is an almost unbroken series of statements of amounts spent on various activities, strung together paratactically with little except repeated "and" for connection. Case endings are occasionally a problem.

Almost the whole of this letter is occupied with information about materials for spinning and weaving. If the date is in fact in Apollonia's hand, it confirms that she is to be seen more as an entrepreneur or business agent than as simply engaged in her household weaving; indeed, she contracts some work out.

NOTES

woof: The threads running at right angles to the warp on the loom.

We greet you: The writer uses singular forms elsewhere.

LOCATION OF OBJECT

Oxford, Papyrology Rooms, Sackler Library.

BIBLIOGRAPHY

Rowlandson 1998: 269, no. 205.

P.Oxy. 59.3991

Sarapias to Ischyrion
Second–third century AD

LOCATION WRITTEN Unknown
LOCATION OF ADDRESSEE Unknown
LOCATION FOUND Oxyrhynchos

Greek

Sarapias to Ischyrion her brother, greetings. I was overjoyed when your letter was received, because you are coming to us for the festival. A lot of supplies, which we were going to send to you, we held back expecting your presence. Your mother made you the cotton tunic. We were looking for someone reliable who could deliver it. Your mother and Sinthonis and your father greet you. Greet Epaphroditos and Demetrios and Herakleides. We had been in no small anxiety because no letter of yours had been received for a long time. Farewell. Tybi 16.

(ADDRESS): From Sarapias to Ischyrion.

THE HAND IS SEMILIGATURED, becoming rather more cursive as it goes on. The writer had some difficulty controlling the flow of ink, and too frequent dippings of the pen can be identified. Apart from that, however, the hand is a competent, practiced one.

The language is mostly straightforward and unadorned, although the word order is more complicated—even sophisticated—than one might expect, with verbs held back toward the end of the sentence at times and relative clauses inserted in the middle of the main clause. There are a couple of corrections and various bits of colloquial spelling.

Sarapias expresses her pleasure at Ischyrion's plans to come for an approaching festival, perhaps about a week away at the time of writing. His long silence had worried them, and they had accumulated some provisions to send him, which they will now hold for his arrival.

NOTES

festival: The editor notes that Oxyrhynchos had a known festival connected with the gymnasium which took place around Tybi 24.

cotton: Relatively rare in Roman Egypt, despite its later importance in the Egyptian economy. It is a summer crop and thus could not be grown on inundated land, which was under water in the summer. It is now known to have been grown in the western oases, where there was no inundation.

Tybi 16: 11 or 12 January.

SB 6.9026

Areskousa to Herakles about cotton
Second century AD

LOCATION WRITTEN   Unknown
LOCATION OF ADDRESSEE   Unknown
LOCATION FOUND   Unknown

Greek

∾ ∾ ∾

Areskousa to Herakles her brother, greeting. You wrote to me about the sow
either to sell it, or to take it home with me, or to supply the cost of its
support. While I wish to supply the cost, they submitted significant
accounts, but I did not dare to undergo such an expense without (asking)
your opinion. But I gave them 8 drachmas on account until you arrive and
know what you have agreed upon. For the litter, however, I supply what
they ask. By all means send me by this shipment 20 drachmas of cotton of
good thread, but make sure not to forget because your brothers do not have
their outer garments, since their cotton garments are worn out, and they
need them because—you know—they work in the field all the time. Salute
all your people each by name. Charmos salutes you as well as Herakleides
and Tanechotes and Sarapion and the little Seuthes and Tauris and
Apollonarion and all the people by us. Farewell.

(ADDRESS ON PAPYRUS FRONT): To my brother Herakles from Areskousa.

∾ ∾ ∾

THE WRITER WAS A first-rate professional. This hand has rhythm, a sense of
proportion, and grace. The characters are mostly separated, but epsilon, which
is unligatured, is formed cursively.

The text is well written in every respect—orthography, morphology, and
syntax. Note the articular infinitives and the consistent use of connectives.
The writer occasionally employs recherché words.

When Areskousa writes to Herakles, whom she calls "brother," she has two
pressing concerns: The care of a sow and its litter, and cotton to make outer
garments for her brothers. This letter is a rare but important testimony to the
use of cotton in Egypt. The people sending their salutations are neatly divided
into three groups: men, children, and women.

Ann Arbor, University of Michigan Library, Papyrus Collection, inv. 1648.

SB 14.11881

Allous to Faustina concerning orphaned children
Fourth century AD

LOCATION WRITTEN   Unknown
LOCATION OF ADDRESSEE   Unknown
LOCATION FOUND   Unknown

Greek

Allous to my lady mother Faustina, greetings in the Lord. Having chanced upon a letter carrier, I greet your motherly disposition, my lady. Since the things you wrote to me show . . . that it is possible . . . to come . . . [long lacuna] the (needs) of the orphaned children of my brother for which, being a woman, I am unable to suffice. Therefore, if you have enough, send me through the letter carrier 2 pounds of tow so that I could spin and spend them for them. I greet you heartily. The little children salute you. I salute mother Kyriake. I pray for your health.

WRITTEN THROUGHOUT BY AN experienced hand, which is not particularly attractive. The slight sense of unevenness mostly derives from the thick pen used. The letters are small, clear and mostly separated. It seems that the writer could go much faster.

In spite of only a few connective particles and relatively short sentences, this letter shows a good command of Greek, with correct use of tenses and no phonetic spelling errors. Note the Christian convention of the contraction of the *nomen sacrum* "Lord."

Allous writes to Faustina asking her to help her out in providing for the orphaned children of her own brother. It is unsure whether Faustina was the woman's real mother or an older, esteemed lady. Probably the second hypothesis is preferable, considering that at the end of the letter another lady is also greeted as "mother."

LOCATION OF OBJECT
Ann Arbor, University of Michigan Library, Papyrus Collection, inv. 430.

P.Abinn. 34

A mother appeals for military leave for her son
Ca. AD 340–350

LOCATION WRITTEN   Arsinoite nome
LOCATION OF ADDRESSEE   Dionysias
LOCATION FOUND   Perhaps Philadelphia

Greek

To my lord and patron the praepositus, (from) the mother of Moses. You
sent for Heron, lord patron, so he went with the barbarians. After God we
have no help other than you. So I sent Athioeis to you, my lord. I beg your
feet, lord patron, since you also know that "the five days are the whole
year," I beg you and beseech you, lord, to permit him the few days. If you
order something, lord, tell Athioeis. I pray for your health, lord patron.

THE LETTER IS WRITTEN in a rapid, rather cursive letter hand with some measure of stylishness, experienced and fluent. The concluding wish for health is
in the same hand, but written more rapidly. The writer is clearly a professional.

The orthography of the letter is more than ordinarily reflective of the
spoken language, with many nonstandard spellings. More striking still is the
abruptness of the letter, with one short, jerky phrase following another. Despite the professional quality of the handwriting, the letter must reflect a direct
transcription of the woman's dictation.

The unnamed mother of Moses writes to Abinnaeus, the praepositus of an
army unit stationed at the fort at Dionysias (northwest corner of the Fayyum)
to ask for a few days' leave for her son. She tells us that Heron, evidently
another son, had been called up by Abinnaeus; just what Moses's status was,
we do not learn.

with the barbarians: The editor takes this to mean joining the military.

five days: Although five days are a common accounting period, as the editor points out, the force of the apparently proverbial expression here is not clear.

LOCATION OF OBJECT

London, British Library, Papyrus 410. Plate in *P.Lond.* Atlas II, pl. 102.

P.Mich. 3.202

Valeria and Thermouthas ask Thermouthion to be the nurse of a child
AD 105

LOCATION WRITTEN   Unknown
LOCATION OF ADDRESSEE   Unknown
LOCATION FOUND   Unknown

Greek

∾ ∾ ∾

Valeria and Thermouthas both together to sister Thermouthion, greeting. As I have asked you on sailing down about the child of Thermouthas to rear it and nurse it, you (will be) happy if you do it. With regard to the two houses you are going to enjoy and be fulfilled. Take 5 staters (or: experience a change from taking 5 staters). If you decide to be a nurse, you are going to find higher wages, because it is a freeborn child, and your fulfillment, and you are going to find parents, if you do it. Sail down in the boat so that you may go upstream with us and the child. Bring from my mother 5 staters if you sail down so that we may go upcountry, or take what you want. I am asking you to sail down in order that you may be happy, for a freeborn child is one thing but a slave is another. Farewell. Year 8 of Trajan the lord. Pachon 10.

(ADDRESS ON BACK): Give it to Thermoutheion in Poeso (at the house) of Theodoros from Valeria.

∾ ∾ ∾

THE HAND IS LARGE, round, and very clear. The letter occupies the entire sheet. It is written slowly, with mostly separated characters. It betrays some

familiarity with writing but no real proficiency. The characters are a bit wobbly, and the inclination varies from upright to bent backward.

The letter shows a good command of Greek but is almost like a conversation. There are practically no connectives. The letter ends abruptly without
final salutations, not even to the writer's mother.

Two women ask a third woman to become the nurse of the child of one of
them. Thermouthion, who was probably very young, lives upcountry, is rearing
a slave child, and knows the mother of Valeria, the writer. Valeria claims that
she will be happier and earn higher wages if she takes up this new job.

NOTES

Valeria and Thermouthas: There is much emphasis on the fact that this
letter is sent by both women. Probably Valeria wants to underline that this
is not only her initiative.

sister: In this case the word does not indicate a family relationship.

parents: This allusion makes it likely that Thermouthion was quite young.

LOCATION OF OBJECT

Ann Arbor, University of Michigan Library, Papyrus Collection, inv. 122.
Plate VII in ed.prin.

BIBLIOGRAPHY

Reprinted as Pestman 1994: no. 26. For the reading Poeso in the address,
see *BL* 3.111.

P.Oxy. 10.1295

Tasois to Dionysios about his treatment of her son
Second–third century AD

LOCATION WRITTEN   Unknown
LOCATION OF ADDRESSEE   Unknown
LOCATION FOUND   Oxyrhynchos

Greek

∽ ∽ ∽

Tasois to her most esteemed Dionysios, greetings. Look, I did not imitate
you by trying to take away my son, but if you intend to rebuke him in this
way, I shall send Ptolemaios and remove him. When his father died, I gave
1,300 drachmas for him and I expended 60 drachmas on his clothing. For
this reason, therefore, stop trying to persuade him to be away from me, or I
shall take him and leave him in Alexandria as a pledge. Now please send
me two months' salary by the man who brings you the letter and the
clothing, and let me know how much money you have given to him and if
you received the clothing. Send the hooded cloak to your brother. Farewell.

(ADDRESS): To Dionysios from Tasois.

∽ ∽ ∽

THIS IS A SMALL, flattened hand with few ligatures and rigid characters. The
thick pen increases the generally unattractive look. It is a hand, however, that
can be trusted to do much writing.

The letter is emotionally forceful by the standards of papyrus letters; its
language is correspondingly strong and lacking in expressive subtlety. The
Greek is, however, formally grammatical.

Tasois remonstrates with Dionysios for attempting to alienate her son from
her. Almost everything else is unclear. From the mention of two months'
salary, it has been supposed that the relationship involved a work contract,
in which the boy was put to work for a salary paid to his mother. But the role
of the 1,300 drachmas mentioned is unclear; it is vastly in excess of anything
one would pay a master for teaching an apprentice. Even for a teacher in
letters it would be substantial. But Tasois's threat to use the boy as a pledge
(presumably for a loan) in Alexandria makes no sense if he does not have
some value. In any event, the mother's control of the boy after his father's
death is underlined by her threats.

NOTE

1,300 drachmas: A sizable sum of money, at least half a year's income for an
average family at this period.

LOCATION OF OBJECT
Shropshire, the Library, Shrewsbury School.

BIBLIOGRAPHY
Sel.Pap. 1.129; Hengstl 1978: no. 116; Gonis 1999: 212, line 10.

P.Oxy. 12.1581

Apia to Zoilos
Second century AD

LOCATION WRITTEN   Unknown
LOCATION OF ADDRESSEE   Unknown
LOCATION FOUND   Oxyrhynchos

Greek

Apia to Zoilos her brother, greetings. Before everything I pray that you are well. At my request, brother, do not let Sarapion be idle and roam aimlessly, but put him to work. I made the loaves of bread. I will send them to you by Ptolemaios when Ptolemaios himself gets them. Greet Modestas and his son; you will hand some over also to Modestas from whatever you receive. Always keep an eye on Sarapion. Greet also Hermione and Herakleides and his son. My father —is greets you and Sarapion.

(ADDRESS): From Apia to Zoilos [her brother?].

THE HANDWRITING IS FLUENT and rapid, evincing much experience.

The writer makes a valiant effort to compose felicitous Greek prose, but the results are mechanical and jerky. The writing is mostly correct, with some accurate use of iota adscript. The overall effect is of a fairly competent scribe attempting to soften the harsh asyndeton and jerkiness of Apia's dictation, but doing so semicompetently.

Apart from the usual greetings, the letter has two concerns. The more pressing is keeping Sarapion, perhaps Apia's son, busy and out of mischief. The other is bread, which Apia has made and promises to send to Zoilos, who in turn is to share it with Modestas.

LOCATION OF OBJECT
Hampstead, Caroline Skeel Library, Westfield College, University of London.

SB 5.7737

Senpikos to her son Melas
First–second century AD

LOCATION WRITTEN Unknown
LOCATION OF ADDRESSEE Unknown
LOCATION FOUND Unknown

Greek

∾ ∾ ∾

Senpikos to her son Melas, many greetings. I wish you to know that your brother . . .thotes was designated to accompany on ship the grain to Alexandria and he gave a guarantee in writing and is receiving the grain already. Now, if he is traveling, I cannot come to you: I am making loaves of bread for him and I am getting him ready. I salute Tapenis and Aplonarion and put shoes on her because of scorpions. Ioulas salutes you. Once your brother leaves, I (will) dye the wool and take it. Farewell.

∾ ∾ ∾

THE LINES ARE WELL spaced, and the flow of the writing is evenly maintained. Because of lack of space, the last lines are more crowded.

This letter, which is rather correct except for some phonetic spellings, presents relatively short and simple sentences joined by "and" and only one connective particle.

Senpikos is torn between her two sons, one who would like her to visit him bringing some dyed wool and the other who has the official task of taking grain to Alexandria. She chooses to help out the latter in his preparations.

LOCATION OF OBJECT
Cairo, Egyptian Museum, Journal d'Entrée 60329.

8. JOURNEYS ∾

BGU 3.843

Takalis to Serenos
First–second century AD

LOCATION WRITTEN   Alexandria
LOCATION OF ADDRESSEE   Unknown
LOCATION FOUND   Unknown

Greek

∾ ∾ ∾

Takalis to Serenos her brother, many greetings. Before everything I pray that you are well, and I make your obeisance before the lord Sarapis. I want you to know that thanks to the gods I arrived in Alexandria in six days . . . a ring for my right finger . . . The (child?) of Panis thanks you because you received your sister well. I greet my mother. I said to your son to send you a chiton and the money Quintus didn't give you. I greet my sister and . . . everyone. I greet Sarapias and all her people. I greet . . . and her son . . . Ptolemaios (greets?) Serenos . . . I pray for your health.

∾ ∾ ∾

"UNPRACTICED HAND" SAYS THE editor.

There are several corrections in the Greek, but not enough. The intended case of "days" is left uncertain by the form written, and endings are sometimes omitted on a definite article and on the verb "send."

Damage to the papyrus makes some of the details of the letter unclear. Takalis is in Alexandria, but the reasons for her trip are not evident.

LOCATION OF OBJECT
Berlin, Staatliche Museen, Papyrussammlung, P. 7205; sent to Greifswald, at present unlocated.

BIBLIOGRAPHY
BL 1.71 (on line 8).

BGU 7.1680

Isis to Thermouthion
Third century AD

LOCATION WRITTEN   Alexandria
LOCATION OF ADDRESSEE   Philadelphia (?)
LOCATION FOUND   Philadelphia

Greek

Isis to Thermouthion her mother, many greetings. I make obeisance for you each day before the lord Sarapis and the associated gods. I want you to know that I have arrived well and safely in Alexandria in four days. I greet my sister and the children, and Elouath and his wife, and Dioskorous and her husband and children, and Tamalis and her husband and her son, and Heron, and Ammonarion and her children and her husband, and Sanpat and her children. And if Aion wants to join the army, let him go; for everyone is joining the army. I pray for your health with all your household.

(ADDRESS): [To Thermouthion] from Isis her daughter.

ISIS USED A PROFESSIONAL scribe in Alexandria to write this letter for her. The characters are large and very fluent, and sometimes the writer prolongs boldly some strokes. The letter is written relatively fast with a good number of ligatures, but legibility is excellent. The professionalism of the writer also shows in the use of an apostrophe and of diaeresis.

The Greek of the letter is generally good, with a few corrections. There is little style, but the aorist and present are used accurately in the concluding sentence, and the writer gives a sense of command of the letter form.

Most of the letter is occupied with greetings, and its main purpose was certainly just to let Thermouthion know that Isis had arrived from Philadelphia in four days, a very good time for the journey from the Fayyum to Alexandria. The remark at the end may suggest a time of general mobilization for war.

NOTE
Elouath, Sanpat, Tamalis: The first of these is perhaps a Semitic name. The second has an apostrophe after it, indicating that the writer recognized it as a name lacking Greek declensional endings.

LOCATION OF OBJECT
Berlin, Staatliche Museen, Papyrussammlung, P. 11494.

BIBLIOGRAPHY

Schubart 1923: 102, no. 73 (translation); *Sel.Pap.* 1.134 (translation). Cf. *BL* 10.21 (on the restoration of a name in line 6).

BGU 13.2350

Aphrodite is stepped on by a horse
Second century AD (?)

LOCATION WRITTEN Unknown
LOCATION OF ADDRESSEE Unknown
LOCATION FOUND Unknown

Greek

Aphrodite to Taonnophris her sister, many greetings. Before everything I pray that you are well; and I want you to know that . . . to go to Alexandria, my foot was trodden by a horse and I was in danger, so that I have been healed at great expense, and until today I have been out of action. So I ask you, if you do not have at your place the key of the storeroom which . . . jar of . . .

(ADDRESS): Deliver to Taonnophris.

THE HAND IS SMALL, smooth, and practiced. It does not use real ligatures but sometimes links some of the letters. It intentionally maintains a low speed and only occasionally lets itself go. This is the hand of someone who could write a text of any length at any speed but here opted for good legibility.

The style is colloquial and paratactic, the orthography mildly phonetic.

Aphrodite was in transit to Alexandria, but her foot was stepped on by a horse; recovery has taken considerable time and money.

LOCATION OF OBJECT
Berlin, Staatliche Museen, Papyrussammlung, P. 21468.

BIBLIOGRAPHY
BL 8.59 (corrections to lines 9 and 13).

P.Bingen 74

Herais to Lucretias
Second century AD, after 130

LOCATION WRITTEN   Probably Alexandria
LOCATION OF ADDRESSEE   Unknown
LOCATION FOUND   Unknown

Greek

Herais to her sister Lucretias, greetings. Before everything I pray that you
are in good health and your children without harm. I and my children are
in good health too, making obeisance for you before the lord Sarapis. Don't
be concerned about Antonius. Up to now, he has not yet enlisted in the
army. I want you to know that those who sojourn in Egypt are under the
authority of the epistrategos. If you travel up to Antinoopolis, write me at
once so that I may come to see you. But if it turns out that you are not
going, then write me too so that I won't go uselessly from this place to that.
Know that when I arrived downriver I found Eros locked up, and I went to
your brother. No matter how often I asked him, he did not want to set him
free, but said, "If he wishes to go upstream, then he shall pay dues to the
orphans." On the fourth day after I came to the city, Nephotianus came
too. Write us whether you have received the purple dye from Peteesios the
boatman. Greet Lucretias, Eutychos, and Apphys [[and Apollonia]].
Antonius, Koprous and Nephotianus greet you.

(ADDRESS): Deliver to Lucretias from Herais.

THE HAND IS LARGELY detached, with letters of uneven size but made with
experience. One forms the impression of someone used to writing in a faster—
but not very regular—hand, deliberately trying to produce a letter hand—
someone used to writing on business. There are three corrections with crossed-
out words, one of them erroneous. The editors suggest that the last represents
a misunderstanding between Herais dictating the letter and her amanuensis.

Phonetic spelling is commonplace. The style overall is somewhat rambling,
with occasional attempts at connective particles but for the most part rather
abrupt paratactic constructions.

This letter is a classic example of a letter dealing with significant business
matters in an allusive fashion opaque to unintended readers, including us.
Herais has made a major trip downriver, with a stop along the way attempting
to settle the matter of a freedman or slave who has been detained over a
dispute about rights to payments by him to some orphans. She reports that
one family member has not yet enlisted in the army before going on to inform

Lucretias about the competence of the regional governor, the epistrategos, over persons (Alexandrians? Antinoites?) in the Egyptian countryside. Herais then says that she will travel to Antinoopolis, presumably for litigation in front of the epistrategos, if Lucretias goes there; but if not, not.

NOTES

[[and Apollonia]]: The double brackets indicate that the writer deleted these words.

LOCATION OF OBJECT

Ann Arbor, University of Michigan Library, Papyrus Collection, inv. 3241.

P.Köln 1.56

Diodora to Valerius Maximus
First–second century AD

LOCATION WRITTEN   Unknown
LOCATION OF ADDRESSEE   Unknown
LOCATION FOUND   Unknown

Greek

∽ ∽ ∽

Diodora to Valerius Maximus greetings and be in all good health. I want you to know that it is ten days that we came first to the metropolis and I went straightaway to your sister and right away I wrote to you that I am free from harm and we were saved with the gods' will. Salute the mother and Paulina and Poplis (Publius) and Diodoros and Grania and Tyche. And please write to me . . . and if I (complete) what is incumbent and I am free from harm I will sail down quickly. Phaophi 1. Farewell.

(ADDRESS ON BACK): Give to Maximus from Diodo(ra).

∽ ∽ ∽

THE ENTIRE TEXT, INCLUDING the address, is written slowly in one hand, with multistroke letters, frequent dipping, and strokes retraced. The result is a very coarse and unproficient hand somehow reminiscent of a literary hand. This might well be Diodora's own hand. The final greeting does not show any more fluency.

The style of the letter is simple and paratactic. There are iotacistic errors and others due to lack of sensitivity to vowel quantity.

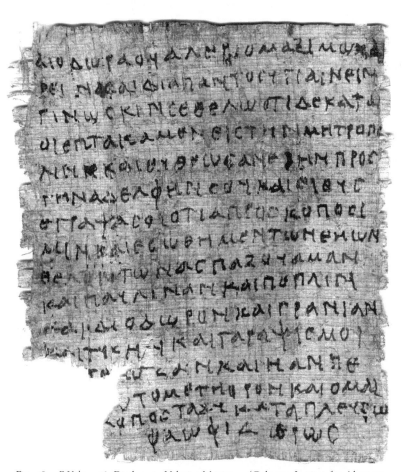

Fig. 28. *P.Köln* 1.56. Diodora to Valerius Maximus. (Cologne, Institut für Altertumskunde, Papyrussammlung, inv. 21. Photograph courtesy of the Digitization Project, Cologne Papyri, sponsored by the Deutsche Forschungsgemeinschaft.)

Diodora writes to Valerius Maximus, who was probably a soldier and perhaps her husband. She is reporting to him ten days after she arrived in a certain nome capital to take care of some business.

NOTES
Diodora: See the remarks of the editor on the relationship of Diodora and Maximus.

we: It is likely that Diodora went to the city accompanied by other people.

Grania: It is uncertain whether this name is feminine or is instead to be taken as Granias, masculine.

Diodo(ra): In the address the name *Diodoras* abbreviated to *Diodo* may represent a nickname.

LOCATION OF OBJECT
Cologne, Institut für Altertumskunde, Papyrussammlung, inv. 21.

BIBLIOGRAPHY
Rea 1980: 262, which sees *Granian* as a feminine name and *aman* as *amman*, a term that indicates a foster mother, a nurse, a head of a convent, or a simple nun (Lampe: 89).

P.Oxy. 14.1773

Eutychis to her mother Ametrion
Third century AD

LOCATION WRITTEN   Antinoopolis
LOCATION OF ADDRESSEE   Oxyrhynchos
LOCATION FOUND   Oxyrhynchos

Greek

Eutychis to Ametrion her mother, many greetings. Before everything I pray to God to find you well. I want you to know that I came to the Tyrannion on the 30th of Tybi, and I could not find any way to come to you, because the camel drivers refused to go to the Oxyrhynchite. Not only that, but I went up to Antinoou(polis) for a boat and did not find any. So now I considered bringing my loads to Antinoou and staying there until I find a boat and sail down. Please give the people who deliver to you this letter of mine two and a half talents of new coinage, that is, 2 tal. 3,000 dr., in return for that which I asked for and got from them in the Tyrannion on account of transport charges, and don't detain them even one hour . . . Receive from them two thousand ninety-two drachmas of old (coinage), that is, 2,092 dr. in full, and my donkey with the saddle cloth. But if you know that you don't have (the money) in your hands, borrow from . . . and pay them, since they cannot wait one hour. See to it that you do not blunder and hinder the men who have benefited me. Greet for me all in the house and all our friends; I'll be coming to you soon. I pray for your health.

(BACK) (ADDRESS): to the Camp, where . . . ask for . . .

(ADDRESS): To Ametrion her mother, from Taurine.

THE HAND IS SEMIDETACHED, but the fluency and shapes of the individual letters, a few ligatures, and a bit of a rightward slant combine to give the impression of a more cursive character than the handwriting actually has.

For the most part the letter is well composed. Ordinary connectives are used as needed. The spelling is phonetic. The writer clearly had some experience with writing business documents, to judge both from the handwriting and from the practiced way in which an abbreviation is written, along with the symbols for talents and drachmas and the numerals.

Eutychis recounts her difficulties in traveling to Oxyrhynchos from an unknown point in the Thebaid. She is evidently heavily loaded with goods, and her first plan was to travel by camel. But for whatever reason the camel drivers refused to make the trip. Next she decided to travel by boat, but that too has been frustrated by the lack of any vessel in Antinoopolis. She has for the moment decided to stay there until a suitable vessel appears. It is not said how the men delivering the letter are traveling to Oxyrhynchos.

NOTES

Antinoou(polis): Hadrian's foundation, located about 80 km south of Oxyrhynchos and across the river from Hermopolis.

Camp: A quarter of Oxyrhynchos.

Taurine: There is no obvious explanation for the appearance of a different name for the sender here.

LOCATION OF OBJECT

Bolton, Lancashire, Bolton Museum, Art Gallery and Aquarium, inv. 17.22.4.

BIBLIOGRAPHY

Ghedini 1923: no. 8; Naldini 1998: no. 10.

SB 5.8027

Tarem. . . to her father Chairemon
Second–third century AD

LOCATION WRITTEN Unknown
LOCATION OF ADDRESSEE Arsinoite nome
LOCATION FOUND Arsinoite nome

Greek

Tarem. . . to Chairemon her father, very many greetings and before everything I pray for your health and I am well myself with my relatives and I do the obeisance for you before the local gods. He is repentant for what he did; this did not happen to him alone. We are thankful to the gods that he has recovered his mind and his health. Do not trouble yourself to come up—the trouble indeed is not little—if you find the occasion. Taking Persion with me I will sail downriver with him. I salute my sisters and their children and their husbands and my brother. And Panisneus salutes you all each by name and my son Ancharenis salutes you.

(ADDRESS ON BACK): Deliver to . . . village of the Arsinoite . . . from his daughter.

THE LETTER WAS WRITTEN slowly, with the characters separated and somewhat rigid but not badly formed. Even though the writer did not make writing his daily concern, he was not too incompetent. Note that letter size varies and alignment leaves much to be desired, particularly in the address.

The text is in correlation with the hand: it shows a decent command of Greek but no preoccupations with style. It consists of short clauses often connected by *kai*. There are phonetic mistakes and vowel interchange.

Tarem. . . tells her father who lives in the Arsinoite not to come to her because she will try to reach him herself, taking someone else to accompany her. In the central part she alludes to some trouble encountered by another person, but everything is obscure for us.

LOCATION OF OBJECT
Brussels, Musées Royaux d'Art et d'Histoire, inv. E. 7147. Plate in *Chronique d'Égypte* 12 (1937) 96 (first edition).

9. LITERACY AND EDUCATION ⌒

P.Athen. 60

Apollonia and Eunous to Rasion and Demarion
First century BC

LOCATION WRITTEN Unknown
LOCATION OF ADDRESSEE Unknown
LOCATION FOUND Unknown

Greek

Apollonia and Eunous (?) to their sisters Rasion and Demarion, greeting. If you are well, it is good; we are also well. You should light up the lamp in the shrine and shake the pillows. Devote your attention to learning and do not worry about mother, for she is well already. Wait for us. Farewell.

(Postscript): And do not play in the courtyard, but behave well inside (be good and stay inside). Take care of Titoas and Sphairos.

(ADDRESS): From Apollonia and (Eunous) to their sisters Rasion and Demarion.

THE HAND RESEMBLES A book hand. The letters are entirely separated, they vary in size, and the alignment is irregular. The amateurish impression that this letter conveys is also increased by the fact that the writer used a thick pen.

The syntax of this letter is rather simple, but the text is correct and free of phonetic mistakes. It mainly consists of a series of imperatives.

Two sisters, who are perhaps away from the family home, write to their younger sisters. The letter is full of domestic recommendations such as taking care of the family shrine and shaking the pillows. It is conceivable that the exhortation about learning refers to learning to read and write, since one of the older sisters may have been literate. The postscript defines in some way what was the acceptable behavior for a girl: staying inside the house, not playing outside, and taking care of two children who were probably younger relatives.

NOTE

shrine: Perhaps a family shrine to the gods.

LOCATION OF OBJECT

Athens, Greek Papyrological Society.

BIBLIOGRAPHY

BL 4.86, on the epistolary phraseology of lines 3–4.

P.Oxy. 6.930

A mother to her son Ptolemaios
Second–third century AD

LOCATION WRITTEN   Unknown
LOCATION OF ADDRESSEE   Unknown
LOCATION FOUND   Oxyrhynchos

Greek

∾ ∾ ∾

. . . do not hesitate to write to me also about whatever you need from here. I was grieved to learn from the daughter of our teacher Diogenes that he had sailed downriver, for I was free from care about him, knowing that he would look after you as far as possible. I took care to send and inquire about your health and to learn what you were reading. And he said the 6th book, and he testified a great deal concerning your paidagogos. So now, child, you and your paidagogos must take care to place you with a suitable teacher. Your sisters and the children of Theonis, whom the evil eye does not touch, and all our people greet you individually. Greet your esteemed paidagogos Eros. . . .

(ADDRESS): . . . to her son Ptolemaios.

∾ ∾ ∾

THE HAND IS FAIRLY practiced and neat but somewhat irregular; it is mainly detached, with no true ligatures and only a few extension strokes joining alpha or epsilon to following letters. The lines are uneven in baseline and placed rather too close together. It is a respectable but not particularly attractive letter hand.

The Greek style is competent and correct, with basic connective particles used as necessary. There are no pretensions to any higher stylistic characteristics. Errors are absent except for banal vowel interchanges.

This well-known letter is one of the most important witnesses to the structure of secondary education in Greek letters. The recipient has left home, perhaps in the Oxyrhynchite countryside, and moved to Oxyrhynchos to advance his education. As was customary in elite families, he was followed by his pedagogue. Even Oxyrhynchos has turned out to have its difficulties, as professional advancement has caused the tutor engaged by the family to move. The writer is identifiable as female by a participial form, and there is no reason not to take "son" in the address and "child" (*teknon*) in the body of the letter literally. It is noteworthy that she is interested not only in taking care of Ptolemaios's needs for supplies (mainly food, one would suppose) and in his health, but in following the course of his studies. The reference to the *Iliad* is written as if the mother were familiar with it. The boy's father is not mentioned as sending greetings, but this does not tell us if he is dead or merely away from home on business.

NOTES

teacher: Gk. *kathegetes*, giving secondary instruction on a tutorial basis and therefore often itinerant (Cribiore 1996: 16). Diogenes has probably left for Alexandria to look for better opportunities.

the 6th book: "The zeta," as the sixth book of the *Iliad* was called using just the sixth letter of the Greek alphabet. It was a staple of Greek education.

paidagogos: The attendant of the boy, probably a family slave (with a typically servile name) who followed the boy to school. Cf. Cribiore 2001a: 47–50. He may have had some part in the boy's elementary instruction.

LOCATION OF OBJECT

Glasgow, Special Collections Department, Glasgow University Library.

BIBLIOGRAPHY

W.Chr. 138; *Sel.Pap.* 1.130; transl. in Schubart 1923: no. 65. Cf. *BL* 4.60 (on sentence division in line 4); Cribiore 1996: 16; Cribiore 2001a: 48, 50, 54, 138, and 195.

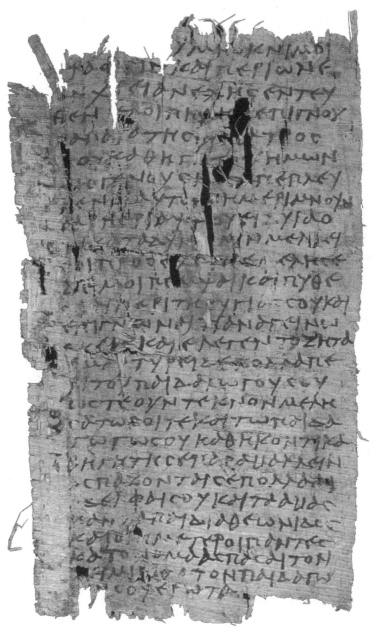

Fig. 29. P.Oxy. 6.930. A mother to her son Ptolemaios. (Glasgow, Special Collections Department, Glasgow University Library. Photograph courtesy of the Glasgow University Library, Department of Special Collections.)

P.Oxy. 56.3860

Taesis to Tiron
Late fourth century AD

LOCATION WRITTEN Unknown
LOCATION OF ADDRESSEE Unknown
LOCATION FOUND Oxyrhynchos

Greek

To my lord husband Tiron, Taesis, many greetings. Before all I pray to the Lord God that the letter from me finds you in good health and spirits. Your sweetest son December greets you and asks after you very frequently. Although you wrote to me, "Pamis is coming to you and bringing you goods," look, he didn't come yet so that I might be free from anxiety, but I am very worried because he did not come. Sabinianos did not come either to bring me the things you have at Oxyrhynchos. If you find someone coming to Oxyrhynchos, write to him or to the guest and to your mother for them to send them to me quickly, while there is water in the canal. If these two months pass, they will not find water in the canal and will no longer be able to come down here. Look, I wrote to Sabinianos and to the guest also concerning what I received from Diogenes, eight spathia and fifty-five myriads, and what I received from Pabion, forty-five knidia and one cover for a dining couch and two solidi, and what I received from Silas, a mattress and two white tunics and a leopard-pattern (garment) and five knidia of pickled olives and a Eulalian quaternion. And your brother sent me fifty sextarii of radish oil for Pamis. I received only these out of everything. Although I wrote to you, "I received twenty-five myriads for the *vestis,*" I did not receive them nor the clothing. Plores has the receipts for everything. Because he said to me "I'm giving these to you on this account on that day," I therefore wrote to you. But on that day I received only the linen tunic. And concerning the mule, I cannot send Argyris [text in margin] because I need him and he is getting the annona for me; and if the goods come from the boat, he is bringing them. [On the back:] And look, my lord, do not be neglectful because of what I wrote you: six mnas of purple (yarn) and a hanging lamp and a lamp stand and a good hand basin and two pounds of good incense and two cups, one small and one big. And look, I am weaving your cloak. And send us a jar of honey, and hurry to come to us quickly. And if you cannot come to us quickly, at least write to us when you are coming, so that we may be in good spirits. Argyris greets you, and Jovinus and Triscentia. Your guest Alexandros greets you, with his wife and children, and I Alexandros wore myself out writing you the letters. And the letter was written on the first of Mecheir. And know that

Mucianus took the mule and four myriads. Send us . . . for our . . . , and a strainer. Send me . . . and a strainer.

(ADDRESS): Deliver to Tiron . . . the officialis of the dux, from Taesis.

THIS REMARKABLE LETTER WAS written on both sides of an almost square piece of papyrus, crowded up against the edges on the front. Virtually all the letters are detached except the combinations *ai* and *ar*; the lines are too close together; and the letters have more vigor than grace. It is not a fast hand, although it is not a very slow one either. The address is larger in size but otherwise identical. This is not the hand of someone who wrote extensively or daily, but rather that of someone with limited schooling. The writer identifies himself: "Your guest Alexandros greets you, together with his wife and children, and it is I, Alexandros, who tired himself out writing you the letter." Clearly this long a letter was indeed exhausting for someone who wrote so slowly.

There are sixty-five corrections or errors in about 390 words. At the begining the writer makes some effort at style, but he cannot keep it up for long and stumbles over almost anything ambitious. After that we revert to "and," only to turn after a bit to sentences that avoid all connective particles. Perhaps the writer became aware of the repeated "and" but lacked the skill to deploy other particles. After a while, "and" reasserts itself and gallops triumphantly on to the end. But there are compensations: the author uses a lot of unusual (even unique) vocabulary. Direct discourse after *hoti* is used with great vigor. On the whole, it seems unlikely that Alexandros was in sufficient command of writing as a skill to have both taken dictation and redone Taesis's prose very much as he did so. We ought to be hearing Taesis almost unvarnished.

The letter covers a range of household business, mostly concerning various items of clothing, furniture, and food. There are also allusions to tax payments. From some references we can deduce that Taesis is located on a country property situated on a seasonal canal. The family house in Oxyrhynchos is currently occupied by her mother-in-law and perhaps a lodger. Tiron himself is elsewhere, perhaps on official business. As we learn from the address, he was an officialis, a civil servant, on the staff of the military governor of the province. That such a position was profitable is indicated by the frequent mentions of luxury goods in the course of the letter.

NOTES

December: The tones in which he is mentioned suggest that he is very young.

guest: Greek transliteration of Latin *hospes*. The exact sense here is unclear; perhaps a lodger?

to Oxyrhynchos: Evidently this is Tiron's home, but he is currently somewhere else, and Taesis is hoping that someone will pass by the home and get things for her. A *hospes* and Tiron's mother are living there at the moment.

water in the canal: Mecheir 1, the date of the letter, is 26 or 27 January. Taesis believes that by late March there will not be enough water in the canal (probably a minor one) to move a boat; one would then have to wait until the summer inundation brought a renewed water supply.

Eulalian quaternion: The term also appears in Diocletian's price edict, but the meaning is unknown.

vestis: Presumably the tax known as *vestis militaris*, intended to pay for clothing for the military.

receipts: It seems that Taesis had written in anticipation of actually receiving the money but then did not get it.

LOCATION OF OBJECT
Oxford, Papyrology Rooms, Sackler Library.

Fig. 30. *P.Oxy.* 56.3860. Taesis to Tiron. (Oxford, Papyrology Rooms, Sackler Library. Photograph courtesy of the Egypt Exploration Society.)

10. RELIGION

Enchoria 25 (1999) 178–82

Two requests for consultation of oracles
Third–second century BC

LOCATION WRITTEN Unknown
LOCATION OF ADDRESSEE Unknown
LOCATION FOUND Qasr Ibrim

Demotic

Prymhy daughter of Senpeteuris greets Kollanthion. Let it be asked (of the oracle) on my behalf before Amun as follows: Since the day, when I departed from the the place of my marriage up to the day, on which Psenosiris gave me the royal (dwelling?), I have not slept and I have not had intercourse with any man except Paonuris the son of Grymya.

Tamandoulis greets Kollanthion. The room where the dung is—if I am to throw him (or her) into it, or into (the room) which is behind it—write to me about this. And have someone take care for Psenparyt, to deal with his inquiries and the things that he will need. And have the goddess give orders to prevent anyone's making trouble.

THE SHEET CONTAINS TWO letters addressed to Kollanthion, both containing business before the oracle, but coming from different women. The first, from a woman with a Nubian name (doubtfully read), represents itself as a question, but is in fact a statement, the truth of which the woman presumably wants the oracle to confirm. It is identical to the oath often taken by women after the end of a marriage, swearing to their marital fidelity.

The second comes from a woman with an Egyptian name formed on the Nubian god Mandoulis. She first asks to have a question put to an unnamed goddess about where a child is to be exposed, then asks Kollanthion to take care of the needs of an otherwise unidentified man, and finally, rather obscurely, apparently asks Kollanthion to make sure the goddess delivers the right answer.

Whether the use of an intermediary here results from the two women's living at a distance from Qasr Ibrim—whether Kollanthion lived there or was only planning to visit—or was simply the local style of consultation of the oracle is unclear.

LOCATION OF OBJECT
Cairo, Egyptian Museum, Journal d'Entrée 95205.

P.Mert. 2.81

Epoeris to Demetrios
Second century AD

LOCATION WRITTEN   Unknown
LOCATION OF ADDRESSEE   Unknown
LOCATION FOUND   Unknown

Greek

Epoeris to Demetrios her son, greeting. Before all things I pray for your health. Do not suppose that I have been neglectful about you. Every ten days I consult the oracle about you on each occasion. So, because I found that good opportunities did not serve you in the present three months, I did not write to you for this reason. You wrote to me concerning the affair of the priest; accordingly, your brother approached him about this and made too much of it, so that the priest said, "It is no longer the concern of the gods." So, after this . . . to him, and you blamed the same excessively, because he himself approached the man about the affair, and . . . (line 32) first and to choose either that you should remain or proceed to Rome. So, if you sail there . . . , when are you intending to return? Be on your guard against those with whom you eat and drink. Everyone in the house greets you; greet all in the house with you. I pray for your well-being. I am very grateful to your mother. I greet Dionysios warmly.

THE HAND IS PARTLY ligatured and obviously experienced, but the writing is rather uneven. There are many corrections.

The style is a bit choppy, although connectives are used correctly. Sentences and clauses tend to be short. The writer has a good vocabulary, however, and spelling irregularities are relatively few.

The letter offers two important points of interest. One is the consultation of the oracle about Demetrios's prospects, together with his "brother's" attempt to intervene directly with the priests—with bad results, as his persistence was met with a rebuff. The other is his impending trip to Rome, on what kind of business cannot be told. Epoeris's motherly concern about Demetrios's companions is candidly expressed.

NOTES

those with whom you eat and drink: It is not clear if this is meant generally or has specific reference either to the house he is currently staying in or to the unknown people he may meet in Rome.

your mother: Probably in this case a term of respect for the lady of the house in which Demetrios is currently living.

LOCATION OF OBJECT
Dublin, Chester Beatty Library.

SB 12.10840

Euthalios and Mike to their mother concerning Easter
Fourth century AD

LOCATION WRITTEN Unknown
LOCATION OF ADDRESSEE Unknown
LOCATION FOUND Unknown

Greek

To my lady mother Syra . . . Euthalios and Mike, many greetings. Before everything I pray for your health before the Lord God. I wanted to come to you before the celebration (and) my sister Mike stopped me, telling me, "Arrive at our mother first for the end of the fast." Shake the. . . . in the basket. Expect my sister. I am coming for the celebration. I wanted to send you things for you to have before the fast but I do not have an intimate friend. Do not be anxious about the fare for Mike that I can give instead of you. I salute you. Nonna salutes you heartily. Silvana salutes you. Annoutis and Theonilas and Ischyrion salute you. I greet Apion and the overseer and his wife and children. And I Mike salute the overseer with the children and his wife. Write to Kala . . . about his sweet child that he should bear it. We cannot (do) anything against death. You know yourself that . . . I pray for you together with my son Dorotheos. I salute my lord father. Pharmouthi 1. I pray for your health for a long time.

THE HAND IS FASTER and more fluent than the usual letter hand, and there are quite a few ligatures. The lines slope uniformly downward. Altogether this is a professional product.

The orthography of this text is so extremely phonetic that the editor thought it necessary to produce a normalized version. There are almost no connective particles and the syntax of the text is rather simple.

This letter from two siblings to their mother is primarily concerned with planning a visit to her during Lent and Easter. On the advice of his sister Euthalios has decided to wait, but Mike will go by boat, with her brother paying the fare for her. Her voice emerges in the second part of the letter as she salutes people and sends condolence for the death of a child.

NOTE

overseer: The nature of the relationship of both brother and sister with the overseer is uncertain. Note that Mike starts her message by saluting him.

LOCATION OF OBJECT
Florence, Biblioteca Medicea Laurenziana, *PSI* 831.

II. EPISTOLARY TYPES: URGENT! ∾

P.Ryl. 2.232

A warning about a liturgy
Second century AD

LOCATION WRITTEN   Probably Herakleia
LOCATION OF ADDRESSEE   Unknown
LOCATION FOUND   Arsinoite nome

Greek

∾ ∾ ∾

Tap- to Ammonaphris . . . greetings. As soon as the strategos arrived at Herakleia, he inquired about you concerning the secretaryship of the cultivators, and the officials reported to him that you were staying in the village. I write to you therefore so that you may know.

(ADDRESS): To Ammonaphris.

∾ ∾ ∾

CLEAR HANDWRITING WITHOUT LIGATURES and some inclination to the right. The writer was experienced. The level of the hand corresponds to that of the text. No salutations are included.

The syntax is businesslike, the orthography good. But the letter was perhaps written in haste, for two things had to be rewritten, one word was written twice, and an entire syllable was omitted.

The author writes to Ammonaphris to inform him that the strategos had come to the village of Herakleia and asked about him in connection with the secretaryship of the cultivators, an important and burdensome liturgical post. The village officials had replied "that you are staying in the village." It is not completely clear whether Ammonaphris was currently the secretary, or rather that the strategos was thinking of appointing him to that post. Nor is it evident what the officials' reply means. Obviously the letter shows that Ammonaphris was not in Herakleia at that point, but we do not know what other village can be meant.

LOCATION OF OBJECT
Manchester, John Rylands University Library, *P.Ryl.* 232.

P.Wisc. 2.74

Kyra and Aia to Aphynchios
Fourth century AD

LOCATION WRITTEN   Unknown
LOCATION OF ADDRESSEE   Unknown
LOCATION FOUND   Unknown

Greek

~ ~ ~

To my lord brother Aphynchios Kyra and Aia, many greetings. Putting off
everything, at once come to us since our mother died and we need very
much your presence. Do not wish then to remain at your place so that you
do (not) meet us and we will ruin our household. You too know that we
cannot do anything [while awaiting?] your presence. Because of this we
have also sent our brother Martyrios in order that you may come to us at
once with him. Gratitude toward him should be the greatest because he
took upon himself the trouble (to come) to you with us providing him with
a compensation. We salute our sister your wife and her children free from
the evil eye and all your people each by name. I pray for your health
through a long time, our lord brother. Do not be neglectful and then repent
later on. Come at once so that you may set everything in due order.

~ ~ ~

WRITTEN FASTER THAN A standard letter hand with more ligatures and characters inclined to the right. The writer seems to have been at home with
writing documents. He shows competence and fluency and seems to check
continuously his tendency to proceed faster.

Besides a considerable number of phonetic spellings and errors in vowel
quantity, the letter shows a decent command of Greek and good use of connective particles. The syntax is not very elaborate but generally correct. The
letter was dictated by one of the sisters who kept on switching between singular and plural personal pronouns. Although she seems to have been responsible for the text and the initiative to write, she felt periodically compelled
to associate her sister in order to make her request more binding.

A letter full of urgency where the presence of a brother is requested at a
mother's death, presumably to set in order family affairs. Not only do Kyra
and Aia think his presence is indispensable, but they dispatch another brother
to fetch him. Even though Aphynchios lived far away and was married, he
was still considered the head of his family of origin.

LOCATION OF OBJECT
Madison, University of Wisconsin Library, inv. 71. Plate XXIX in edition.

BIBLIOGRAPHY
Photo in Boswinkel and Sijpesteijn 1968: pl. 36. Reprinted in Horsley 1982: no. 103. About *eleuthera* (line 16), see *BL* 7.282. *BL* 11.291, probably to be dated around 350–400.

12. EPISTOLARY TYPES: JUST GREETINGS AND GOOD WISHES ᖌ

BGU 1.332

Serapias to her children
Second–third century AD

LOCATION WRITTEN   Alexandria
LOCATION OF ADDRESSEE   Unknown
LOCATION FOUND   Arsinoite nome

Greek

ᖌ ᖌ ᖌ

Serapias to her children Ptolemaios and Apolinaria and Ptolemaios, many greetings. Before all I pray that you are well, which is the most important of all for me. I make your obeisance before the lord Serapis, praying to find you well, as I pray that (you) have been successful. I was delighted to receive a letter to the effect that you have come through well. Greet Ammonous with her children and husband, and those who love you. Kyrilla greets you, and the daughter of Hermias, Hermias, Hermanoubis the nurse, Athenais the teacher, Kyrilla, Kasia, . . . , S-anos, Empis, all those here. Please write me about what you're doing, knowing that if I receive a letter from you I am happy about your well-being. I pray for your health.

(ADDRESS IN SECOND HAND): Deliver to Ptolemaios the brother of Apolinaria.

(ADDRESS IN FIRST HAND): Deliver to Ptolemaios her son. Greet . . .

ᖌ ᖌ ᖌ

WRITTEN SLOWLY WITH A thick pen, letters mostly separated, and faulty alignment. The final greetings are in the same hand and are only slightly more fluent.

The language is mainly straightforward and unadorned, with a scattering of phonetic spellings. The grammar is reasonably complex, but the syntax of the third sentence is a bit unclear.

The letter is entirely an act of connection, thanking the recipients for their letter, expressing wishes for their health and success, urging them to write again, and conveying greetings.

Serapis: This is the evidence that the letter was written in Alexandria.

Hermias: The name is given twice, both times in the nominative, despite the fact that after "daughter" it should be genitive. It is possible that the repetition is simply a slip, and it seems a bit odd for Hermias to be mentioned only after his unnamed daughter, but letter writers often think of people to mention in an unsystematic order.

Hermanoubis: Elsewhere a masculine name, but the feminine article before Gk. *trophos*, "nurse," is decisive.

teacher: Gk. *deskalos*, a form of the usual *didaskalos* specially used of women teachers; see Cribiore 1996: 23–24.

LOCATION OF OBJECT
Berlin, Staatliche Museen, Papyrussammlung, P. 6811.

BIBLIOGRAPHY
BL 1.39 (on lines 1, 11, and 12–13); 5.11 (on *deskalos*); Cribiore 1996: 22–24 (on *deskalos*).

P.Berl.Zill. 12

Athanasia greets her mother
Third–fourth century AD

LOCATION WRITTEN   Unknown
LOCATION OF ADDRESSEE   Unknown
LOCATION FOUND   Unknown (Arsinoite nome?)

Greek

∾ ∾ ∾

To my lady mothers from Athanasia, greetings. Before everything I pray to
our lord God that you are well and healthy. Know, my lady mother, that I
make obeisance on your behalf. Don't worry about me, for we give thanks
to our lord God that he has watched over our affairs to this day. I greet my
lord father and my lady mother and my sister Horigeneia and Thais and
Sophia and Lucilla and Eudaimon and Herakleides and Dionysios. I greet
my lord brother Pekyllos and his children. I greet Zosimos and Kalopos and
Hellaliben and Makedonios and Thatres and Piperis and Nike and Zosime
and all your people by name. I pray for your health, my lady mother. I greet
all your people by name. Farewell.

(ADDRESS): To my lady mother, from her daughter Athanasia.

∾ ∾ ∾

THE HAND IS ENTIRELY detached, with slowly made letters, somewhat wan-
dering lines, and many corrections. Many of the individual letters, however,
are competently made, and the overall impression is of a private individual
with an "evolving" hand.

The spelling is phonetic, including the omission of unaccented vowels on
occasion, dropping of a final nu on an accusative, and some difficulty settling
on the declension of *meter*, "mother." The expression otherwise is simple,
largely paratactic and with few other particles.

The letter conveys greetings, assurances that the writer is fine, and wishes
for good health for the recipients. Naldini includes it in his corpus of Christian
letters on the basis of the prayer to the *kyrios theos*, "Lord God." That is not
decisive, and there are no other explicit marks of Christianity, but Athanasia's
name itself may be a sign of Christianity.

NOTE
mothers: Athanasia then shifts into the singular, but another "mother" is
referred to in the greetings and was probably included in this plural.

LOCATION OF OBJECT
Berlin, Staatliche Museen, Papyrussammlung, P. 11042. Plate in Youtie 1974:
pl. VII.

BIBLIOGRAPHY

Text, translation, and notes in Naldini 1998: 147–49, no. 26, using corrections by H. C. Youtie (see *BL* 6.23). Further corrections in Youtie 1974: 31–32, with notes on 40–41 (*BL* 7.29).

P.Oxy. 14.1761

Kallirhoe to Sarapias
Second–third century AD

LOCATION WRITTEN Alexandria
LOCATION OF ADDRESSEE Unknown
LOCATION FOUND Oxyrhynchos

Greek

Kallirhoe to Sarapias her lady, greeting. I make your obeisance each day before the lord Sarapis. Since the day you left, we are searching for your turds, wishing to see you. Greet Thermouthis and Helias and Ploution and Aphrodite and Nemesianos. Karabos and Harpokration greet you and all those in the household. I pray for your health.

(ADDRESS): Deliver to Sarapias from Kallirhoe.

THE LETTERS ARE ADEQUATELY made but rather uneven, and the lines wander a bit. The hand is mainly detached, with a few joined letters. At the end of 5 "and" is canceled, and there is one correction. Although not a beginner's, the handwriting is not very fluent.

The orthography is extremely phonetic, with numerous vocalic interchanges. In all, there are some fourteen words (out of fifty-three) needing correction. Stylistically, the letter is straightforward and lacking in embellishments like connective particles. Altogether the impression is of a writer not quite in control of the language.

The contents are entirely of the "reaching out to touch" variety: obeisance before Sarapis, missing the addressee, and greetings. Only a unique expression of longing gives a distinctive character to the letter.

NOTE

Sarapis: An indication of writing in Alexandria.

turds: A unique indication of longing.

Wellesley, Mass., Wellesley College Library.

PSI 12.1247

Ammonous to Apollonianos and Spartiates
Ca. AD 235–238

LOCATION WRITTEN   Unknown
LOCATION OF ADDRESSEE   Oxyrhynchos (?)
LOCATION FOUND   Oxyrhynchos

Greek

∾ ∾ ∾

Ammonous to Apollonianos and Spartiates my lords and sweetest father and brother, very many greetings. I write embracing you and praying that you may have the good things in life, and urging you to write to me frequently about your well-being, knowing that, if I receive a letter from you, I celebrate a festival. Greet my sweetest children and my sister Dioskouriaina. Your children greet you.

(second hand) (Postscript): Greet Isidora and her children. I pray that you may be well and fortunate throughout your life. The soldier bothered us earlier because of . . . you instructed him. Diogenes will tell you the affair.

∾ ∾ ∾

AMMONOUS DICTATED HER LETTER to a professional scribe, who wrote fast, ligatured characters inclined to the right but strove to maintain some legibility. Her long postscript, however, shows that she could have written the whole text herself. Her hand shows well-formed, separated letters written slowly but with some gracefulness. It maintains some rhythm and is well proportioned.

The letter, although short, has pretensions to style. Only in the part written by Ammonous herself at the end are there even iotacistic errors.

Ammonous was the daughter of Sarapion alias Apollonianos, whom she addresses here simply as Apollonianos. The father is the central figure of an important dossier (about fifty papyri) and the best-known representative of a wealthy Oxyrhynchite family which provided strategoi of the Hermopolite in three generations. The letter as dictated contains nothing except greetings and a somewhat literary request for a letter back. Ammonous added a more serious matter of business in a postscript in her own hand, but left it to Diogenes (whose identity is unknown to us) to explain it.

Dioskouriaina: Actually her sister-in-law, the wife of Spartiates.

Florence, Biblioteca Medicea Laurenziana, *PSI* 1247. Plate of the recto (the official document) in the edition, Tav. I, and in *Aegyptus* 45 (1965) after p. 249, Tav. 4 (as part of a study of chancery-style writing).

Corrections to lines 17 and 25 in *BL* 6.186 and 8.409. See *P.Rain.Cent.*, p. 365, for the date.

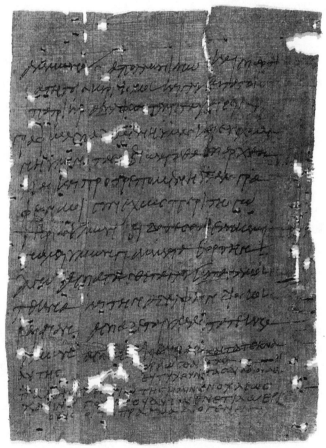

Fig. 31. *PSI* 12.1247. Ammonous to Apollonianos and Spartiates. (Florence, Biblioteca Medicea Laurenziana, *PSI* 1247. Photograph courtesy of the Ministero per i Beni e le Attività Culturali. All further reproduction by any means is prohibited.)

13. DOUBLE LETTERS ON A SHEET ∾

BGU 2.615

Ammonous to her father, followed by Celer to Antonius his brother
Second century AD

LOCATION WRITTEN   Unknown
LOCATION OF ADDRESSEE   Unknown
LOCATION FOUND   Arsinoite nome

Greek

∾ ∾ ∾

Ammonous to her sweetest father, greetings. When I received your letter and learned that you were, the gods willing, safe, I was extremely delighted. And finding an opportunity the same hour, I wrote you this letter, eager to embrace you. Take care of the pressing matters quickly. If the little girl says anything, . . . If the man bringing you the letter brings you a basket, I am sending it. All your people greet you individually. Celer and all his people greet you. I pray for your health.

Celer to Antonius his brother, many greetings. When I received your . . . letter and learned that you were, the gods willing, safe, I was extremely delighted. You wrote to me, how Anthestios received a subscription to his requests. Exercise yourself with experienced people, what to do on our account, and if you learn anything . . . , inform me quickly, and transmit it also to our brother Longinus, and at the same time greet him. All my people greet you individually. I pray for your health.

At the same hour that I received your letter I found an opportunity and wrote back. Mesore 17.

(ADDRESS): . . . from Ammonous his daughter.

∾ ∾ ∾

THE WRITING IS CALLED a "clear cursive." Both letters are written in the same hand, but the editor notes that the health formulas at the end of both are written in a faster hand, perhaps different from that of the body of the letters.

The syntax of the two letters is generally correct and the vocabulary considerable, but the two letters begin with the identical expression of pleasure at learning of Antonius's safety. The Greek is generally correct, with only relatively trivial orthographic deviations.

The letters were written in a hurry, evidently with a messenger waiting to leave, and Ammonous's has little else except greetings, a general injunction to deal with important business, and a remark about the *mikra*, the little girl, which remains unclear. Celer is more explicit about business matters, but only a little clearer.

NOTES

Exercise yourself: The exact point of this remark escapes us. Presumably Celer is asking Antonius to get experienced help in dealing with the matter, which may have had to do with legal business before an official, perhaps in the metropolis of the Arsinoite nome, if that is where Antonius was when he received these letters.

found an opportunity: That is, to send a letter by way of a suitable person traveling in the right direction.

LOCATION OF OBJECT

Formerly Berlin, Staatliche Museen, Papyrussammlung, P. 7946; burned in Münster.

P.Grenf. 1.53

Artemis to Theodoros
Fourth century AD

LOCATION WRITTEN Unknown
LOCATION OF ADDRESSEE Unknown
LOCATION FOUND Unknown

Greek

∾ ∾ ∾

Artemis to Theodoros my lord husband, greetings in God. Before everything I pray the lord God that we find you in all good health. I sent you through Apion, your fellow soldier, letters and a cloak. I pray for your health. Your children salute you and Allous sends you many threats because you wrote often and saluted everyone but you did not salute her only. Allous (?) salutes you.

Artemis writes to Sarapion also called Isidoros. If you are a soldier, you are crazy, but the commander quickly lessens craziness. You are writing to us with the intention of amazing us, saying that the commander does not want people who ruin houses. If you want to draw conclusions about the fornications of your daughters, do not question me but the Elders of the church, how the two of them leapt up saying, "We want men" and how Loukra was found beside her lover, making herself a courtesan. Therefore, they are full of grudge because we handed them to Soucharos. And if we had to be specific about family, this again we show first, who is of better birth, since we utterly deny that we were born from a slave. This I am writing to you, Theodoros: do everything about the present situation, and it is necessary to show him the letter.

∾ ∾ ∾

THE HAND IS DESCRIBED as a small cursive. The letter was probably the work of a scribe.

The letter shows a decent command of Greek and displays a good variety of clauses. Connectives are many but almost exclusively consist of *de*. There are phonetic mistakes, repetitions, and an omitted syllable. The voice of Artemis comes through quite clearly in the pace of the text and in the colorful vocabulary (as, e.g., in "threaten" or "leapt up"). The usual *chairein* is replaced on the page by the impersonal and cold *graphei*.

The first letter serves only to accompany the sending of the cloak and the other letter. Even in this one, however, Artemis is outspoken when she mentions the "threats" that Allous, perhaps her daughter, sends Theodoros. The second letter, which is addressed to a Sarapion, a fellow soldier of Theodoros, is full of tantalizing details about a certain business involving his daughters.

Artemis (and perhaps other people, she always speaks in the first-person plural) apparently was actively involved in denouncing the two girls' behavior and was accused by their father of "ruining their house" and being of low birth.

NOTES

courtesan: "*Gadeitana,*" that is, "woman of Cadiz."

grudge: It seems likely that the subject of *phthonousi* (bear a grudge) are the girls themselves. It is unclear who Soucharos was.

LOCATION OF OBJECT
Dublin, Trinity College Library.

BIBLIOGRAPHY
Naldini 1998: no. 56, with complete bibliography.

P.Mich. 8.508

Thaisarion to Serenus and Serapous: two letters from Alexandria
Second–third century AD

LOCATION WRITTEN Alexandria
LOCATION OF ADDRESSEE Unknown
LOCATION FOUND Unknown

Greek

Thaisarion to Serenus and . . . her brothers, many greeting. Before everything I pray for your health and make obeisance for you before our lord Serapis. I wish you to know that I received from Nilos . . . you too (sing.) receive therefore from him a bundle of reeds (or pens) and 4 pairs of sandals for Herais, 2 for Serenus, 1 (pair) for Ammonios, and 1 for Ch. . . and rouge. When the sister . . . well send me a letter in a hurry. I salute Ammonios and Sampous. Ptolemaios and Alexandros salute you all.

Thaisarion to Serapous her sister and to her brothers, many greetings. Before everything I pray that you are well and I make obeisance for you before our lord Serapis. I wish you to know that our brother Ptolemaios went upcountry early in the morning in the . . . hour, Epeiph 9 and I used for his dinner what you sent me. And you, send me the half—2 jars of radish oil—of the value of the one I used, for I need them when I give birth. And in any case he is also your brother. Ammonios sailed upriver with the prefect, since he is part of his staff, and wherever he is he will visit you. If my mother thinks of coming with him, let her make herself ready. But you did not think it worthy to send me a single letter. And send me a jar of salve . . . farewell.

(ADDRESS ON BACK): give it to Serenus . . .

THE HAND IS DESCRIBED by the editor as "large and ungainly," but the writer was a professional scribe probably used to writing documents, and the hand is not ungainly. The few ligatures do not impair clarity.

Both letters mostly consist of commands in the imperative and finite clauses connected with "and." Connective particles are limited to a minimum. The style is repetitive and jerky.

Thaisarion writes two letters from Alexandria, one for her brothers and another for her sister and brothers. The first is shorter and is mainly concerned with sandals that she would like to receive for various family members. The second letter mentions expenses that she has incurred because of another brother who traveled upcountry. She would like to be partly refunded, taking advantage of the fact that Ammonios—perhaps the same man mentioned in the first letter—is sailing upriver in the retinue of the prefect and could take things back to her. Her mother is also preparing herself to visit Thaisarion in Alexandria.

NOTES

phukarion: Rouge from seaweeds.

radish oil: This cheap oil was used to cook food for guests celebrating the birth.

LOCATION OF OBJECT

Formerly Ann Arbor, University of Michigan Library, Papyrus collection, inv. 4776d,e; now in Cairo, Egyptian Museum.

BIBLIOGRAPHY

See *BL* 10.124 on the restoration of line 18.

P.Oxy. 31.2599

Two letters of Tauris
Third–fourth century AD

LOCATION WRITTEN Unknown
LOCATION OF ADDRESSEE Unknown
LOCATION FOUND Oxyrhynchos

Greek

To my lord father Apitheon, Tauris (sends) greetings. Send us two weaver's combs and two ounces of storax, and also two large combs for the head. As you told me, "I am sending you things like that to the farm," send (them). The purple (yarn) which you said "I'm buying," buy (it). So then, tell the sister of the wife of Dioskoros to say to Didyme, "As you said, if you are working on *dikarytida*, make them; if you're not doing it, on my father's purple (yarn) and tow." I greet Esther and your sister Susanna. As you said, lady, "I'm sending you some towels," send (them), and I'm sending you the Egyptian ones. I greet you, lady, and your sister and the sister of your mother.

To my lord brother Theodoros, Tauris (sends) many greetings. Buy three towels for me, my lord brother, and the boots which you mentioned and three pairs of slippers for the baths. Take the half-pound of fine tow (?) which I gave you to use and make it into a facecloth, or bring the price of it. Send me two large combs. As you said "I'm buying . . . ," when you come out remember your oath. As to the little *manuale* in the bag, do not give it to anyone. Bring it when you come. As to the half-pound of fine tow (?) . . . Tell the son of Herakleianos, ". . . the two talents, if you think proper, . . . and buy purple." I greet you, Herakl. . . and your husband. I greet Theod. . . Come quickly so we may see you.

THE HAND IS A business cursive, faster than the hands found in most private letters; the writer has difficulty maintaining straight lines in the longer line length of the letter to Theodoros.

There is much very phonetic spelling, but it is a minor point compared to the entirely new word formations sprinkled through the text. The use of singular forms after "two" may point to a writer more at home in spoken Egyptian, as the construction resembles that with "two" in Coptic.

The two letters are almost entirely concerned with getting and sending various goods, mainly things connected with the making of fabric, clothing, and footwear. It is in both letters at times difficult to be sure where to put quotation marks around what Tauris tells her correspondent to say to a third person. The appearance of biblical names is interesting. At this date it is hard to say whether they are more likely to belong to Jews or Christians.

NOTE

manuale: This word has several meanings; it is not clear which is meant here.

LOCATION OF OBJECT

Oxford, Papyrology Rooms, Sackler Library.

P.Oxy. 36.2789

Two letters of Kleopatra about tax payments
Third century AD (ca. 245–302)

LOCATION WRITTEN   Unknown
LOCATION OF ADDRESSEE   Unknown
LOCATION FOUND   Oxyrhynchos

Greek

Kleopatra to Epaphroditos her father, many greetings. Take care to measure out to Moros the mason five artabas of barley, since I am being pressed by the dekaprotos; for I am to be locked up. See to it that you do not neglect this. I pray for your health.

Kleopatra to Moros her brother, greetings. I wrote to my father Epaphroditos to measure out to you five artabas of barley, so that you may take care of the matter of the *dekaprotos*; and from now on you are on your own in this matter. See to it that you do not neglect this. I pray for your health.

THESE TWO LETTERS WERE written on a single sheet and never detached. Both are written, body and subscription, in a single hand, which is a scribal cursive, rather faster than a normal letter hand. It is the sort of hand one would expect to find in a contract or a tax receipt. This is presumably a professional hand.

The language also suggests this professionalism. The letters are accurate, with only one phonetic spelling and the omission of a lambda in one word. They organize sentences with conjunctions and particles and use the articular infinitive once. There is nothing very stylish about them, but they are good business prose, giving the main body of each letter in a single complex sentence.

Both letters concern a single item of business, the need for Epaphroditos, addressed as Kleopatra's "father," to give five artabas of barley to Moros the mason (*oikodomos*), so that she can settle an obligation to the tax collectors called *dekaprotoi* and avoid being thrown into prison. Moros is addressed as "brother," obviously not to be taken literally. What Moros's role in the affair was, is not evident; Kleopatra gives notice that once he gets these five artabas he is going to be self-sufficient in the matter, that is, she will no longer be involved.

NOTE

dekaprotos: The *dekaprotoi* were a board of tax-collection supervisors drawn from the elite of the metropolis and responsible for the taxes in grain on the land of the whole nome. The office existed in Egypt only from the mid-240s until 302.

LOCATION OF OBJECT

Oxford, Papyrology Rooms, Sackler Library.

BIBLIOGRAPHY

Rowlandson 1998: 236–37, no. 173(b).

P.Oxy. 62.4340

Two letters to Didyme

Ca. AD 250–275

LOCATION WRITTEN Unknown

LOCATION OF ADDRESSEE Unknown

LOCATION FOUND Oxyrhynchos

Greek

Petosiris to Didyme, many greetings. The purple (yarn) which you sent to us has not been made up. Send us ten bundles of . . . balls in green, about the color of your cape. Sell the cloak you have for 48 (?) drachmas. If you don't get the price, don't sell, but take care of the 40 drachmas and send them to us quickly. Inquire about the health of the son of Nilous and write us if necessary about him. Collect 40 dr. as delivery charges from Teeus, the daughter of Herakleides son of Sarammon.

Thaesis to her daughter Didyme, many greetings. I delivered 7 ½ metretai of wine to Herakleides Selmon and Capitolius, and I returned the balance of the money to them along with the price of 18½ metretai at the rate of 64 dr. per metretes. You wrote to me—your wife in your name—and I sold the wine at twice what I bought it for, and I signed for — dr. Soeis is bothering me about the artaba of grain. Send me straightaway a jar of oil for Herakleides Selmon and 1 basket. I greet you and all yours many times. Eseis greets you many times, and Theonilla and Nilous Didyme. Menas' son-in-law has given me nothing. I pray for your health.

(ADDRESS): From Didyme [sic] from Thaesis and Petosiris.

THE RECTANGULAR SHEET CONTAINS two letters, divided by a short paragraphos stroke. They are written throughout in the same hand, although the greeting is written much faster than the body. The overall impression is of an experienced writer, but it remains a letter hand rather than anything faster.

The writer is by no means in command of flawless, educated Greek. Syllables are omitted at least three times and a relative pronoun once; a syllable is repeated. Violations of standard grammar are frequent, including the article in place of the relative, mistaken cases, active for middle, and a botched address. There are also numerous phonetic spellings and many remakings or corrections of letters. In short, the letter displays a vigorous but sloppy, colloquial, and perhaps Egyptian-tinged Greek.

The first letter, from Petosiris to Didyme, concerns mostly matters of clothing; Petosiris also inquires after the health of a boy and instructs Didyme to collect some money. The second letter, from Thaesis, is focused on a wine transaction, but it also asks for some goods and (unlike Petosiris's letter) includes the usual greetings. It shows Thaesis actively engaged in wine speculation. Most remarkable, however, is the phrase (addressed to a woman) "You wrote to me—your wife in your name—etc."

NOTE

wine: It seems that the two men had provided Thaesis with a sum of money out of which she bought 26 metretai of wine at 32 drachmas per metretes. This was perhaps all the wine she could find at an attractive price. She then sold part of the wine for 64 drachmas per metretetes. Now she has turned back to the men the remaining wine, the proceeds from the sale, and the money never invested.

LOCATION OF OBJECT

Oxford, Papyrology Rooms, Sackler Library.

BIBLIOGRAPHY

Bagnall 1998 [2000], for an argument that the writer (perhaps Thaesis writing on behalf of both, since her name comes first in the address?) has forgotten for the moment that she is not writing to Didyme's husband but (nominally at least) to Didyme. That is, possibly she is replying to a letter written in Petosiris's name by Didyme, and the "you" she is thinking about here is Petosiris.

SB 20.14132

Ptolema to her mother and sister about receiving items
First–second century AD

LOCATION WRITTEN Alexandria (?)
LOCATION OF ADDRESSEE Unknown
LOCATION FOUND Unknown

Greek

Ptolema to Beleous her mother and lady, very many greetings. Before
everything I pray that you are well together with Heros and . . . ; For I did
not want (to wait?) until you came, because I have no one (here?). I sent
you a basket containing 5 pairs of loaves. You know, my lady, that I do not
have anything now. And if I . . . , I'll give you my thanks. I greet Nemesas
and Kottara.

Ptolema to Heros her sister, greeting. I regret, sister, that I did not see you
when I was leaving for Alexandria. I do not have anything until now. Send
for what I sent to you, sandals and 5 pairs of loaves. Receive these from
Trophimos. Salute your sister-in-law and your husband and your brother-in-
law. Farewell. Epeiph 6.

THE WRITER WAS ABLE to produce a fairly long text but was not completely
experienced. At the end, the lines start running downward and the hand
becomes visibly worse. The size of the letters is not always consistent. The
final salutations are in much larger letters and may have been written by
Ptolema.

Both letters consist of short, simple sentences replete with phonetic and
orthographic mistakes. Besides the most common errors, there are syllables
skipped and plenty of vowel changes. The writer had trouble with syllabic
division at the end of lines. The linguistic errors are in correlation with the
clumsy appearance of the handwriting.

Two letters written by Ptolema to her mother and sister. They both concern
the sending of items that Ptolema needs and that she has previously requested
by letter. She seems to be in Alexandria and declares that she is in need of
everything.

LOCATION OF OBJECT
Ann Arbor, University of Michigan Library, Papyrus Collection, inv. 4203.

BIBLIOGRAPHY
Gonis 1997b (with extensive corrections).

Fig. 32.   *SB* 20.14132. Ptolema to her mother and sister about receiving items.
(Ann Arbor, University of Michigan Library, Papyrus Collection, inv. 4203.)

Bibliography

Cely Letters = Hanham, Alison, ed. 1975. *The Cely Letters, 1472–1488*. Early English Text Society 273. Oxford.

Paston Letters = Davis, Norman, ed. 1971–76. *Paston Letters and Papers of the Fifteenth Century*. 2 vols. Oxford. A selection is given in Davis, Norman, ed. 1958. *Paston Letters*. Oxford.

Plumpton Letters = Kirby, Joan, ed. 1996. *The Plumpton Letters and Papers*. Camden Fifth Series 8. Cambridge.

Stonor Letters = Kingsford, Charles L., ed. 1919. *The Stonor Letters and Papers, 1290–1483*. Camden Third Series 29–30. London. Second ed., with introduction and additional notes, Carpenter, Christine, ed. 1996. *Kingsford's Stonor Letters and Papers, 1290–1483*. Cambridge. Citations are from the second edition.

Abu-Lughod, Lila. 1993. *Writing Women's Worlds: Bedouin Stories*. Berkeley.

Alston, Richard. 1995. *Soldier and Society in Roman Egypt: A Social History*. London.

Bacot, Seÿna. 1999. "Avous-nous retrouvé la grand-mère de Koloje?" *Ägypten und Nubien in spätantiker und christlicher Zeit* (Wiesbaden) 2:241–47.

Bagnall, Roger S. 1985. *Currency and Inflation in Fourth Century Egypt*. Atlanta.

———. 1993. *Egypt in Late Antiquity*. Princeton.

———. 1995. *Reading Papyri, Writing Ancient History*. London.

———. 1997. "For the Visit of My Father Sarapion: CPR VIII 52." *Tyche* 12:245–46.

———. 1998 [2000]. "'Your Wife in Your Name': P.Oxy. LXII 4340." *Greek, Roman, and Byzantine Studies* 39:157–67.

———. 1999. "Eirene to Epaphrys: P. Yale I 77 Revised." *Chronique d'Égypte* 74:109–17.

———. 2001. "Les lettres privées des femmes: Un choix de langue en Égypte byzantine." *Bulletin de la Classe des Lettres, Académie Royale de Belgique*, 6 ser. 12:133–53.

———. 2001 [2002]. "Monks and Property: Rhetoric, Law, and Patronage in the Apophthegmata Patrum and the Papyri." *Greek, Roman, and Byzantine Studies* 42:7–24.

Bagnall, Roger S., and Bruce W. Frier. 1994. *The Demography of Roman Egypt*. Cambridge.

Baumann, Gerd, ed. 1986. *The Written Word: Literacy in Transition*. Oxford.

Beaucamp, Joëlle. 1990–92. *Le statut de la femme à Byzance*. 2 vols. Paris.

———. 1993. "Organisation domestique et rôles sexuels: Les papyrus byzantins." *Dumbarton Oaks Papers* 47:185–94.

Bennett, H. S. 1932. *The Pastons and Their England: Studies in an Age of Transition*. 2nd ed. Cambridge.

Borg, Barbara. 1998. '*Der zierlichste Anblick der Welt*': *Ägyptische Porträtmumien*. Mainz am Rhein.

Boswinkel, Ernst, and P. J. Sijpesteijn. 1968. *Greek Papyri*. Amsterdam.

Bowersock, G. W. 1971. "A Report on Arabia Provincia." *Journal of Roman Studies* 61:232–33.

Burkhalter, Fabienne. 1990. "Les statuettes en bronze d'Aphrodite en Égypte romaine d'après les documents papyrologiques." *Revue archéologique:* 51–60.

Carpenter, Christine. 1986. "The Fifteenth-Century English Gentry and Their Estates." In M. Jones, ed., *Gentry and Lesser Nobility in Late Medieval Europe*, 36–60. Gloucester and New York.

Chapa, Juan. 1998. *Letters of Condolence in Greek Papyri*. Florence.

Clarysse, Willy. 1990. "An Epistolary Formula." *Chronique d'Égypte* 65:103–6.

———. 1993. "Egyptian Scribes Writing Greek." *Chronique d'Égypte* 68:195–99.

Clarysse, Willy, and Katelijn Vandorpe. 1995. *Zénon, un homme d'affaires grec à l'ombre des pyramides*. Leuven.

Coles, R. A., A. Geissen, and L. Koenen. 1973. "Some Corrections and Notes to P. Fouad." *Zeitschrift für Papyrologie und Epigraphik* 11:235–39.

Conybeare, C. 2000. *Paulinus Noster: Self and Symbols in the Letters of Paulinus of Nola*. Oxford.

Cribiore, Raffaella. 1996. *Writing, Teachers, and Students in Graeco-Roman Egypt*. American Studies in Papyrology 36. Atlanta.

———. 2001a. *Gymnastics of the Mind: Greek Education in Hellenistic and Roman Egypt*. Princeton.

———. 2001b. "Windows on a Woman's World: Some Letters from Roman Egypt." In A. Lardinois and L. McClure, eds., *Making Silence Speak: Women's Voices in Greek Literature and Society*, 223–39. Princeton.

———. 2002. "The Women in the Apollonios Archive and Their Use of Literacy." In H. Melaerts and L. Mooren, eds., *Le rôle et le statut de la femme en Égypte hellénistique, romaine, et byzantine*, 149–66. Leuven.

Cugusi, Paolo. 1983. *Evoluzione e forme dell'epistolografia latina*. Rome.

———. 2002. *Corpus Epistularum Latinarum Papyris Tabulis Ostracis Servatarum* III. Florence.

Cuvigny, Hélène. 2002. "Remarques sur l'emploi de *idios* dans le praescriptum épistolaire." *Bulletin de l'Institut Français d'Archéologie Orientale* 102:143–53.

Davis, Norman. 1949. "The Text of Margaret Paston's Letters." *Medium Aevum* 18:12–28.

———. 1954. "The Language of the Pastons." *Proceedings of the British Academy* 40:119–39.

Deissmann, A. 1923. *Licht vom Osten*. 4th ed. Tübingen.

Dickey, Eleanor. 1996. *Greek Forms of Address: From Herodotus to Lucian*. Oxford.

Drescher, J. 1944. "A Widow's Petition." *Bulletin de la Société d'Archéologie Copte* 10:91–96, with plates I–II.

Edgar, C. C. 1923. "Selected Papyri from the Archives of Zenon." *Annales du Service des Antiquités de l'Égypte* 23:187–209.

Eitrem, Sam, and Leiv Amundsen. 1951. "Three Private Letters from the Oslo Collection." *Aegyptus* 31:177–83.

Elm, Susanna. 1994. '*Virgins of God*': *The Making of Asceticism in Late Antiquity*. Oxford.

Emmet, A. 1984. "A Female Monastic Community in Egypt?" In A. Moffat, ed., *Maistor: Classical, Byzantine, and Renaissance Studies for Robert Browning* 77–83. Byzantina Australiensia 5, Canberra.

Farid, Farouk. 1979. "Sarapis-Proskynema in the Light of SB III 6263." *Actes XVe Congrès Internationale de Papyrologie* (Brussels) 4:141–47.

Ferrante, Joan M. 1997. *To the Glory of Her Sex: Women's Roles in the Composition of Medieval Texts.* Bloomington.

Geraci, Giovanni. 1971. "Ricerche sul Proskynema." *Aegyptus* 51:3–211.

Ghedini, G. 1923. *Lettere cristiane dai papiri greci del III e IV secolo.* Milan.

Gonis, Nikolaos. 1997a. "Remarks on Private Letters." *Zeitschrift für Papyrologie und Epigraphik* 119:135–47.

———. 1997b. "Ptolema's Distress Away from Home (SB XX 14132 Revised)." *Bulletin of the American Society of Papyrologists* 34:111–18.

———. 2003. "Remarks on Private Letters II." *Zeitschrift für Papyrologie und Epigraphik* 142:163–70.

Grassi, E. 1956. "Papyrologica." *La parola del passato* 11:204–5.

Hagedorn, Dieter. 2001. "Bemerkungen zu Urkunden." *Zeitschrift für Papyrologie und Epigraphik* 136:149–50.

Haines-Eitzen, Kim. 2000. *Guardians of Letters.* Oxford.

Hanson, Ann Ellis. 1989. "Village Officials at Philadelphia." In L. Criscuolo and G. Geraci, eds., *Egitto e storia antica dall'ellenismo all'età araba,* 429–40. Bologna.

Harris, William V. 1989. *Ancient Literacy.* Cambridge, Mass.

Hengstl, Joachim. 1978. *Griechische Papyri aus Ägypten als Zeugnisse des öffentlichen und privaten Lebens.* Munich.

Hohlwein, N. 1927. "La Papyrologie grecque." *Musée Belge* 31:5–19.

Hombert, Marcel. 1935. "Récents Travaux sur les Lettres Privées." *Chronique d'Égypte* 10:405–6.

———. 1954. Review of Traversa, "Dai papiri inediti della Raccolta Milanese." *Aegyptus* 33 (1953): 57–59, in *Chronique d'Égypte* 29:329–31.

Horsfall, Nicholas. 1995. "Rome without Spectacles." *Greece and Rome* 42:49–56.

Horsley, G. H. R. 1982. *New Documents Illustrating Early Christianity* (1977). North Ryde, N.S.W., Australia.

Husson, Geneviève. 1983. *OIKIA: Le vocabulaire de la maison privée en Égypte d'après les papyrus grecs.* Paris.

Keenan, James G. 1975. "On Law and Society in Late Roman Egypt." *Zeitschrift für Papyrologie und Epigraphik* 17:237–50.

Kiessling, Emil. 1927. "Die Aposkeuai und die prozessrechtliche Stellung der Ehefrauen im ptolemäischen Ägypten." *Archiv für Papyrusforschung* 8:240–49.

Kortus, Michael. 1999. *Briefe des Apollonios-Archives aus der Sammlung Papyri Gissenses.* Giessen.

Lewis, Naphtali. 1974. *Papyrus in Classical Antiquity.* Oxford.

Llewelyn, Stephen. 1994. "The εἰς (τὴν) οἰκίαν Formula and the Delivery of Letters to Third Persons or to Their Property." *Zeitschrift für Papyrologie und Epigraphik* 101:71–78.

Lukaszewicz, Adam. 1992. "Antoninus the Κόρυφος (Note on P.Oxy. XLVI 3298.2)." *Journal of Juristic Papyrology* 22:43–46.

MacCoull, L. S. B. 1998 [2000]. "Prophethood, Texts, and Artifacts: The Monastery of Epiphanius." *GRBS* 39:307–24.

Malherbe, A. J. 1988. *Ancient Epistolary Theorists.* Atlanta.

McDonnell, Myles. 1996. "Writing, Copying, and Autograph Manuscripts in Ancient Rome." *Classical Quarterly* 46:469–91.

Mondini, Maria. 1916. "Lettere femminili nei papiri greco-egizi." *Studî della Scuola Papirologica* 2:29–50.

Naldini, Mario. 1998. *Il cristianesimo in Egitto*. 2nd ed. (1st ed. 1968.) Florence.

Oates, John F., et al. 2001. *Checklist of Editions of Greek, Latin, Demotic, and Coptic Papyri, Ostraca, and Tablets*. Oakville, Conn.

O'Callahan, J. 1963. *Cartas cristianas griegas del siglo V*. Barcelona.

Olsson, Bror. 1925. *Papyrusbriefe aus der frühesten Römerzeit*. Uppsala.

Papathomas, Amphilochios. 1995. "Textbeiträge zu CPR XIV." *Tyche* 10:143–54.

Parsons, P. J. 1980–81. "Background: The Papyrus Letter." *Didactica Classica Gandensia* 20–21:3–19.

———. 1985. Review of Bagnall, *The Florida Ostraka*. *Journal of Egyptian Archaeology* 71:210–11.

Pestman, P. W. 1994. *The New Papyrological Primer*. 2nd ed. Leiden.

Pomeroy, Sarah B. 1977. "Technikai kai mousikai." *American Journal of Ancient History* 2:51–68.

———. 1984. *Women in Hellenistic Egypt: From Alexander to Cleopatra*. New York.

Preisigke, Friedrich, et al. 1915–. *Berichtigungsliste der griechischen Papyrusurkunden aus Ägypten*. 11 vols. Berlin/Leipzig, Heidelberg, Leiden.

Rea, John R. 1980. "Cologne Papyri." *Classical Review* 30:260–62.

Rémondon, Roger. 1964. "Problèmes du bilinguisme dans l'Égypte lagide (U.P.Z. I, 148)." *Chronique d'Egypte* 39:126–46.

———. 1972. "L' Église dans la société égyptienne à l'époque byzantine." *Chronique d'Égypte* 47:254–77.

Richlin, Amy. 1993. "The Ethnographic Dilemma and the Dream of a Lost Golden Age." In N. S. Rabinowitz and A. Richlin, eds., *Feminist Theory and the Classics*, 272–303. New York.

Richmond, Colin. 1990. *The Paston Family in the Fifteenth Century: The First Phase*. Cambridge.

———. 1996. *The Paston Family in the Fifteenth Century: Fastolf's Will*. Cambridge.

Rowlandson, Jane, ed. 1998. *Women and Society in Greek and Roman Egypt: A Sourcebook*. Cambridge.

Scholl, R. 1990. *Corpus der ptolemäischen Sklaventexte*. Stuttgart.

Schubart, Wilhelm. 1918. *Einführung in die Papyruskunde*. Berlin.

———. 1923. *Ein Jahrtausend am Nil: Briefe aus dem Altertum*. 2nd ed. Berlin.

———. 1925. *Griechische Paläographie*. Munich.

Schubert, Paul. 2000. "P.Gen. I 74 et le procès de Drusilla." *Zeitschrift für Papyrologie und Epigraphik* 130:211–17.

Schwartz, Jacques. 1962. "En marge du dossier d'Apollonios le stratège." *Chronique d'Égypte* 37:348–54.

Scott, Joan Wallach. 1986. "Gender: A Useful Category of Historical Analysis." *American Historical Review* 91:1053–75. Reprinted in Joan Wallach Scott, ed., *Feminism and History: Oxford Readings in Feminism*, 152–80. Oxford, 1996.

Skeat, T. C. 1993. *The Reign of Augustus in Egypt*. Munich.

———. 1995. "Was Papyrus Regarded as 'Cheap' or 'Expensive' in the Ancient World?" *Aegyptus* 75:85–87.

Sweeney, Deborah. 2001. *Correspondence and Dialogue: Pragmatic Factors in Late Ramesside Letter Writing*. Wiesbaden.

Thomas, J. David. 1978. "O. Florida 14: Man or Woman?" *Chronique d'Égypte* 53:142–44.

Thomas, Keith. 1986. "The Meaning of Literacy in Early Modern England." In Gerd Baumann, ed., *The Written Word: Literacy in Transition*, 97–131. Oxford.

Thornton, Tamara P. 1996. *Handwriting in America: A Cultural History*. New Haven.

Tibiletti, G. 1979. *Le lettere private nei papiri greci del III e IV secolo d.C.: Tra paganesimo e cristianesimo*. Milan.

Trapp, M. 2003. *Greek and Latin Letters: An Anthology, with Translation*. Cambridge.

Traversa, A. 1953. "Dai papiri inediti della raccolta milanese." *Aegyptus* 33:57–79.

Turner, Eric G. 1960. "A Booklover's Papyri." *Classical Review* 10:215–17.

Vandorpe, Katelijn. 1995. *Breaking the Seal of Secrecy*. Leiden.

Van Rengen, Wilfried. 1979. Review of Bagnall, *The Florida Ostraka*. *Chronique d'Égypte* 54:332–36.

Watt, Diane. 1993. "'No Writing for Writing's Sake': The Language of Service and Household Rhetoric in the Letters of the Paston Women." In Karen Cherewatuk and Ulrike Wiethaus, eds., *Dear Sister: Medieval Women and the Epistolary Genre*, 122–38. Philadelphia.

Wente, Edward. 1990. *Letters from Ancient Egypt*. Atlanta.

White, John L. 1986. *Light from Ancient Letters*. Philadelphia.

Whitehorne, John. 1994. "Religious Expressions in the Correspondence of the Strategus Apollonius." *Analecta Papyrologica* 6:21–36.

Wilcken, Ulrich. 1927. "Papyrus-Urkunden." *Archiv für Papyrusforschung* 8:66–114.

———. 1937. "Urkunden-Referat." *Archiv für Papyrusforschung* 12:74–102.

Wilfong, Terry G. 1990. "The Archive of a Family of Moneylenders from Jeme." *Bulletin of the American Society of Papyrologists* 27:169–81.

———. 2002. *Women of Jeme*. Ann Arbor.

Winkworth, L. E. 1992. "A Request for Purgatives: P. Oxy. I 187." *Zeitschrift für Papyrologie und Epigraphik* 91:85–87.

Winter, J. G. 1927. "The Family Letters of Paniskos." *Journal of Egyptian Archaeology* 13:73–74.

Wipszycka, Ewa. 1975. "Les terres de la congrégation pachômienne dans une liste de payements pour les apora." In J. Bingen, G. Cambier, and G. Nachtergael, eds., *Le monde grec: Pensée, littérature, histoire, documents — Hommages à Claire Préaux*. Brussels.

———. 2002a. "Del buon uso delle lettere private: Commento a SB III, 7243 e P.Oxy. XIV, 1774." In J.-M. Carrié and R. Testa, eds. *Humana sapit: Études d'antiquité tardive offertes à Lellia Cracco Ruggini*, 469–73. Turnhout.

———. 2002b. "L'ascéticisme féminin dans l'Égypte de l'antiquité tardive: Topoi littéraires et formes d'ascèse." In H. Melaerts and L. Mooren, eds., *Le rôle et le statut de la femme en Égypte hellénistique, romaine, et byzantine*, 355–96. Leuven.

Witkowski, S. 1911. *Epistulae privatae graecae quae in papyris aetatis Lagidarum servantur*. 2nd ed. Leipzig.

Worp, Klaas A. 1995. "Letters of Condolence in the Greek Papyri: Some Observations." *Analecta Papyrologica* 7:149–54.

Youtie, H. C. 1958. "Notes on Papyri and Ostraca." *Transactions of the American Philological Association* 89:374–76. Reprinted in *Scriptiunculae* 1 (1973): 284–86.

———. 1964. "Notes on Papyri." *Bulletin of the Institute of Classical Studies* 11:22–25. Reprinted in *Scriptiunculae* 2 (1973): 1008–11.

———. 1974. *The Textual Criticism of Documentary Papyri*. 2nd ed. London.

———. 1978. "Grenfell's Gift to Lumbroso." *Illinois Classical Studies* 3:90–99. Reprinted in *Scriptiunculae Posteriores* 1 (1981): 36–45.

Zuckerman, Constantin. 1995. "The Hapless Recruit Psois and the Mighty Anchorite, Apa John." *Bulletin of the American Society of Papyrologists* 32:184–94.

Index

Pachomian monasticism, 206
paidagogos, 375
palaeographical dates, 55
Palladius, 204
palm tree, 312
Paniskos, archive of, 294
papas, 199, 321
Papnouthis and Dorotheos, archive of, 70
Papnouthis, monk, 205
papyri, deposition of, 22
papyri, documentary, chronological distribution of, 19
papyrus, 33–35, 299, 322; blank, 191; reuse of, 35
parchment, 34
Parsons, Peter J., 12
Paston family, correspondence of, 26–32
Paston, Margaret, 26
pawnshops, 295–96
Pedo, L. Antonius, prefect of Egypt, 322
Pelusium 80, 82, 305; language use in, 56
periodic style, 17
Persians, occupation of Egypt, 73, 242, 245, 249, 253
personal hands, 45, 54
Petesouchos, *proskynema* before, 276–77
petitions, 10, 16, 101, 102, 209, 313, 321
Philotera on the Red Sea, 165
Phoibasia, 17, 52, 60, 235–36; hand of, 236
pigeons, 311
pigs, slaughtering of, 274
Pisentius, bishop, 34, 73, 239–43
plague, 268
Plumpton family, correspondence of, 26–32
Pompeius, archive of, 50, 70, 126–34
postscripts, 63, 142, 144, 184, 393
prefect, 314, 399
pregnancy, 283
priests, 309, 312, 383
prison, 402
prisoners, 246
privileged groups, 69
professional hands, 7, 46
propertied class, 73

property, ownership and management of by women, 80, 82, 162
proskynema formulas, 89–90, 165, 177–79; Demotic equivalent, 310
Ptolemaios, recluse of Sarapieion, 112
public business, 81
public life, Greek used in, 21
punctuation, 209

Ramesside letters, 15
rare words, 65
regnal years, dates by, 92
relatives, use of for writing, 45
religion in letters, 14
rents, collection of, 300
reply, failure to, 299
request letters, 13
ribbed ostraca, 54
riots, 287
Rome, journey to, 383
Rowlandson, Jane, 1

Sahidic dialect, 223
sale of land, 293
salutations. *See* greetings
Sarapieion of Memphis, 111
Sarapion alias Apollonianos, dossier of, 393
Sarapis, 288; worship of, 89–90, 177–79
Sassanians. *See* Persians
school exercises, 35, 41, 44
school hands, 55, 109
schools, 13, 347
Schubart, Wilhelm, 12
scribe, professional, 43–44, 47, 365; professional, 393, 399; apprentice, 13; Christian, 42; Egyptian, 103; female, 42
seamstresses, 241, 352
second hands, 46, 236, 354
secretaries, 41, 176; hands of, 7
sections in letters, 46
servants, 140, 149, 160–61
sexual fidelity, 382
shrine, family, 375
shrine, healing, 153
sibling marriage, 86
size, in handwriting, 44
slaves, 40, 125, 143, 336, 367

Sobek (Souchos), god, 128–29, 136
soldiers, 306, 347–48, 370, 397
solidus, 91
Souchos. *See* Sobek
speed, in handwriting, 44
spelling, phonetic, 259
spinning, 77–79, 354
starvation, 246
status, social, 48, 70
Stonor family, correspondence of,
    26–32
strategos, 139
students, practice of letter writing
    by, 13
style, colloquial, 18
style, epistolary, 43
style, formal, 18
style, oral, 223, 259
style, periodic, 17
subscriptions, on medieval letters,
    28–30
suicide, 280
symmachos, 39
syntax, sophistication of, 151
Syria, 260

Tasoucharion, dossier of, 70, 80, 86,
    176–82
taxation and tax collection, 132, 189,
    211, 297; taxes in grain, 191
teachers, 361, 375–76; women, 77, 348,
    389–90; chair of, 333
Tebtunis, 183
Terentianus, Julius, archive of, 347–48
textiles, 77–79
Thermouthas, dossier of, 70, 188–92
thought process in dictated letters, 62
Tiberianus, archive of, 70, 135–38
torture, 246
toys, 301

trash dumps, 22
travel, 81–83, 189, 196–97, 300, 371
traveling allowance, 99
tribune, 204

usury, 296

vestis militaris, 378
village scribe, 309
vineyard, 329
voices, of women, 6, 60, 138
votive limbs, 153

Wadi Fawakhir, 35
water, 350
waterwheel, 346
wealth, 48, 70, 231, 297, 330
weaving, 77–79, 104, 140, 159, 299,
    352–57
wedding, 235
wet-nursing, 76, 169, 265. *See also*
    nurses
wheat, price of, 125
widows, 220, 242, 321
woman teacher, 348, 389–90
women scribes, 42
women, education of, 48, 61, 65–66
wooden boards, 34, 219
wool and wool-working, 77–79, 196,
    212–13, 224–25, 231, 233–34, 283,
    317, 341, 353
words, rare, 65
writing skills, poor, 52

Youtie, Herbert, 41

Zenon, archive of, 15–16, 23, 42, 68,
    97–104
Zeus Kasios, 305

Index of Letters

References in bold indicate the page(s) on which the text appears.

P.Rain.Cent. 70: 61, 277–78
P.Ryl. 2.232: 386
P.Ryl. 2.243: 350–51
P.Ryl.Copt. 310: 321
PSI 3.177: 77, 280–81
PSI 9.1080: 301
PSI 9.1082: 64, 341
PSI 12.1247: 52, 63, 393–94
PSI 14.1418: 342
P.Tebt. 2.413: 40, 336–37
P.Tebt. 2.414: 38, 337–38
P.Wash.Univ. 2.106: 322–23
P.Wisc. 2.74: 387–88
P.Würzb. 21: 279–80
P.Yale 1.77: 62, 339–40
SB 3.6264: 282
SB 5.7572: 64, 76, 283
SB 5.7737: 82, 363
SB 5.7743: 52, 343
SB 5.8027: 82, 373
SB 5.8092: 232
SB 6.9026: 356–57
SB 6.9120: 129–30
SB 6.9121: 130–31

SB 6.9122: 132–33
SB 8.9746 = SB 3.7243: 196–97
SB 12.10840: 82, 385
SB 14.11492: 233–34
SB 14.11580: 81, 284
SB 14.11585: 344–45
SB 14.11588: 302–3
SB 14.11881: 78, 357
SB 14.12085: 234–35
SB 16.12326: 285–286
SB 16.12589: 287
SB 16.12981: 36, 303–4
SB 18.13612: 209
SB 18.13762: 52: 235–36
SB 20.14132: 405–6
SB 20.14226: 237–38
SB 20.15180: 174–75
SB 20.15192: 210
SB 22.15276: 104
SB Kopt. 1.295: 242–43
UPZ 1.59: 45, 48, 111–12
UPZ 1.148: 113
W.Chr. 100: 288
W.Chr. 499: 289–90